Modelling Dynamic Systems Using PcFiml 9.0 for Windows®

Jurgen A. Doornik
David F. Hendry

INTERNATIONAL THOMSON BUSINESS PRESS
I(T)P® An International Thomson Publishing Company

London • Bonn • Boston • Johannesburg • Madrid • Melbourne • Mexico City • New York • Paris
Singapore • Tokyo • Toronto • Albany, NY • Belmont, CA • Cincinnati, OH • Detroit, MI

Modelling Dynamic Systems Using PcFiml 9.0 for Windows®

First published 1997 by International Thomson Business Press

I(T)P® A division of International Thomson Publishing Inc.
The ITP logo is a trademark under licence

PcFiml is a computer program designed for Econometric analysis. It is the micro-computer, interactive descendant of GIVE and RALS from the library AUTOREG (Hendry and Srba, 1980). The acronym GIVE is from Generalized Instrumental Variables Estimators (see Sargan, 1959 and Hendry, 1976).

To facilitate replication and validation of empirical findings, **PcFiml** should be cited in all reports and publications involving its application.

British Library Cataloguing-in-Publication Data
A catalogue record for this book is available from the British Library

Library of Congress Cataloging-in-Publication Data
A catalog record for this book is available from the Library of Congress

---

First edition 1997

Printed in the UK by Clays Ltd, St Ives plc

ISBN 1-86152-058-1

International Thomson Business Press
Berkshire House
High Holborn
London WClV 7AA
UK

International Thomson Business Press
20 Park Plaza
14th Floor
Boston MA 02116
USA

http://www.itbp.com

Contents

Tables

Preface

PcFiml version 9 for Windows is the latest in a long line of descendants of the original GIVE and FIML programs, and many scholars, researchers and students have contributed to its present form. We are grateful to them all for their help and encouragement.

The release of PcGive Professional version 9 sees a further enhancement of graphical presentations and another shift in approach towards a practical textbook of applied systems modelling (the pre-computer usage of the term 'manual'). The documentation now comprises very extensive tutorials conducting a complete modelling exercise, teaching econometric modelling conjointly with learning program usage, the econometrics of PcFiml and a technical discussion of the statistical output – the computer instruction manual has now vanished.

The original mainframe ancestor was written in Fortran, PC versions in a mixture of Fortran, C and Assembler, whereas version 9 is entirely written in C and C++.

Sections of code in earlier versions were contributed by Neil Ericsson, Adrian Neale, Denis Sargan, Frank Srba and Juri Sylvestrowicz, and their important contributions are gratefully acknowledged. We are also grateful to Bernard Silverman for permission to include his code for density estimation. Version 9 relies on Microsoft Visual C++ and the Microsoft Foundation Class for its interface.

A special thanks goes to Gunnar Bårdsen for his detailed checking of early versions of PcFiml 9. We also wish to thank Peter Boswijk, Mike Clements, Neil Ericsson, Henrik Hansen, Grayham Mizon and Marius Ooms, for kindly commenting on various versions of PcFiml. We are grateful to the Oxford Institute of Economics and Statistics, especially to Gillian Coates, Candy Watts, and Alison Berry for help with earlier versions. We also wish to thank Maureen Baker and Nuffield College for their support.

The documentation for GIVE has evolved dramatically over the years. We are indebted to Mary Morgan and Frank Srba for their help in preparing the first (mainframe) version of a manual. Our thanks also to Manuel Arellano, Giorgio Bodo, Peter Boswijk, Julia Campos, Mike Clements, Neil Ericsson, Carlo Favero, Chris Gilbert, Henrik Hansen, Søren Johansen, Marius Ooms, Adrian Neale, Ed Nelson, Bent Nielsen, Robert Parks, Jean-François Richard, Timo Teräsvirta and Giovanni Urga for their many helpful comments on the documentation.

Scientific Word in combination with emTeX and DVIPS eased the development of the documentation for version 9 in LaTeX, further facilitated by the more self-contained nature of PcFiml 9 and its in-built help system. The editing was also undertaken using

OxEdit, which allowed flexible incorporation of PcFiml output, and SnapShot/32 (with PSP for conversion to PostScript) which enabled the screen captures.

Over the years, many users and generations of students have written with helpful suggestions for improving and extending PcFiml, and while version 9 will undoubtedly not yet satisfy all of their wishes, we remain grateful for their comments and hope that they will continue to write with good ideas and *report any bugs*!

DFH owes a considerable debt to Evelyn and Vivien during the hundreds of hours he has spent on this project: their support and encouragement were essential, even though they could benefit but indirectly from the end product. In a similar fashion, JAD is delighted to thank Kate Dewhurst. We hope the benefits derived by others compensate.

We wish you enjoyable and productive use of

PcFiml for Windows

Part I

Prologue

Chapter 1

Introduction to PcFiml

1.1 General information

PcFiml is an interactive menu-driven program for econometric modelling of linear dynamic economic systems. Version 9 for Windows, to which this documentation refers, runs on IBM-compatible machines operating under Windows (3.1 after the Win32S extender version 1.30 is installed, but preferably under Windows 95 or NT). There is also a version which works on Dec-Alpha machines running Windows NT. **PcFiml** is part of the AUTOREG Library (see Hendry and Srba, 1980, Hendry, 1986, 1993, Doornik and Hendry, 1992, 1994a, 1994b and Hendry and Doornik, 1996b).

PcFiml is designed for modelling multivariate time-series data when the precise formulation of the economic system under analysis is not known *a priori*. The current version is for systems that are linear in variables, which could comprise jointly determined, weakly or strongly exogenous, predetermined and lagged endogenous variables. A wide range of system and model estimation methods is available; stochastic and identity equations are handled. Particular features of the program are its ease of use, familiar interface, flexible data handling, structured approach, extensive set of preprogrammed diagnostic tests, its focus on recursive methods, and its powerful graphics. An extensive batch language is also supported.

The main design concepts underlying PcFiml centre on the need to avoid information overload when modelling a system of dynamic equations (as the number of parameters can become very large), to remain easy and enjoyable to use, to offer the frontier techniques, and to implement a coherent modelling strategy. Specifically, it seeks to achieve all of these objectives simultaneously. The size of system that can be analysed pushes the limits of PCs capacities, data availability, econometric technique and comprehension of dynamic models. The documentation is especially extensive to fully explain the econometric methods, the modelling approach and the techniques used, as well as bridge the vast gap between the theory and practice in this area by a detailed description of a modelling exercise in operation. Like the companion volume on single-equation modelling (see Hendry and Doornik, 1996b), this book transcends the old ideas of 'textbooks' and 'computer manuals' by linking the learning of econometric methods and concepts to the outcomes achieved when they are applied by the user at the computer. Because the program is so easy to learn and use, the main focus is on its econometrics and application to data analysis. Detailed tutorials in Chapters 3–7 teach econometric modelling of dynamic systems for possibly non-stationary data by walking the user through the program in organised steps. This is supported by clear explanations of the associated econometric methods in Chapters 8–13. The material spans the level from introductory to frontier research, with an emphatic orientation to practical modelling. The exact definitions of all statistics calculated by PcFiml are described in Chapter 14. The appendices in Chapters A1–A2 are for reference to details about PcFiml languages, and data sets. The context-sensitive help system supports this approach by offering help on both the program and the econometrics at every stage.

This chapter describes the special features of PcFiml, discusses how to use the documentation, provides background information on data storage, interactive operation, help, results storage and filenames, sketches the basics of how to use the program and describes its graphics capabilities, illustrated throughout later chapters.

1.2 The special features of PcFiml

(1) *Ease of use*

- PcFiml is **user friendly**, being a **fully interactive and menu-driven** approach to econometric system modelling: pull-down menus offer options, and dialog boxes provide easy access to the available functions.
- PcFiml has a very **high level of error protection** making it suitable for live teaching in the classroom, student use, and systematic analyses – as well as fraught late-night research.
- PcFiml provides an extensive context-sensitive **help system** explaining both the program usage and the econometrics.
- **High quality screen presentations** in edit windows allow documentation of results as analysis proceeds, with easy review of previous results, and cutting and pasting within or between windows.
- Text and graphics can be controlled by a **mouse**, allowing powerful and flexible editing, rapid menu and dialog access, and easy documentation of graphs.
- **Estimation options** can be set to automatically activate or inhibit model evaluation procedures for systems and models, control the format for presentation of results, and determine the level of detail and sophistication of the output reported.

(2) *Advanced graphics*

- PcFml supports **text and graphics together on screen**, with easy adjustment of graph types, layout and colours using the powerful yet flexible features provided in **GiveWin** (see Hendry and Doornik, 1996a).
- Up to **36 graphs** can be shown simultaneously in any one window, with easy user control or automatic selection: many graph windows can be open at once.
- **Graphs can be documented and edited** via direct screen access with reading from the graph.
- **Time series and cross-plots** are supported with flexible adjustment and scaling options, as well as histograms and data densities.
- **Descriptive results, recursive statistics, cointegration output, diagnostic tests, cross-equation relationships, likelihood projections and forecasts** all can be graphed for every equation jointly in the system (up to blocks of 36 equations).

(3) *Flexible data handling in GiveWin*

- The **data handling system provides convenient storage** of large data sets with easy loading to PcFiml either as a unit, or for subsamples or subsets of variables.
- **Excel and Lotus spreadsheet files** can be loaded directly, or using 'cut and paste' facilities.
- **Large data sets** can be analysed, with as many variables and observations as memory allows.
- Database variables can be transformed by a **calculator**, or by entering **mathematical formulae** in an editor with easy storage for reuse; the database is easily viewed, incorrect observations are simple to revise, and variables can be documented on-line.
- **Extending** data sets is simple, and the data used for estimation can be any subset of the data in the database.
- **Several data sets** can be open simultaneously, with easy switching between the database, and copy & paste to merge compatible data.

(4) *Efficient modelling*

- The underlying **C algorithms** are **fast, efficient, accurate** and carefully **tested**; all **data are stored in double precision**, and numerical operations use 80-bit arithmetic.

- PcFiml is specially designed for **modelling multivariate time-series** data, and analyses dynamic responses and long-run relations with ease; it is simple to change sample, or forecast, periods or estimation methods: models are retained for further analysis, and general-to-specific sequential simplifications are monitored for reduction tests.
- The **structured modelling approach** is fully discussed in this book, and guides the ordering of menus and dialogs, but application of the program is completely at the user's control.
- A **vast range of estimators** is supported, including multivariate least squares, system cointegration techniques, and most simultaneous equations estimators (centered around FIML), providing automatic handling of identities and checking of identification, and allowing non-linear cross-equation constraints; powerful numerical optimization algorithms are embedded in the program with easy user control, and most methods can be calculated recursively over the available sample.
- PcFiml offers **powerful preprogrammed testing facilities** for a wide range of specification hypotheses, including tests for dynamic specification, lag length, cointegration, tests on cointegration vectors and parsimonious encompassing; Wald tests of linear and non-linear restrictions are easily conducted.
- **System and model revision is straightforward** since PcFiml remembers as much as possible of the previous specification for the next formulation.
- A **batch language** allows storage for automatic estimation and evaluation of models, and can be used to prepare a PcFiml session for teaching.

(5) *Powerful evaluation*

- **System and simultaneous-equations mis-specification tests are automatically provided,** including vector residual autocorrelation, vector heteroscedasticity, system functional form mis-specification, and vector normality.
- **Individual equation diagnostic information** is also provided including ARCH and (for example) plots of correlograms and residual density functions.
- The **recursive estimators provide easy graphing** of residuals with their confidence intervals, log-likelihoods, and parameter-constancy statistics (scaled by selected nominal significance levels); these are calculated for systems, cointegration analyses and models – see recursive FIML in action.
- All estimators provide **graphs** of fitted/actual values, residuals, and **forecasts** with error bars or bands for 1-step (against outcomes in that case), h-step and dynamic forecasts; perturbation and impulse response analyses are also supported.

(6) *Extensive batch language*

- **PcFiml formulates the batch commands** needed to rerun a system and model as an interactive session proceeds – all you have to do is save the file if desired.
- The **batch language** supports commands for data loading; transformation; system formulation, estimation and testing; cointegration analyses and tests; model formulation, estimation and testing; imposing restrictions. All these can be stored as simple batch commands, to be extended, revised and/or edited with ease. Batch files can be run in whole or in part from within an interactive session.

(7) *Output*

- **Graphs can be saved** in several file formats for later recall and further editing, or printing and importing into many popular word processors, as well as directly by 'cut and paste'.
- **Results window** information can be saved as an ASCII (human-readable) document for input to most word processors, or directly input by 'cut and paste'.

We now consider some of these special features in greater detail.

(1) *Ease of use*

- By avoiding a complicated command language that has to be learned in detail prior to efficient use, PcFiml is remarkably easy to use relative to the complexities of the dynamic modelling tasks it can perform.
- The program facilitates progress by automatically handling many aspects of model formulation, identification, estimation, numerical optimization, and transformation.
- A focus on graphical output and summary statistics helps avoid information overload that can become a serious difficulty when modelling multivariate relationships.
- Program options allow control over the detail of output presented and how it is formatted, as well as setting automatic evaluation and graphic analyses or batch testing after estimation – or only when required.

(2) *Advanced graphics*

- Users have full control over **screen and graph colours**. The colour, type (solid, dotted, dashed etc.), and thickness of each line in a graph can be set; graphs can be drawn inside boxes, and with or without grids; axis values can be automatic or user defined; areas highlighted as desired; and so on.
- Up to **36 different graphs** can be shown simultaneously in one window on-screen, which is especially valuable for graphical evaluation of equations and recursive methods. Combinations of graphs displaying different attributes of data can be shown simultaneously – examples are reported below.
- Once on-screen, text can be entered for **graph documentation**, or a mouse used to highlight interesting features during live presentations. Graphs can be both rapidly saved and instantly recalled. Coordinates can be read from each graph, however many graphs are displayed at once.
- The option to see **multiple graphs** allows for more efficient evaluation of large amounts of information. Blocks of graphs can simultaneously incorporate descriptive results (fitted and actual values, scaled residuals and forecasts etc.) and diagnostic test information; or show many single-parameter likelihood grids.
- Much of PcFiml's output is provided in graphical form which is why it is an interactive (rather than a batch) program. The option to see multiple graphs allows for efficient processing of large amounts of information. Blocks of graphs for up to 36 equations can be viewed simultaneously, incorporating descriptive results (fitted and actual values, scaled residuals etc.), recursive statistics, cointegration output (time series of cointegration vectors, or recursive eigenvalues), single-equation diagnostic test information, cross-equation relationships (such as residual cross-plots), single-parameter likelihood grids, and a wide range of forecasts.

(3) *Efficient modelling sequence*

- Modelling dynamic econometric systems involves creating and naming lags, controlling sample periods, assigning the appropriate status to variables (endogenous, non-modelled etc.), so such operations are either automatic or very easy. The basic PcFiml operator is a lag polynomial matrix. Long-run system solutions, cointegration tests, the significance of blocks of lagged variables, the choice between deterministic or stochastic dynamics, and roots of long-run and lag-polynomial matrices are all calculated. When the recommended general-to-specific approach is adopted, the sequence of reductions is monitored for both systems and models, and reduction F-tests and system information criteria are reported.

- This **extensive book** seeks to bridge the gap between econometric theory and empirical modelling: the tutorials in Part II walk the user through every step from inputting data to the final selected econometric model of the vector of variables under analysis. The econometrics chapters in Part III explain all the necessary econometrics for system modelling and evaluation with reference to the program, offering detailed explanations of all the estimators and tests. The statistical output chapter carefully defines all the estimators and tests produced by PcFiml.
- The **ordering of the menus and dialogs** is determined by the underlying theory: first establish a data-coherent, constant-parameter dynamic system; then investigate cointegration, and reduce the system to a stationary, near orthogonal and simplified representation; next develop a model to characterize that system in a parsimonious and interpretable form; and finally check for parsimonious encompassing of the system: see Hendry, Neale and Srba (1988), Hendry and Mizon (1993) and Hendry (1993, 1995) for further details. Nevertheless, the application and sequence of the program's facilities remain completely under the user's control.
- The estimators supported are based on the estimator generating equation approach in Hendry (1976), and include handling of identities and automatic checking of identification. Estimation methods include Multivariate Ordinary (OLS) and Recursive Least Squares (RLS); Johansen's reduced-rank cointegration analysis for systems with both its recursive and constrained implementations; Single-equation OLS (for large systems and small samples, denoted 1SLS), Two-Stage Least Squares (2SLS), Three-Stage Least Squares (3SLS), Limited-Information Instrumental Variables (LIVE), Full-Information Instrumental Variables (FIVE), Limited-Information Maximum Likelihood (LIML), Full-Information Maximum Likelihood (FIML), Recursive FIML (RFIML), and constrained FIML (CFIML: with possibly non-linear cross-equation constraints for models; also available recursively, and denoted RCFIML). Systems and models are easily revised, transformed and simplified since as much as possible of a previous specification is retained. Up to 100 models are remembered for easy recall and progress evaluation.
- Powerful testing facilities for a wide range of specification hypotheses of interest to econometricians and economists undertaking substantive empirical research are preprogrammed for automatic calculation. Available tests include dynamic specification, lag length, cointegration rank, hypothesis tests on cointegration vectors and/or adjustment coefficients, and tests of reduction or parsimonious encompassing. Wald tests of (non-)linear linear restrictions are easily conducted using the constraints editor and such constraints can be imposed for estimation by cutting and pasting, then using CFIML.

(4) *Powerful evaluation*

- **Evaluation tests** can be either automatically calculated, calculated in a block as a summary test option, or implemented singly or in sets merely by selecting the relevant dialog option. A comprehensive and powerful range of mis-specification tests is offered in order to sustain the methodological recommendations about model evaluation. System and simultaneous-equations models mis-specification tests include vector residual autocorrelation, vector heteroscedasticity, system functional form mis-specification and vector normality (the test proposed in Doornik and Hansen, 1994). Individual-equation diagnostic information is also provided, including scalar versions of all the above tests as well as ARCH, and (for example) plots of correlograms and residual density functions. When the system is in fact a single equation, tests in common with PcGive have been designed to deliver the same answer with the same degrees of freedom.
- Much of the power of PcFiml resides in its extensive use of recursive estimators for systems, cointegration analyses and models. The output can be voluminous (1-step residuals and their standard errors, constancy tests etc. at every sample size for every equation), but recursive statistics can be graphed for easy presentation and appraisal (up to 36 graphs simultaneously). The size of systems is really only restricted by the available memory and length of data samples. Recursive cointegration analysis and recursive FIML are surprisingly easy and amazingly fast – given the enormous numbers of calculations involved.
- All estimators provide time-series graphs of residuals, fitted and actual values and their cross-plots. 1-step forecasts and outcomes with 95% confidence intervals shown by error bars or bands can be graphed, as can dynamic simulation (within sample), dynamic forecasts (*ex ante*) or even h-step ahead forecasts for any choice of h – all with approximate 95% confidence bars. Forecasts can be conducted under alternative scenarios.
- Full graphics facilities can be applied to any or all of these graphs (e.g., adding regression lines etc.).

(5) *Extensive batch language*

- To minimize complexity and enhance speed of learning and use, PcFiml formulates the batch commands needed to rerun a system and model as an interactive session proceeds. Once the batch file is saved, it can be loaded and run in whole or in part from within an interactive session, perhaps edited or appropriately extended at the time. The latest model is saved on exit.

- The batch language supports commands for selecting module (pcFiml, PcGive etc.); data loading; data transformation; system formulation, estimation and testing; cointegration analyses, tests and constraints; dynamic analysis; model formulation, estimation and testing; evaluation tests; dynamic forecasts and simulation; and/or implementation of estimation restrictions. All these can be stored as simple batch commands, to be extended, revised and/or edited with ease. The available commands are always listed in the batch editor for instant entry to a batch file.

Considerable experience has demonstrated the practicality and value of using PcFiml live in classroom teaching as a complementary adjunct to theoretical derivations. On the research side, the incisive recursive estimators and the wide range of preprogrammed tests make PcFiml the most powerful interactive econometric modelling program available. Part II records its application to a practical econometric modelling problem. These roles are enhanced by the flexible and informative graphics options provided.

1.3 Documentation conventions

The convention for instructions that you should type is that they are shown in `Typewriter` font. Capitals and lower case are only distinguished as the names of variables in the program and the mathematical formulae you type. Once GiveWin has started, then from the keyboard, the `Alt` key accesses line menus (at the top of the screen); from a mouse, click on the item to be selected using the left button. Common commands have a shortcut on the toolbar, the purpose of which can be ascertained by placing the mouse on the relevant icon. Icons that can currently operate are highlighted. Commands on menus, toolbar buttons, and dialog items (buttons, checkboxes etc.) are shown in Sans Serif font: click on highlighted options to implement.

Equations are numbered as (chapter.number); for example, (8.1) refers to equation 8.1, which is the first equation in Chapter 8. References to sections have the form §chapter.section, for example, §8.1 is Section 8.1 in Chapter 8. Tables and Figures are shown as Figure chapter.number; for example, Figure 5.2 for the second Figure in Chapter 5. Multiple graphs are numbered from left to right and top to bottom, so (b) is the top-right graph of four, and (c) the bottom left.

1.4 Using PcFiml documentation

This book comes in five main parts: Part I comprises this introductory chapter, and instructions on starting the program. Part II has five extensive tutorials on dynamic system modelling; these emphasise the modelling aspects yet explain program usage en route. Part III has six chapters discussing the econometrics of PcFiml from system formulation to dynamic forecasting. Part IV offers a detailed description of the statistical and econometric output of PcFiml. Finally, Part V contains appendices. The documentation ends with references, and author and subject indices. As discussed above, the aim is to provide a practical textbook of systems modelling, linking the econometrics of PcFiml to empirical practice through tutorials which implement an applied modelling exercise. In more detail:

(1) A separate book explains and documents the companion program **GiveWin** which records the output and provides the data loading and graphing facilities. It also describes how to use its editor, data transformation facilities, and graphics control.

(2) The **Prologue** introduces the main features provided by PcFiml, sketches how to use the program and illustrates some of its output.

(3) The **Tutorials** in Chapters 3 to 7 are specifically designed for joint learning of the econometric analyses and use of the program. They describe system formulation, estimation and evaluation; cointegration procedures; reduction of the system to a stationary representation; econometric modelling of that system; and advanced features. By implementing a complete empirical research exercise, they allow rapid mastery of PcFiml while acquiring an understanding of how the econometric theory operates in practice.

(4) The **Econometric Overview** in Chapter 8 reviews the various econometric procedures included in PcFiml.

(5) The **Econometric Theory** in Chapters 9 to 12 explain in technical detail the econometrics of PcFiml.

(6) Chapters 13 and 14 concern numerical optimization and the detailed description of the statistical output of PcFiml. Chapter 14 is to some extent self-contained, as it briefly repeats the basic notation employed in Chapters 9 to 12.

(7) The **Appendices** in Chapters A1 to A2 document the remaining functions of PcFiml. Chapter A1 documents the various languages (such as Algebra and Batch) used in PcFiml. Most information about menus, dialogs etc., is available in the on-line help. These chapters should be needed for reference only, but it may be helpful to read them once.

The appropriate sequence is first to follow the instructions in the **installation procedure** to copy and install PcFiml 9 on your system. Next, read the remainder of this introduction, then follow the step-by-step guidance given in the **tutorials** to become familiar with the operation of PcFiml. The **appendices** should be needed for reference only, but it may be helpful to read them once, especially A1. The technical description of the econometrics procedures used by PcFiml is provided in Part III.

To use the documentation, either check the index for the subject, topic, menu, or dialog that seems relevant, or look up the part relevant to your current activity (for example, econometrics, tutorials or manuals) in the **Contents**, and scan for the most likely keyword. The references point to relevant publications that analyse the methodology and methods embodied in PcFiml.

1.5 An overview of PcFiml menus

There are five main groups of menus relevant to:

(1) File: which enables exiting the program and keeping it visible;

(2) Model: system and model formulation and estimation;

(3) Test: formal and graphical analysis and testing of both systems and models;

(4) View: determines whether tool, and status, bars are shown;

(5) Help: accesses the help system.

Entry to further dialogs is always via one of these, which pulls down the relevant set of choices. The use of the various menus is explained in the tutorials in Chapters 3–7, and detailed descriptions can be found in the help.

1.6 Citation

To facilitate replication and validation of empirical findings, PcFiml and PcGive should be cited in all reports and publications involving their application. The appropriate form is to cite this book about PcFiml in the list of references.

1.7 World Wide Web

Consult `http://www.nuff.ox.ac.uk/Users/Doornik/` for pointers to additional information relevant to the current and future versions of PcGive and PcFiml.

1.8 Some data sets

The data used in Hendry (1995) is provided in the files UKM1.IN7/UKM1.BN7. The DHSY data (see Davidson, Hendry, Srba and Yeo, 1978) is supplied in the files DHSY.IN7/DHSY.BN7. For the data sets used in Hendry and Morgan (1995), consult: `ftp://hicks.nuff.ox.ac.uk/pub/economic/hendry/histects`.

Chapter 2

Getting Started

2.1 Introduction

We assume that you have the basic skills to operate programs under the Windows operating system (the GiveWin and PcGive books provide hints). PcFiml works on Windows 3.1, Windows NT, or Windows 95, but the screen appearance of the program and dialogs will reflect the operating system you are using. The captures in this book were made under Windows NT.

Even though PcFiml and GiveWin are separate programs, they work closely together: GiveWin provides the data which PcFiml analyses, and receives all the text output and graphs which you create in PcFiml. When you start PcFiml, it automatically starts up GiveWin (or will connect to the version which is already active). Then GiveWin will ask PcFiml if it can handle batch commands (which it can). Note that GiveWin will *not* automatically start PcFiml (when you close GiveWin, you must also close PcFiml to restart).

The operation of PcFiml is similar to PcGive, and both share the GiveWin edit window for results and its graphics. We assume that users of PcFiml have previously used PcGive, so will only sketch the mechanics of data input, transformation, menu selection, editing, and graphics. For detailed instructions on how to load and transform data using the calculator or algebra, and create sophisticated graphs, consult the GiveWin book.

The convention for instructions that you should type is that they are shown in `Typewriter` font. Capitals and lower case are only distinguished as the names of variables in the program and the mathematical formulae you type. Once GiveWin and PcFiml have started, then from the keyboard, the `Alt` key accesses line menus (at the top of the screen); from a mouse, click on the item to be selected. Commands on menus, toolbar buttons, and dialog items (buttons, checkboxes etc.) are shown in Sans Serif font. Common commands have a shortcut on the toolbar. If the text says 'Press `Alt+h`' you have to press and hold down the Alt key and continue holding it down while you press `h`. 'Press `Alt+f,x`' requires you to press `Alt+f` (to access the File menu) and then `x` (for Exit). This exits the program. After a modelling session PcFiml will ask you whether you really wish to exit.

If at any time you get stuck, press `F1` for context-sensitive help. Or access the help index (`Alt+h, i`) to find out about specific topics (including relevant econometric information).

In these tutorials we shall mainly use the mouse. Most tasks can also be performed using the keyboard — use whatever you feel more comfortable with.

2.2 Starting PcFiml

Double click on the PcFiml icon to start it. If this is the first time you have used PcFiml, you might wish to reduce it to a smaller size. Your screen could then look like the capture shown below. The message window is currently empty.

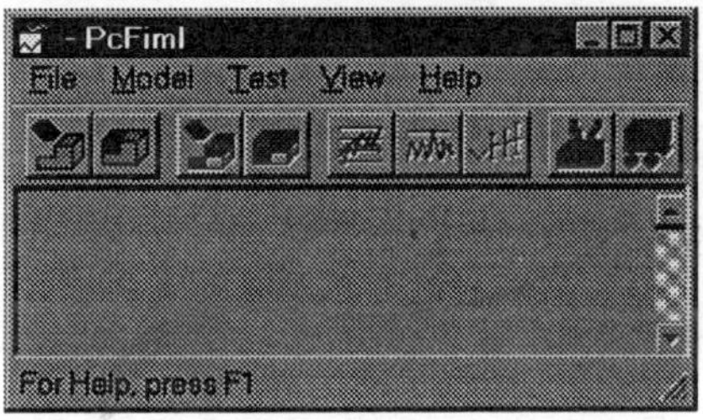

2.3 Loading and viewing the PcFiml tutorial data set

Without data, PcFiml cannot operate, so the first step is to load data into GiveWin which PcFiml can then access. Load the tutorial data set for the following exercises: access GiveWin, click the mouse on 'File', or type `Alt+f`. The IN7 extension indicates a PcGive 7 data file (a format which remains the same for versions 8 and 9). The IN7 file is a human-readable file, describing the data. There is a companion BN7 file, which holds the actual numbers (in binary format, so this file cannot be edited). GiveWin can handle a wide range of data files, among them Excel (.XLS up to version 4) and Lotus files (.WKS and .WK1), and, of course, plain human-readable (ASCII) files. You can also cut and paste data between Excel and GiveWin. Details are in the GiveWin book.

Access the File menu in GiveWin:

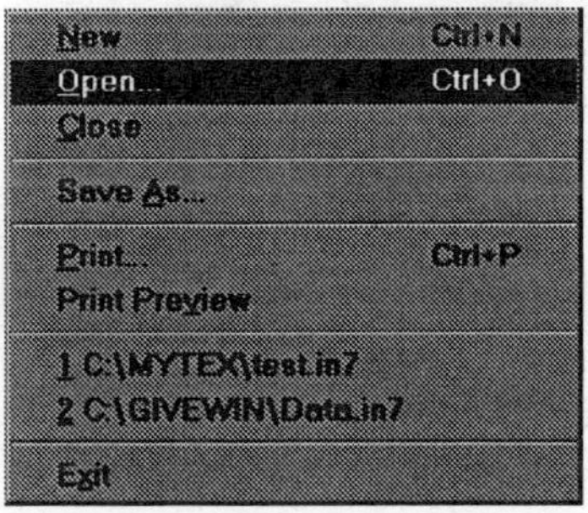

and choose Open. If you installed in the default directory structure, the data will be in the `\Program Files\GiveWin\PcFiml` subdirectory, so locate that directory and select pcftut1:

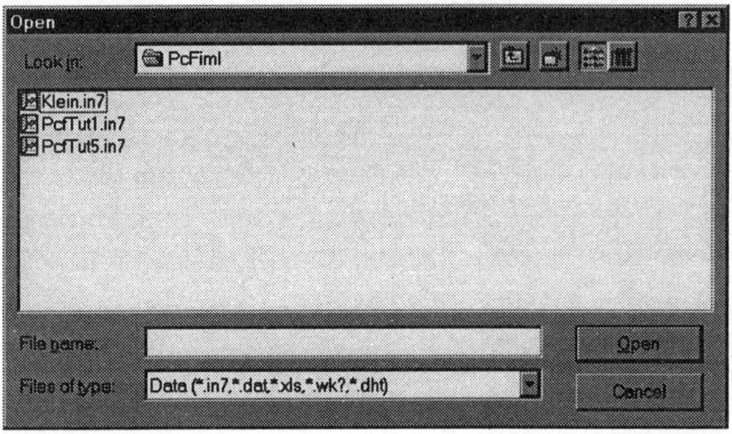

The data file will be loaded, and displayed minimized at the lower left of the GiveWin window:

The data set comprises four stochastic variables, denoted *Ya*, *Yb*, *Yc* and *Yd*; a *Constant*, *Seasonal* and *Trend* are automatically created by PcFiml when required. The data are computer-generated, to mimic a realization of a monthly vector stochastic process representable by a (log)linear dynamic system. The tutorials will explain the use of PcFiml by analysing and modelling these four variables over their sample period of 240 observations, 1974(1)–1993(12). We retain the data points 1994(1)–1998(12), where there are no outcomes (signalled by the number −9999.99 for missing data), for multi-step forecasting exercises later.

Bring the window into view by clicking on the icon with two overlapping boxes (Windows NT and 95; for Windows 3.1: double click on the database) to show the actual database (note that the left-most panel of GiveWin's status bar shows the data value with maximum accuracy):

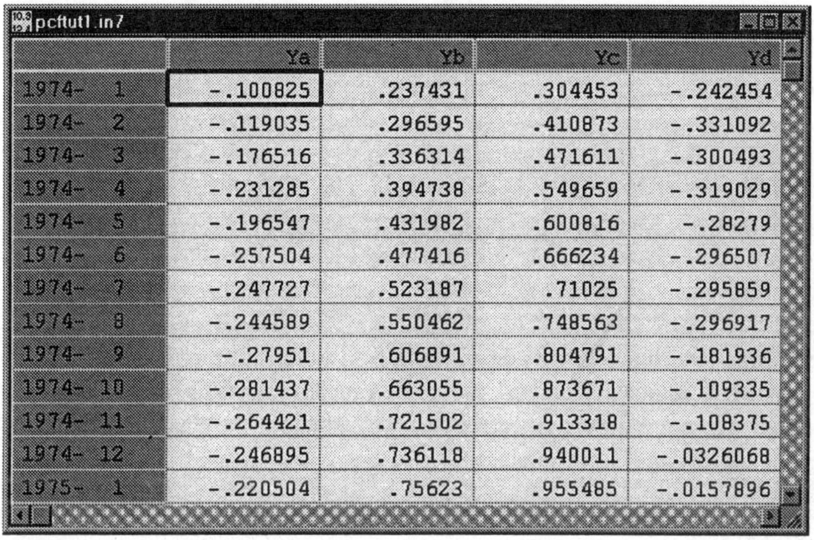

pcftut1.in7

	Ya	Yb	Yc	Yd
1974- 1	-.100825	.237431	.304453	-.242454
1974- 2	-.119035	.296595	.410873	-.331092
1974- 3	-.176516	.336314	.471611	-.300493
1974- 4	-.231285	.394738	.549659	-.319029
1974- 5	-.196547	.431982	.600816	-.28279
1974- 6	-.257504	.477416	.666234	-.296507
1974- 7	-.247727	.523187	.71025	-.295859
1974- 8	-.244589	.550462	.748563	-.296917
1974- 9	-.27951	.606891	.804791	-.181936
1974- 10	-.281437	.663055	.873671	-.109335
1974- 11	-.264421	.721502	.913318	-.108375
1974- 12	-.246895	.736118	.940011	-.0326068
1975- 1	-.220504	.75623	.955485	-.0157896

Double clicking on the variable name shows the documentation of the variable. For the *Ya* variable:

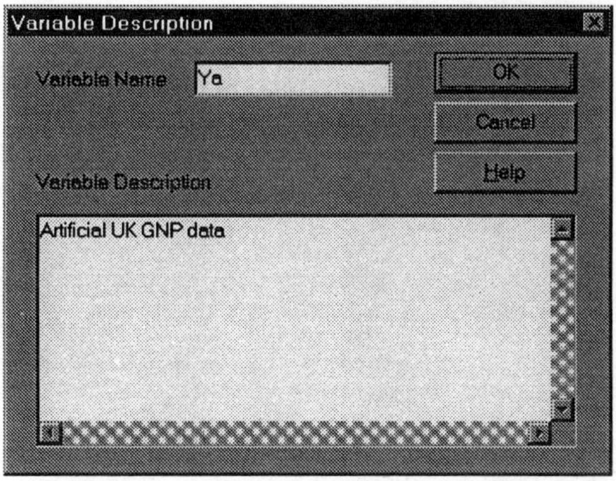

The data can be manipulated, much like in a spreadsheet program. Here we shall not need these facilities, so *minimize* the window again: click on the first button in the right-hand side of the window (Windows NT and 95; in Windows 3.1: click on the downward-pointing button). Do not click on the cross: this closes the database, thus removing it from GiveWin and so PcFiml (this operates differently from version 8).

2.4 Data description

After loading a new data set for use in PcFiml, it is important to check the data (for typing errors; with human-readable files, did we accidentally transpose the data matrix?). This is best done using the powerful graphical tools of GiveWin. You can graph one or many variables over time, create cross-plots and all this for up to 36 graphs at a time. Graphs in these tutorials were saved as PostScript files (.eps) using the black/white/gray colour model. If you changed line thickness etc., the graphs will look slightly different.

The graphics facilities of GiveWin are easy to use. This section will show you how to make time plots and cross plots of variables in the database. GiveWin offers automatic selections of scaling etc., but you will be able to edit these graphs, and change the default layout such as line colours and line types. Graphs can also be saved in a variety of formats for later use in a word processor or for reloading to GiveWin. All these issues are fully described in the GiveWin manual.

2.4.1 A first graph

Graphics is the first entry on the Tools menu. Activate the command to see the following dialog box (or click on the cross-plot graphics icon on the toolbar):

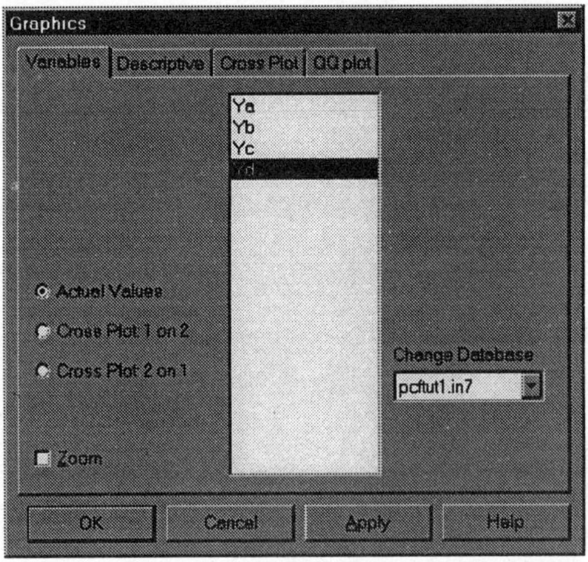

This is the first example of a dialog with a multiple selection list box. In such a list box you can mark as many items as you want. Here we mark all the variables we wish to graph. With the keyboard you can only mark a single variable (by using the arrow up and down keys) or range of variables (hold the shift key down while using the arrow up or down keys).

With the mouse there is more flexibility:

- single click to select one variable;
- hold the left mouse button down to select a range of variables;
- hold the `Ctrl` key down and click to select additional variables;
- hold the `Shift` key down and click to extend the selection range.

In this example, we select *Ya*, then press the Apply button. The graph which appears beneath the dialog box shows one Figure. Here, we will also plot the other three variables, so select *Yb*, Apply, then *Yc*, Apply, and finally *Yd*, pressing the OK button after the fourth. The outcome is shown in Figure 2.1 (there may be minor differences in the positions of the legends or the axis lengths). You can pick the legend up with the mouse, and move it to another position in the graph as desired.

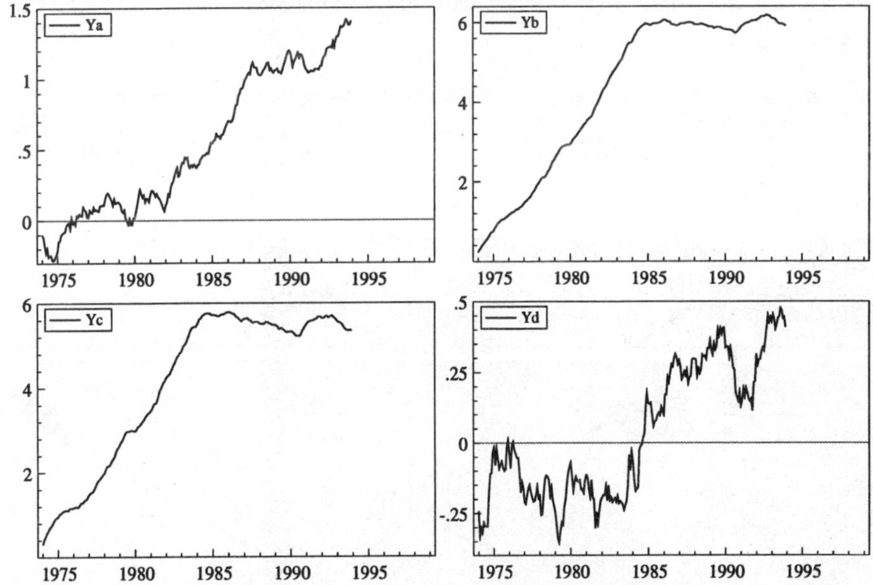

Figure 2.1 Time-series of the four variables.

The first series resembles the log of UK GNP (see, for example, Hendry and Doornik, 1994), the second and third resemble logs of Dutch Consumers' expenditure and income (see Winder and Palm, 1989), and the last is like the log of a floating real exchange rate. There are clear upward trends in all four series, but this is erratic in the first and especially the fourth, and there appears to a break in the trend growth of *Yb* and *Yc* around late 1984. Such behaviour is compatible with the series being integrated (possibly of order 1, denoted by I(1)), but does not preclude other explanations (for example, stationary around a deterministic – but perhaps split – trend). However, there is no obvious seasonality in the data. Throughout these tutorials we will consider the data to be in log form.

Most graphs in this book are boxed in, obtainable by choosing Graphics Setup from the View menu, and selecting the Layout page then clicking on Boxed. The View and Edit menu show the available options for graphs: while you have it open, click on Keep Graph, so later graphs will appear in new windows. Alternatively, to add further graphs to those on-screen, just click on the Graphics toolbar again and select the desired variables.

Next, we will plot the data both over time and against each other, in pairs (*Ya*,*Yd*) and (*Yb*,*Yc*). Selection is similar to that for single series, but now mark both (*Ya*,*Yd*), then press the Apply button. To cross plot these variables, select *Ya* and *Yd* again, and click on Cross Plot 1 on 2 then press the Apply button. Repeat the two operations for time-series and cross plots of *Yb* and *Yc*, pressing the OK button after the fourth. The outcome is shown in Figure 2.2 (again perhaps subject to minor differences: we have matched the time series of *Ya* and *Yd* for both scale and range, and comment on the regression lines momentarily).

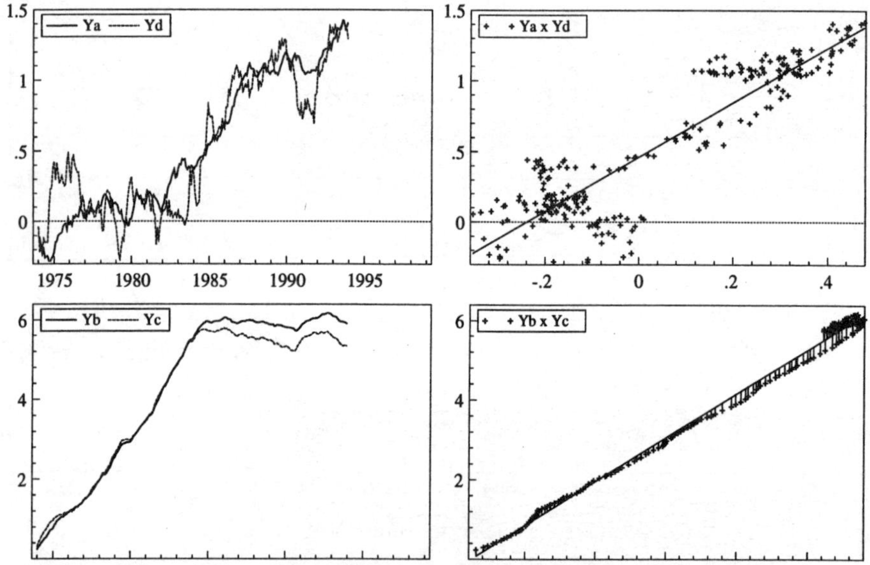

Figure 2.2 Time series and cross-plots for pairs of variables.

Clearly, the two sets are highly correlated within pairs, but behave differently between. Further, (*Yb*,*Yc*) seem to have moved closely together at the start of the sample, but diverged later, at the point when rapid growth stopped.

GiveWin graphs can be edited while on screen: double click on the first cross plot, select the Regression, Scale page in the Graphics Properties dialog, and add a regression line as shown in Figure 2.2. We have also added a linear regression to the second cross plot, including projections from the line to the points. To access that facility, simply mark Projections when selecting the Regression, Scale page in the Graphics Properties dialog. The GiveWin book describes the available facilities in detail.

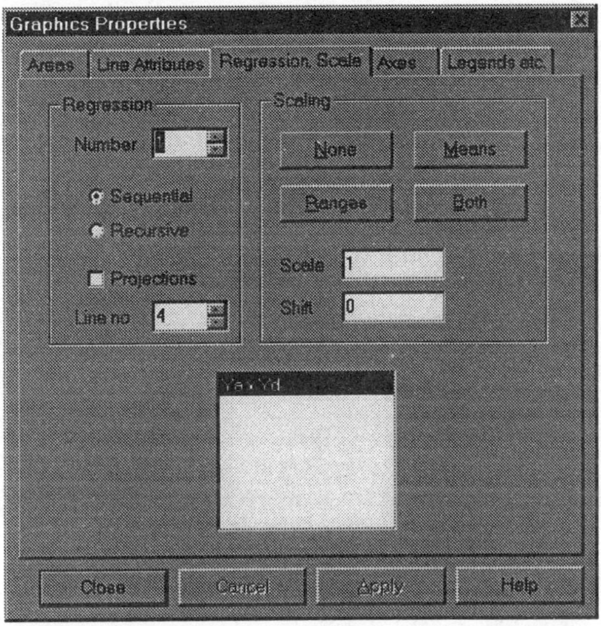

2.4.2 Calculator

Since the data series are individually non-stationary, other features may be more evident in graphs of the first differences of the variables. To create these, access the calculator; click on its icon, or on Tools, then Calculator.

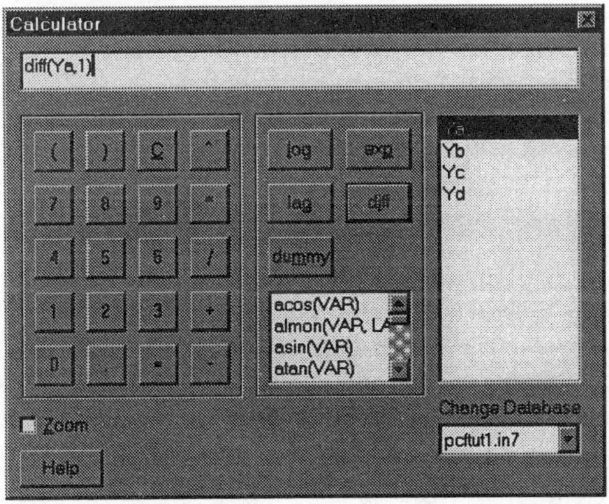

Highlight *Ya* (click with the mouse) then double click on 'diff', and finally click on '=' (or type =). Accept the name *DYa* offered by GiveWin. Repeat for *Yb*, *Yc*, *Yd*, then press `Esc` to return to the Results window. Repeat the operations used to obtain Figure 2.2, but now for the differenced series. This leads to Figure 2.3.

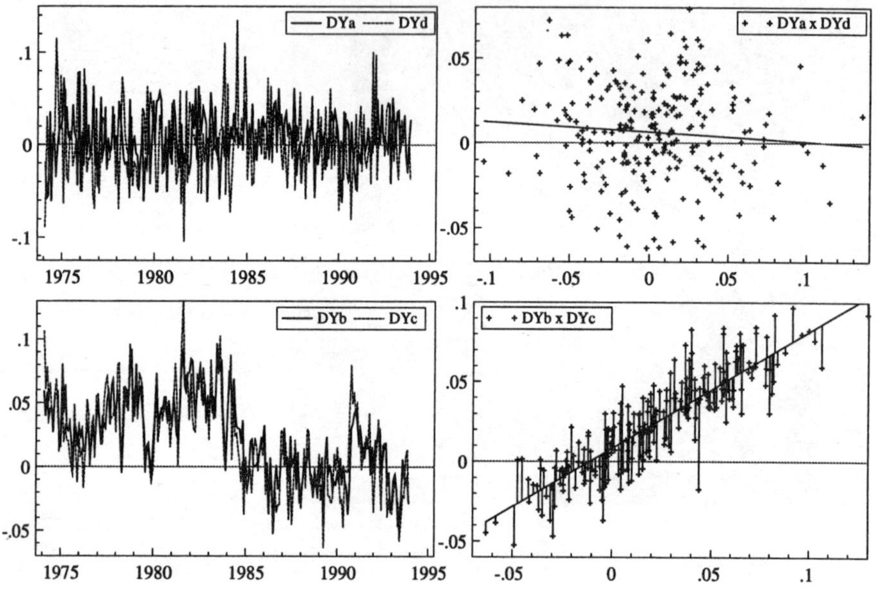
DYa DYd
+ DYa x DYd
DYb DYc
+ DYb x DYc

Figure 2.3 Time series and cross-plots for pairs of differences.

The differences do not seem to be integrated, although (*DYb*,*DYc*) show noticeable serial and cross correlation. Since the differences are autocorrelated, a lag length of 2 is the minimum needed to characterize the outcomes. The possible change in the growth rate of (*Yb*,*Yc*) is visible as a small shift downwards in the region where (*DYb*, *DYc*) fluctuate. We have added linear regression lines to the two cross plots, including projections from the line to the points in the last graph.Results

Calculator transformations are logged to the Results window, which currently resembles:

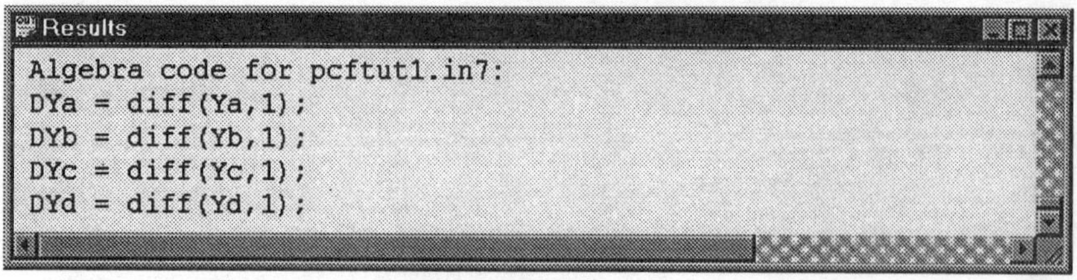
Results
Algebra code for pcftut1.in7:
DYa = diff(Ya,1);
DYb = diff(Yb,1);
DYc = diff(Yc,1);
DYd = diff(Yd,1);

These can be copied to the clipboard (the 'two-pages' icon), then pasted into the Algebra Editor obtained by clicking on the Alg icon:

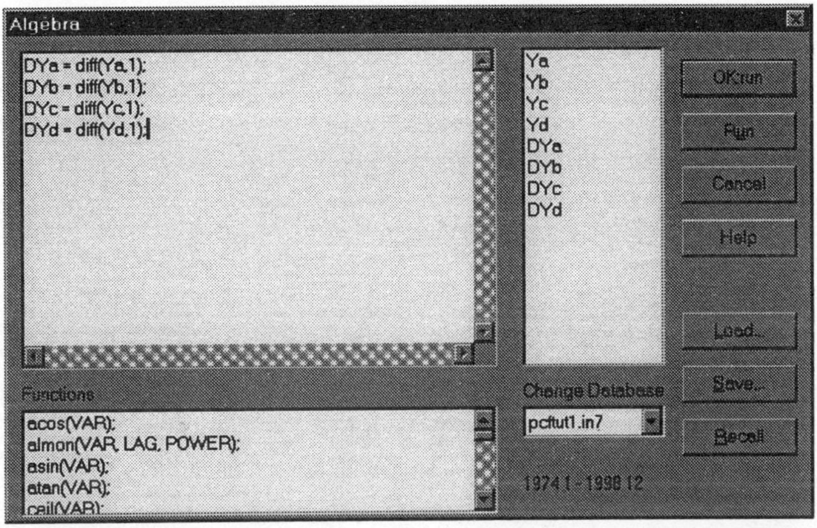

Such operations can be saved as an .ALG file for later use to economize on the size of databases.

2.4.3 Graph saving and printing

To print a graph directly to the printer, click on the printer icon in the toolbar. You can preview the result first using the Print Preview command from the File menu.

Graphs can be saved to disk in various formats:

- Windows metafile (.WMF);
- Enhanced metafile (.EMF, Windows 95 and Windows NT only);
- Encapsulated PostScript (.EPS), which is the format used to produce all the graphs in this book;
- GiveWin Graphics File (.GWG).

The GWG format is particular to GiveWin; no other program can read it and no printer can handle it. However, it is the only format which you can reload into GiveWin for further editing, saving later in the appropriate format for your word processor.

This completes the getting started chapter. We hope that you're now ready for the more substantial econometric modelling of dynamic systems.

Part II

PcFiml Tutorials

Chapter 3

System Formulation, Estimation and Evaluation

3.1 Introduction to dynamic systems

The Formulate System command on the Model menu is used for dynamic system formulation: formulate (or reformulate) a system for estimation by selecting variables and lag lengths in the Data selection dialog box. When you press OK, you will be taken automatically to the Estimation dialog.

The modelling process in PcFiml starts by focusing on the *system*, often called the *unrestricted reduced form* (URF), which can be written as (using simple dynamics):

$$\mathbf{y}_t = \boldsymbol{\pi}_1 \mathbf{y}_{t-1} + \boldsymbol{\Gamma}_1 \mathbf{z}_t + \mathbf{v}_t, \mathbf{v}_t \sim \mathsf{IN}_n \left[\mathbf{0}, \boldsymbol{\Omega}\right],$$

where $\mathbf{y}_t, \mathbf{z}_t$ are respectively $(n \times 1)$ and $(q \times 1)$ vectors of observations at time t, for $t = 1 \ldots T$, on the endogenous and non-modelled variables. A *vector autoregression* (VAR) arises when there are no $\mathbf{z}$ (but there could be a constant, seasonals or trend), and all $\mathbf{y}$ have the same lag length. An example of a two-equation system is:

$$\begin{aligned} Ya_t &= \delta_0 + \delta_1\, Ya_{t-1} + \delta_2\, Yb_{t-1} + \delta_3\, Ya_{t-2} + \delta_4\, Yb_{t-2} + \delta_5\, Yc_t \\ Yb_t &= \delta_6 + \delta_7\, Ya_{t-1} + \delta_8\, Yb_{t-1} + \delta_9\, Ya_{t-2} + \delta_{10}\, Yb_{t-2} + \delta_{11}\, Yc_t \end{aligned} \tag{3.1}$$

In a system each equation has the same variables on the right-hand side; here with one lag on *Ya*, 2 on *Yb*, and none on *Yc*. This system would be a VAR when $\delta_5 = \delta_{11} = 0$.

A more compact way of writing the system is:

$$\mathbf{y}_t = \boldsymbol{\Pi}_u \mathbf{w}_t + \mathbf{v}_t, \tag{3.2}$$

where $\mathbf{w}$ contains $\mathbf{z}$, lags of $\mathbf{z}$ and lags of $\mathbf{y}$.

An in-depth discussion of the econometric analysis of a dynamic system is given in Chapter 10.

3.2 Formulating a system

Select the Model menu on PcFiml, and choose Formulate System (which should be highlighted).

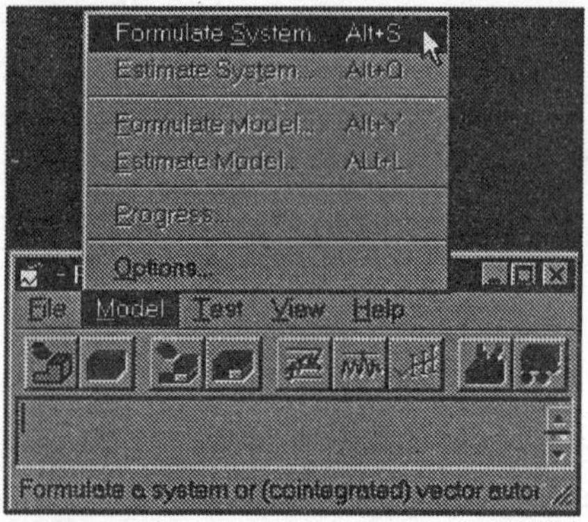

The key information required by PcFiml in order to formulate the system comprises:

- the menu of endogenous variables (here *Ya* to *Yd*);
- their lag lengths (here 3; a common length is needed later for cointegration analysis);
- the choice of deterministic variables (e.g., Constant and Trend);
- and their status (unrestricted, or whether they enter only the long-run solution of the system);
- any additional unmodelled variables (none here).
- Later, estimation choices will need to specify the sample period and the method of estimation. The next two dialogs elicit this information in a direct way.

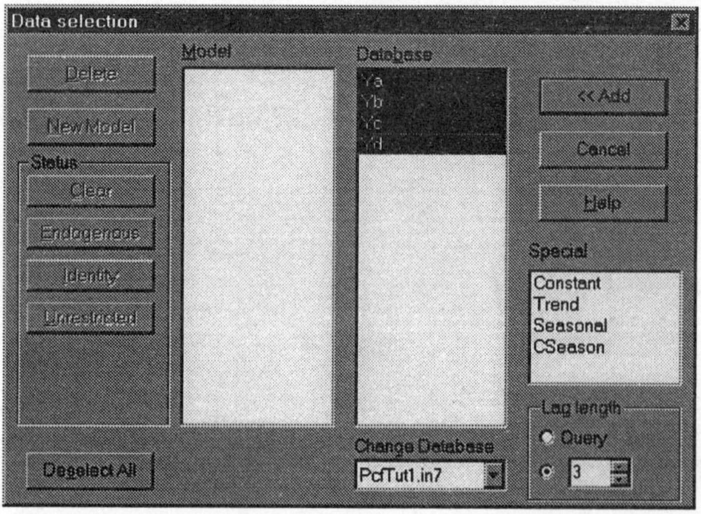

First set the lag length to three (in the bottom right corner). Mark *Ya*, *Yb*, *Yc*, *Yd*, *Trend* (refer to page 18 for a discussion of multiple selection list boxes), press the Add button. Current-dated variables are automatically denoted as E(ndogenous) unless they are selected from the list of special variables (*Constant*, *Trend* and seasonals here; these are by default classified as U(nrestricted)). Lags of system variables are not created. The next two sections discuss these issues.

Change the status of *Trend* from U(nrestricted) to exogenous (so it can be restricted in a later tutorial to enter the long run only, precluding a quadratic trend in the levels if some of the variables are found to have unit roots). To achieve this, mark *Trend* in the model list, and press the Clear button to clear its status. The following capture shows the dialog just before pressing Clear:

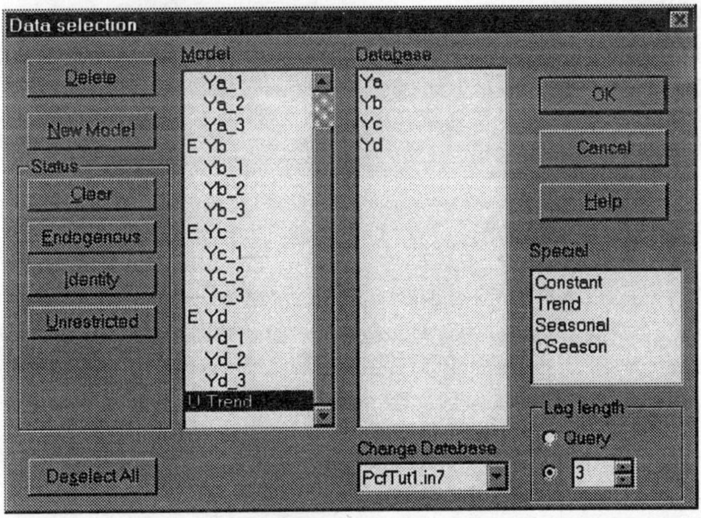

Other mouse-based operations are: double clicking on a variable in the database or a special variable will add that variable to the system specification; double clicking on a system variable will clear its status.

Press the OK button to accept the system as formulated, to bring up the estimation dialog.

3.3 Special variables

The list of special variables contains the deterministic variables which are frequently used in a model. For annual data, these are the *Constant* and the *Trend*. The constant always has the value 1. The trend is 1 for the first database observation, 2 for the second, etc.

For non-annual data, PcFiml automatically creates a seasonal. The Seasonal is non-centred, whereas CSeason is centred (mean 0). An example using quarterly data is:

	Trend	Seasonal	CSeason	Seasonal_1	Seasonal_2	Seasonal_3
1980 1	1	1	0.75	0	0	0
1980 2	2	0	−0.25	1	0	0
1980 3	3	0	−0.25	0	1	0
1980 4	4	0	−0.25	0	0	1
1981 1	5	1	0.75	0	0	0
1981 2	6	0	−0.25	1	0	0
1981 3	7	0	−0.25	0	1	0
1981 4	8	0	−0.25	0	0	1

Seasonal will always be 1 in quarter 1, independent of the first observation in the sample. When adding the seasonal to a model which already has a constant term, PcFiml will add Seasonal, Seasonal_1 and Seasonal_2. That corresponds to Q(1), Q(2) and Q(3). When there is no constant, Seasonal_3 is also added.

3.4 Unrestricted variables

Variables can be classified as *unrestricted*. Such variables will be partialled out, prior to estimation, and their coefficients will be reconstructed afterwards. Suppose, for example, that the constant in the above example is set to unrestricted. Then *Ya*, *Ya_1*, *Yb_1*, *Ya_2*, *Yb_2* and *Yc* are regressed on the constant; in subsequent estimation, PcFiml will use the residuals from these regressions and omit the constant (the coefficients $\delta_1 \ldots \delta_5$ and $\delta_7 \ldots \delta_{11}$ in (3.1) are unaffected). Although unrestricted variables do not affect the basic estimation, there are some important differences:

(1) Following estimation: the R^2 measures and corresponding F-test are relative to the unrestricted variables.

(2) In recursive estimation: the coefficients of unrestricted variables are fixed at the full sample values.

(3) In cointegration analysis: unrestricted variables are partialled out together with the short-run dynamics, whereas restricted variables (other than lags of the endogenous variables) are restricted to lie in the cointegrating space.

(4) In FIML estimation: again, the result does not depend on the fact whether a variable is unrestricted or not, but estimation of the smaller model could improve convergence properties of the non-linear estimation process.

(5) In heteroscedasticity tests: squares and cross-products of unrestricted variables are not included in the tests.

3.5 Estimating a system

After pressing the OK button to accept the system as formulated, PcFiml brings up the Estimation dialog:

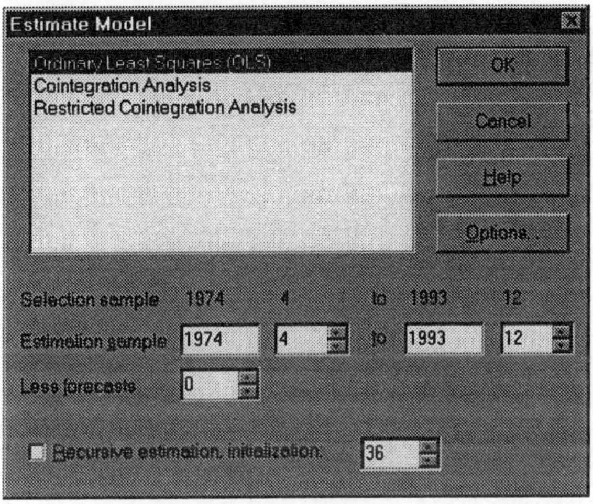

Check that the estimation sample is set to 1974(4)–1993(12), to ensure a common sample for all that follows. Ordinary Least Squares (OLS) should be highlighted: click on OK to produce the estimation output. The Message window shows the state of computation, and any warnings or other messages as they occur.

Even in such a small system as the present one, a fair volume of output appears: yet we have in fact set the Options dialog to produce minimum output, and adding tests, forecasts etc., will magnify the output considerably. Recursive estimation will produce a potentially enormous output. If there are n endogenous variables with m lags, and q non-modelled variables with r lags, then each equation has $k = nm + (r+1)q$ regressors. With T observations and $M-1$ retained for initialization, there will be $nk(T-M+1)$ coefficients, standard errors etc. plus $\frac{1}{2}n\,(n+1)\,(T-M+1)$ error variances. Here, that would produce about 15 000 basic numbers to handle – hardly 'data reduction', and hardly comprehensible if presented as pure numerical information. This problem of InfoGlut is tackled in PcFiml by using graphical presentations as far as possible to guide modelling. The complete estimation output is shown in §3.14 at the end of this chapter. We will draw on and report here only those items of most relevance as they are required. Thus, we now consider a few of the summary statistics.

First, the goodness of fit is best measured by the standard deviations of the residuals, as these are either in the same units as the associated dependent variables, or for log models, are a proportion. Moreover, they are invariant under linear transforms of the variables in each equation. They are presented with each equation as σ and collected at the end of the equation output. Here we have truncated the number of digits reported for readability:

```
      standard deviations of URF residuals
         Ya          Yb          Yc          Yd
    0.02633     0.01733     0.02337     0.03800
```

Consequently, the residual standard deviations are about 2.6%, 1.7%, 2.2% and 3.8% respectively. Assuming that three lags were sufficient to produce white noise errors on the system (an issue considered shortly), then these provide the baseline innovation standard errors. Next, the correlations between the residuals (also shown at the end of the output) are:

```
correlation of URF residuals
                 Ya          Yb          Yc          Yd
 Ya         1.00000
 Yb         0.08637      1.0000
 Yc        -0.05150      0.7153      1.0000
 Yd        -0.05394     -0.3995     -0.5235       1.000
```

There is one large positive correlation between *Yb* and *Yc* and two large negative correlations between *Yb* and *Yd*, and *Yc* and *Yd* respectively. Such features invite modelling. Finally, the correlations between fitted values and outcomes in each equation are:

```
correlation of actual and fitted
                Ya          Yb          Yc          Yd
            0.9987      1.0000      0.9999      0.9876
```

The squares of these correlations are the nearest equivalent to R^2 in a multivariate context, and as least-squares on each equation is valid here, their squares do coincide with the conventional coefficient of multiple correlation squared R^2. The correlation of actual and fitted remains useful when a model is developed, but no unique R^2 measure is calculable. The extremely high values reflect the non-stationarity apparent in the data and do not by themselves ensure a sensible model. The 1.0000 is simply owing to the number of digits reported and does not indicate a perfect fit. A full listing of the output is at the end of this chapter.

3.6 Graphic analysis and multivariate testing

Rather than peruse the detailed output of coefficients, standard errors and so on to try and interpret the system, we will now view the graphical output. Click on the Test menu and select the highlighted item Graphic Analysis (also available by clicking on the 'two graph lines' icon – the graphs in red and blue). Mark the first three options, namely Actual and fitted, Cross plot of actual and fitted values, and Residuals (scaled): with four endogenous variables, there will be 12 graphs.

Press OK on the graphics dialog. The graphs will appear all at once in GiveWin as shown in Figure 3.1. (When graphs get small, the legends are automatically removed; double click on a graph and use the legends dialog page to reinstate the legends.)

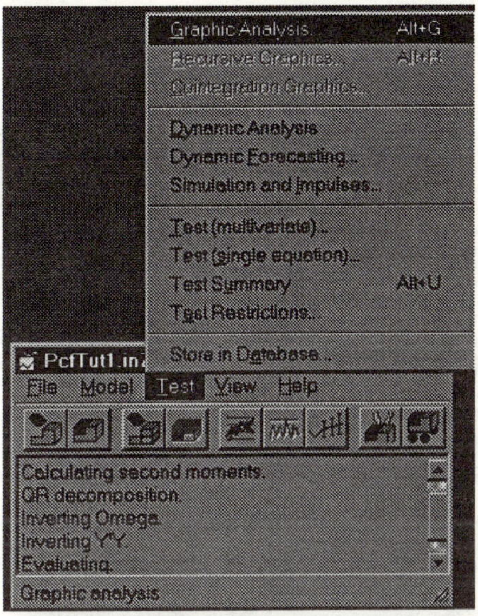

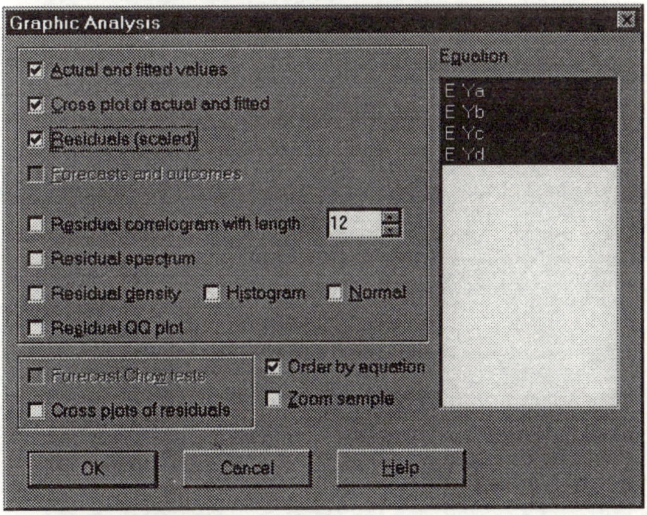

The obvious features of the graphs are the very close fits (owing to the integrated and non-stationary nature of the variables and, as before, should not be taken as evidence for the goodness of the system representation); the close tracking of the apparent change in trend (again, a *post-hoc* feature which least-squares essentially ensures will occur irrespective of its correctness); and the relatively random (white noise) appearance of the residuals in the final column. Further, the residuals seem to be relatively homoscedastic with few outliers visible.

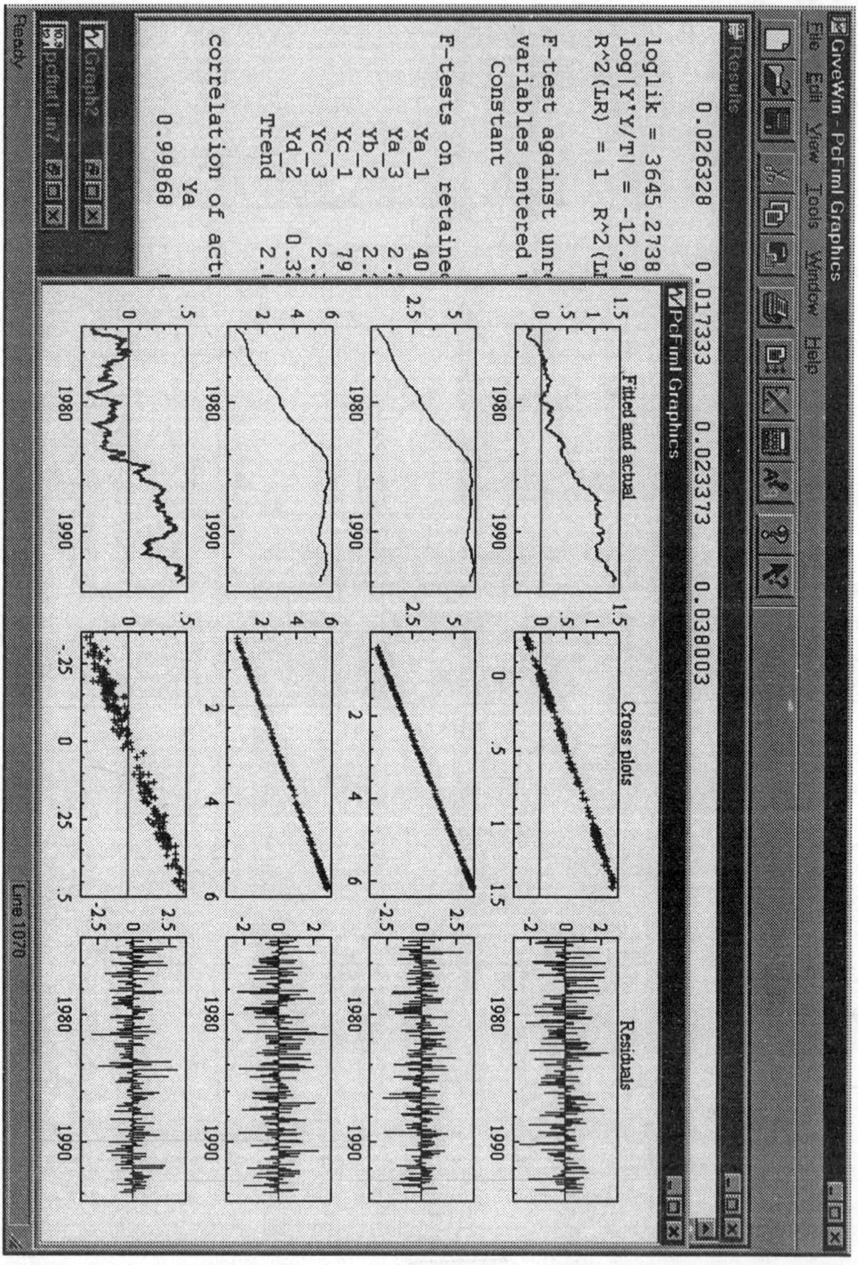

At this stage a complete screen capture of GiveWin will look approximately as above.

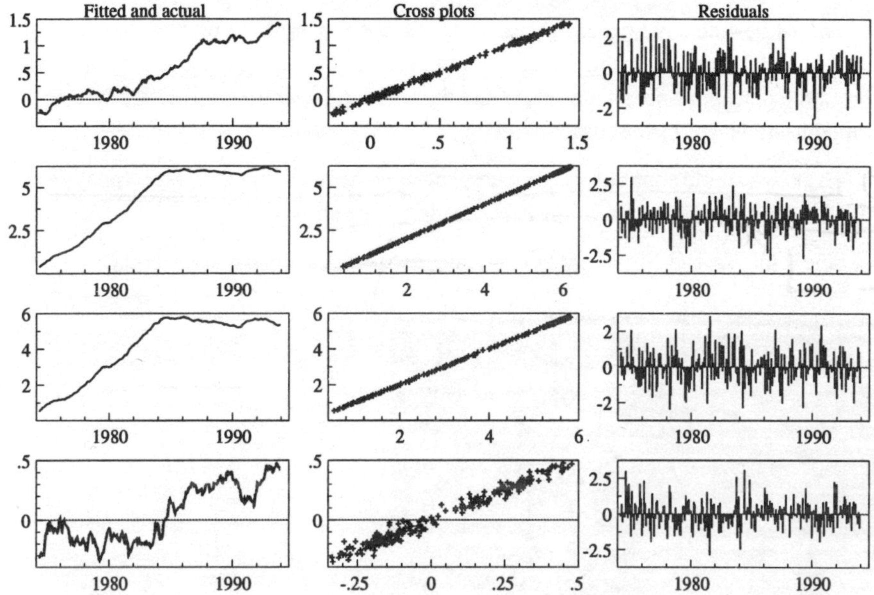

Figure 3.1 Actual and fitted values, their cross-plots, and scaled residuals.

We can investigate some of these aspects further by returning to the Graphic analysis, but now selecting residual correlogram, residual density, residual histogram and residual (cumulative) distribution (12 graphs again) as shown Figure 3.2.

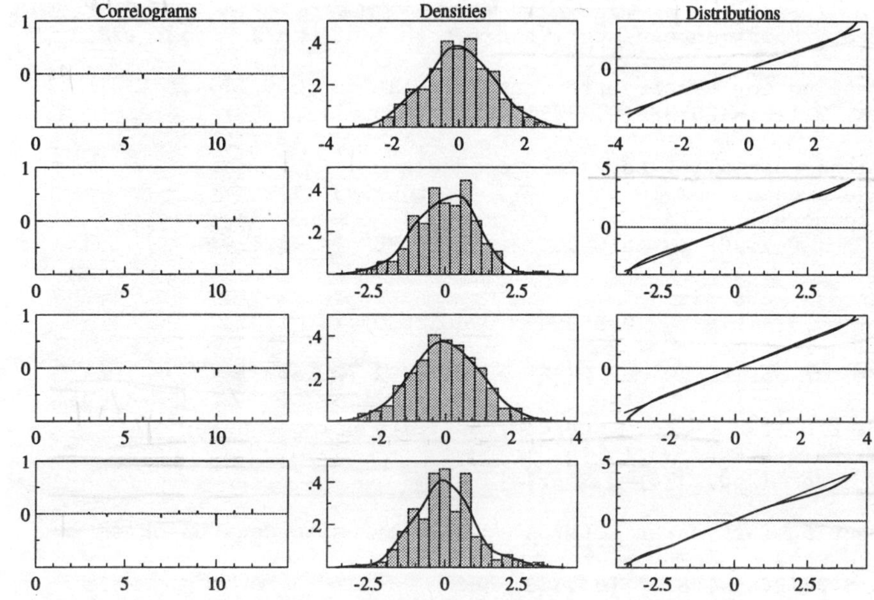

Figure 3.2 Residual correlograms, densities, histograms and distributions.

The white-noise nature of the residuals is loosely confirmed by the absence of any residual serial correlations in the correlograms, and normality seems a fair approximation to the distributional shape. Note that the standardized cumulative distributions are plotted beside N(0, 1) for comparison.

These are single equation diagnostics, and appropriate system mis-specification tests must be conducted for data congruency before proceeding.

Select the Test (Multivariate) menu, choose Test, and mark every entry:

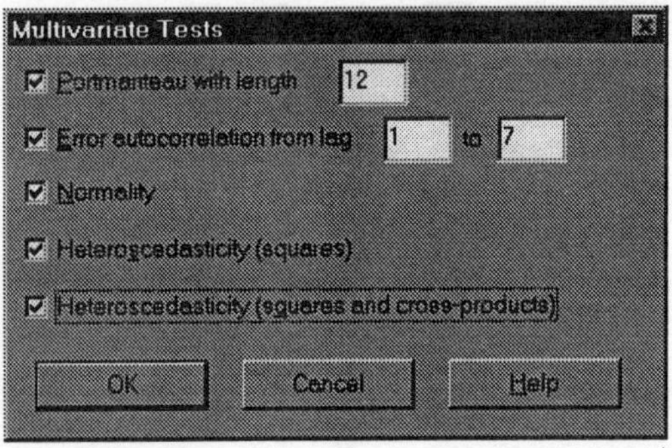

to obtain (after a suitable computational delay for the calculation of these more demanding statistics):

```
Vector portmanteau statistic for 12 lags and 237 obs: 178.9

Testing for vector error autocorrelation from lags 1 to 7
Chi^2(112)=120.38 [0.2773]  and  F-form(112,765)=1.0101 [0.4578]

Vector normality test for residuals
The present sample is:  1974 (4) to 1993 (12)
Skewness
     -0.20098    -0.97365      0.68936       2.7704

Excess kurtosis
     -0.41119    -0.55594   0.0013589        1.4747

Vector normality Chi^2( 8)=    11.792 [0.1608]

Testing for vector heteroscedasticity using squares
Chi^2(260)=264.93 [0.4037] and
  F-form(260,1776)=0.95021 [0.6974]

Testing for vector heteroscedasticity using squares&cross-
products
Chi^2(1040)=1061.1 [0.3179] and
  F-form(1040,1118)=0.91465 [0.9282]
```

If the χ^2 tests for heteroscedasticity have 240 and 900 degrees of freedom on your screen, then you forgot to clear the status of the *Trend*.

No test reveals any substantive problem, so we treat the system as data congruent for the time being. The degrees of freedom of these tests tend to be very large, so considerable mis-specification could be hidden within an insignificant test, but without some notion as to its form, little more can be done. Should many individual tests be conducted, it is important to control the overall size of the procedure. However, we have also ignored the integrated (I(1)) nature of the data in setting implicit critical values: since these should usually be larger, and no hypothesis as yet suggests rejection, no practical problems result.

3.7 System reduction

We now return to the system specification-test information, and consider the F-tests for the various variables in the system. The first of these is for the overall significance in the system of each regressor in turn (that is, its contribution to all four equations taken together):

```
F-tests on retained regressors, F(4, 220)
   Ya_1      40.7047 [0.0000]**   Ya_2       1.37460 [0.2437]
   Ya_3      2.20961 [0.0689]     Yb_1       81.8847 [0.0000]**
   Yb_2      2.25769 [0.0639]     Yb_3      0.630489 [0.6412]
   Yc_1      79.1999 [0.0000]**   Yc_2       4.05550 [0.0034]**
   Yc_3      2.35642 [0.0547]     Yd_1       46.6737 [0.0000]**
   Yd_2     0.328333 [0.8588]     Yd_3      0.856701 [0.4908]
  Trend      2.02149 [0.0924]
```

Five system regressors are significant at the 1% level, and a further two at (nearly) the 5% level, with the *Trend* close to the 5% level. Conversely, *Yb*_3, *Yd*_2 and *Yd*_3 have high probability values (that is, are not at all significant) and seem redundant. Care is needed when eliminating variables that are highly intercorrelated (for example, *Yd*_2 and *Yd*_3), and since a common lag length is needed for the cointegration analysis, we first investigate deleting all lags at length 3, since none is very significant. Thus, select Model, Formulate System, and mark *Ya*_3, *Yb*_3, *Yc*_3 and *Yd*_3, and then Delete. Accept the reduced system, *keeping the estimation sample period unchanged*, estimate and the output appears. Again the details are reported at the end of this chapter, and here we note the same summary statistics as before:

```
correlation of URF residuals
                   Ya            Yb            Yc            Yd
 Ya            1.0000
 Yb          0.096181        1.0000
 Yc         -0.035921       0.71091        1.0000
 Yd         -0.063725      -0.38380      -0.52008        1.0000
```

```
standard deviations of URF residuals
           Ya           Yb           Yc           Yd
     0.026377     0.017372     0.023294     0.038148

correlation of actual and fitted
           Ya           Yb           Yc           Yd
      0.99865      0.99996      0.99991      0.98725
```

The residual standard deviations are essentially unaltered, confirming the unimportance for fit of the eliminated variables.

Next select Model, Progress to check the statistical relevance of the deletions. The Progress dialog is:

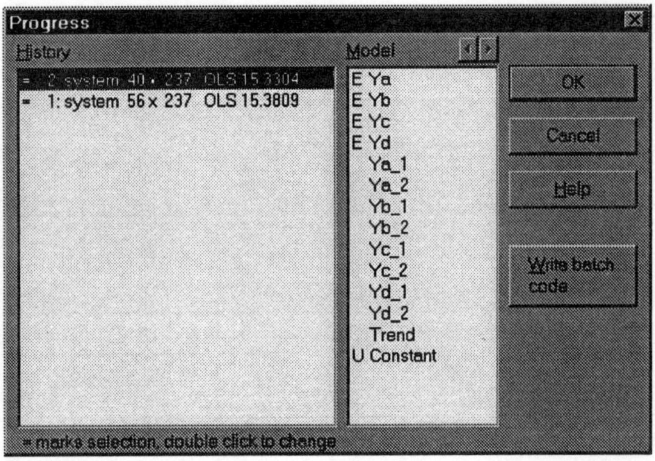

Accept to see the output:

```
Progress to date
system    T     p         log-likelihood         SC         HQ        AIC
3   237    40   OLS       3633.3104       -29.738    -30.087    -30.661
2     237    56   OLS          3645.2738    -29.470    -29.959    -30.762

Tests of system reduction
System  1 --> System  2: F(16, 672) =     1.4127 [0.1289]
```

The reduction by 16 parameters for eliminating lag length 3 is acceptable on the overall F-test, and reduces the 'costs' as measured by the model-selection criteria which seek to balance fit with degrees of freedom.

The summary F-statistics suggest that some lag-2 variables matter greatly, and the *Trend* remains borderline significant using conventional significance levels, so we retain it until after the more appropriate cointegration analysis in the next tutorial.

```
F-tests on retained regressors, F(4, 224)
  Ya_1     40.6206 [0.0000] **     Ya_2    0.394858 [0.8122]
  Yb_1     92.4701 [0.0000] **     Yb_2     8.03435 [0.0000] **
  Yc_1     85.0977 [0.0000] **     Yc_2     4.74698 [0.0011] **
```

```
 Yd_1     44.7151 [0.0000] **     Yd_2    0.210826 [0.9323]
 Trend    2.08552 [0.0836]
```

3.8 Dynamic analysis

As a prelude to cointegration analysis, we consider several features of the dynamics of the system. Chapter 10 explains the mathematics. Select Test, Dynamic Analysis which will produce extensive output as follows:

```
Dynamic analysis of the system
Lag-1 multipliers
                    Trend
 Ya            0.00029502
 Yb            0.00020480
 Yc            8.2633e-005
 Yd            0.00014370

Mean lag matrix
                       Ya          Yb          Yc          Yd
 Ya              -0.91496     0.14773   -0.032664    -0.13888
 Yb             -0.037509    -0.59272   -0.030256    0.033615
 Yc             -0.019612   -0.069637    -0.66901     0.15243
 Yd              0.085489   -0.041152    0.061909     -1.0146

Long-run matrix \Pi(1)-I = Po
                       Ya          Yb          Yc          Yd
 Ya              -0.12517    0.057707   -0.053269     0.11624
 Yb              0.025793    -0.11125     0.10976   -0.037207
 Yc              0.022914   0.0085615   -0.012237    -0.13002
 Yd           -0.00023537   -0.027224    0.028584   -0.022932

Long-run covariance
                       Ya          Yb          Yc          Yd
 Ya               0.28136
 Yb                8.8734      455.97
 Yc                8.8246      455.24      454.53
 Yd              -0.12881     -8.8055     -8.8067     0.20213

Long-run multipliers
                    Trend
 Ya             0.0045874
 Yb             -0.017839
 Yc             -0.019927
 Yd             0.0020836

Static long run
                    Trend
 Ya             0.0045874
 Yb             -0.017839
 Yc             -0.019927
 Yd             0.0020836
```

```
Standard errors of static long run
                     Trend
 Ya              0.0025150
 Yb                0.10125
 Yc                0.10109
 Yd              0.0021317

Eigenvalues of \Pi(1)-I
        real       complex       modulus
     -0.1325        0.0000        0.1325
   -0.004201        0.0000      0.004201
    -0.06746       0.02231       0.07105
    -0.06746      -0.02231       0.07105

Eigenvalues of companion matrix
        real       complex       modulus
    -0.04335       0.02839       0.05182
    -0.04335      -0.02839       0.05182
      0.3512       0.05705        0.3558
      0.3512      -0.05705        0.3558
      0.7929        0.0000        0.7929
      0.9938        0.0000        0.9938
      0.9316      0.007853        0.9316
      0.9316     -0.007853        0.9316
```

From the eigenvalues of $\hat{\mathbf{P}}_0 = \hat{\pi}(1) - \mathbf{I}_n$, the rank of the long-run matrix seems to be less than 4 (there is one very small eigenvalue), consistent with the apparent non-stationarity of the data. However, the rank is also greater than zero, suggesting some long-run relations, or cointegration, between the variables. The companion matrix shows no roots outside the unit circle, which might signal an explosive system, nor more roots close to unity than the dimension of the long-run matrix, consistent with the system being I(1), rather than I(2). Nevertheless, the three eigenvalues greater than 0.9 suggest at most 2 long-run relations: and more would cast doubt on our tentative classification. The non-stationarity is reflected in the huge values on the diagonal of the long-run covariance matrix, and the poorly determined static long-run multipliers. However, the long-run trend is nearly significant for *Ya*, supporting retaining it as a system regressor.

3.9 Recursive estimation

The next main feature to be described concerns graphical examination of parameter constancy using recursive methods. Select Model, Estimate, and tick the box for Recursive estimation. The output in the results window will be identical to OLS, but selecting Test reveals that Recursive Graphics is now a feasible selection. Choose it to bring up the Recursive Graphics dialog (also available by clicking on the 'Chow-test' icon – the red graph with the straight line):

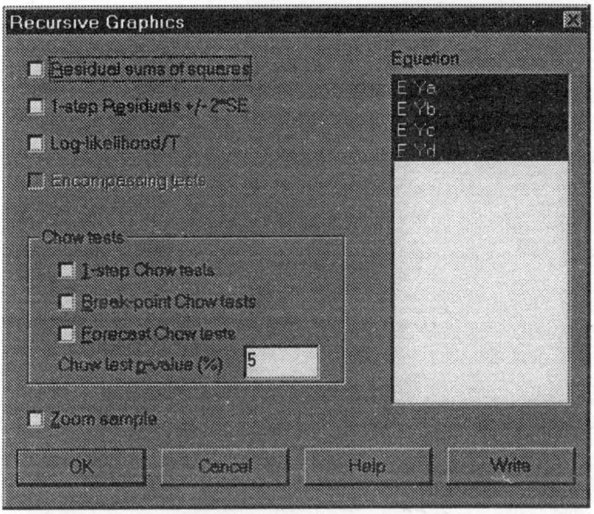

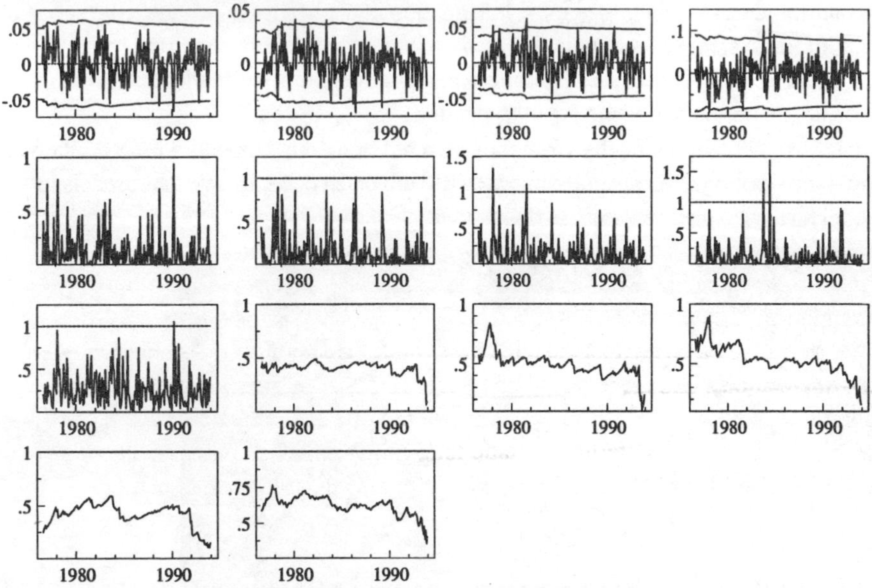

Figure 3.3 Recursive estimation statistics.

Mark 1-step residuals, 1-step Chow tests, and break-point Chow tests; set the significance level to 1% given that there are over 200 statistics per equation. There will be 14 graphs: 1-step residuals, 1-step and $N\downarrow$ (or break-point) Chows for each of the four equations, plus 1-step and $N\downarrow$ Chows for the system as a whole (called 'Chow' in the Figure). The output looks like Figure 3.3. The vast majority of the 1-step residuals lie within their anticipated 95% confidence intervals (that is, $0 \pm 2\tilde{\sigma}_t$). About 1% of the

1-step tests should be significant etc. Overall, constancy is not rejected, so the system with two lags seems acceptable on the analysis thus far.

The next stage is to consider the integration and cointegration properties of the system, which is the subject of the second tutorial. Prior to that, we note the use of PcFiml for forecasting, although in econometric terms, that would be best undertaken after the system has been reduced to I(0). But first we save the current system specification as a batch file.

3.10 Batch editor

While we have been formulating our system, PcFiml has been quietly recording the resulting form, and this can be viewed in the batch editor. Switch to GiveWin and activate the Batch Editor to see the system record as shown in the next screen capture (its icon is the page with 3 red arrows pointing right). This batch file should be saved before exiting the batch editor, so that it can be rerun on restarting to resume the analysis wherever it was terminated. As can be seen, the information in the batch file relates to the specification of the system (which variables are involved, their classification into endogenous, non-modelled and unrestricted variables, and the method of estimation with its associated sample period and recursive initialization).

PcFiml will automatically write the batch file of the final model to the Results window when exiting. It is also possible to write the batch code for selected models in the model history using the Progress dialog.

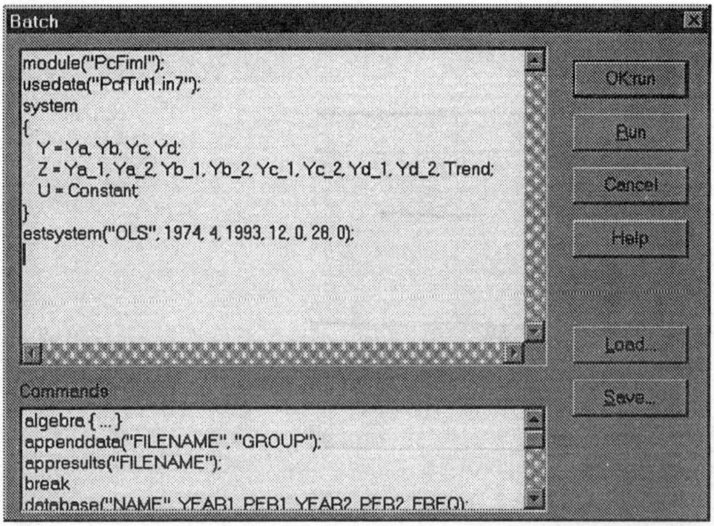

Finally, to run a batch file, click on OK. A full overview of the syntax is available through the help system, by pressing the Help button. Also see Appendix A1. If both PcGive and PcFiml are active, you can switch between the two by running the `module("PcFiml");` and `module("PcGive");` batch commands respectively.

Here we make a few changes. We keep the recursive estimation (to remove it, change the number 28 in `estsystem` to 0), but add in some batch code to create first differences, which we will use later. The final code is:

```
module("PcFiml");
usedata("pcftut1.in7");
algebra
{
  DYa = diff(Ya, 1);
  DYb = diff(Yb, 1);
  DYc = diff(Yc, 1);
  DYd = diff(Yd, 1);
}
system
{
  Y = Ya, Yb, Yc, Yd;
  Z = Ya_1, Ya_2, Yb_1, Yb_2, Yc_1, Yc_2, Yd_1, Yd_2, Trend;
  U = Constant;
}
estsystem("OLS", 1974, 4, 1993, 12, 0, 28, 0);
```

There is no need to save this file, as it is supplied with PcFiml as `pcftut1.fl` in the PcFiml directory.

3.11 Output options

The output written to the Results window depends on the options set from the Options dialog accessed from the Model menu. As can be seen, a wide variety of combinations of settings is feasible, from minimal to maximal output.

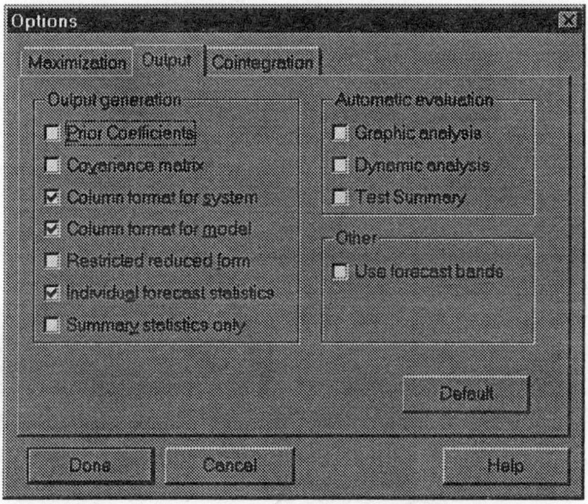

The following control is available over the generated output:

(1) Whether or not to report coefficients of variables marked unrestricted in the system;
(2) Whether or not to print the covariance matrix of the model coefficients and the restricted covariance matrix of the test for general restrictions;
(3) Whether or not to print the estimated system in the PcGive columnar format (otherwise the matrix format is used);
(4) Whether or not to print the estimated model in the PcGive columnar format (otherwise the equation format is used);
(5) Whether or not to report the restricted reduced form;
(6) Whether or not to report the individual forecast statistics, and the descriptive statistics of the forecast errors;
(7) Whether or not to report summary statistics only.

Whether or not to automatically invoke upon successful estimation:

(1) Graphic analysis;
(2) Dynamic analysis;
(3) Test summary.

Finally, whether to use forecast-error bars or bands.

The default uses the settings shown just above.

3.12 Forecasting

PcFiml supports three distinct types of forecast analysis. First, within the available data sample, sequences of 1-step-ahead out-of-estimation-sample forecasts can be generated. Select Model, Estimate, deselect recursive estimation and set the number of forecasts to 20, then accept.

The following summary statistics are reported (the profile can be used to set more extensive output):

```
1-step (ex post) forecast analysis 1992 (5) to 1993 (12)
Parameter constancy forecast tests:
using \Omega Chi^2(80)=69.177[0.8007] F(80,207)=0.86472[0.7713]
using  V[e]  Chi^2(80)=64.416[0.8978] F(80,207)= 0.8052[0.8676]
using  V[E]  Chi^2(80)=65.757[0.8743] F(80,207)=0.82197[0.8433]
```

Again, graphics provide a convenient medium, so select Test, Graphic Analysis, and mark forecasts and forecast Chow test, creating five graphs. The output is in Figure 3.4. The forecasts lie within their 95% confidence intervals (shown by the vertical error bars of ±2SE, based on the 1-step ahead forecast error variances), and the system constancy test is not significant at the 5% level at any horizon (this is an unscaled χ^2 test, with the 5% significance line as shown).

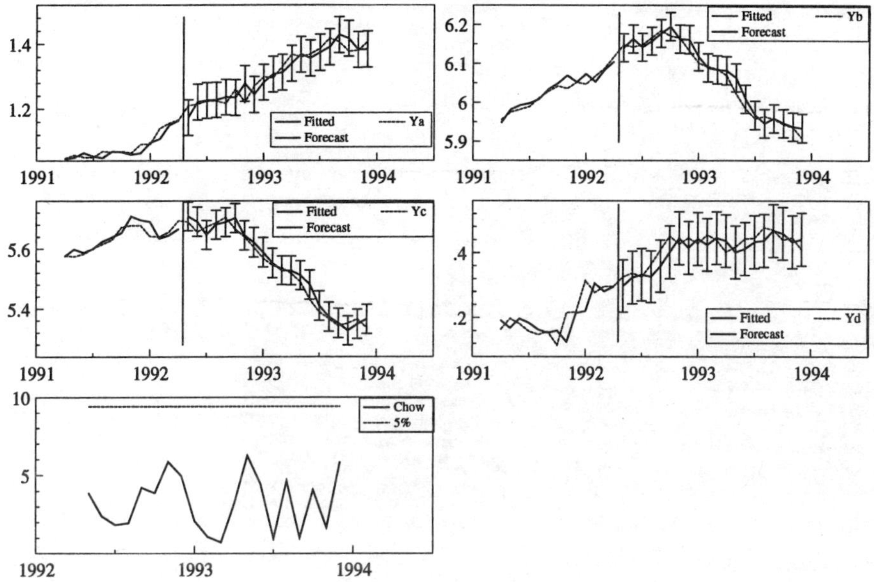

Figure 3.4 Forecast statistics.

For purely *ex ante* dynamic forecasts, select Dynamic Forecasting from the Test menu. The two types of forecasts available here are:

(1) Dynamic forecasts
(2) h-step forecasts
Up to h forecasts, the graphs will be identical to the dynamic forecasts. Thereafter, h-step forecasts will be graphed: at $T+h$ the dynamic forecast for $T+h$ starting from T, at $T+h+1$ the dynamic forecast for that period starting at $T+1$, at $T+h+2$ the dynamic forecast starting at $T+2$, etc.

Forecasts are drawn with or without 95% error bars or bands, but by default only the innovation uncertainty (error variance) is allowed for in the computed forecast error variances. Optionally, parameter uncertainty can be taken into account when computing the forecast error variances (but not for h-step forecasts), and is allowed only when there are no unrestricted variables.

In the dialog, set 44 periods, and mark the error variance option and accept to produce Figure 3.5. Note that you can switch between showing error bars and error bands in the Options dialog. Once a graph is on screen, you can switch between bands and bars as follows: double click on the graph, select Forecast x (time), and error band settings appear on the line attributes property page.

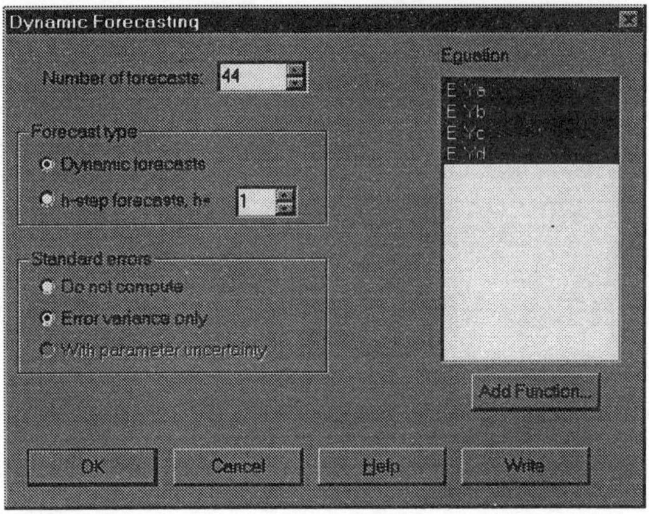

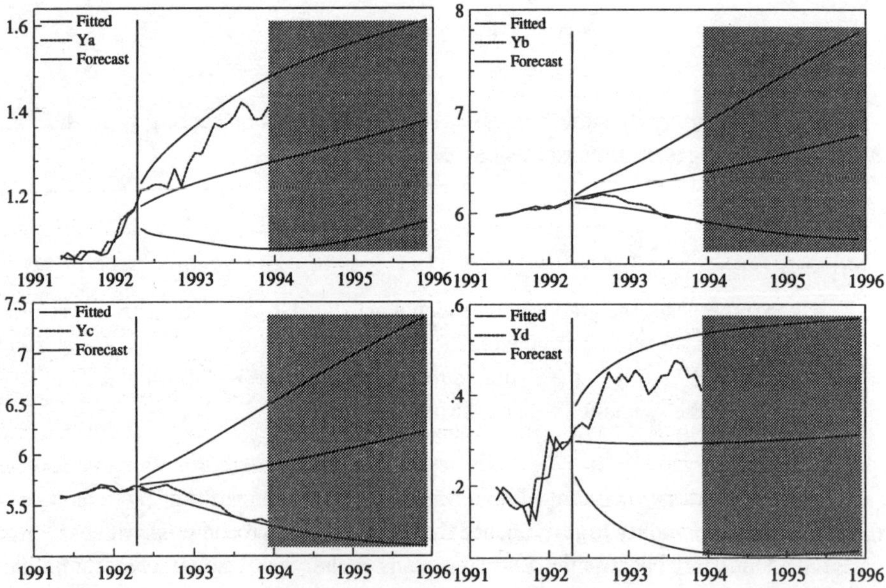

Figure 3.5 Dynamic forecasts.

We have highlighted the ex ante period. The uncertainty about the future increases rapidly, and little confidence can be held in the end-of-sample predictions. This is a natural consequence of the implicit unit roots in the system, and matches the large increases seen above between the conditional 1-step residual variances and the long-run variances. The data were actually available for the first 20 'out of sample' values, and as shown in

Figure 3.5, reveal the large potential departures between multi-step forecasts and outcomes that are compatible with even a considerable degree of forecast uncertainty.

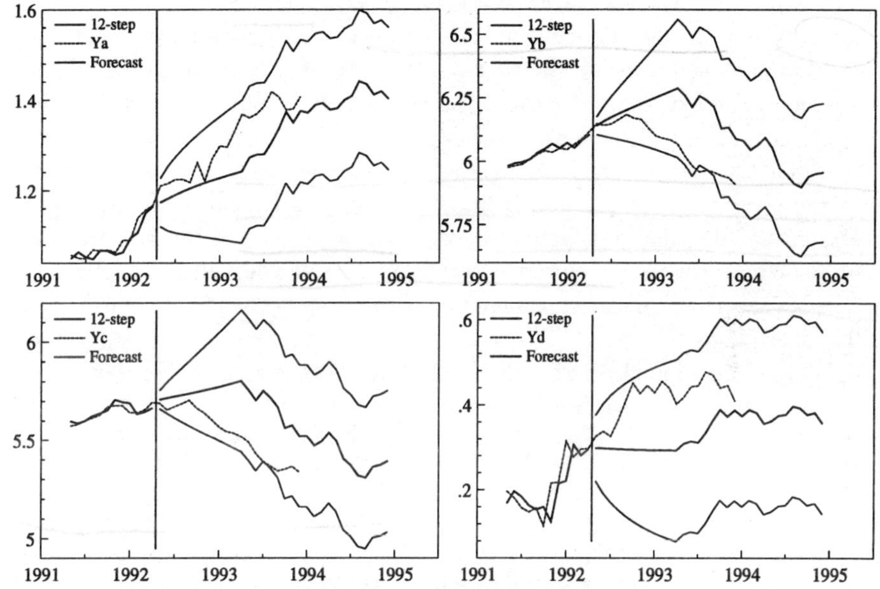

Figure 3.6 12-step forecasts.

The final forecast mode shown in Figure 3.6 is a sequence of h-step-ahead out-of-estimation-sample forecasts for any choice of h. Select Test, Dynamic Forecasting. The selection now follows the same path as the previous choice except that h-step must be marked in the Dynamic Forecasting dialog, and the desired value of h entered (set $h =$ 12 here, given that the frequency is monthly). Thus, choose 32 periods, mark the error bars and 1-step, but set the number of steps to 12. The output will coincide with that from dynamic forecasts for the first 12 steps, then continue at 12 steps for the remainder of the forecast period up to 12 periods beyond. In effect, therefore, dynamic forecasts correspond to setting h equal to the forecast period. The uncertainty remains constant from 12 steps onwards in Figure 3.6, and the forecasts start to behave more like the actual data. This happens because the 13th forecast is actually the 12-step forecast starting at $T + 2$, etc.

The outcomes are rather poor, even though the system in fact coincides with the reduced form of the data generation process (a secret we shall not reveal at this stage). The error bands are based on an asymptotic approximation which neglects parameter uncertainty, and this can substantially underestimate forecast error variances in small samples. One potential advantage of a more restricted model of the system is that parameter variability may be considerably reduced.

3.13 Equilibrium-correction representation

This is a simple yet useful transform of a dynamic system which can facilitate the interpretation of systems by mapping from $\mathbf{y}_t, \mathbf{y}_{t-1}, \mathbf{y}_{t-2}, \mathbf{y}_{t-3}$ etc. to $\Delta\mathbf{y}_t, \Delta\mathbf{y}_{t-1}, \Delta\mathbf{y}_{t-2}$, and $\mathbf{y}_{t-1}$ where only the first lag remains in levels. Linear systems are invariant under linear transforms in that the likelihood is unaltered, and if $\widehat{\mathbf{\Pi}}$ is the original estimate of a coefficient matrix $\mathbf{\Pi}$, and we map to $\mathbf{A\Pi}$, then the estimate of the transformed matrix $\widehat{\mathbf{A\Pi}}$ is equal to $\mathbf{A}\widehat{\mathbf{\Pi}}$. Unit roots are still estimated if any are present, but graphs and many specification test statistics are easier to interpret. Since the residuals are unaltered, diagnostic tests are not changed, nor are such calculations as dynamic analysis, dynamic forecasting and dynamic simulation. However, graphical analysis (such as actual and fitted, static forecasts etc.) will change to match the use of a dependent variable in differences. Note that this transformation was called error-correction form in the previous edition of this book.

In terms of the example in §3.1 (differenced variable names are prefixed by a D):

$$\begin{aligned} DYa_t &= \alpha_0 + \alpha_1 DYa_{t-1} + \alpha_2 DYb_{t-1} + \alpha_3 Ya_{t-1} + \alpha_4 Yb_{t-1} + \alpha_5 Yc_t \\ DYb_t &= \alpha_6 + \alpha_7 DYa_{t-1} + \alpha_8 DYb_{t-1} + \alpha_9 Ya_{t-1} + \alpha_{10} Yb_{t-1} + \alpha_{11} Yc_t \end{aligned}$$

Table 3.1 Comparison of ECF to levels and differenced system.

	Levels	Differenced
coefficients, t-values, etc.	√	
$\mathbf{\Omega}$, loglik, etc.	√	√
$\log\lvert\mathbf{Y}'\mathbf{Y}\rvert$		√
R^2, F-tests		√
actual and fitted		√
1-step forecasts		√
1-step forecasts parameter constancy tests	√	√
graphical analysis		√
recursive graphics	√	√
cointegration and cointegration graphics	√	
dynamic forecasting and simulation	√	
dynamic analysis	√[1]	
heteroscedasticity tests[2]		√
other mis-specification tests	√	√
general restrictions		√

[1]ECF does not report Lag-1 multipliers and standard errors of static long run.
[2]ECF different from levels owing to inclusion of squares.

Creating the equilibrium-correction form requires creating the first differences (using the calculator, or algebra code), then specifying the system using these differences, together with the first lag of the levels. In this case, since PcFiml will not recognize the relation between the lagged level and the differenced level in the differenced system, some results will not match. Call the manually-created system the *differenced system*. Imagine if PcFiml created the same representation internally, keeping track of the levels-differences identities: call this the ECF. Table 3.1 compares what the ECF would deliver to the system in levels and the differenced system; a $\surd$ indicates the results which are identical.

We have already created the differences using the Calculator in §2.4.2 (create them if you skipped this), so access the Formulate System dialog, select New Model, mark *DYa* to *DYd*, using 1 lag (as this extends back to 2 periods with $\Delta Ya_{t-1} = Ya_{t-1} - Ya_{t-2}$), now mark *Ya* to *Yd* again with 1 lag, and delete the current values of these (marked by E in the Model column), add the Trend (clear status), then click OK. The capture shows the setup prior to accepting:

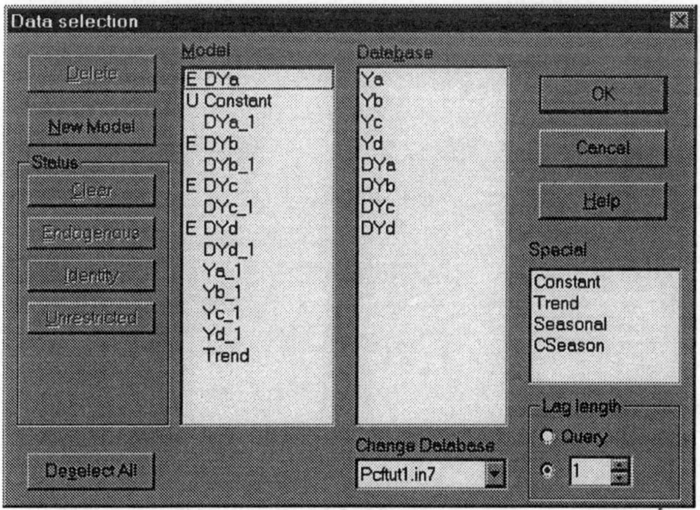

Choose OLS with 0 forecasts, still starting in 1974 (4), then accept. We only note the summary information on F-tests as most other statistics are unaltered (coefficient estimates are linear functions of those reported at the end of this chapter).

```
loglik = 3633.3104  log|\Omega| = -30.6608
|\Omega| = 4.8324e-014  T = 237
log|Y'Y/T| = -28.865
R^2(LR) = 0.834017  R^2(LM) = 0.278252

F-test on all regressors except unrestricted,
  F(36,841) = 14.366 [0.0000] **
variables entered unrestricted:
  Constant
```

```
F-tests on retained regressors, F(4, 224)
  DYa_1     0.394858 [0.8122]         DYb_1      8.03435 [0.0000] **
  DYc_1      4.74698 [0.0011] **     DYd_1     0.210826 [0.9323]
   Ya_1      5.78515 [0.0002] **      Yb_1      6.98141 [0.0000] **
   Yc_1      7.03095 [0.0000] **      Yd_1      14.1499 [0.0000] **
  Trend      2.08552 [0.0836]

correlation of actual and fitted
            DYa           DYb           DYc           DYd
        0.40771       0.83122       0.76312       0.17646
```

We have commented on many of the statistics above. The new ones concern the likelihood measures (several are reported for convenience), and the two R^2 measures, based on the likelihood ratio and Lagrange-multiplier principle (see Chapter 10).

The actual and fitted graphs are perhaps the most changed as Figure 3.7 shows (click the graphics icon, or `Alt+t,g`, and mark the first three options). The less than spectacular fits are clear, especially the much lower correlations implicit in the cross plots, although the scaled residuals graphs are identical to those shown above.

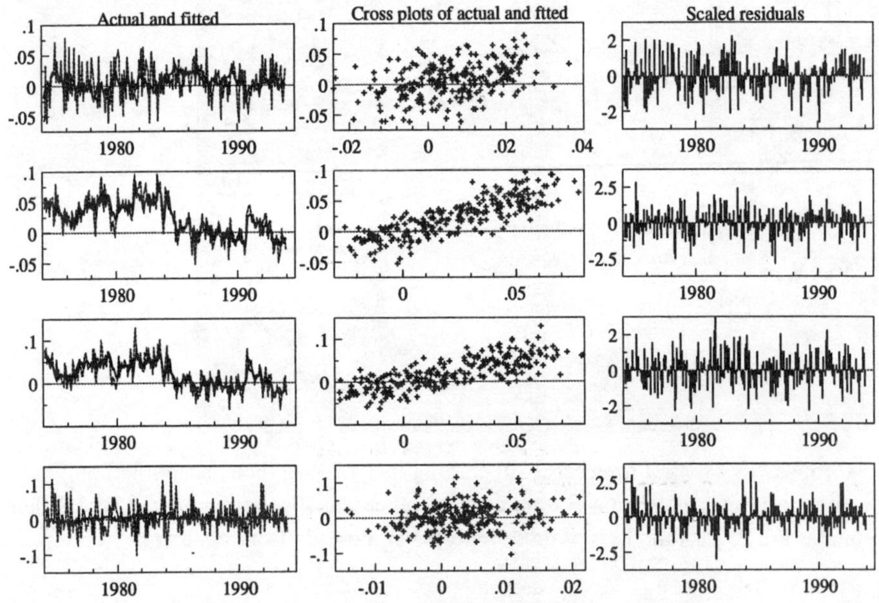

Figure 3.7 Fitted and actual values for differences.

There are many aspects that can now be explored without further guidance from us: try the test summary for additional single equation diagnostics; try forecasting without error bars, noting how misleading such results are, and compare them with the output from dynamic simulation.

This concludes the first tutorial on formulating, estimating, testing, and analysing a dynamic system. You can exit PcFiml, and turn to the next chapter. If you wish, you can save the Results window, but there is no need to save the database: remember that we changed it at the very start by creating differences; we shall recreate these in Chapter 5. The batch file is already provided, but otherwise it is easy to save the algebra file, or better still, add the algebra commands to the start of a batch file.

3.14 Listing of estimation output

```
--- PcFiml 9 session started at 12:49:17 on Wed. 11 Dec. 1996 ---

EQ(1) Estimating the unrestr.red. form by OLS (using PcfTut1.in7)
The present sample is:  1974 (4) to 1993 (12)

URF Equation 1 for Ya
Variable      Coefficient      Std.Error  t-value  t-prob
Ya_1              0.83355       0.067439   12.360  0.0000
Ya_2              0.12437       0.088392    1.407  0.1608
Ya_3            -0.078558       0.064784   -1.213  0.2266
Yb_1              0.21343        0.14548    1.467  0.1438
Yb_2            -0.026977        0.22052   -0.122  0.9027
Yb_3             -0.14439        0.13478   -1.071  0.2852
Yc_1            -0.091132        0.11724   -0.777  0.4378
Yc_2            -0.090933        0.17893   -0.508  0.6118
Yc_3              0.14369        0.11897    1.208  0.2284
Yd_1             0.097068       0.054249    1.789  0.0749
Yd_2            -0.022127       0.071338   -0.310  0.7567
Yd_3             0.040990       0.052049    0.788  0.4318
Trend          0.00033357     0.00014976    2.227  0.0269
Constant       0.00048046      0.0062565    0.077  0.9389

\sigma = 0.026328   RSS = 0.1545756338

URF Equation 2 for Yb
Variable      Coefficient      Std.Error  t-value  t-prob
Ya_1             0.011928       0.044398    0.269  0.7884
Ya_2           -0.0040349       0.058193   -0.069  0.9448
Ya_3             0.028708       0.042650    0.673  0.5016
Yb_1               1.1740       0.095777   12.257  0.0000
Yb_2             -0.21242        0.14518   -1.463  0.1448
Yb_3            -0.096526       0.088729   -1.088  0.2778
Yc_1              0.22896       0.077182    2.967  0.0033
Yc_2             -0.26585        0.11780   -2.257  0.0250
Yc_3              0.17003       0.078322    2.171  0.0310
Yd_1            -0.027632       0.035715   -0.774  0.4399
Yd_2            -0.050225       0.046965   -1.069  0.2860
Yd_3             0.037865       0.034266    1.105  0.2703
Trend          0.00016567    9.8594e-005    1.680  0.0943
Constant        0.0082488      0.0041189    2.003  0.0464

\sigma = 0.017333   RSS = 0.06699682846

URF Equation 3 for Yc
Variable      Coefficient      Std.Error  t-value  t-prob
Ya_1             0.026424       0.059868    0.441  0.6594
Ya_2             0.060322       0.078470    0.769  0.4429
Ya_3            -0.060013       0.057511   -1.043  0.2979
Yb_1            -0.073624        0.12915   -0.570  0.5692
Yb_2              0.14515        0.19577    0.741  0.4592
Yb_3            -0.069574        0.11965   -0.581  0.5615
Yc_1               1.3346        0.10408   12.824  0.0000
Yc_2             -0.42665        0.15885   -2.686  0.0078
Yc_3             0.085796        0.10561    0.812  0.4174
Yd_1             -0.10392       0.048160   -2.158  0.0320
Yd_2            -0.041504       0.063330   -0.655  0.5129
Yd_3             0.010405       0.046206    0.225  0.8220
Trend         9.2518e-005     0.00013295    0.696  0.4872
Constant         0.012011      0.0055542    2.163  0.0316

\sigma = 0.0233726   RSS = 0.1218198699

URF Equation 4 for Yd
Variable      Coefficient      Std.Error  t-value  t-prob
Ya_1             0.084159       0.097343    0.865  0.3882
Ya_2             -0.19727        0.12759   -1.546  0.1235
Ya_3              0.13580       0.093511    1.452  0.1479
Yb_1            -0.050796        0.20999   -0.242  0.8091
Yb_2             0.042642        0.31831    0.134  0.8936
Yb_3            -0.023777        0.19454   -0.122  0.9028
Yc_1              0.14639        0.16922    0.865  0.3879
```

```
Yc_2          -0.26604        0.25828    -1.030  0.3041
Yc_3           0.15280        0.17172     0.890  0.3745
Yd_1           0.96986       0.078306    12.386  0.0000
Yd_2          0.070855        0.10297     0.688  0.4921
Yd_3         -0.087596       0.075129    -1.166  0.2449
Trend       4.4629e-005    0.00021617     0.206  0.8366
Constant     -0.011389      0.0090308    -1.261  0.2086

\sigma = 0.0380028    RSS = 0.3220593788

correlation of URF residuals
                    Ya            Yb            Yc            Yd
 Ya             1.0000
 Yb           0.086368        1.0000
 Yc          -0.051501       0.71531        1.0000
 Yd          -0.053940      -0.39947      -0.52353        1.0000

standard deviations of URF residuals
        Ya            Yb            Yc            Yd
    0.026328      0.017333      0.023373      0.038003

loglik=3645.2738 log|\Omega|=-30.7618 |\Omega|=4.36836e-014 T=237
log|Y'Y/T| = -12.9023
R^2(LR) = 1  R^2(LM) = 0.896346

F-test on all regressors except unrestricted,
  F(52,854)=1636.3 [0.0000] **
variables entered unrestricted:
  Constant

F-tests on retained regressors, F(4, 220)
    Ya_1      40.7047 [0.0000] **      Ya_2       1.37460 [0.2437]
    Ya_3      2.20961 [0.0689]         Yb_1       81.8847 [0.0000] **
    Yb_2      2.25769 [0.0639]         Yb_3      0.630489 [0.6412]
    Yc_1      79.1999 [0.0000] **      Yc_2       4.05550 [0.0034] **
    Yc_3      2.35642 [0.0547]         Yd_1       46.6737 [0.0000] **
    Yd_2     0.328333 [0.8588]         Yd_3      0.856701 [0.4908]
   Trend      2.02149 [0.0924]

correlation of actual and fitted
        Ya            Yb            Yc            Yd
     0.99868       0.99996       0.99992       0.98757

Vector portmanteau statistic for 12 lags and 237 obs: 178.9

Testing for vector error autocorrelation from lags 1 to 7
Chi^2(112)=120.38 [0.2773]  and F-form(112,765) = 1.0101 [0.4578]

Vector normality test for residuals
The present sample is:  1974 (4) to 1993 (12)
Skewness
     -0.20098      -0.97365       0.68936        2.7704

Excess kurtosis
     -0.41119      -0.55594     0.0013589        1.4747

Vector normality Chi^2( 8)=      11.792 [0.1608]

Testing for vector heteroscedasticity using squares
Chi^2(260)=264.93 [0.4037]   and
    F-form(260,1776)=0.95021 [0.6974]

Testing for vector heterosc. using squares and cross-products
Chi^2(1040)=1061.1 [0.3179]   and
    F-form(1040,1118)=0.91465 [0.9282]


EQ( 2) Estimating the unrestr.red. form by OLS (using PcfTut1.in7)
The present sample is:  1974 (4) to 1993 (12)

URF Equation 1 for Ya
Variable      Coefficient     Std.Error  t-value  t-prob
Ya_1             0.83470       0.067482   12.369  0.0000
Ya_2            0.040134       0.064652    0.621  0.5354
Yb_1             0.26315        0.13568    1.939  0.0537
Yb_2            -0.20544        0.12631   -1.627  0.1052
Yc_1            -0.13920        0.11234   -1.239  0.2166
Yc_2            0.085933        0.11423    0.752  0.4527
Yd_1            0.093599       0.053097    1.763  0.0793
Yd_2            0.022638       0.052129    0.434  0.6645
Trend         0.00029995     0.00014656    2.047  0.0418
Constant       0.0018400      0.0061923    0.297  0.7666

\sigma = 0.0263775    RSS = 0.1579402802

URF Equation 2 for Yb
Variable      Coefficient     Std.Error  t-value  t-prob
Ya_1            0.014077       0.044444    0.317  0.7517
Ya_2            0.011716       0.042580    0.275  0.7835
Yb_1              1.1848       0.089361   13.258  0.0000
Yb_2            -0.29603       0.083185   -3.559  0.0005
```

```
Yc_1             0.18927      0.073988     2.558  0.0112
Yc_2           -0.079506      0.075231    -1.057  0.2917
Yd_1           -0.040800      0.034970    -1.167  0.2445
Yd_2           0.0035925      0.034332     0.105  0.9168
Trend         0.00016194   9.6526e-005     1.678  0.0948
Constant       0.0080034     0.0040783     1.962  0.0509

\sigma = 0.0173724   RSS = 0.0685085908

URF Equation 3 for Yc
Variable     Coefficient     Std.Error   t-value  t-prob
Ya_1            0.026216      0.059593     0.440  0.6604
Ya_2         -0.0033020       0.057094    -0.058  0.9539
Yb_1           -0.052514       0.11982    -0.438  0.6616
Yb_2            0.061076       0.11154     0.548  0.5845
Yc_1              1.3065      0.099207    13.170  0.0000
Yc_2            -0.31875       0.10087    -3.160  0.0018
Yd_1            -0.10762      0.046890    -2.295  0.0226
Yd_2           -0.022407      0.046035    -0.487  0.6269
Trend        7.4677e-005    0.00012943     0.577  0.5645
Constant        0.012773     0.0054685     2.336  0.0204

\sigma = 0.023294   RSS = 0.1231723675

URF Equation 4 for Yd
Variable     Coefficient     Std.Error   t-value  t-prob
Ya_1            0.085018      0.097596     0.871  0.3846
Ya_2           -0.085254      0.093502    -0.912  0.3629
Yb_1           -0.095601       0.19623    -0.487  0.6266
Yb_2            0.068377       0.18267     0.374  0.7085
Yc_1             0.11908       0.16247     0.733  0.4644
Yc_2           -0.090493       0.16520    -0.548  0.5844
Yd_1             0.93953      0.076791    12.235  0.0000
Yd_2            0.037541      0.075391     0.498  0.6190
Trend         0.00013281    0.00021196     0.627  0.5316
Constant       -0.013770     0.0089556    -1.538  0.1255

\sigma = 0.0381484   RSS = 0.3303524573

correlation of URF residuals
                      Ya            Yb            Yc            Yd
 Ya               1.0000
 Yb             0.096181        1.0000
 Yc            -0.035921       0.71091        1.0000
 Yd            -0.063725      -0.38380      -0.52008        1.0000

standard deviations of URF residuals
           Ya           Yb           Yc           Yd
     0.026377     0.017372     0.023294     0.038148

loglik=3633.3104 log|\Omega|=-30.6608 |\Omega|=4.8324e-014  T=237
log|Y'Y/T| = -12.9023
R^2(LR) = 1  R^2(LM) = 0.893559

F-test on all regressors except unrestricted,
  F(36,841)=2647.4 [0.0000] **
variables entered unrestricted:
  Constant

F-tests on retained regressors, F(4, 224)
   Ya_1     40.6206 [0.0000] **      Ya_2     0.394858 [0.8122]
   Yb_1     92.4701 [0.0000] **      Yb_2      8.03435 [0.0000] **
   Yc_1     85.0977 [0.0000] **      Yc_2      4.74698 [0.0011] **
   Yd_1     44.7151 [0.0000] **      Yd_2     0.210826 [0.9323]
  Trend     2.08552 [0.0836]

correlation of actual and fitted
           Ya           Yb           Yc           Yd
      0.99865      0.99996      0.99991      0.98725


Progress to date
system    T    p        log-likelihood       SC       HQ      AIC
    3   237   40  OLS        3633.3104  -29.738  -30.087  -30.661
    2   237   56  OLS        3645.2738  -29.470  -29.959  -30.762

Tests of system reduction
System  1 --> System  2: F(16, 672) =     1.4127 [0.1289]


Dynamic analysis of the system
Lag-1 multipliers
                   Trend
 Ya           0.00029502
 Yb           0.00020480
 Yc          8.2633e-005
 Yd           0.00014370

Mean lag matrix
                      Ya            Yb            Yc            Yd
 Ya             -0.91496       0.14773     -0.032664      -0.13888
 Yb            -0.037509      -0.59272     -0.030256      0.033615
```

```
 Yc                -0.019612   -0.069637     -0.66901      0.15243
 Yd                 0.085489   -0.041152     0.061909      -1.0146

Long-run matrix \Pi(1)-I = Po
                          Ya          Yb           Yc           Yd
 Ya                -0.12517    0.057707    -0.053269      0.11624
 Yb                0.025793    -0.11125      0.10976    -0.037207
 Yc                0.022914   0.0085615    -0.012237     -0.13002
 Yd             -0.00023537   -0.027224     0.028584    -0.022932

Long-run covariance
                          Ya          Yb           Yc           Yd
 Ya                 0.28136
 Yb                  8.8734      455.97
 Yc                  8.8246      455.24       454.53
 Yd                -0.12881     -8.8055      -8.8067      0.20213

Long-run multipliers
                       Trend
 Ya                0.0045874
 Yb                -0.017839
 Yc                -0.019927
 Yd                0.0020836

Static long run
                       Trend
 Ya                0.0045874
 Yb                -0.017839
 Yc                -0.019927
 Yd                0.0020836

Standard errors of static long run
                       Trend
 Ya                0.0025150
 Yb                  0.10125
 Yc                  0.10109
 Yd                0.0021317

Eigenvalues of \Pi(1)-I
         real      complex      modulus
      -0.1325       0.0000       0.1325
    -0.004201       0.0000     0.004201
     -0.06746      0.02231      0.07105
     -0.06746     -0.02231      0.07105

Eigenvalues of companion matrix
         real      complex      modulus
     -0.04335      0.02839      0.05182
     -0.04335     -0.02839      0.05182
       0.3512      0.05705       0.3558
       0.3512     -0.05705       0.3558
       0.7929       0.0000       0.7929
       0.9938       0.0000       0.9938
       0.9316     0.007853       0.9316
       0.9316    -0.007853       0.9316

EQ( 3) Estimating the unrestr.red. form by OLS (using PcfTut1.in7)
The present sample is:  1974 (4) to 1993 (12)

URF Equation 1 for Ya
Variable      Coefficient     Std.Error   t-value   t-prob
Ya_1              0.83470      0.067482    12.369   0.0000
Ya_2             0.040134      0.064652     0.621   0.5354
Yb_1              0.26315       0.13568     1.939   0.0537
Yb_2             -0.20544       0.12631    -1.627   0.1052
Yc_1             -0.13920       0.11234    -1.239   0.2166
Yc_2             0.085933       0.11423     0.752   0.4527
Yd_1             0.093599      0.053097     1.763   0.0793
Yd_2             0.022638      0.052129     0.434   0.6645
Trend          0.00029995    0.00014656     2.047   0.0418
Constant        0.0018400     0.0061923     0.297   0.7666

\sigma = 0.0263775    RSS = 0.1579402802

URF Equation 2 for Yb
Variable      Coefficient     Std.Error   t-value   t-prob
Ya_1             0.014077      0.044444     0.317   0.7517
Ya_2             0.011716      0.042580     0.275   0.7835
Yb_1               1.1848      0.089361    13.258   0.0000
Yb_2             -0.29603      0.083185    -3.559   0.0005
Yc_1              0.18927      0.073988     2.558   0.0112
Yc_2            -0.079506      0.075231    -1.057   0.2917
Yd_1            -0.040800      0.034970    -1.167   0.2445
Yd_2            0.0035925      0.034332     0.105   0.9168
Trend          0.00016194   9.6526e-005     1.678   0.0948
Constant        0.0080034     0.0040783     1.962   0.0509

\sigma = 0.0173724    RSS = 0.0685085908
```

```
URF Equation 3 for Yc
Variable      Coefficient      Std.Error  t-value  t-prob
Ya_1             0.026216       0.059593    0.440  0.6604
Ya_2          -0.0033020        0.057094   -0.058  0.9539
Yb_1           -0.052514         0.11982   -0.438  0.6616
Yb_2            0.061076         0.11154    0.548  0.5845
Yc_1              1.3065        0.099207   13.170  0.0000
Yc_2            -0.31875         0.10087   -3.160  0.0018
Yd_1            -0.10762        0.046890   -2.295  0.0226
Yd_2           -0.022407        0.046035   -0.487  0.6269
Trend        7.4677e-005      0.00012943    0.577  0.5645
Constant        0.012773       0.0054685    2.336  0.0204

\sigma = 0.023294    RSS = 0.1231723675

URF Equation 4 for Yd
Variable      Coefficient      Std.Error  t-value  t-prob
Ya_1            0.085018        0.097596    0.871  0.3846
Ya_2           -0.085254        0.093502   -0.912  0.3629
Yb_1           -0.095601         0.19623   -0.487  0.6266
Yb_2            0.068377         0.18267    0.374  0.7085
Yc_1             0.11908         0.16247    0.733  0.4644
Yc_2           -0.090493         0.16520   -0.548  0.5844
Yd_1             0.93953        0.076791   12.235  0.0000
Yd_2            0.037541        0.075391    0.498  0.6190
Trend         0.00013281      0.00021196    0.627  0.5316
Constant       -0.013770       0.0089556   -1.538  0.1255

\sigma = 0.0381484    RSS = 0.3303524573

correlation of URF residuals
                      Ya           Yb            Yc            Yd
 Ya               1.0000
 Yb             0.096181       1.0000
 Yc            -0.035921      0.71091        1.0000
 Yd            -0.063725     -0.38380      -0.52008        1.0000

standard deviations of URF residuals
          Ya           Yb           Yc           Yd
    0.026377     0.017372     0.023294     0.038148

loglik=3633.3104 log|\Omega|=-30.6608 |\Omega|=4.8324e-014  T=237
log|Y'Y/T| = -12.9023
R^2(LR) = 1  R^2(LM) = 0.893559

F-test on all regressors except
  unrestricted, F(36,841)=2647.4 [0.0000] **
variables entered unrestricted:
  Constant

F-tests on retained regressors, F(4, 224)
   Ya_1     40.6206 [0.0000] **      Ya_2     0.394858 [0.8122]
   Yb_1     92.4701 [0.0000] **      Yb_2      8.03435 [0.0000] **
   Yc_1     85.0977 [0.0000] **      Yc_2      4.74698 [0.0011] **
   Yd_1     44.7151 [0.0000] **      Yd_2     0.210826 [0.9323]
  Trend     2.08552 [0.0836]

correlation of actual and fitted
          Ya           Yb           Yc           Yd
     0.99865      0.99996      0.99991      0.98725

EQ( 4) Estimating the unrestr.red. form by OLS (using PcfTut1.in7)
The present sample is:  1974 (4) to 1993 (12) less 20 forecasts
The forecast period is: 1992 (5) to 1993 (12)

URF Equation 1 for Ya
Variable      Coefficient      Std.Error  t-value  t-prob
Ya_1             0.84792        0.070592   12.012  0.0000
Ya_2            0.030862        0.067468    0.457  0.6478
Yb_1             0.29847         0.14211    2.100  0.0369
Yb_2            -0.23438         0.13251   -1.769  0.0784
Yc_1            -0.17537         0.11746   -1.493  0.1369
Yc_2             0.11616         0.12042    0.965  0.3359
Yd_1            0.093517        0.055184    1.695  0.0916
Yd_2            0.016102        0.053774    0.299  0.7649
Trend         0.00025321      0.00017059    1.484  0.1393
Constant       0.0023711       0.0062999    0.376  0.7070

\sigma = 0.0265969    RSS = 0.1464303811

URF Equation 2 for Yb
Variable      Coefficient      Std.Error  t-value  t-prob
Ya_1            0.014322        0.046379    0.309  0.7578
Ya_2           0.0088178        0.044326    0.199  0.8425
Yb_1              1.1675        0.093369   12.504  0.0000
Yb_2            -0.28881        0.087059   -3.317  0.0011
Yc_1             0.20035        0.077170    2.596  0.0101
Yc_2           -0.081845        0.079118   -1.034  0.3021
Yd_1           -0.040942        0.036256   -1.129  0.2601
Yd_2           0.0099059        0.035329    0.280  0.7795
```

```
Trend           0.00023986   0.00011208     2.140  0.0335
Constant         0.0076699    0.0041390     1.853  0.0653

\sigma = 0.017474    RSS = 0.06320523423

URF Equation 3 for Yc
Variable       Coefficient     Std.Error  t-value  t-prob
Ya_1              0.046317     0.062368     0.743  0.4585
Ya_2             -0.022402     0.059608    -0.376  0.7074
Yb_1             -0.098625      0.12556    -0.785  0.4331
Yb_2              0.086757      0.11707     0.741  0.4595
Yc_1                1.3381      0.10377    12.895  0.0000
Yc_2              -0.33163      0.10639    -3.117  0.0021
Yd_1             -0.096606     0.048755    -1.981  0.0489
Yd_2             -0.026842     0.047509    -0.565  0.5727
Trend           0.00016801   0.00015072     1.115  0.2663
Constant          0.012018    0.0055659     2.159  0.0320

\sigma = 0.0234982    RSS = 0.114298245

URF Equation 4 for Yd
Variable       Coefficient     Std.Error  t-value  t-prob
Ya_1               0.10126      0.10374     0.976  0.3302
Ya_2              -0.10111     0.099151    -1.020  0.3091
Yb_1             -0.090145      0.20885    -0.432  0.6665
Yb_2              0.082979      0.19474     0.426  0.6705
Yc_1               0.10590      0.17262     0.613  0.5402
Yc_2             -0.095790      0.17697    -0.541  0.5889
Yd_1               0.93363     0.081098    11.512  0.0000
Yd_2              0.033461     0.079026     0.423  0.6724
Trend          3.4564e-005   0.00025070     0.138  0.8905
Constant         -0.012369    0.0092583    -1.336  0.1830

\sigma = 0.0390866    RSS = 0.3162462009

correlation of URF residuals
                      Ya            Yb             Yc            Yd
 Ya               1.0000
 Yb              0.12322        1.0000
 Yc          -0.0042800        0.71153         1.0000
 Yd           -0.079425       -0.40894       -0.53709        1.0000

standard deviations of URF residuals
          Ya            Yb            Yc            Yd
    0.026597      0.017474      0.023498      0.039087

loglik=3321.3502 log|\Omega|=-30.6115  |\Omega|=5.07673e-014 T=217
log|Y'Y/T| = -12.9588
R^2(LR) = 1   R^2(LM) = 0.895111

F-test on all regressors except
  unrestricted, F(36,766)=2343.7 [0.0000] **
variables entered unrestricted:
  Constant

F-tests on retained regressors, F(4, 204)
   Ya_1      39.1032 [0.0000] **      Ya_2      0.651210 [0.6266]
   Yb_1      85.7184 [0.0000] **      Yb_2       7.77494 [0.0000] **
   Yc_1      80.7173 [0.0000] **      Yc_2       4.74366 [0.0011] **
   Yd_1      40.8889 [0.0000] **      Yd_2      0.324532 [0.8613]
  Trend      1.82729 [0.1249]

correlation of actual and fitted
          Ya            Yb            Yc            Yd
     0.99839       0.99996       0.99992       0.98396

1-step (ex post) forecast analysis 1992 (5) to 1993 (12)
Parameter constancy forecast tests:
using \Omega Chi^2(80)=69.177  [0.8007] F(80,207)=0.86472 [0.7713]
using  V[e]  Chi^2(80)=64.416  [0.8978] F(80,207)= 0.8052 [0.8676]
using  V[E]  Chi^2(80)=65.757  [0.8743] F(80,207)=0.82197 [0.8433]

Algebra code for PcfTut1.in7:
DYa = diff(Ya,1);
DYb = diff(Yb,1);
DYc = diff(Yc,1);
DYd = diff(Yd,1);


EQ( 5) Estimating the unrestr.red. form by OLS (using PcfTut1.in7)
The present sample is:  1974 (4) to 1993 (12)

URF Equation 1 for DYa
Variable       Coefficient     Std.Error  t-value  t-prob
DYa_1            -0.040134     0.064652    -0.621  0.5354
DYb_1              0.20544      0.12631     1.627  0.1052
DYc_1            -0.085933      0.11423    -0.752  0.4527
DYd_1            -0.022638     0.052129    -0.434  0.6645
Ya_1              -0.12517     0.028332    -4.418  0.0000
Yb_1              0.057707     0.050904     1.134  0.2581
```

```
Yc_1            -0.053269        0.050632    -1.052   0.2939
Yd_1              0.11624        0.028330     4.103   0.0001
Trend          0.00029995      0.00014656     2.047   0.0418
Constant        0.0018400       0.0061923     0.297   0.7666

\sigma = 0.0263775   RSS = 0.1579402802

URF Equation 2 for DYb
Variable      Coefficient       Std.Error   t-value   t-prob
DYa_1           -0.011716        0.042580    -0.275   0.7835
DYb_1             0.29603        0.083185     3.559   0.0005
DYc_1            0.079506        0.075231     1.057   0.2917
DYd_1          -0.0035925        0.034332    -0.105   0.9168
Ya_1             0.025793        0.018660     1.382   0.1682
Yb_1             -0.11125        0.033526    -3.318   0.0011
Yc_1              0.10976        0.033347     3.292   0.0012
Yd_1            -0.037207        0.018659    -1.994   0.0473
Trend          0.00016194     9.6526e-005     1.678   0.0948
Constant        0.0080034       0.0040783     1.962   0.0509

\sigma = 0.0173724   RSS = 0.0685085908

URF Equation 3 for DYc
Variable      Coefficient       Std.Error   t-value   t-prob
DYa_1           0.0033020        0.057094     0.058   0.9539
DYb_1           -0.061076         0.11154    -0.548   0.5845
DYc_1             0.31875         0.10087     3.160   0.0018
DYd_1            0.022407        0.046035     0.487   0.6269
Ya_1             0.022914        0.025020     0.916   0.3607
Yb_1            0.0085615        0.044954     0.190   0.8491
Yc_1            -0.012237        0.044713    -0.274   0.7846
Yd_1             -0.13002        0.025019    -5.197   0.0000
Trend         7.4677e-005      0.00012943     0.577   0.5645
Constant         0.012773       0.0054685     2.336   0.0204

\sigma = 0.023294   RSS = 0.1231723675

URF Equation 4 for DYd
Variable      Coefficient       Std.Error   t-value   t-prob
DYa_1            0.085254        0.093502     0.912   0.3629
DYb_1           -0.068377         0.18267    -0.374   0.7085
DYc_1            0.090493         0.16520     0.548   0.5844
DYd_1           -0.037541        0.075391    -0.498   0.6190
Ya_1          -0.00023537        0.040976    -0.006   0.9954
Yb_1            -0.027224        0.073620    -0.370   0.7119
Yc_1             0.028584        0.073227     0.390   0.6966
Yd_1            -0.022932        0.040973    -0.560   0.5762
Trend          0.00013281      0.00021196     0.627   0.5316
Constant        -0.013770       0.0089556    -1.538   0.1255

\sigma = 0.0381484   RSS = 0.3303524573

correlation of URF residuals
                      DYa          DYb          DYc          DYd
 DYa               1.0000
 DYb             0.096181       1.0000
 DYc            -0.035921      0.71091       1.0000
 DYd            -0.063725     -0.38380     -0.52008       1.0000

standard deviations of URF residuals
         DYa          DYb          DYc          DYd
    0.026377     0.017372     0.023294     0.038148

loglik=3633.3104 log|\Omega|=-30.6608 |\Omega|=4.8324e-014  T=237
log|Y'Y/T| = -28.865
R^2(LR) = 0.834017  R^2(LM) = 0.278252

F-test on all regressors except
  unrestricted, F(36,841)=14.366 [0.0000] **
variables entered unrestricted:
  Constant

F-tests on retained regressors, F(4, 224)
  DYa_1    0.394858 [0.8122]        DYb_1      8.03435 [0.0000] **
  DYc_1     4.74698 [0.0011] **     DYd_1     0.210826 [0.9323]
   Ya_1     5.78515 [0.0002] **      Yb_1      6.98141 [0.0000] **
   Yc_1     7.03095 [0.0000] **      Yd_1      14.1499 [0.0000] **
  Trend     2.08552 [0.0836]

correlation of actual and fitted
         DYa          DYb          DYc          DYd
     0.40771      0.83122      0.76312      0.17646
```

Chapter 4

Cointegration

4.1 Introduction to cointegration analysis

A crucial property of any economic variable influencing the behaviour of statistics in econometric models is the extent to which the variable is *stationary*. A simple example of a univariate non-stationary process is:

$$y_t = \alpha + \beta y_{t-1} + \epsilon_t, \quad \text{where } \beta = 1, \tag{4.1}$$

which generates a random walk (with drift if $\alpha \neq 0$). Here the autoregressive coefficient is unity and stationarity is violated. A process with no unit roots is said to be $\mathsf{I}(0)$, 'Integrated of order 0'; a process is $\mathsf{I}(d)$ if it needs to be differenced exactly d times to become $\mathsf{I}(0)$.

To study integration when there are n variables, we start with a first-order VAR as estimated in the previous chapter:

$$\mathbf{y}_t = \boldsymbol{\pi}_1 \mathbf{y}_{t-1} + \mathbf{v}_t, \quad \mathbf{v}_t \sim \mathsf{IN}_n\left[\mathbf{0}, \boldsymbol{\Omega}\right]. \tag{4.2}$$

This can be rewritten as (by subtracting $\mathbf{y}_{t-1}$ from both sides):

$$\Delta \mathbf{y}_t = \mathbf{P}_0 \mathbf{y}_{t-1} + \mathbf{v}_t. \tag{4.3}$$

$\mathbf{P}_0 = \boldsymbol{\pi}_1 - \mathbf{I}_n$ is the matrix of long-run responses. Although $\mathbf{v}_t \sim \mathsf{IN}_n[\mathbf{0}, \boldsymbol{\Omega}]$, and so is stationary, the n variables in $\mathbf{y}_t$ need not all be stationary. Express $\mathbf{P}_0$ as $\boldsymbol{\alpha}\boldsymbol{\beta}'$, then its rank p determines how many linear combinations of variables are stationary. If $p = n$ all variables in $\mathbf{y}_t$ are stationary, whereas $p = 0$ implies that $\Delta \mathbf{y}_t$ is stationary. For $0 < p < n$ there are p cointegrated (stationary) linear combinations of $\mathbf{y}_t$. Then $\boldsymbol{\alpha}$ is a $(n \times p)$ and $\boldsymbol{\beta}'$ a $(p \times n)$ matrix both of rank p.

The approach in PcFiml to determining cointegration rank and the associated cointegrating vectors is based on Johansen (1988), extended for various tests as described below. Chapter 11 explains the mathematics and statistics. Other useful references which provide more extensive and expository treatments include Banerjee, Dolado, Galbraith and Hendry (1993), Hendry (1995) and Johansen (1995b). The aim is to establish relationships that have stationary deviations even though the variables involved are individually non-stationary. Since it is very important how variables which are not part of the VAR are treated, we turn to that issue.

4.2 Unrestricted variables

The status of the non-modelled variables can importantly affect the outcome of a cointegration analysis. This is because of the implicit conditioning involved in different assignments. Here, the *Constant* is *Unrestricted*. This allows for non-zero drift in any unit-root processes found by the cointegration analysis. Unless there are good reasons to the contrary, it is usually unwise to force the constant to lie in the cointegration space: however, when modelling variables with no possibility of inherent drift, such as interest rates, it can be useful to restrict the constant.

The *Trend* is another matter altogether. Generally, a quadratic deterministic trend in levels of economic variables is not a sensible long-run outcome, so the *Trend* should usually be forced to lie in the cointegration space, thereby restricting the system to at most a linear deterministic trend in levels. That is the specification of our present system as suggested in Chapter 3.

4.3 Restarting

If you did not exit GiveWin at the end of the previous tutorial, skip to the start of the next section. If you are starting completely afresh, to resume where the previous tutorial ended, load the data set by clicking on File, Open, locate the PcFiml directory and double click on the dataset named PCFTUT1.IN7. Next, select Model, Batch editor and load PCFTUT1.FL (also in provided in the PcFiml directory) as the batch file for the system with two lags; click on OK:run (or Tab to OK:run and press enter), and replicate the output of EQ(3) as listed in §3.14. If you did not save the batch file, set up the two-lag version of the four-variable system in levels as explained in Chapter 3 (clear the status of the *Trend*; 1974(4) is the first observation used for estimation in this chapter).

Depending on how you returned here, the estimator may be OLS or recursive least squares (RLS; the distinction in the batch file lies in the arguments of the OLS function: both are now called OLS, which is a change from earlier versions; similarly MLS is renamed OLS). For the rest of the tutorial, we assume the recursive method was used, so you should re-estimate accordingly. The cointegration analysis is conducted recursively only if the system is estimated recursively, and the same initial values and sample period are used.

4.4 Cointegration analysis

Cointegration analysis on the Estimate System dialog provides full cointegration analysis of the system using the maximum likelihood method developed by Sören Johansen. It is only available if all endogenous variables have the same lag length. Identities are simply ignored.

Select Model, Estimate System, Cointegration Analysis, and estimation immediately occurs. The Message window shows the progress of the recursive calculations, and the output specific to cointegration comprises:

```
Cointegration analysis 1974 (4) to 1993 (12)

eigenvalue μi      loglik for rank
                     3566.26    0
     0.27105         3603.72    1
    0.147176         3622.59    2
   0.0745108         3631.77    3
    0.012949         3633.31    4

Ho:rank=p -Tlog(1-μ) T-nm   95%   -Tlog(1-μ) T-nm       95%
p ==  0  74.93**   72.4**   31.5  134.1**    129.6**   63.0
p <=  1  37.73**  36.46**   25.5  59.17**    57.17**   42.4
p <=  2  18.35    17.73     19.0  21.44      20.72     25.3
p <=  3  3.089    2.985     12.3  3.089      2.985     12.3

standardized β' eigenvectors
       Ya          Yb          Yc          Yd        Trend
   1.0000     -1.3665      1.3034     -2.3040    0.0018082
  0.17072      1.0000     -1.0176    -0.66528   -0.0018356
  0.65409     -1.0088      1.0000    0.092266   -0.0012609
  0.31652   -0.011820   -0.083780      1.0000   -0.0054159

standardized α coefficients
Ya    -0.025114      -0.10396      -0.12625   0.00086099
Yb     0.035792     -0.062866 -0.00056734      0.0034884
Yc     0.049439      0.025752    -0.049998     0.0056299
Yd    0.0077430     -0.016783 5.2146e-005    -0.016262

long-run matrix Po=αβ', rank 4
        Ya          Yb          Yc          Yd        Trend
Ya    -0.12517   0.057707 -0.053269     0.11624   0.00029995
Yb    0.025793   -0.11125   0.10976  -0.037207   0.00016194
Yc    0.022914  0.0085615 -0.012237   -0.13002  7.4677e-005
Yd -0.00023537 -0.027224   0.028584  -0.022932   0.00013281

Number of lags used in the analysis: 2

Variables entered unrestricted:    Constant
Variables entered restricted:        Trend
```

There is one very small eigenvalue and two judged significant at the 1% level on the critical values (see Osterwald-Lenum, 1992), even when adjusted for degrees of freedom (see Reimers, 1992). This outcome determines the rank of $\widehat{\mathbf{P}}_0$ as 2 (that is, we reject H_0: $p = 1$). However, one other eigenvalue is close to significance at the 5% level, leaving open the possibility that the rank is in fact $p = 3$. The first two (three) rows of eigenvectors (normalized on the diagonal, so the ordering of variables can matter) report the estimated cointegration vectors as representative of the cointegration space: any linear combinations of these are also admissible, so the long-run relations are not identified in that sense. To uniquely determine cointegration vectors relevant to an economic analysis requires the subject matter input, which is difficult to accomplish for artificial data. One possibility is just to accept the combinations as shown, but these are unlikely to coincide with the structural relations. Another, which we follow below in order to illustrate the various tests and restricted estimators, is to impose some theory structure.

Interpret *Yb* and *Yc* as consumption and income respectively, with *Ya* as productivity and *Yd* as the real exchange rate. The last is then likely to be close to a random walk empirically on the limited information set used here. The first could depend on a deterministic trend (as a proxy for slowly evolving stocks of knowledge, human capital and physical capital), as well as on the real exchange rate, but is unlikely to depend directly on consumption. Consumption and income are likely to be cointegrated with a unit coefficient, not dependent on a deterministic linear trend, but perhaps depending on either of the other two variables.

The system with 2 lags and deterministic factors can be expressed as:

$$\Delta \mathbf{x}_t = \boldsymbol{\alpha\beta}'\mathbf{x}_{t-1} + \boldsymbol{\Gamma}\Delta\mathbf{x}_{t-1} + \boldsymbol{\Phi}\mathbf{d}_t + \mathbf{e}_t,$$

where $\mathbf{x}_t$ is defined as $(Ya\ Yb\ Yc\ Yd)'_t$ and $\mathbf{d}_t = (1, t)'$. The α coefficients corresponding to the standardized β reported above show marked feedbacks of $\widehat{\beta}'_3\mathbf{x}_t$ onto *Ya*, and of $\widehat{\beta}'_2\mathbf{x}_t$ onto *Yb*. The remaining $\alpha_{i,j}$ are small, but below we test various hypotheses that they are zero. The long-run matrix $\mathbf{P}_0 = \boldsymbol{\alpha\beta}'$, although computed differently from the dynamic analysis in Chapter 3, should be identical to that reported earlier (except for the additional column for the *Trend*). For rank $p = 4$, the log-likelihood should also match the value for the system in the previous chapter.

Before testing any of the claimed 'theory', we will peruse the cointegration results graphically.

4.5 Cointegration graphics

Select Test and Cointegration Graphics.

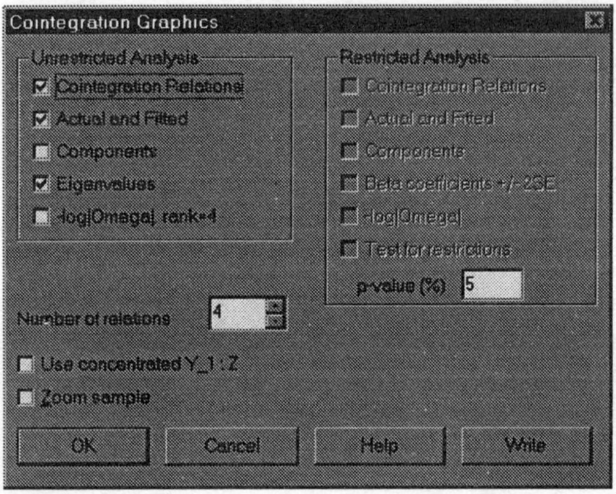

This leads to the Cointegration Graphics dialog as shown above. Only the first column is relevant as yet. Mark the first two entries for cointegration relations, and actual and fitted, as well as the entry for (recursive) eigenvalues. Set 4 relations, then click OK to see Figure 4.1 (the vertical axis scale of the first two recursive eigenvalues has been edited to the full interval 0–1 to show their relative constancy).

The first column of Figure 4.1 shows the linear combinations $\widehat{\beta}'\mathbf{x}_t$, the next plots the sum of the non-normalized coefficients (with the opposite sign as in regression, namely $-\sum_{j\neq i}\widehat{\beta}_j x_{jt}$) against the normalized variable (that is, long-run fitted and actual), and the third column shows the values of the recursively calculated eigenvalues (having partialled out the full-sample dynamics and unrestricted variables). The first three cointegration vectors look fairly stationary (indeed, none much more so than the others), but the last looks distinctly non-stationary. The fitted and actuals are reasonably close for the first three plots as well. The eigenvalues are relatively constant, the first two at non-zero values, the third much smaller but visibly above zero, and the last at close to zero throughout. However, these are conditional on having partialled out the full-sample dynamics and unrestricted variables, so are more 'constant' than would have been found at the time on a smaller sample. Conversely, the $\widehat{\beta}'\mathbf{x}_t$ do not correct for short-run dynamics, so would look more stationary still if Use concentrated Y_1: Z was marked.

To set options for cointegration analysis, access Model, Options, Cointegration to see the Cointegration options dialog:

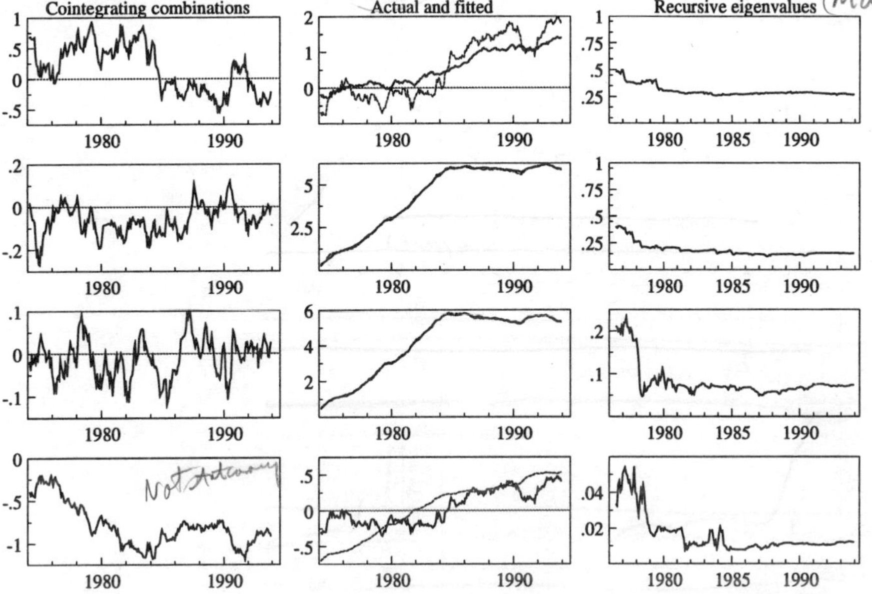

Figure 4.1 Time series of cointegration vectors and recursive eigenvalues.

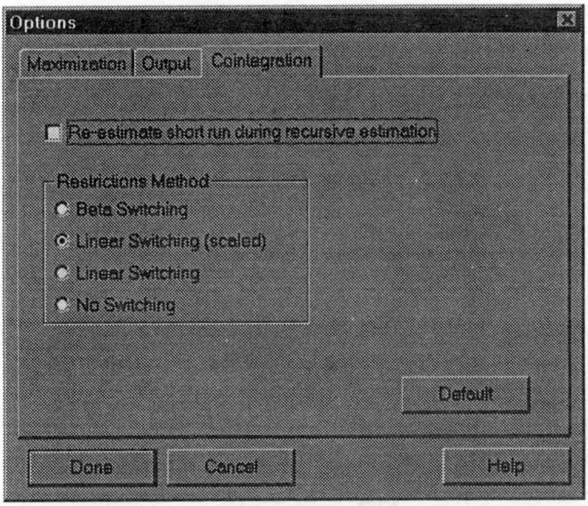

Set the option to re-estimate the short-run dynamics in every period, and recalculate the recursive eigenvalues. Figure 4.2 shows the comparison of the two sets; the lines showing larger changes are those where we have removed the short run each period, equivalent to what an investigator at the time would have found.

The β coefficients **cannot** be graphed when no restrictions are imposed on either scale or rotations, as any linear transform is an admissible vector. Such graphs can be

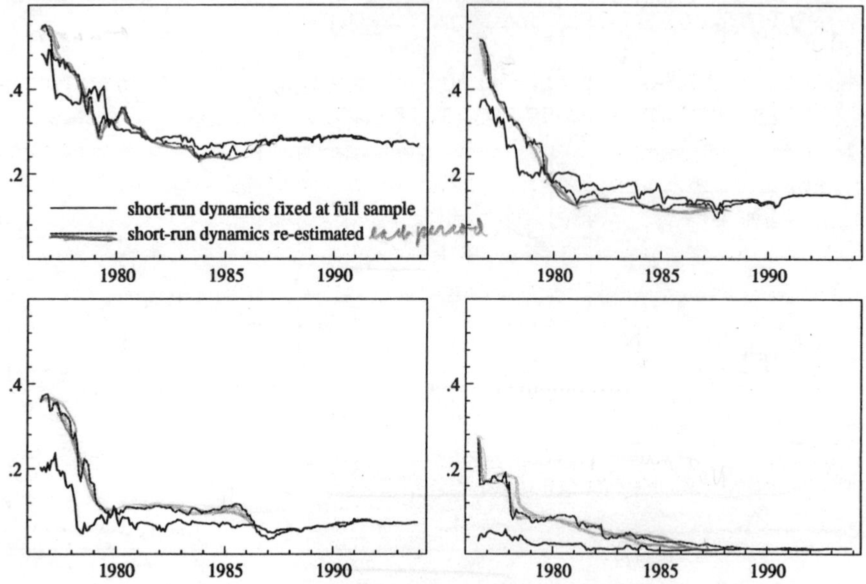

Figure 4.2 Recursive eigenvalues with and without partialling.

erratic and hard to interpret: Figure 4.3 shows what you would see for the outcome when the short-run is partialled out over the whole period.

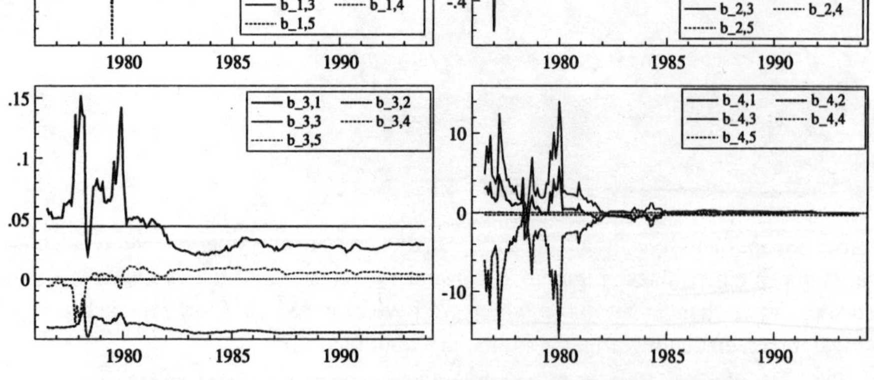

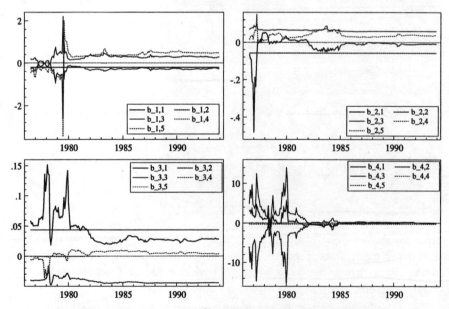

Figure 4.3 Recursive β coefficients without restrictions.

4.6 Testing cointegration restrictions

PcFiml offers a uniform approach to testing all forms of restrictions on both cointegration vectors and feedback coefficients. It is based on the transparency of explicitly setting the restrictions to be imposed on elements of α and β. A restrictions editor is provided, which shows the numbering of all the elements, and within which restrictions are defined by statements of the form &4=0 to set the element corresponding to parameter 5 to zero (numbering commences with &0). Several examples will now be provided, and related to alternative approaches (such as Johansen and Juselius, 1990, and Johansen, 1991). The addendum to this chapter discusses the so-called H and A forms of linear restrictions.

The easiest first step is to compute $\widehat{\mathbf{P}}_0$ when only a rank restriction is imposed. Select Model, Estimate System, to see:

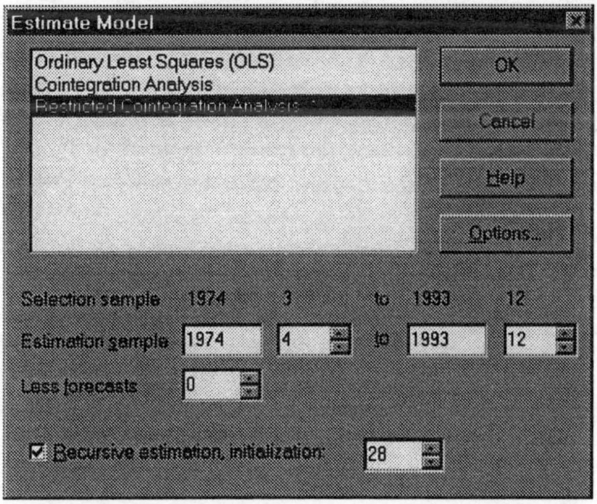

Deselect recursive estimation, and click on Restricted Cointegration Analysis as we wish to impose a reduced rank of 2 on $\mathbf{P}_0$.

The Restricted Cointegration Analysis dialog appears as:

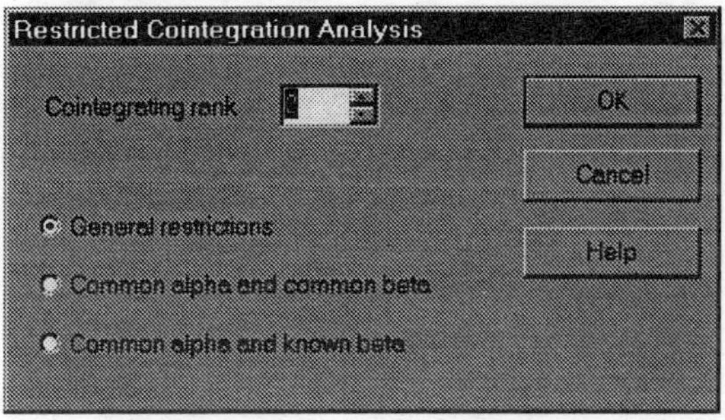

Set the rank to 2 and the General Restrictions dialog will appear as shown:

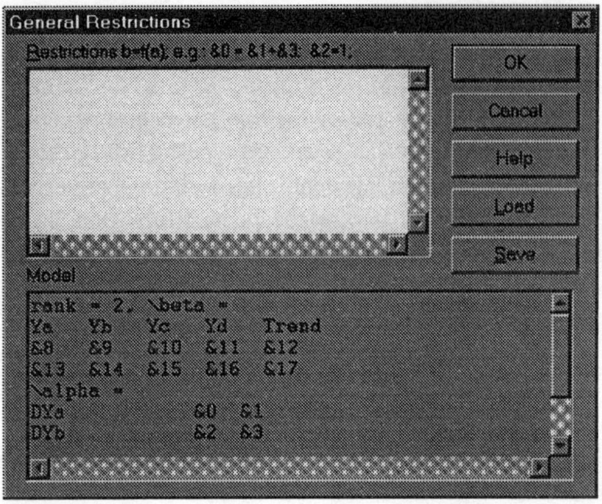

Press OK to accept without imposing any restrictions. What happens next depends on your options settings: if automatic maximization is set, the results appear immediately. Otherwise the Maximization Control dialog appears: press Estimate and then OK to produce:

```
General cointegration restrictions:
Analysis of restrictions on α and β:
- α is unrestricted
- β is unrestricted
- restrictions do not identify all cointegrating vectors

General cointegration test 1974 (4) to 1993 (12)

β'
      Ya          Yb          Yc          Yd        Trend
   1.0000     -1.3665      1.3034     -2.3040    0.0018082
  0.17072      1.0000     -1.0176    -0.66528   -0.0018356

α
Ya  -0.025114     -0.10396
Yb   0.035792    -0.062866
Yc   0.049439     0.025752
Yd  0.0077430    -0.016783

standard errors of α
Ya  0.0084229     0.029945
Yb  0.0054328     0.019315
Yc  0.0073225     0.026033
Yd   0.011990     0.042626
```

```
Restricted long-run matrix  Po=αβ', rank 2
          Ya          Yb          Yc          Yd        Trend
Ya  -0.042862   -0.069643    0.073057     0.12703   0.00014542
Yb   0.025060    -0.11178     0.11062   -0.040643   0.00018011
Yc   0.053835   -0.041808    0.038233    -0.13104  4.2124e-005
Yd  0.0048778   -0.027364    0.027170  -0.0066748  4.4807e-005

Reduced form β'
          Yc          Yd        Trend
Ya  0.070698      2.6053   0.00056778
Yb    1.0055     0.22050    0.0017387

Standard errors of long-run matrix
Ya   0.0098529  0.032081   0.032389   0.027812  5.7038e-005
Yb   0.0063551  0.020692   0.020891   0.017939  3.6789e-005
Yc   0.0085656  0.027890   0.028157   0.024178  4.9586e-005
Yd    0.014026  0.045667   0.046105   0.039590  8.1192e-005

Moving average impact matrix
Ya   0.49619      1.3289       1.2876      0.15551
Yb   -4.0889     0.97989       1.3266      -1.6054
Yc   -4.1329     0.86783       1.2182      -1.6194
Yd   0.30260     0.48654      0.46114      0.10363

Restrictions do not identify all cointegrating vectors.
loglik = 3622.5901  -log|Ω| = 30.570381  unr.loglik = 3622.5901
Zero degrees of freedom in LR-test,
no binding restrictions imposed.
```

We will discuss the moving-average impact matrix below. When $p = 2$ is imposed, $\mathbf{P}_0$ is somewhat different from its counterpart without any rank restrictions. The difference between the rank of 2 and 4 in $\mathbf{P}_0$ suggests also considering $p = 3$, which yields (imposing no restrictions again):

```
General cointegration restrictions:

Analysis of restrictions on α and β:
- α is unrestricted
- β is unrestricted
- restrictions do not identify all cointegrating vectors

General cointegration test 1974 (4) to 1993 (12)

β'
       Ya         Yb         Yc         Yd       Trend
   1.0000    -1.3665     1.3034    -2.3040   0.0018082
  0.17072     1.0000    -1.0176   -0.66528  -0.0018356
  0.65409    -1.0088     1.0000   0.092266  -0.0012609
```

```
α
Ya   -0.025114     -0.10396     -0.12625
Yb    0.035792    -0.062866 -0.00056734
Yc    0.049439     0.025752    -0.049998
Yd   0.0077430    -0.016783 5.2146e-005

standard errors of α
Ya   0.0082554     0.029349     0.039167
Yb   0.0054447     0.019357     0.025832
Yc   0.0073053     0.025972     0.034659
Yd    0.012016     0.042720     0.057010

long-run matrix Po=αβ', rank 3
           Ya          Yb          Yc          Yd        Trend
Ya   -0.12544  0.057717 -0.053197     0.11538  0.00030462
Yb   0.024689  -0.11121    0.11005  -0.040696  0.00018083
Yc   0.021132 0.0086281 -0.011765   -0.13565  0.00010517
Yd  0.0049119 -0.027416   0.027222 -0.0066700 4.4741e-005

Reduced form β'
           Yd        Trend
Ya   -0.88108    0.0064232
Yb    -49.365     0.085018
Yc    -49.314     0.082823

Standard errors of long-run matrix
Ya  0.027378    0.050495  0.050416  0.027497 7.4593e-005
Yb  0.018057    0.033303  0.033251  0.018135 4.9197e-005
Yc  0.024227    0.044683  0.044613  0.024332 6.6008e-005
Yd  0.039851    0.073498  0.073383  0.040024  0.00010858

Moving average impact matrix
Ya   -0.0012604    -0.070616    -0.070543    0.0014305
Yb    -0.070616      -3.9565      -3.9524     0.080147
Yc    -0.070543      -3.9524      -3.9483     0.080064
Yd    0.0014305     0.080147     0.080064   -0.0016236

Restrictions do not identify all cointegrating vectors.
loglik = 3631.7659  -log|Ω| = 30.64781 unr.loglik = 3631.7659
Zero degrees of freedom in LR-test,
no binding restrictions imposed.
```

This is close to the unrestricted outcome, consistent with the selected rank, but that is unsurprising since $\mathbf{P}_0$ is not much restricted by $p = 3$. The reduced-form cointegration vectors correspond to the triangular representation (see Phillips, 1991). The large long-run effects from *Yd* on *Yb* and *Yc* suggest that the observed rise in the real exchange rate is a major determinant of the altered growth rate. Note that the 'loglik' values of the two restricted-rank cases match those for the corresponding case in the unrestricted analysis.

To illustrate how the general approach in PcFiml operates, we consider testing whether the first cointegration vector is given by $(0, 1, -1, 0, 0)$. This entails that *Yb*$-$*Yc* is stationary, and is a testable restriction: see Chapter 11.

When the cointegration rank is p, the elements of α are notionally numbered from 0 to $np - 1$ in the form (for $n = 4, p = 2$):

```
&0   &1
&2   &3
&4   ...
```

The elements of β are then numbered in rows from np to $np + p(n + q_r) - 1$ for q_r non-modelled variables in the cointegration vector. For $n = 4, p = 2$ and $q_r = 1$:

```
&8    &9    &10   &11   &12
&13   &14   ...
```

Note that the numbering of the elements alters as the rank of $\mathbf{P}_0$ changes. To implement the desired restrictions, access the Model menu, Estimate system, Restricted cointegration analysis, input the rank as 2 and accept. This will lead to the constraints editor shown above. Delete any contents (position the cursor at the beginning, hold down `Shift` while moving the cursor to the end of the text, release `Shift`, and press `Del` to remove any marked text block). The numbering of the elements in the system is shown in the lower box as an *aide mémoire*.

An alternative way to implement the same test would be through the batch editor, which requires the information to be entered as:

```
option("shortrun", 0);// relevant for recursive estimation
testcoint
{   2                     // set rank to two
    &8  = 0;  &9  = 1;// specify restrictions
    &10 =-1;  &11 = 0;
    &12 = 0;
}                         // non-recursive estimation by "RCOINT"
estsystem("RCOINT", 1974, 4, 1993, 12, 0, 0, 0);
```

Here we use the General restrictions editor. Set the restrictions as:

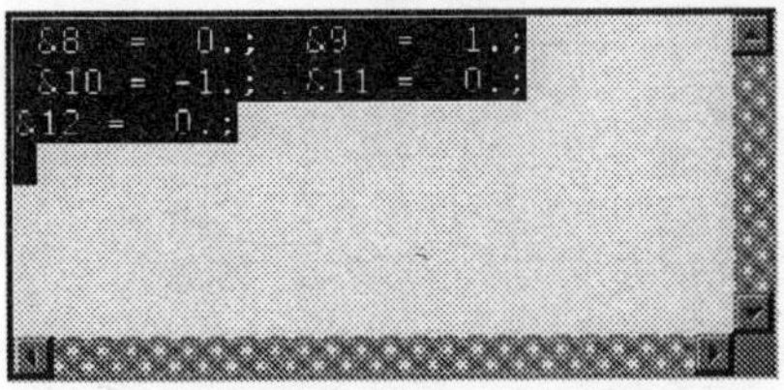

Pressing OK leads to maximization, which involves step-wise maximization of the likelihood function (linear switching algorithm), so may take some time to calculate. When 'Inverting Var[Theta]' shows at the end of the message window, click to see the results.

If the Maximization Control dialog appears; click Estimate to implement; when 'Strong convergence' shows at the top of the dialog, click OK to write the results. This dialog can be switched off in the Options dialog, and is discussed in §4.8 below. The output is similar to the unrestricted analysis, with an additional statistic testing the validity of the restriction, which is decisively rejected. Since $p = 2$ is preserved, these tests have conventional asymptotic χ^2-distributions.

```
General cointegration restrictions:
 &8  =  0.;  &9  =  1.;
 &10 = -1.;  &11 =  0.;
 &12 =  0.;
Analysis of restrictions on α and β:
- linear restrictions
- α x β restrictions are variation free
- α is unrestricted
- β has only within-equation restrictions
- restrictions do not identify all cointegrating vectors
- β equality restrictions rewritten

Restricted Cointegration analysis 1974 (4) to 1993 (12)

β'
      Ya         Yb        Yc         Yd          Trend
 0.00000     1.0000   -1.0000    0.00000        0.00000
 0.22283    0.12657  -0.14088   -0.52231 -9.7895e-005

α
Ya    0.017058     -0.24346
Yb   -0.049957     0.099475
Yc   -0.063686      0.23589
Yd   0.0021177     0.057779

standard errors of α
Ya    0.011667     0.051939
Yb   0.0077074     0.034312
Yc    0.010135     0.045120
Yd    0.016635     0.074057

Restricted long-run matrix Po=αβ', rank 2
            Ya         Yb          Yc          Yd        Trend
Ya   -0.054249 -0.013756   0.017241     0.12716  2.3833e-005
Yb    0.022166 -0.037367   0.035943 -0.051957 -9.7381e-006
Yc    0.052563 -0.033829   0.030453   -0.12321 -2.3093e-005
Yd    0.012875 0.0094307 -0.010258 -0.030179 -5.6563e-006

Reduced form β'
           Yc             Yd          Trend
Ya   0.064225         2.3440     0.00043933
Yb     1.0000 -1.8688e-016 -3.5026e-020

Standard errors of long-run matrix
Ya    0.011573    0.010894    0.011052   0.027128 5.0845e-006
Yb   0.0076457   0.0071967   0.0073010   0.017922 3.3590e-006
Yc    0.010054   0.0094636   0.0096008   0.023567 4.4170e-006
Yd    0.016502    0.015533    0.015758   0.038681 7.2498e-006
```

```
Moving average impact matrix
Ya     1.2655      0.42124      0.42124      0.52833
Yb     7.1842      -173.17      -173.17       7.8098
Yc     7.1842      -173.17      -173.17       7.8098
Yd    0.34303       4.9246       4.9246     0.011409

Restrictions do not identify all cointegrating vectors.
loglik = 3612.0414    unrestricted loglik = 3622.5901
LR-test, rank=2: Chi^2(3) = 21.098 [0.0001] **
```

If we believed that the cointegration rank was unity, and that the resulting cointegration vector only affected the first variable, then we could set to zero the last three elements in the first (and only) column of α, leaving β unrestricted (other than normalization). This time, select Model, Estimate system, Restricted cointegration analysis, set the rank to 1, and type &4=1; &1=0; &2=0; &3=0; so the output is:

```
General cointegration restrictions:
&4=1; &1=0; &2=0; &3=0;
Analysis of restrictions on α and β:
- linear restrictions
- α x β restrictions are variation free
- α has only within-equation restrictions
- α restrictions are homogenous
- α restrictions are simple
- β has only within-equation restrictions

Restricted Cointegration analysis 1974 (4) to 1993 (12)

β'
     Ya        Yb        Yc        Yd       Trend
  1.0000  -0.77671  0.74554  -0.69809  -0.0021321

standard errors of β'
     Ya        Yb        Yc        Yd       Trend
 0.00000   0.29357  0.29128   0.20905   0.00091587

α
Ya      -0.12783
Yb       0.00000
Yc       0.00000
Yd       0.00000

standard errors of α
Ya      0.02392
Yb      0.00000
Yc      0.00000
Yd      0.00000

Restricted long-run matrix Po=αβ', rank 1
           Ya          Yb          Yc          Yd         Trend
Ya    -0.12783     0.09929    -0.09530     0.08924   0.00027255
Yb     0.00000     0.00000     0.00000     0.00000      0.00000
```

```
Yc     0.00000   0.00000    0.00000   0.00000     0.00000
Yd     0.00000   0.00000    0.00000   0.00000     0.00000

Reduced form β'
        Yb         Yc         Yd       Trend
Ya   0.77671  -0.74554  0.69809  0.0021321

Moving average impact matrix
Ya     1.2640      0.78841    -0.55501      0.34077
Yb    0.57550       1.2176     0.34196     -0.16513
Yc   -0.70443    0.089298      1.2488      0.22524
Yd    0.41809    -0.12996     0.15816      0.91243

loglik = 3579.4624  unrestricted loglik = 3603.7247
LR-test, rank=1: Chi^2(3) = 48.525 [0.0000] **
```

Unsurprisingly, this restriction is also rejected ($\mathsf{SE}[\mathbf{P}_0]$ is not reported if α is restricted).

The forms of linear restrictions that can be imposed on $\boldsymbol{\alpha}$ or $\boldsymbol{\beta}$ in this set of selections is essentially unlimited. As you saw, PcFiml checks whether the restrictions uniquely identify the parameters or not. However, non-linear, or cross $\alpha\&\beta$ restrictions are also easily imposed, so we turn to a detailed analysis of general cointegration restrictions.

4.7 Determining unique cointegration relations

Now we consider more substantive applications, by restricting the elements of the first two cointegration vectors to obtain unique representations. The subject-matter theory postulated above suggested that *Yb* and *Yc* cointegrated with a unit coefficient, but might depend on either of the other two variables. *Yc* probably depends on *Yd* (as a proxy for leisure increasing as output per head does), but *Yb* may depend on *Ya* (that is, real income falls as the real exchange rate rises). However, both of these variables (that is, *Yb* and *Yc*) could be excluded from the first cointegrating vector and *Trend* from the other. The theory also essentially entailed that neither of the cointegrating vectors affected *Yd*. Finally, we consider the possibility that the first vector affects neither *Yb* nor *Yc*, and the other affects *Ya*. Generally, application of analysis, experience, and reasoning are required to determine cointegration vectors uniquely. The general theory of identification (uniqueness) in econometrics is discussed in Chapter 12.

We first test for the restrictions on α alone, without restrictions on β using rank 2 (Alt+m, t, Enter, 2, OK):

```
&2=0; &4=0; &6=0;
&1=0; &7=0;
```

Note that the variable designations have been switched in the text.
Ya → Yd   Yd → Ya
Yb → Yc   Yc → Yb

Implementing these restrictions leads to:

General cointegration restrictions:
&2=0; &4=0; &6=0;
&1=0; &7=0;
Analysis of restrictions on α and β:
- linear restrictions
- α x β restrictions are variation free
- α has only within-equation restrictions
- α restrictions are homogenous
- α restrictions are simple
- β is unrestricted
- restrictions do not identify all cointegrating vectors

General cointegration test 1974 (4) to 1993 (12)

β'

Ya	Yb	Yc	Yd	Trend
0.36285	-0.28440	0.27298	-0.25865	-0.00075933
-0.11078	0.25105	-0.24053	0.42033	-0.00068224

α

Ya	-0.35398	0.00000
Yb	0.00000	-0.18633
Yc	0.00000	-0.24753
Yd	0.00000	0.00000

standard errors of α

Ya	0.065899	0.00000
Yb	0.00000	0.024290
Yc	0.00000	0.029871
Yd	0.00000	0.00000

Restricted long-run matrix Po=$\alpha\beta'$, rank 3

	Ya	Yb	Yc	Yd	Trend
Ya	-0.12844	0.10067	-0.096629	0.091557	0.00026879
Yb	0.020641	-0.046777	0.044817	-0.078319	0.00012712
Yc	0.027421	-0.062142	0.059538	-0.10405	0.00016887
Yd	0.00000	0.00000	0.00000	0.00000	0.00000

Reduced form β'

	Yc	Yd	Trend
Ya	-0.0020852	-0.91646	0.0064553
Yb	0.95718	-2.0787	0.0055661

Moving average impact matrix

Ya	2.7615	15.145	9.2329	-3.0342
Yb	-84.055	-508.21	-330.13	92.468
Yc	-93.895	-564.05	-364.97	103.28
Yd	-2.7995	-15.242	-9.2441	3.0758

Restrictions do not identify all cointegrating vectors.
loglik = 3614.4882 unrestricted loglik = 3622.5901

```
LR-test, rank=2: Chi^2(3) = 16.204 [0.0010] **
```

These restrictions on α are strongly rejected.

Next we consider the hypotheses about unique cointegrating vectors $\boldsymbol{\beta}$, noting that their joint imposition has important implications for long-run weak exogeneity, namely whether or not the cointegration vectors are cross linked between equations. We only allow for the possibility that *Ya* and *Yd* satisfy the necessary conditions for being weakly exogenous in the *Yb* and *Yc* equations. We hypothesise the normalized relations:

$$\begin{aligned} CI1 &= Ya - a_1 Yd - a_2 t, \\ CI2 &= Yb - b_1 Ya - b_2 Yc + b_3 Yd. \end{aligned}$$

These equations define unique vectors, and we will test $b_2 = 1$ shortly. The value of prior information from a long-run theoretical analysis is clear here. In terms of PcFiml, the restrictions become, together with excluding cointegration vectors from *Yd*:

```
&8=1;  &9=0;  &10=0;
&14=1; &17=0;
&6=0;  &7=0;
```

These $\boldsymbol{\beta}$ restrictions lead to (after convergence, which might be weak or strong, depending on the convergence criterion and the method selected; the obtained results will depend somewhat on the used value for the convergence criteria):

```
General cointegration test 1974 (4) to 1993 (12)
β'
        Ya         Yb         Yc          Yd         Trend
    1.0000    0.00000    0.00000    -2.7695    -0.0024169
  -0.67617     1.0000    -1.0065     1.6059       0.00000

standard errors of β'
        Ya         Yb          Yc         Yd         Trend
   0.00000    0.00000     0.00000    0.25253    0.00057859
  0.078545    0.00000    0.010153    0.21556       0.00000

α
Ya   -0.091549   -0.086439
Yb   -0.047818    -0.10626
Yc    0.032631   -0.024644
Yd     0.00000     0.00000

standard errors of α
Ya    0.026477    0.033775
Yb    0.015709    0.020039
Yc    0.019629    0.025039
Yd     0.00000     0.00000

Restricted long-run matrix Po=αβ', rank 3
          Ya          Yb          Yc           Yd          Trend
Ya  -0.033102   -0.086439    0.087000     0.11473     0.00022127
Yb   0.024033    -0.10626     0.10695   -0.038220     0.00011557
Yc   0.049295   -0.024644    0.024804    -0.12995   -7.8868e-005
```

```
Yd     0.00000     0.00000     0.00000     0.00000     0.00000

Reduced form β'
        Yc          Yd        Trend
Ya    0.00000    2.7695    0.0024169
Yb     1.0065   0.26669    0.0016342

Moving average impact matrix
Ya     1.7459     0.76021      0.58827      0.63041
Yb    -19.411      7.5634       9.3718      -7.0088
Yc    -19.453      7.4419       9.2551      -7.0240
Yd    0.63041     0.27450      0.21241      0.22763

loglik = 3619.6453   -log|
Omega| = 30.54553   unrestr. loglik = 3622.5901
LR-test, rank=2: Chi^2(3) = 5.8897 [0.1171]
```

The restrictions are jointly acceptable, although the additional β restriction is barely accepted. To verify that statement, rerun the restricted cointegration analysis with just the α restrictions to obtain $\chi^2(2) = 0.56388[0.7543]$, then access the GiveWin Tools menu, Tail probability to see the following dialog.

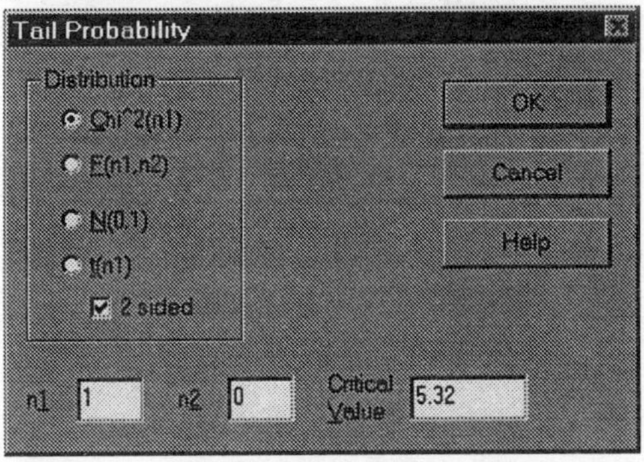

Mark Chi^2, input 1 degree of freedom, then a value of 5.32 (the difference between the two chi^{2}s), and accept to obtain:

```
Chi^2(1)  =  5.32  [0.0211]  *
```

which rejects at the 5% (but not the 1%) level.

As $b_2 = 1$ seems acceptable from the reported standard errors, imposing that, the combined sets of restrictions identify the two cointegrating relations:

$$\begin{aligned} Ya &= c_1\, Yd + c_2 t \\ Yb - Yc &= d_1\, Ya + d_2\, Yd \end{aligned} \tag{4.4}$$

Thus, productivity trends at (approximately) 2.5% ($0.0023 \times 12 \times 100$ per annum), since all variables are in logs, but as output is unlikely to increase as the real exchange rate rises, we interpret the long-run relation as one where the real exchange rate is positively linked to the deviation of productivity from trend. Also, consumption is proportional to income, such that this deviation increases with increases in productivity, and falls with rises in the real exchange rate. From the standard errors, all these elements are significantly different from zero.

The trend matters greatly in the long run, as can be seen from its tiny standard error. Adding the restriction that &15=-1 is fully acceptable as $\chi^2(4) = 6.11[0.19]$. The additional constraint induces $\chi^2(1) = 0.22$, as GiveWin's Tail probability confirms.

The coefficients in the cointegration vectors allow a simplification, in that the relation of *Ya* to *Yd* in the second can be removed by using the first to deliver:

```
&8=1; &9=0; &10=0;
&14=1; &13=0; &16=0;
&15=-1;
&6=0; &7=0;
β'
        Ya          Yb          Yc          Yd          Trend
    1.0000     0.00000     0.00000     -2.5998     -0.0025725
   0.00000      1.0000     -1.0000     0.00000     -0.0021264

standard errors of β'
        Ya          Yb          Yc          Yd          Trend
   0.00000     0.00000     0.00000     0.26038     0.00065399
   0.00000     0.00000     0.00000     0.00000     0.00016658

α
Ya      -0.045194     -0.080242
Yb       0.015524     -0.097462
Yc       0.048636     -0.033821
Yd        0.00000       0.00000

standard errors of α
Ya       0.010512      0.029545
Yb      0.0062523      0.017572
Yc      0.0078182      0.021973
Yd        0.00000       0.00000

Moving average impact matrix
Ya    1.4804      0.73797       0.73797       0.56941
Yb   -21.195       10.471        10.471       -8.1524
Yc   -21.195       10.471        10.471       -8.1524
Yd   0.56941      0.28385       0.28385       0.21902

loglik = 3619.3702   unrestricted loglik = 3622.5901
LR-test, rank=2: Chi^2(5) = 6.4398 [0.2657]
```

However, these violate long-run weak exogeneity. These restricted cointegration vectors can be plotted via Cointegration graphics, and are shown in Figure 4.4.

If one is willing to wait a short time, then the recursive restricted cointegration coefficients can be graphed. The options also allow a transform of the likelihood, and the test of the overidentifying restrictions to be graphed. In this case we keep the short-run fixed (remember: this is set in the Options dialog.

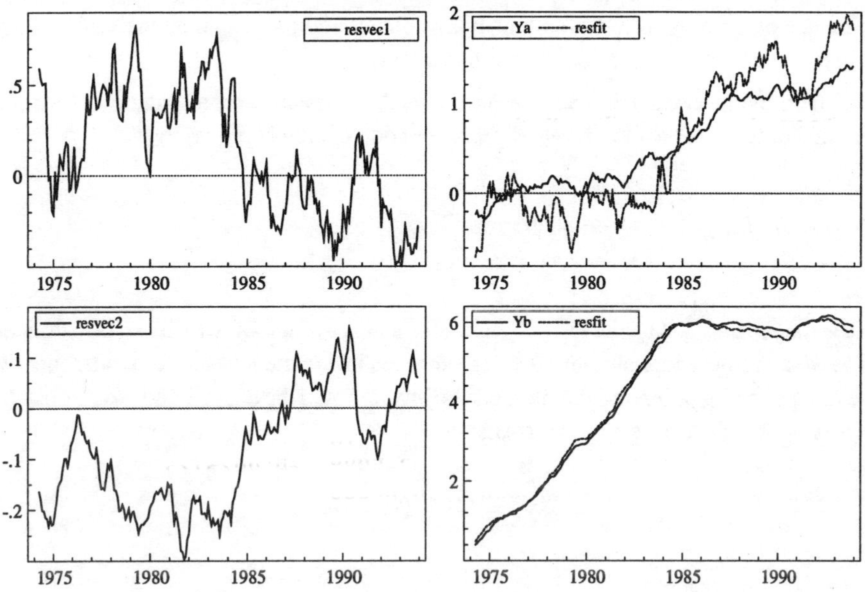

Figure 4.4 Time series of restricted cointegration vectors.

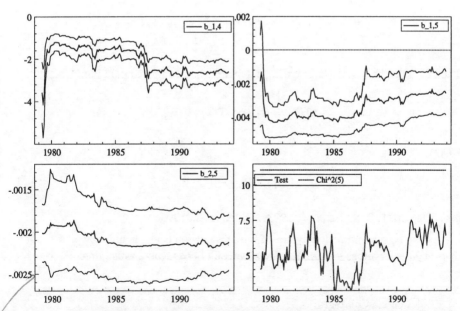

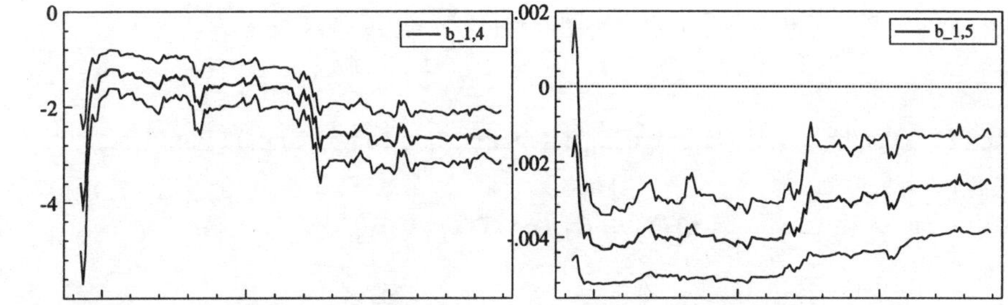

Figure 4.5 Time series of restricted cointegration coefficients.

Figure 4.5 shows the graphs of the three remaining unrestricted $\widehat{\beta}_{i,j,t} \pm 2\widehat{\mathsf{SE}}_t$, using 60 initial values (otherwise, the variation at the start swamps that later), together with the

Estimate System (OK)
Restricted Coint analysis
General restrictions (OK)
Cointegration Graphics
Beta coefficients +/- 2SE (if available)

sequence of χ^2 tests of the overidentifying cointegration restrictions; their 5% critical values are shown (alternative p-values can be set).

The moving-average impact matrix shows the alternative representation of a cointegrated process. Consider the VAR representation of an I(1) process $\mathbf{y}_t$:

$$\mathbf{y}_t = \boldsymbol{\mu} + \sum_{i=1}^{m} \boldsymbol{\pi}_i \mathbf{y}_{t-i} + \boldsymbol{\epsilon}_t.$$

Since the process is I(1), the lag polynomial contains a unit root, which can be extracted to leave a lag polynomial with all its eigenvalues inside the unit circle. Consequently, the remainder lag polynomial matrix can be inverted, and the differenced process can be expressed in a moving-average form as:

$$\Delta \mathbf{y}_t = \mathbf{C}(L)(\boldsymbol{\mu} + \boldsymbol{\epsilon}_t).$$

and solving for levels:

$$\mathbf{y}_t = \mathbf{y}_0 + \mathbf{C}(1)\boldsymbol{\mu} t + \mathbf{C}(1)\sum_{i=1}^{t} \boldsymbol{\epsilon}_i + \mathbf{C}(L)\boldsymbol{\epsilon}_t.$$

Then $\mathbf{C}(1)$ is the moving-average impact matrix. It is computed in PcFiml from:

$$\mathbf{C}(1) = \boldsymbol{\beta}_\perp \left(\boldsymbol{\alpha}_\perp' \boldsymbol{\Upsilon} \boldsymbol{\beta}_\perp\right)^{-1} \boldsymbol{\alpha}_\perp'$$

where

$$\mathrm{r}\left(\boldsymbol{\alpha}_\perp' \boldsymbol{\Upsilon} \boldsymbol{\beta}_\perp\right) = n - p \tag{4.5}$$

(see Chapter 11, Banerjee *et al.*, 1993, and Johansen, 1995b).

As can be seen immediately, the MA representation is identical for *Yb* and *Yc*; and that for *Ya* is 2.6 times that for *Yd*. Thus, here, $\mathbf{C}(1)$ has rank 2 as required.

4.8 The switching algorithm

We now take a more detailed look at the switching algorithm. Click on the Model menu, Options to see:

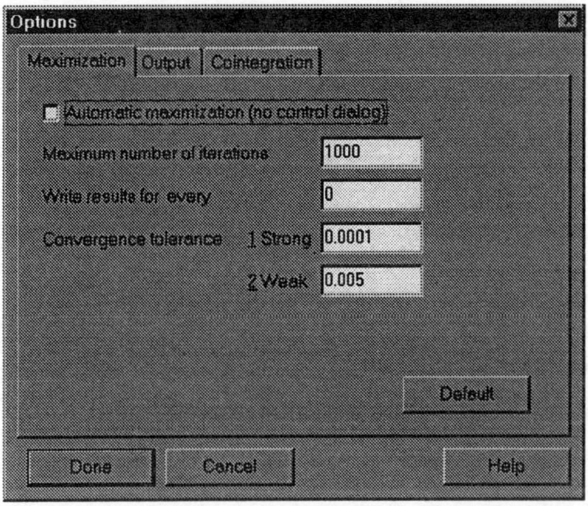

Click on Automatic maximization (so the 'tick' disappears), and then Done to end and save the dialog. Again use rank two, and non-recursive estimation. Now, after entering the restrictions and accepting, the Maximization control dialog appears. For example, corresponding to the restrictions in (4.4), with unrestricted α, we set

```
&8=1;  &9=0;   &10=0;
&14=1; &15=-1; &17=0;
```

so that the control dialog is:

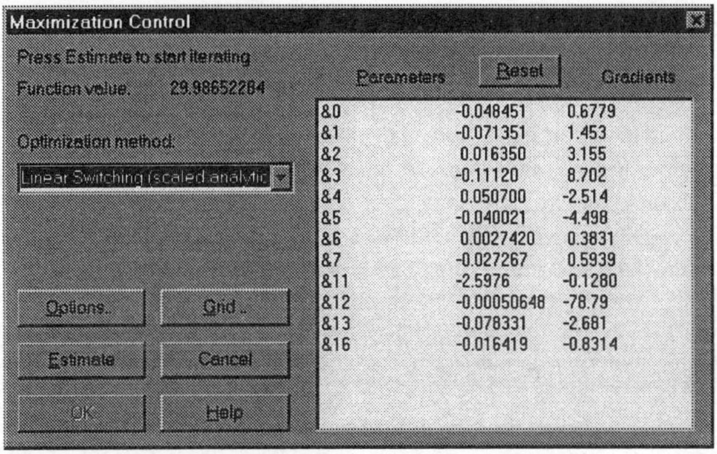

The message at the top of the screen is 'Press Estimate to start iterating', as we have not started the optimization algorithm yet. The reported function value corresponds to $-\log|\Omega|$. The actual log-likelihood as reported in the test output is $T/2$ times this. The list on the right gives the starting values of each of the parameters and the gradients; the former can be changed (double click).

Two ways of computing likelihood derivatives are available: analytical and numerical. The latter computes $\partial\ell\left(\gamma\left(\boldsymbol{\theta}\right)\right)/\partial\theta_i$ by numerical differentiation, where γ denotes the elements of $(\boldsymbol{\alpha},\boldsymbol{\beta})$ in a vector. The former combines the analytical computation of $\partial\ell\left(\gamma\right)/\partial\gamma_i$ with analytical derivatives for $\partial\gamma\left(\boldsymbol{\theta}\right)/\partial\theta_i$. In addition, several algorithms can be used: $\boldsymbol{\beta}$ switching (scaled); linear switching between $\boldsymbol{\alpha}$ and $\boldsymbol{\beta}$, scaled or unscaled; nonlinear switching; and no switching, namely optimization over all parameters γ jointly. Experience up to now suggests that all these methods have their place. Switching is more robust, but often slower. Not switching works better in the presence of a large number of restrictions. The scaled options refer to PcFiml's ability to analyze and rewrite the restrictions (temporarily removing any imposed normalization for example), see Chapter 11 for more information.

PcFiml lets you choose which to try at each stage. Click on the 'down' button beside Linear switching to see some of the options:

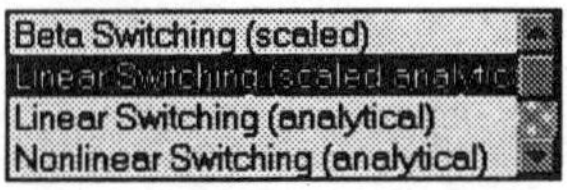

You can scroll down to see the remainder:

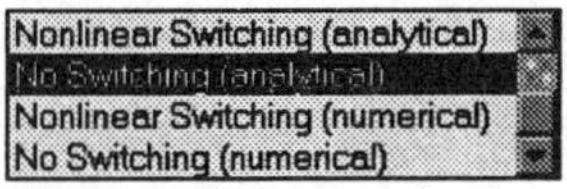

The present optimization problem is potentially awkward, and the dialog gives full control over the process. Among the problems that can happen is that a decrease in an $\boldsymbol{\alpha}$ parameter can be 'absorbed' by an increase in some $\boldsymbol{\beta}$s, leaving the product largely unchanged. Switching usually works, but may not work at poor starting parameter values. The reset button resets the parameters to the original starting values.

First optimize using the No Switching (analytical) choice. The algorithm takes some time (over 60 iterations), then returns the message 'Strong convergence'. The derivatives are relatively small, but far from zero. Clicking several times again on Estimate induces most gradients to become fairly small. Further progress is possible by clicking Estimate again, but is often slow. If the convergence criteria are too tight, repeated attempts to progress can induce 'Weak convergence', with a failure to improve the line search (see Chapter 13 for a discussion of numerical optimization).

Reset the parameters, then reoptimize using a switching algorithm: Linear Switching (scaled analytical). Convergence is fast (49 steps), but leads to weak convergence:

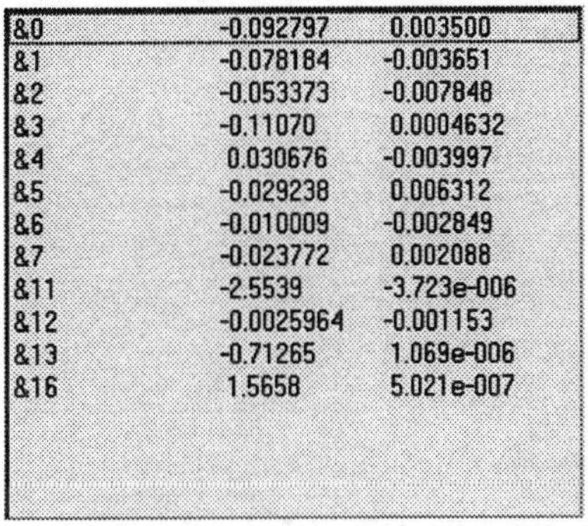

&0	-0.092797	0.003500
&1	-0.078184	-0.003651
&2	-0.053373	-0.007848
&3	-0.11070	0.0004632
&4	0.030676	-0.003997
&5	-0.029238	0.006312
&6	-0.010009	-0.002849
&7	-0.023772	0.002088
&11	-2.5539	-3.723e-006
&12	-0.0025964	-0.001153
&13	-0.71265	1.069e-006
&16	1.5658	5.021e-007

Upon convergence, try to continue with switching. This works, and can lead to strong convergence, confirming that the current point is a maximum. Alternatively, after the convergence shown in the above screen capture, change to the no switching (analytical) algorithm, and continue to discover 'Strong convergence' in about a further 25 iterations.

After optimization, access the Grid dialog as shown:

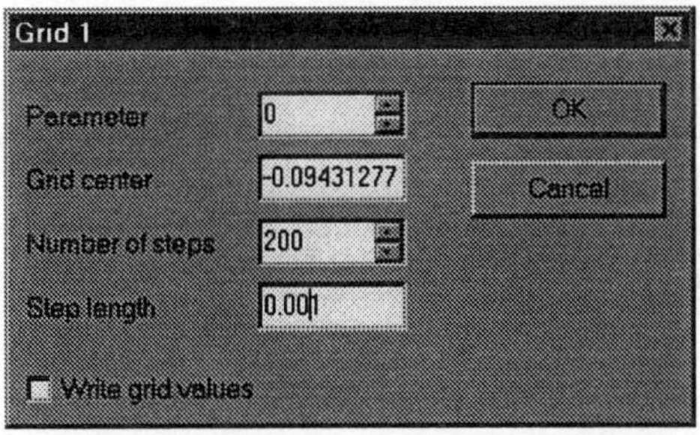

Set 200 steps, and a step length of 0.001 as shown. Select until 'parameter 0' reappears, then cancel to produce the plots of the likelihood grids as in Figure 4.6.

The grids look fine, with the sharper spike deriving from the large scale of that graph (the coefficient of trend).

Press Reset again, as there are two more methods to explore. Since α is unrestricted, Beta Switching is available. Unlike the other switching methods, which alternate between α and β, this method switches over cointegrating vectors, maximizing over one restricted vector at time. Beta switching converges in 32 steps, but again we need to press Estimate a few times to get the gradient on &12 smaller.

The final method is Linear Switching (analytical). The difference with the scaled method is that no rewriting of restrictions is attempted. Convergence requires at least twice as many iterations than the scaled method.

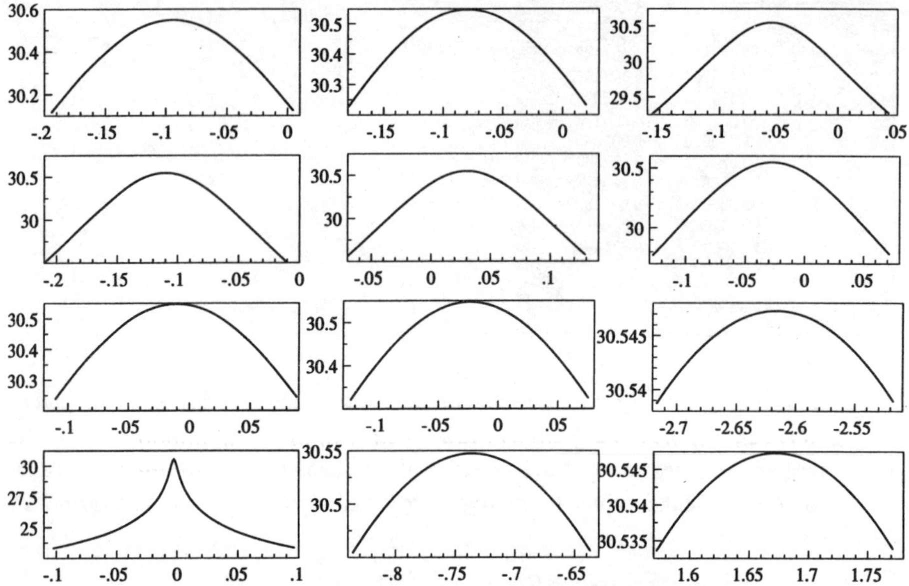

Figure 4.6 Reduced-rank likelihood grids.

4.8.1 Three cointegrating vectors

As we want to explain conditional modelling in later chapters, we will 'cheat' at this stage, and use the cointegration vectors found in the previous edition of this book. These were based on assuming three long-run relationships, and took the form:

```
&1 = 0;  &2 = 0;
&3 = 0;  &6 = 0;  &9 = 0;
&10 = 0; &11 = 0;
&12 = 1; &13 = 0; &14 = 0; &15 = -1;
&17 = 0; &18 = 1; &19 =-1;  &21 = 0;
&23 =-1; &24 = 1; &25 = 0; &26 = 0;
```

β'

Ya	Yb	Yc	Yd	Trend
1.0000	0.00000	0.00000	-1.0000	-0.0043530
0.00000	1.0000	-1.0000	-1.8023	0.00000
0.35272	-1.0000	1.0000	0.00000	0.00000

standard errors of β'

Ya	Yb	Yc	Yd	Trend
0.00000	0.00000	0.00000	0.00000	0.00029702
0.00000	0.00000	0.00000	0.12392	0.00000
0.018440	0.00000	0.00000	0.00000	0.00000

```
α
Ya      -0.10277        0.00000         0.00000
Yb       0.00000        0.026423        0.14211
Yc       0.00000        0.072440        0.060651
Yd       0.00000        0.00000         0.00000

standard errors of α
Ya       0.020502       0.00000         0.00000
Yb       0.00000        0.0085435       0.024417
Yc       0.00000        0.010544        0.030124
Yd       0.00000        0.00000         0.00000

Restricted long-run matrix Po=α*β', rank 3
              Ya          Yb          Yc          Yd        Trend
Ya   -0.10277    0.00000     0.00000     0.10277  0.00044735
Yb   0.050123   -0.11568     0.11568   -0.047623     0.00000
Yc   0.021393   0.011789   -0.011789    -0.13056     0.00000
Yd    0.00000    0.00000     0.00000     0.00000     0.00000

Moving average impact matrix
Ya  0         0         0  0
Yb  0   -31.972   -31.972  0
Yc  0   -31.972   -31.972  0
Yd  0         0         0  0

loglik = 3624.6044  -log|Ω| = 30.587379
unrestr. loglik = 3631.7659
LR-test, rank=3: Chi^2(10) = 14.323 [0.1588]
```

These vectors satisfy the necessary condition for long-weak exogeneity and are uniquely identified. Thus, we retain them for the remaining tutorials. They also allow the interesting demonstration that linear switching (scaled analytic) converges quickly for them; but no switching will not converge; the other linear switching method has problems to beyond weak convergence; beta switching is not available. Click three times on Estimate to get all gradients to 1e-005 or smaller. The moving average impact matrix has rank 1, consistent with the three cointegration vectors specified (we have replaced the very small values with 0).

This concludes the tutorial on cointegration. The next stage is to map the data in the system to I(0), and that is the topic of Chapter 5.

A batch file corresponding to this chapter is provided in a file called PCFTUT2.FL. There are various ways to create such a file, for example by activating the batch editor in Givewin, and saving the specification. For now, exit PcFiml. This will write the most recent specification to the Results window:

```
Batch code for the final specification:
module("PcFiml");
usedata("pcftut1.in7");
system
{
    Y = Ya, Yb, Yc, Yd;
```

```
    Z = Ya_1, Ya_2, Yb_1, Yb_2, Yc_1, Yc_2, Yd_1, Yd_2, Trend;
    U = Constant;
}
testcoint
{
3
&1 = 0;  &2 = 0;
&3 = 0;  &6 = 0;  &9 = 0;
&10 = 0; &11 = 0;
&12 = 1; &13 = 0; &14 = 0; &15 = -1;
&17 = 0; &18 = 1; &19 =-1;  &21 = 0;
&23 =-1; &24 = 1; &25 = 0; &26 = 0;
}
estsystem("RCOINT", 1974, 4, 1993, 12, 0, 0, 0);
```

The header ('Batch code for ...') is not batch language, and has to be removed when saving the code. Finally, in PCFTUT2.FL we changed the `usedata` command (which just selects an already loaded database) to `loaddata` (which will attempt to load the database into GiveWin).

4.9 Addendum: *A* and *H* matrices

Up to this point, we have completely ignored the other two choices for restricted cointegration analysis. This section turns to the final two methods, which will not involve iterative estimation.

The first linear restriction we consider is whether the cointegration vector $(0, 1, -1, 0, 0)$ lies in the cointegration space. The **H** matrix discussed in Chapter 11 then has the form $(0, 1, -1, 0, 0)'$ and is set as follows. Select Model, Estimate system, Restricted cointegration analysis and choose the third item on the mini-menu: Common alpha and known beta.

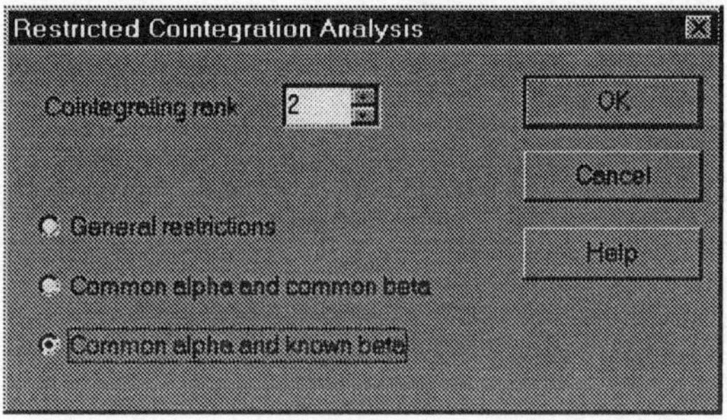

Input a rank of 2, skip the entry for setting α (`Esc`), and alter the dimensions of **H** to $5{\times}1$, typing in the elements of **H** as $(0, 1, -1, 0, 0)'$ in the first column. The matrix editor should look like:

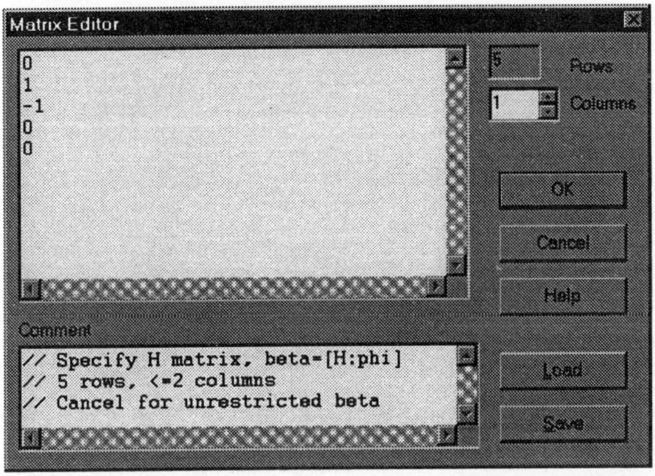

The output is similar to the unrestricted analysis, with an additional statistic testing the validity of the restriction, which is decisively rejected. Since $p = 2$ is preserved, these tests have conventional asymptotic χ^2-distributions.

```
Restricted Cointegration analysis 1974 (4) to 1993 (12)

eigenvalue μi      loglik for rank
                      3583.62   1
     0.213238         3612.04   2
      0.10535         3625.23   3
    0.0650025         3633.20   4
  0.000950861           ---

H matrix, containing known columns of β: β=[H:φ], CΩ=φ
Ya             0.0000
Yb              1.000
Yc             -1.000
Yd             0.0000
Trend          0.0000

standardized β'=[H:φ]' eigenvectors
      Ya          Yb          Yc          Yd          Trend
  0.0000       1.000      -1.000      0.0000         0.0000
 -31.148       1.000       1.000       72.99       0.013646

standardized α coefficients
Ya    -0.015446    0.0017420
Yb    -0.036674 -0.00071218
Yc    -0.032192   -0.0016878
Yd    0.0098340 -0.00041378

Restricted long-run matrix Po=αβ', rank 2
            Ya          Yb          Yc          Yd         Trend
Ya   -0.05426    -0.01370     0.01719      0.1271   0.00002377
```

```
Yb    0.02218   -0.03739    0.03596   -0.05198 -9.719e-006
Yc    0.05257   -0.03388    0.03050    -0.1232 -0.00002303
Yd    0.01289   0.009420   -0.01025   -0.03020 -5.647e-006

Reduced form β'
             Yc           Yd        Trend
Ya      0.06421        2.343    0.0004381
Yb        1.000 -6.271e-018 -1.172e-021

LR-test, rank=2: Chi^2( 3) = 21.098 [0.0001] **
```

These differ from the results reported above only to the extent that the β eigenvectors both normalized here, but as the second is not unique, any linear combination is acceptable. The reduced-form β and $\chi^2(3)$ are identical.

Alternatively, if we believed that the cointegration rank was unity, and that the resulting cointegration vector only affected the first variable then we could set to zero the last three elements in the first (and only) column of α, leaving β unrestricted. This time, click on the estimate icon ('completed block'), accept restricted cointegration analysis, and choose the second item on the mini-menu for common α and β. Set the rank to 1, and accept. On the matrix editor, set the number of columns to 1, and type unity in the first element of α, leaving the other elements at zero; skip the β setting (`Esc`), and the output is:

```
Restricted Cointegration analysis 1974 (4) to 1993 (12)

eigenvalue μi       loglik for rank
                        3566.26    0
      0.105424          3579.46    1

A matrix, imposing linear restrictions on α: α=Aθ
Ya                   1.000
Yb                  0.0000
Yc                  0.0000
Yd                  0.0000

standardized β' eigenvectors
        Ya            Yb            Yc            Yd       Trend
     1.000       -0.7767        0.7455       -0.6981   -0.002132

standardized α=Aθ coefficients
Ya       -0.1278
Yb        0.0000
Yc        0.0000
Yd        0.0000

Restricted long-run matrix Po=αβ', rank 1
             Ya          Yb          Yc          Yd       Trend
Ya      -0.1278     0.09928    -0.09530     0.08923   0.0002726
Yb       0.0000      0.0000      0.0000      0.0000      0.0000
Yc       0.0000      0.0000      0.0000      0.0000      0.0000
```

```
Yd      0.0000     0.0000     0.0000     0.0000     0.0000
```

```
Reduced form β'
           Yb          Yc          Yd       Trend
Ya     0.7767     -0.7455      0.6981    0.002132
```

```
LR-test, rank=1: Chi²(3)  = 48.525 [0.0000] **
```

Unsurprisingly, this restriction is also rejected. Now the log-likelihood value for $p = 0$ should match that for $p = 0$ in the unrestricted cointegration analysis. These results can also be matched against those in §4.6. Note the closeness of the likelihoods and P_0 values, so the apparent differences are due to alternative rotations.

Chapter 5

Reduction to I(0)

5.1 Introduction

The next important step in model construction is to map the data to I(0) series, by differencing and cointegrating combinations. We have determined three unique cointegrating vectors in Chapter 4 and can construct the data analogues either by the algebra, or the calculator. We choose the former first.

If you start afresh, run the batch file PCFTUT2.FL referred to at the end of Chapter 4. This batch file loads the data set, estimates the system, does cointegration analysis, and tests restrictions on α and β. Alternatively, just load the data set PCFTUT1.IN7.

First, we use the algebra editor to create the cointegrating vectors corresponding to (4.4). In GiveWin, type `Alt+a` and enter the algebra code as follows (or load the algebra file called PCFTUT3.ALG):

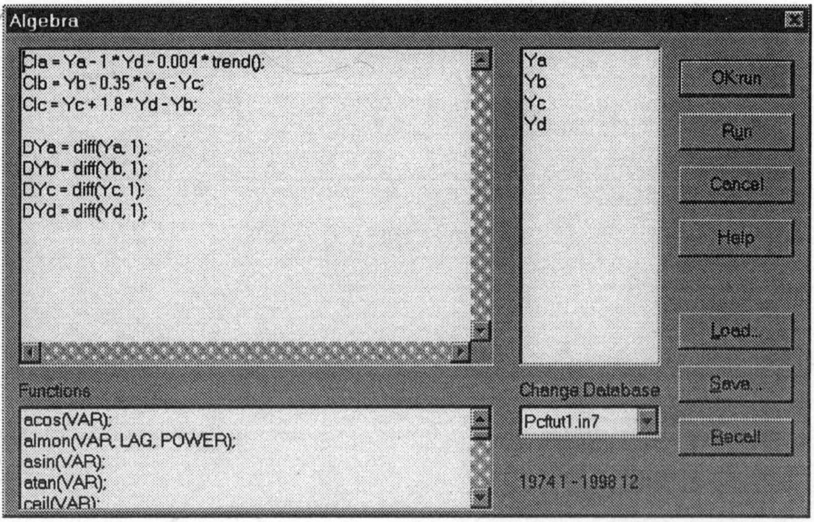

The list on the right gives the database variables that can be accessed in the algebra code; the list below gives the algebra functions. Selecting any of these leads to the item being pasted into the editor. We shall need the differences of all the Y variables in this chapter. We created them using the calculator as explained in §2.4.2, but they are shown in the Algebra edit box for convenience. Click OK to run.

We can now formulate an I(0) system that excludes all I(1) variables, and effects the reduction equivalent to the rank 3 restriction on $\mathbf{P}_0$. The time-series graphs of the restricted cointegrating vectors are shown in Figure 5.1 (in GiveWin: `Alt+g`, mark *CIa*, *CIb*, *CIc* with the mouse, holding down the `Ctrl` key):

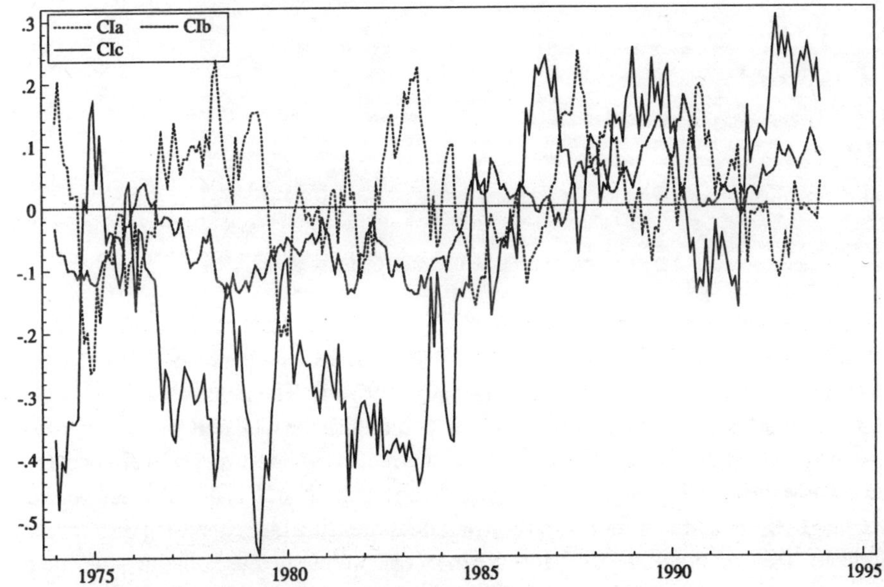

Figure 5.1 Restricted cointegrating relations.

Now select Model, Formulate System (`Alt+m, s` or use the toolbar button). Press the New Model button to clear the existing system, if any. Select one lag, mark *DYa*, *DYb*, *DYc*, *DYd*, *CIa*, *CIb*, *CIc*, press Add. Note that one lag of a difference includes the second lag of the level, matching the reduction to 2 lags obtained in Chapter 3. Switch to the model column (`Alt+m`, or click inside with the mouse, or left arrow), and mark *Constant* then Clear its status. The reason for this will become clear later. Next, mark *CIa*, *CIb*, *CIc* and change their status to identity. PcFiml automatically handles identities in that they are omitted from system estimation (since they are redundant) but included in models of the system. Once the menu of variables included in the identity is defined by the process of model formulation, PcFiml will estimate the coefficients, but will not proceed unless the 'fit' is essentially perfect. The inclusion of identities is a convenient way to approach modelling with cointegrated variables since it avoids having to eliminate two of the differences in terms of levels and differences of cointegrating vectors. Then, for example, dynamic analysis or dynamic forecasts can be conducted. The final result should look like:

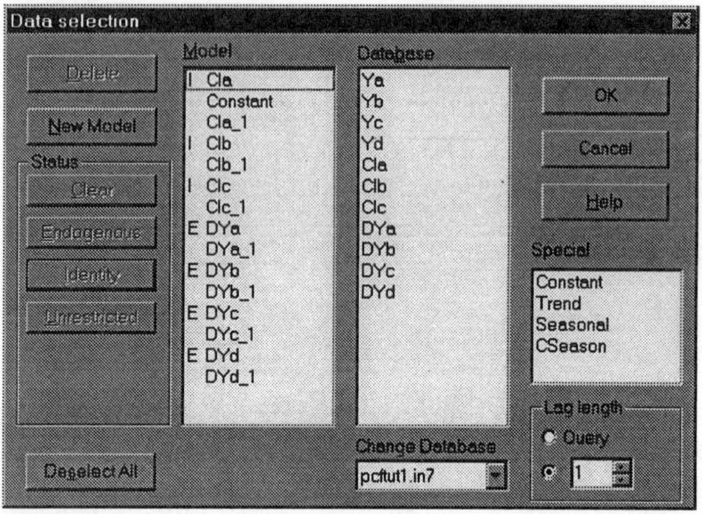

Accept, and estimate by recursive ordinary least squares, since henceforth all tests are in I(0) form, and so have conventional critical values. To exactly match our output, check that the first data point in the estimation sample is 1974(4). The impact of the two reductions (shorter lag and cointegration) has been to diminish the total number of parameters from 66 ($4 \times 14 + 10$) to 42 ($4 \times 8 + 10$). It is incorrect to conduct a direct likelihood-ratio test against the initial system, since that would be a mixture of I(1) distributions (corresponding to estimated unit roots) and conventional (deleting the second-lag differences). However, the equation standard errors are in fact very close to those obtained in Chapter 3, consistent with the validity of the rank restriction.

The output can be presented in columnar or equation format; the following uses the former mode:

```
Data loaded from: pcftut1.in7 and pcftut1.BN7

               **** output from batch run deleted ****

CIa = Ya - 1 * Yd - 0.004 * trend();
CIb = Yb - 0.35 * Ya - Yc;
CIc = Yc + 1.8 * Yd - Yb;

DYa = diff(Ya, 1);
DYb = diff(Yb, 1);
DYc = diff(Yc, 1);
DYd = diff(Yd, 1);

EQ( 2) Estimating the urf by OLS  (using pcftut1.in7)
The present sample is:  1974 (4) to 1993 (12)
```

URF Equation 1 for DYa

Variable	Coefficient	Std.Error	t-value	t-prob
DYa_1	-0.028316	0.064465	-0.439	0.6609
DYb_1	0.21745	0.12650	1.719	0.0870
DYc_1	-0.11459	0.11296	-1.014	0.3114
DYd_1	-0.017049	0.052030	-0.328	0.7435
CIc_1	0.0022507	0.015222	0.148	0.8826
CIa_1	-0.10324	0.021647	-4.769	0.0000
CIb_1	0.054626	0.040657	1.344	0.1804
Constant	0.0068065	0.0024925	2.731	0.0068

σ = 0.0264596 RSS = 0.1603254385

URF Equation 2 for DYb

Variable	Coefficient	Std.Error	t-value	t-prob
DYa_1	-0.016350	0.042254	-0.387	0.6991
DYb_1	0.29463	0.082915	3.553	0.0005
DYc_1	0.092993	0.074041	1.256	0.2104
DYd_1	-0.0025665	0.034103	-0.075	0.9401
CIc_1	-0.029262	0.0099771	-2.933	0.0037
CIa_1	-0.019088	0.014189	-1.345	0.1799
CIb_1	-0.13084	0.026649	-4.910	0.0000
Constant	0.0098576	0.0016337	6.034	0.0000

σ = 0.017343 RSS = 0.06887874734

URF Equation 3 for DYc

Variable	Coefficient	Std.Error	t-value	t-prob
DYa_1	-0.0061329	0.056933	-0.108	0.9143
DYb_1	-0.072372	0.11172	-0.648	0.5178
DYc_1	0.34047	0.099763	3.413	0.0008
DYd_1	0.016286	0.045951	0.354	0.7234
CIc_1	-0.069097	0.013443	-5.140	0.0000
CIa_1	-0.0014310	0.019118	-0.075	0.9404
CIb_1	-0.060184	0.035907	-1.676	0.0951
Constant	0.0073065	0.0022013	3.319	0.0011

σ = 0.0233682 RSS = 0.1250501553

URF Equation 4 for DYd

Variable	Coefficient	Std.Error	t-value	t-prob
DYa_1	0.086187	0.093163	0.925	0.3559
DYb_1	-0.054387	0.18281	-0.297	0.7664
DYc_1	0.097084	0.16325	0.595	0.5526
DYd_1	-0.024429	0.075192	-0.325	0.7456
CIc_1	-0.0099956	0.021998	-0.454	0.6500
CIa_1	0.0051844	0.031284	0.166	0.8685
CIb_1	-0.0078212	0.058757	-0.133	0.8942
Constant	0.00059932	0.0036021	0.166	0.8680

σ = 0.0382385 RSS = 0.3348400575

```
correlation of URF residuals
              DYa           DYb           DYc           DYd
DYa        1.0000
DYb      0.089597        1.0000
DYc     -0.050091       0.70795        1.0000
DYd     -0.056133      -0.37690      -0.52153        1.0000

standard deviations of URF residuals
          DYa           DYb           DYc           DYd
     0.026460      0.017343      0.023368      0.038239

loglik=3627.0657  log|Ω|=-30.6081  |Ω|=5.09389e-014  T=237
log|Y'Y/T|  = -28.3295
R²(LR) = 0.897577  R²(LM) = 0.308092

F-test on all regressors except unrestricted,
F(32,835) = 22.311 [0.0000] **
No variables entered unrestricted.

F-tests on retained regressors, F(4, 226)
DYa_1  0.322710 [0.8626]        DYb_1    8.27498 [0.0000]**
DYc_1   5.44405 [0.0003]**      DYd_1   0.106112 [0.9803]
CIc_1   10.1758 [0.0000]**      CIa_1    5.90593 [0.0002]**
CIb_1   9.04471 [0.0000]**   Constant    11.9607 [0.0000]**

correlation of actual and fitted
          DYa           DYb           DYc           DYd
      0.39196       0.83021       0.75893       0.13408
```

First note that `log|Y'Y/T|` is not the same as that reported in §3.13, even though the explanatory variable and estimation sample are the same. As discussed in Chapter 14, the reported quantities are $\log|\check{\mathbf{Y}}'\check{\mathbf{Y}}|$, that is, based on the dependent variables *after removing the unrestricted variables.* In §3.13, the *Constant* is unrestricted, whereas the equations above have no unrestricted variables. Rerunning the previous estimation with unrestricted *Constant* would produce different $\log|\check{\mathbf{Y}}'\check{\mathbf{Y}}|$ and R^2s.

The coefficients are now becoming interpretable in part. Consider each equation in turn:

(1) *DYa*: *DYa_1*, *DYc_1* and *DYd_1* seem irrelevant as do *CIb_1*, *CIc_1*, matching the earlier cointegration tests on α.

(2) *DYb*: again *DYa_1*, *DYc_1* and *DYd_1* seem irrelevant, but both cointegrating vectors *CIb_1*, *CIc_1* matter, consistent with our previous findings about α.

(3) *DYc*: the only significant stochastic variables are the lag of *DYc* and *CIc_1*.

(4) *DYd*: apparently nothing is significant!

This last outcome is consistent with our interpretation of *Yd* as a real exchange rate, but poses potential modelling problems. If *DYd* were to be retained as endogenous, but no explanatory variables were to be included, then any simultaneous equations model including *DYd* in another equation would fail the rank condition for identification (see

Chapter 12). Thus, either we remain at the system level, or if it enters any equation contemporaneously, we will need to condition on *DYd* below. The F-tests confirm that *DYa_1* and *DYd_1* are not significant in the system as a whole. The correlations of actual and fitted are much lower in I(0) space, and that for *DYd* is close to zero.

Select Test, Graphic analysis, and mark the first three entries in the Graphic analysis dialog, and click OK. Figure 5.2 shows the resulting time series of fitted and actual values, their cross plots, and the scaled residuals for the four endogenous variables. The different goodness of fit of the four equations time-series is not apparent, since fine detail cannot be discerned (it is clearer on a colour screen), but the cross-plots show the markedly different correlation scatters. There is no evidence that the outcomes are markedly affected by any influential observations, nor do the residuals manifest outliers or obvious patterns.

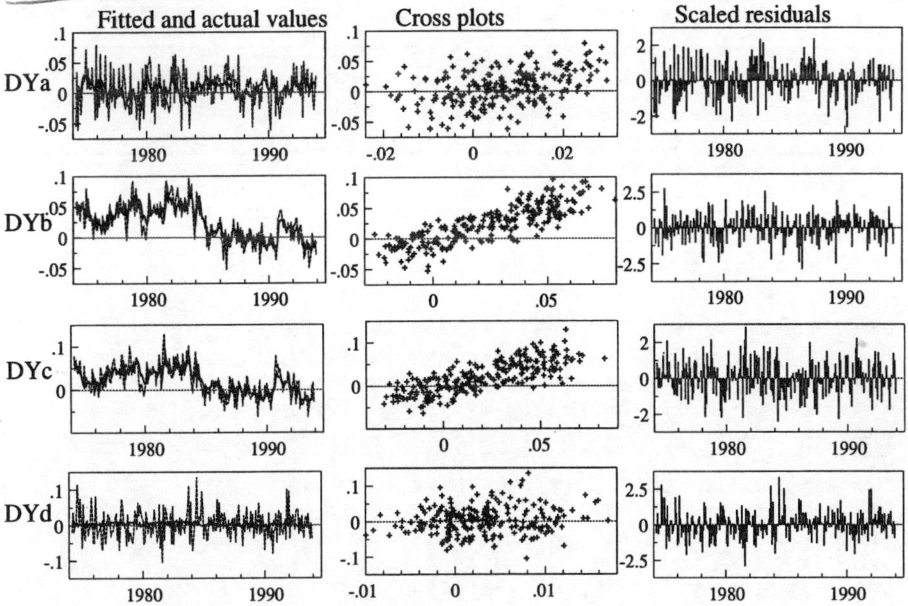

Figure 5.2 Fitted and actual values and scaled residuals.

It is sensible to diagnostically test our reduced system, so we briefly reconsider constancy and data congruence. Select Test, Graphic analysis, and mark the last four entries in the Graphic analysis dialog (including histogram to match our graph), leading to Figure 5.3. There is no evidence of within-equation residual serial correlation, and the densities and distributions are close to normality with no signs of important outliers.

A more powerful diagnostic is given by selecting Test, Test summary which yields:

```
DYa   :Portmanteau 12 lags=    10.843
DYb   :Portmanteau 12 lags=    10.288
DYc   :Portmanteau 12 lags=    6.1469
DYd   :Portmanteau 12 lags=    16.045
```

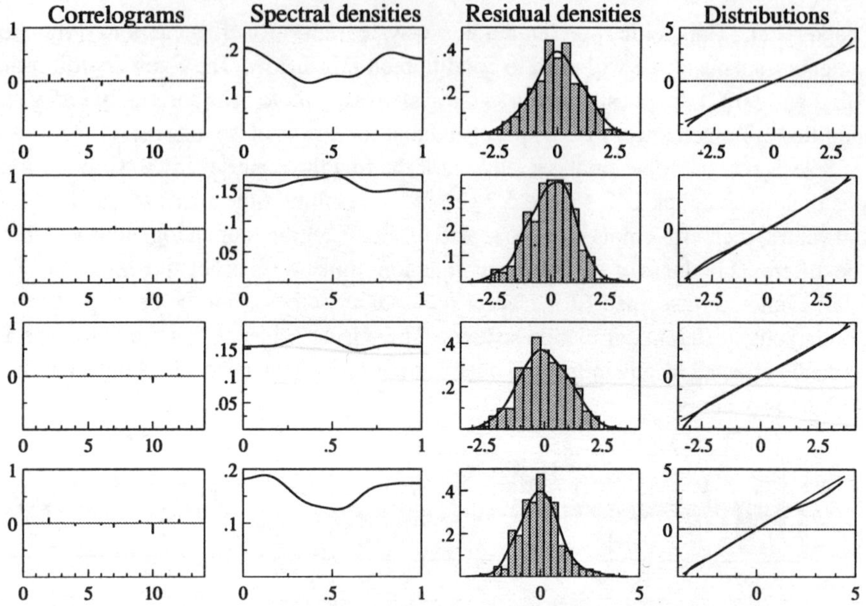

Figure 5.3 Individual-equation graphical diagnostics.

```
DYa  :AR 1- 7 F( 7,222) =    1.5368 [0.1559]
DYb  :AR 1- 7 F( 7,222) =   0.28345 [0.9600]
DYc  :AR 1- 7 F( 7,222) =   0.22749 [0.9785]
DYd  :AR 1- 7 F( 7,222) =    1.0391 [0.4046]
DYa  :Normality Chi^2(2)=   0.78909 [0.6740]
DYb  :Normality Chi^2(2)=    1.8584 [0.3949]
DYc  :Normality Chi^2(2)=   0.71144 [0.7007]
DYd  :Normality Chi^2(2)=    5.2741 [0.0716]
DYa  :ARCH 7  F( 7,215) =    1.9663 [0.0609]
DYb  :ARCH 7  F( 7,215) =   0.44043 [0.8759]
DYc  :ARCH 7  F( 7,215) =    1.0768 [0.3793]
DYd  :ARCH 7  F( 7,215) =   0.77071 [0.6125]
DYa  :Xi^2    F(14,214) =    1.2104 [0.2692]
DYb  :Xi^2    F(14,214) =    2.1508 [0.0106] *
DYc  :Xi^2    F(14,214) =   0.55613 [0.8965]
DYd  :Xi^2    F(14,214) =   0.99314 [0.4614]
DYa  :Xi*Xj   F(35,193) =    1.4097 [0.0764]
DYb  :Xi*Xj   F(35,193) =    1.4779 [0.0519]
DYc  :Xi*Xj   F(35,193) =   0.59911 [0.9634]
DYd  :Xi*Xj   F(35,193) =   0.83936 [0.7252]

Vector portmanteau 12 lags=  189.59
Vector AR 1-7 F(112,788)  =    1.0468 [0.3604]
Vector normality Chi^2( 8)=   11.608  [0.1696]
Vector  Xi^2  F(140,1699) =    1.1243 [0.1604]
Vector  Xi*Xj F(350,1800) =    0.9643 [0.6626]
```

The first block shows single equation statistics, and the second the system tests. None of the tests is significant at the 1% level, and only a heteroscedasticity statistic for *Yb* matters at 5%, which may need reconsideration when a model of the system has been constructed and evaluated.

Finally, select Test, Recursive graphics (or click on its icon).

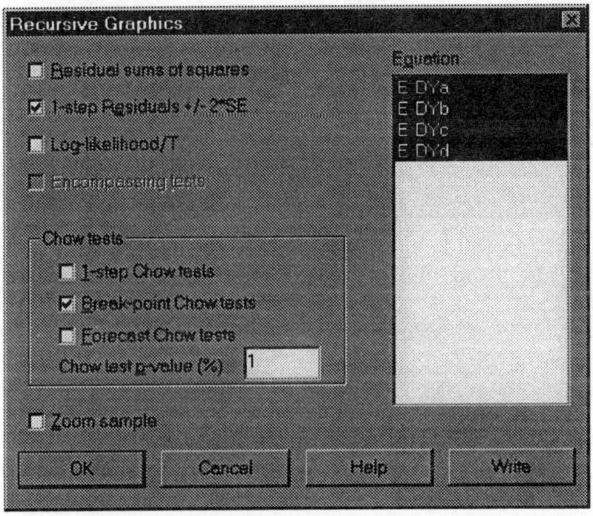

Mark the entries in the dialog for 1-step residuals and break-point Chow tests with a 1% significance level, and accept to see Figure 5.4. The 1-step errors lie within their approximate 95% confidence bands with constant standard errors (the first four plots), and no break-point Chow test is anywhere significant (the 1% line is the top of each of the last five boxes). The last plot is the overall system constancy test. Thus, constancy cannot be rejected, suggesting that the system is in fact managing to 'explain' the termination of growth in *Yb* and *Yc* around 1984 as an endogenous feature.

5.2 A parsimonious VAR

The only major remaining reduction to a parsimonious VAR that can be implemented at the level of the system is to eliminate *DYa_1* and *DYd_1*. This is because variables must be dropped from the system altogether since all equations have the same formulation by construction; later, when we construct a model of the system, the equations can differ in their specifications. Nevertheless, the resulting system provides a stiff competitor for any model thereof since there are no redundant variables to camouflage poor restrictions in other directions.

Select Model, Formulate System, mark *DYa_1* and *DYd_1*, and delete them, then re-estimate by OLS (so deselect recursive estimation).

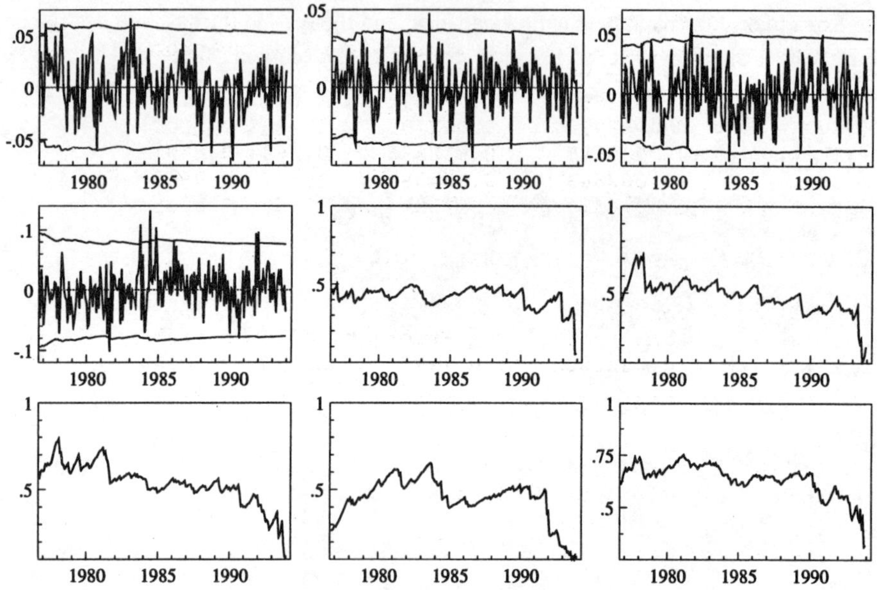

Figure 5.4 Recursive constancy statistics.

```
EQ( 3) Estimating the urf by OLS  (using pcftut1.in7)
The present sample is:  1974 (4) to 1993 (12)

URF Equation 1 for DYa
Variable      Coefficient     Std.Error  t-value  t-prob
DYb_1             0.20253       0.12234    1.656  0.0992
DYc_1           -0.093582       0.10430   -0.897  0.3705
CIc_1          0.00096294      0.014945    0.064  0.9487
CIa_1            -0.10274      0.021061   -4.878  0.0000
CIb_1            0.059501      0.038957    1.527  0.1280
Constant        0.0064346     0.0023641    2.722  0.0070

σ = 0.0263594   RSS = 0.1605025931

URF Equation 2 for DYb
Variable      Coefficient     Std.Error  t-value  t-prob
DYb_1             0.28727      0.080168    3.583  0.0004
DYc_1             0.10130      0.068349    1.482  0.1397
CIc_1           -0.029864     0.0097936   -3.049  0.0026
CIa_1           -0.019432      0.013801   -1.408  0.1605
CIb_1            -0.12938      0.025529   -5.068  0.0000
Constant        0.0097176     0.0015492    6.273  0.0000

σ = 0.0172734   RSS = 0.06892378563
```

```
URF Equation 3 for DYc
Variable       Coefficient     Std.Error  t-value  t-prob
DYb_1            -0.072180       0.10802   -0.668  0.5047
DYc_1              0.33452      0.092095    3.632  0.0003
CIc_1            -0.068990      0.013196   -5.228  0.0000
CIa_1           -0.0030685      0.018596   -0.165  0.8691
CIb_1            -0.062849      0.034398   -1.827  0.0690
Constant         0.0074310     0.0020874    3.560  0.0005

σ = 0.0232748    RSS = 0.1251368136

URF Equation 4 for DYd
Variable       Coefficient     Std.Error  t-value  t-prob
DYb_1            -0.022060       0.17713   -0.125  0.9010
DYc_1             0.073244       0.15102    0.485  0.6281
CIc_1           -0.0075531      0.021639   -0.349  0.7274
CIa_1             0.010316      0.030494    0.338  0.7354
CIb_1           -0.0084430      0.056406   -0.150  0.8811
Constant        0.00094813     0.0034229    0.277  0.7820

σ = 0.0381661    RSS = 0.3364858831

       correlation of URF residuals
           DYa         DYb          DYc          DYd
DYa     1.0000
DYb    0.09026      1.0000
DYc   -0.05025      0.7077        1.000
DYd   -0.05718     -0.3774      -0.5214        1.000

       standard deviations of URF residuals
         DYa        DYb        DYc        DYd
     0.02636    0.01727    0.02327    0.03817

loglik=3626.1448  log|Ω|=-30.6004  |Ω|=5.13363e-014  T=237
log|Y'Y/T| = -28.3295
R^2(LR) = 0.896778  R^2(LM) = 0.306412

F-test against unrestricted regressors,
F(24,796) = 30.449 [0.0000] **
No variables entered unrestricted.

F-tests on retained regressors, F(4, 228)
   DYb_1  8.37700 [0.0000]**  DYc_1  5.73757 [0.0002]**
Constant  12.9747 [0.0000]**  CIa_1  6.15368 [0.0001]**
   CIb_1  9.64306 [0.0000]**  CIc_1  10.2625 [0.0000]**

correlation of actual and fitted
        DYa         DYb         DYc         DYd
    0.39077     0.83009     0.75874     0.11467
```

Every variable now matters to the system, if not to every equation in it, but the fit has changed little.

5.3 A restricted system

It is possible to remain in the context of VAR modelling, yet impose specific restrictions on each equation. To do so, however, requires formulating a model of the system, and initially PcFiml takes that model to be the system itself, augmented with any necessary identities. The identities must be specified in the form:

$$\begin{aligned} CIa &: DYa, DYd, Constant, CIa\_1; \\ CIb &: DYb, DYa, DYc, CIb\_1; \\ CIc &: DYb, DYc, DYd, CIc\_1; \end{aligned}$$

corresponding to:

$$\begin{aligned} CIa &= DYa - 1.0 * DYd - 0.004 + CIa\_1; \\ CIb &= DYb - 0.35 * DYa - DYc + CIb\_1; \\ CIc &= DYc - DYb + 1.8 * DYd + CIc\_1; \end{aligned}$$

This specification retains the system in I(0) space (see, for example, Hendry and Mizon, 1993), and is the reason for changing the status of the constant from Unrestricted earlier so it can be included now.

NOTE: If no model existed before, the default specification is the system, with any identities still unspecified. Otherwise PcFiml will try to reuse the previous model specification, even if it belonged to another system (this might lead to the default displaying an unidentified model: only variables that are in the system can appear in the model).

The total number of variables involved in a system must be less than the estimation sample size, but otherwise the size of the system is only limited by available memory.

Now, select Model, Formulate Model to see:

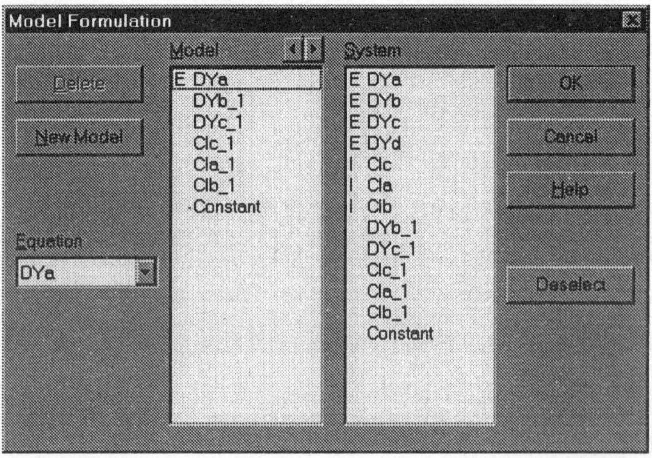

The leftmost column lists the options and which endogenous variable is under analysis; the middle column shows the current model of that endogenous variable; and the next right column the system currently under analysis. Leave the equations for the differenced variables as in the system, and input the three identities. Thus, highlight *CIa*, switch to the system column, mark *DYa*, *DYd*, *Constant* and *CIa*_1 and click Add. Next, click the down-arrow button on the Equation box, select *CIb*, switch to the system column, mark *DYa*, *DYb*, *DYc*, *CIb*_1 and click Add. Repeat for *CIc* with the appropriate variables (*DYb*, *DYc*, *DYd*, *CIc*_1). (If later PcFiml complains that an identity is not exact, a mistake was made here.) Now accept (click OK), and the model estimation dialog appears.

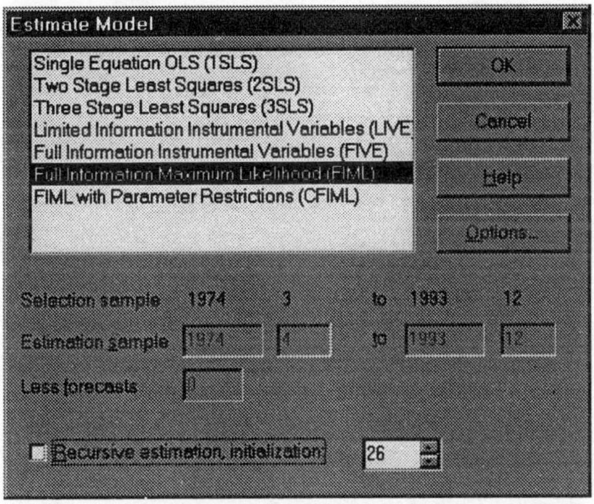

Mark Full Information Maximum Likelihood (FIML) to replicate the previous results, but as a model of the system, clear the recursive extimation box, and accept. This takes us to the FIML Maximization control dialog (if automatic maximization is off):

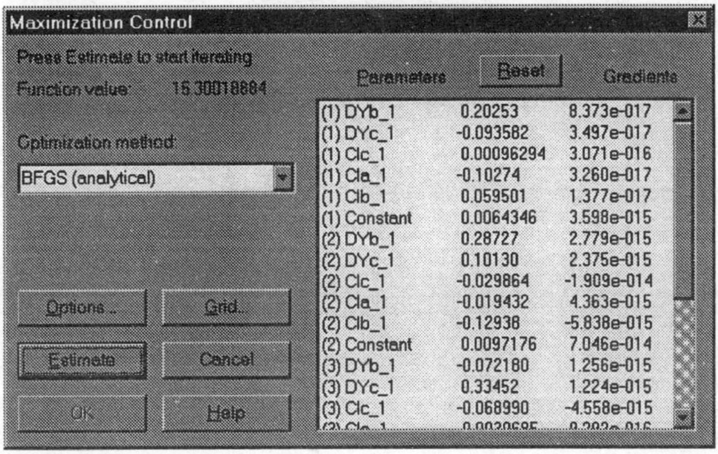

Press Estimate to commence estimation: a full description of the FIML dialog is presented in the next chapter. The message window shows the state of play and on convergence, which should be essentially instantaneous, accept (click OK or ↵), and the estimates will be written to the Results window as:

```
Identity for CIc
DYb            -1.0000
DYc             1.0000
DYd             1.8000
CIc_1           1.0000
R^2 = 1 over 1974 (4) to 1993 (12)
Identity for CIa
DYa             1.0000
DYd            -1.0000
Constant   -0.0040000
CIa_1           1.0000
R^2 = 1 over 1974 (4) to 1993 (12)
Identity for CIb
DYa           -0.35000
DYb             1.0000
DYc            -1.0000
CIb_1           1.0000
R^2 = 1 over 1974 (4) to 1993 (12)

EQ( 4) Estimating the model by FIML  (using pcftut1.in7)
The present sample is:  1974 (4) to 1993 (12)

Equation 1 for DYa
Variable    Coefficient     Std.Error  t-value  t-prob       HCSE
DYb_1           0.20253       0.12234    1.656  0.0992    0.10789
DYc_1         -0.093582       0.10430   -0.897  0.3705   0.089112
CIc_1        0.00096294      0.014945    0.064  0.9487   0.015503
CIa_1          -0.10274      0.021061   -4.878  0.0000   0.021457
CIb_1          0.059501      0.038957    1.527  0.1280   0.035621
Constant      0.0064346     0.0023641    2.722  0.0070  0.0021400

σ = 0.0263594

Equation 2 for DYb
Variable    Coefficient     Std.Error  t-value  t-prob       HCSE
DYb_1           0.28727      0.080168    3.583  0.0004   0.079743
DYc_1           0.10130      0.068349    1.482  0.1397   0.070166
CIc_1         -0.029864     0.0097936   -3.049  0.0026  0.0099298
CIa_1         -0.019432      0.013801   -1.408  0.1605   0.015895
CIb_1          -0.12938      0.025529   -5.068  0.0000   0.028153
Constant      0.0097176     0.0015492    6.273  0.0000  0.0017070

σ = 0.0172734
```

```
Equation 3 for DYc
Variable    Coefficient      Std.Error  t-value  t-prob       HCSE
DYb_1         -0.072180        0.10802   -0.668  0.5047    0.11698
DYc_1           0.33452       0.092095    3.632  0.0003   0.097691
CIc_1         -0.068990       0.013196   -5.228  0.0000   0.013043
CIa_1        -0.0030685       0.018596   -0.165  0.8691   0.019163
CIb_1         -0.062849       0.034398   -1.827  0.0690   0.035216
Constant      0.0074310      0.0020874    3.560  0.0005  0.0021677

σ = 0.0232748

Equation 4 for DYd
Variable    Coefficient      Std.Error  t-value  t-prob       HCSE
DYb_1         -0.022060        0.17713   -0.125  0.9010    0.19085
DYc_1          0.073244        0.15102    0.485  0.6281    0.15237
CIc_1        -0.0075531       0.021639   -0.349  0.7274   0.022096
CIa_1          0.010316       0.030494    0.338  0.7354   0.027656
CIb_1        -0.0084430       0.056406   -0.150  0.8811   0.052701
Constant     0.00094813      0.0034229    0.277  0.7820  0.0030328

σ = 0.0381661

loglik=3626.1448  log|Ω|=-30.6004  |Ω|=5.13363e-014  T=237
correlation of residuals
               DYa          DYb          DYc          DYd
 DYa        1.0000
 DYb      0.090258       1.0000
 DYc     -0.050250      0.70766       1.0000
 DYd     -0.057179     -0.37742     -0.52137       1.0000
```

A full description of FIML output is also reserved for the next chapter: here we merely note that the same numbers are delivered as before.

Since the complete structure of the system is now known, aspects such as dynamic analysis and dynamic forecasts can be implemented. Select Test, Dynamic analysis (the 'rolling cart' icon) to produce:

```
Dynamic analysis of the model
Lag-1 multipliers
          Constant
 DYa     0.0011215
 DYb     0.0035283
 DYc     0.0018177
 DYd    0.00034934
 CIc    -0.0016617
 CIa     0.0022586
 CIb     0.0013525

Long-run matrix π(1)-I = Po
              DYa          DYb          DYc          DYd          CIc
 DYa      -1.0000      0.20253    -0.093582      0.00000   0.00096294
 DYb      0.00000     -0.71273      0.10130      0.00000    -0.029864
 DYc      0.00000    -0.072180     -0.66548      0.00000    -0.068990
```

```
DYd        0.00000    -0.022060      0.073244    -1.0000   -0.0075531
CIc        0.00000     -0.39915       0.36506    0.00000    -0.052721
CIa        0.00000      0.22459      -0.16683    0.00000    0.0085160
CIb        0.00000      0.28856      -0.20047    0.00000     0.038788
               CIa          CIb
DYa       -0.10274     0.059501
DYb      -0.019432     -0.12938
DYc     -0.0030685    -0.062849
DYd       0.010316   -0.0084430
CIc       0.034933     0.051338
CIa       -0.11305     0.067944
CIb       0.019594    -0.087361

Long-run covariance
               DYa          DYb           DYc           DYd         CIc
DYa    5.5295e-020
DYb    1.1134e-016     0.092395
DYc    1.1138e-016     0.092395      0.092395
DYd    9.2234e-020  1.2175e-016   1.2175e-016   1.2979e-019
CIc   -8.5654e-016     -0.69824      -0.69824  -9.3442e-016      5.3547
CIa   -5.2592e-017    -0.055169     -0.055169  -7.0138e-017     0.41303
CIb   -3.0129e-016     -0.25118      -0.25118  -3.3012e-016      1.8921
               CIa          CIb
CIa       0.096012
CIb        0.15116      0.69505

Long-run multipliers
          Constant
DYa      0.0049655
DYb      0.0052563
DYc      0.0035184
DYd     0.00096552
CIc       0.034925
CIa       0.041804
CIb       0.034566

Static long run
          Constant
DYa      0.0049655
DYb      0.0052563
DYc      0.0035184
DYd     0.00096552
CIc       0.034925
CIa       0.041804
CIb       0.034566

Standard errors of static long run
          Constant
DYa      0.0022738
DYb      0.0010352
DYc      0.0014614
DYd      0.0032922
CIc       0.011389
```

```
CIa      0.0041264
CIb      0.0047800

Eigenvalues of π(1)-I
        real        complex        modulus
      -1.000         0.0000          1.000
      -1.000         0.0000          1.000
     -0.6496        0.08118         0.6546
     -0.6496       -0.08118         0.6546
    -0.01429         0.0000        0.01429
     -0.1866         0.0000         0.1866
     -0.1314         0.0000         0.1314

Eigenvalues of companion matrix
        real        complex        modulus
      0.0000         0.0000         0.0000
      0.0000         0.0000         0.0000
      0.3504        0.08118         0.3597
      0.3504       -0.08118         0.3597
      0.9857         0.0000         0.9857
      0.8134         0.0000         0.8134
      0.8686         0.0000         0.8686
```

Since the system is stationary, the long-run outcomes are interpretable (some are redundant given the simplicity of the dynamics in this system). Note that the roots of $\widehat{\pi}(1) - \mathbf{I}_n$ are one minus the roots of the companion matrix, and that the long-run *Constant* is highly significant in every equation except *DYd*. The *Constant* coefficients for the differenced variables are, of course, their long-run trends, and when multiplied by 1200, deliver the annual growth rates as a percentage.

The long-run covariances are not easy to interpret when the identities are retained, since the (7×7) matrix only has rank 4. Here, the 'non-singular' long-run system is given by, for example, *DYc*, *CIa*, *CIb*, *CIc*, which is a valid (full rank) representation.

For dynamic forecasting, select Test, Dynamic forecast and set 24 periods (two years), marking all seven variables (we are using error bars, a choice made under Options), to see Figure 5.5.

The error bars for *DYa* and *DYd* reach their unconditional values almost at once whereas those for *DYb* and *DYc* continue to increase for about six periods, and the error bars for the cointegrating vectors increase for about the first year. The variables therefore rapidly converge to their unconditional means and variances, where the former are non-zero except for *DYd*, and have 'realistic' values. The contrast with the dynamic forecast graphs of Figure 3.5 is marked, and the current model is a much better representation of the information content of the system. When considering the columns of zeros in the long-run covariance matrix, why do the error bars of *DYa* and *DYd* not converge to zero? The answer is that the error bars are based (as $h \to \infty$) on the unconditional error covariance matrix (of the form $\sum_i \mathbf{A}^i \boldsymbol{\Omega} \mathbf{A}^{i\prime}$) whereas the long-run covariance is $(\mathbf{I}_n - \mathbf{A})^{-1} \boldsymbol{\Omega} (\mathbf{I}_n - \mathbf{A}')^{-1}$. See Chapter 10 for a more precise description.

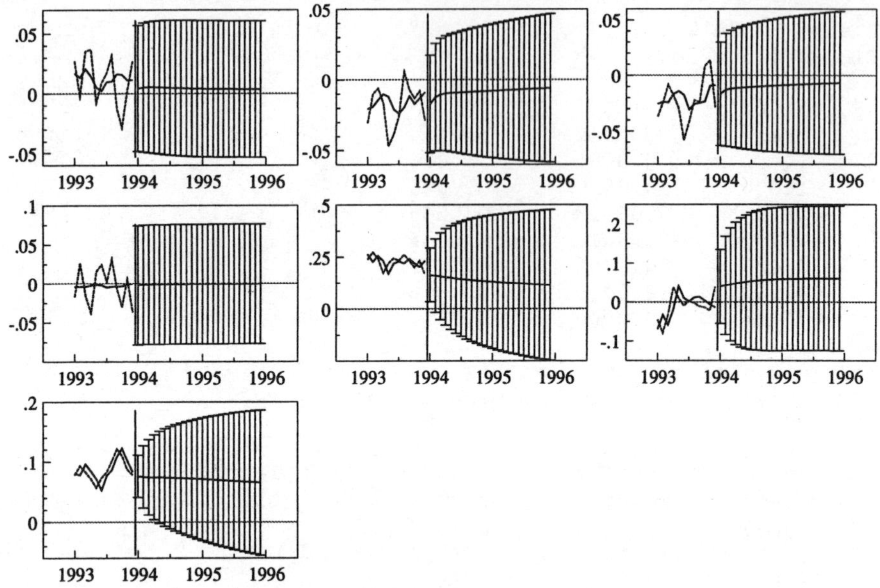

Figure 5.5 Dynamic forecasts in I(0) space.

The final exercise is to impose the restrictions that *CIb_1* and *CIc_1* do not enter the equation for *DYa*; no cointegration vector enters the equation for *DYd*; and *CIa_1* does not enter either equation *DYb* or *DYc*. `Alt+y` is the direct access key for model formulation or click on the second 'completed-block' icon; mark *CIb_1* and *CIc_1* in the first equation and delete; highlight the fourth, mark *CIa_1*, *CIb_1* and *CIc_1* and delete; highlight the equation for *DYb* and delete *CIa_1*; and repeat for *DYc*. Accept, and estimate by FIML again to produce (skipping the output for the identities):

```
EQ( 5) Estimating the model by FIML  (using pcftut1.in7)
The present sample is:  1974 (4) to 1993 (12)
Equation 1 for DYa
Variable    Coefficient     Std.Error  t-value  t-prob       HCSE
DYb_1           0.14364       0.11064    1.298  0.1955   0.096455
DYc_1          -0.15624      0.099068   -1.577  0.1161   0.085116
CIa_1         -0.092817      0.018893   -4.913  0.0000   0.017684
Constant      0.0079032     0.0021945    3.601  0.0004  0.0019600
σ = 0.0264122

Equation 2 for DYb
Variable    Coefficient     Std.Error  t-value  t-prob       HCSE
DYb_1           0.30336      0.077143    3.932  0.0001   0.076061
DYc_1          0.068368      0.065205    1.049  0.2955   0.064815
CIc_1         -0.026421     0.0083268   -3.173  0.0017  0.0085699
CIb_1          -0.14188      0.022760   -6.234  0.0000   0.024469
Constant      0.0098652     0.0015328    6.436  0.0000  0.0016271
σ = 0.0172761
```

Equation 3 for DYc

Variable	Coefficient	Std.Error	t-value	t-prob	HCSE
DYb_1	-0.074418	0.10234	-0.727	0.4679	0.11008
DYc_1	0.32518	0.086755	3.748	0.0002	0.091436
CIc_1	-0.071216	0.010283	-6.925	0.0000	0.0098966
CIb_1	-0.061562	0.028104	-2.191	0.0295	0.027911
Constant	0.0074361	0.0020369	3.651	0.0003	0.0020693

σ = 0.0231793

Equation 4 for DYd

Variable	Coefficient	Std.Error	t-value	t-prob	HCSE
DYb_1	-0.00017985	0.15699	-0.001	0.9991	0.16687
DYc_1	0.11430	0.13554	0.843	0.3999	0.13756
Constant	0.00060945	0.0031581	0.193	0.8471	0.0027694

σ = 0.0380386

loglik=3622.8588 log|Ω|=-30.5726 |Ω|=5.27798e-014 T=237
LR test of over-identifying restrictions: Chi^2(7)=6.57187 [0.4748]

correlation of residuals

	DYa	DYb	DYc	DYd
DYa	1.0000			
DYb	0.093819	1.0000		
DYc	-0.049316	0.70560	1.0000	
DYd	-0.059750	-0.37812	-0.52158	1.0000

The key statistic is the likelihood ratio test of over-identifying restrictions which accepts, matching the weak exogeneity aspect of the cointegration tests in Chapter 4.

It is possible to redo this estimation recursively (this is done remarkably quickly), which gives further useful information in the recursive graphics. Click on their (red graph) icon to see:

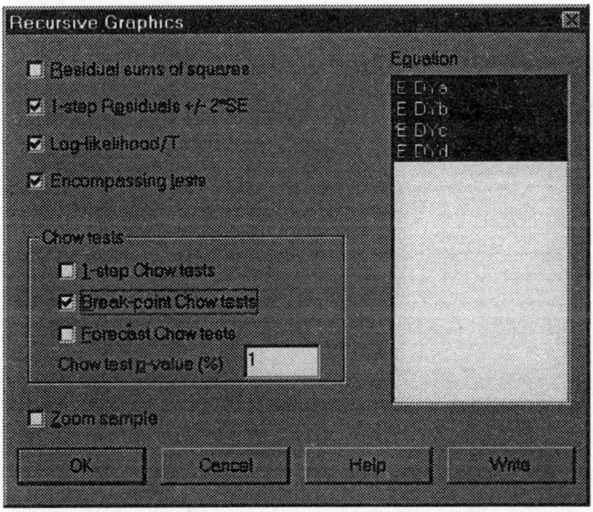

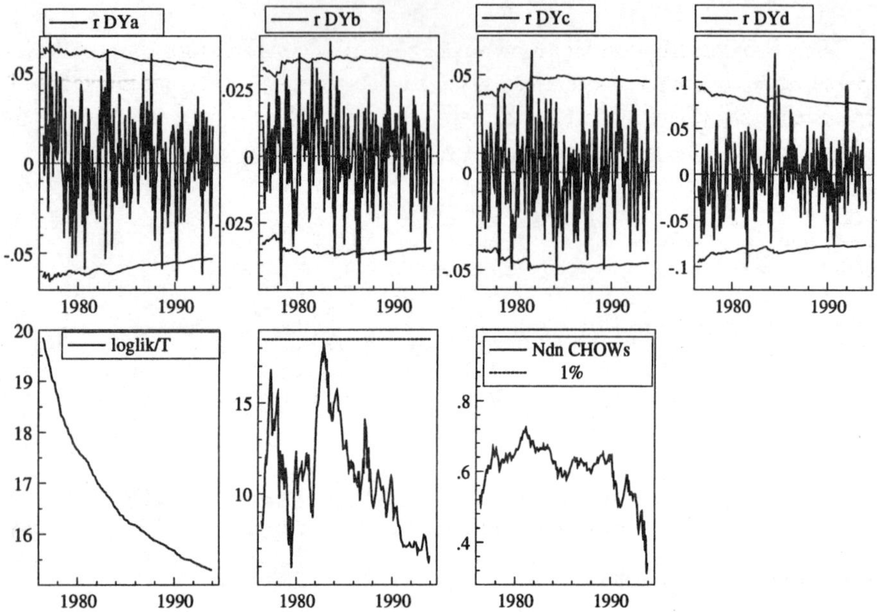

Figure 5.6 Recursive model statistics.

Select the settings shown, to produce Figure 5.6. The first row shows the now familiar recursive residuals with $\pm 2\hat{\sigma}_t$; the second shows the scaled log-likelihood function as T increases, the sequence of scaled tests of the hypothesis that the model parsimoniously encompasses the system (i.e., the recursively-computed likelihood-ratio test of the overidentifying restrictions), and the sequence of break-point Chow tests scaled by their 1% significance (one-off) level. There is no evidence against the specification at this stage (check that the test summary remains acceptable).

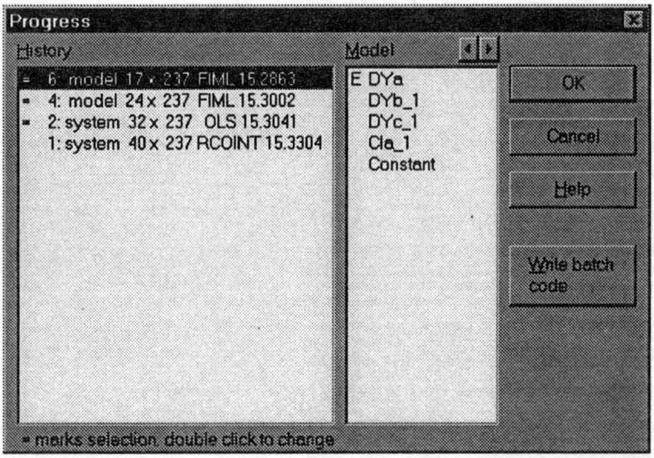

Select Progress from the Model menu (`Alt+m,p`) to conduct a formal test of the last two reductions of both the system and its model. Elegible I(0) systems are marked ('='); the nested case, where $\Delta Ya_1, \Delta Yd_1$ have been deleted is represented by the model thereof, on which the individual-equation restrictions have been imposed.
Accept to obtain:

```
Progress to date
model       T    p         log-likelihood          SC         HQ        AIC
    5     237   17   FIML       3622.8588     -30.180    -30.329    -30.573
    4     237   24   FIML       3626.1448     -30.047    -30.256    -30.600
system      T    p         log-likelihood          SC         HQ        AIC
    3     237   24   OLS        3626.1448     -30.047    -30.256    -30.600
    2     237   32   OLS        3627.0657     -29.870    -30.149    -30.608

Tests of model reduction
Model    4 --> Model    5: Chi^2( 7) =        6.5719 [0.4748]
System   3 --> Model    5: Chi^2( 7) =        6.5719 [0.4748]

Tests of system reduction
System   2 --> System   3: F( 8, 452) =    0.21997 [0.9873]
```

Thus, both reductions are easily accepted, so the individual insignificance of the F-tests on *DYa_1* and *DYd_1* did not camouflage their joint significance as revealed by the last statistic.

Finally, we create a batch file corresponding to this chapter. The current contents of the Batch edit window should be:

```
module("PcFiml");
usedata("Pcftut1.in7");
system
{
    Y = DYa, DYb, DYc, DYd;
    Z = DYb_1, DYc_1, CIc_1, CIa_1, CIb_1, Constant;
    I = CIc, CIa, CIb;
}
estsystem("OLS", 1974, 4, 1993, 12, 0, 26, 0);
model
{
    DYa = DYb_1, DYc_1, CIa_1, Constant;
    DYb = DYb_1, DYc_1, CIc_1, CIb_1, Constant;
    DYc = DYb_1, DYc_1, CIc_1, CIb_1, Constant;
    DYd = DYb_1, DYc_1, Constant;
    CIc = DYb, DYc, DYd, CIc_1;
    CIa = DYa, DYd, CIa_1, Constant;
    CIb = DYa, DYb, DYc, CIb_1;
}
estmodel("FIML", 26);
```

To add all the transformations etc., store this block, then search up in the Results window, to locate the block which records the transformations creating the cointegrating vectors and differences. Mark this block and copy to the internal clipboard (Ctrl+Ins). Access the batch editor, to add the following line: `loaddata("pcftut1.in7");` press ↩ and type `algebra` ↩, { ↩. Next press `Shift+Ins` to copy from the clipboard, and type ↩ } ↩. Finally, add the unrestricted system treated as a model. Now the batch file reads (we also ordered the *CI* identity equations, but have omitted the remainder of the batch file shown above):

```
module("PcFiml");
loaddata("pcftut1.in7");
algebra
{
  CIa = Ya - 1 * Yd - 0.004 * trend();
  CIb = Yb - 0.35 * Ya - Yc;
  CIc = Yc + 1.8 * Yd - Yb;

  DYa = diff(Ya, 1);
  DYb = diff(Yb, 1);
  DYc = diff(Yc, 1);
  DYd = diff(Yd, 1);
}
system
{
  Y = DYa, DYb, DYc, DYd;
  I = CIa, CIb, CIc;
  Z = DYa_1, DYb_1, DYc_1, DYd_1, CIa_1, CIb_1, CIc_1, Constant;
}
estsystem("OLS", 1974, 4, 1993, 12, 0, 0, 0);
model
{
  DYa = DYa_1,DYb_1,DYc_1,DYd_1, CIa_1,CIb_1,CIc_1, Constant;
  DYb = DYa_1,DYb_1,DYc_1,DYd_1, CIa_1,CIb_1,CIc_1, Constant;
  DYc = DYa_1,DYb_1,DYc_1,DYd_1, CIa_1,CIb_1,CIc_1, Constant;
  DYd = DYa_1,DYb_1,DYc_1,DYd_1, CIa_1,CIb_1,CIc_1, Constant;
  CIa = DYa, DYd, CIa_1, Constant;
  CIb = DYa, DYb, DYc, CIb_1;
  CIc = DYb, DYc, DYd, CIc_1;
}
estmodel("FIML", 0);
```

This corresponds to PCFTUT3.FL.

Before exiting, try deleting every regressor from *DYd* to see the identification failure; that course is not viable here because PcFiml requires at least one regressor in each equation. Then try deleting any variable from an identity, and see the resulting error message. The next chapter will consider conditioning to produce an open system, and a simultaneous equations model thereof. This concludes the tutorial on mapping to I(0).

Chapter 6

Modelling the I(0) System

6.1 Introduction to dynamic models

The Formulate Model command on the Model menu is used for dynamic model formulation: formulate (or reformulate) a model for estimation by shaping the system into structural equations in the Formulate Model dialog box. When you press OK, you will be taken automatically to the Model estimation dialog.

To obtain a *simultaneous dynamic model*, premultiply the system (3.2) given in §3.1 by a non-singular, non-diagonal matrix $\mathbf{B}$, which yields:

$$\mathbf{B}\mathbf{y}_t = \mathbf{B}\mathbf{\Pi}_u\mathbf{w}_t + \mathbf{B}\mathbf{v}_{ut}.$$

We shall write this as:

$$\mathbf{B}\mathbf{y}_t + \mathbf{C}\mathbf{w}_t = \mathbf{u}_t, \ \mathbf{u}_t \sim \mathsf{IN}_n\left[\mathbf{0}, \mathbf{\Sigma}\right]$$

with $t = 1, \ldots, T$; or using $\mathbf{A} = (\mathbf{B} : \mathbf{C})$ in which $\mathbf{B}$ is $(n \times n)$ and $\mathbf{C}$ is $(n \times k)$:

$$\mathbf{A}\mathbf{x}_t = \mathbf{u}_t.$$

The *restricted reduced form* (RRF) corresponding to this model is obtained as the solution:

$$\mathbf{y}_t = \mathbf{\Pi}_r\mathbf{w}_t + \mathbf{v}_{rt}, \ \text{ with } \mathbf{\Pi}_r = -\mathbf{B}^{-1}\mathbf{C}.$$

The estimated variance of $\mathbf{u}_t$ is:

$$\widetilde{\mathbf{\Sigma}} = \frac{\widehat{\mathbf{A}}\mathbf{X}'\mathbf{X}\widehat{\mathbf{A}}'}{T-c}.$$

There is a degrees-of-freedom correction c, which equals the average number of parameters per equation (rounded towards 0); this would be k for the system.

Identification of the model, achieved through imposing within-equation restrictions on $\mathbf{A}$, is required for estimation. The *order condition* for identification is only a necessary condition imposed on each equation. PcFiml checks this as each equation is formulated. The *rank condition* is necessary and sufficient, and is checked prior to model estimation by setting each non-zero coefficient to unity plus a uniform random number.

Some equations of the model could be *identities*. Identities in PcFiml are created by marking identity endogenous variables as such during system formulation. These are ignored during system estimation and analysis. Identities come in at the model formulation level, where the identity is specified just like other equations. However, there is no need to specify the coefficients of the identity equation, as PcFiml automatically derives these by estimating the equation.

An example of a model with (3.1) as unrestricted reduced form is:

$$Ya_t = \beta_0 + \beta_1\, Ya_{t-1} + \beta_2\, Yb_t + \beta_3\, Yc_t$$
$$Yb_t = \beta_4 + \beta_5\, Yb1_{t-1}.$$

Here, $\delta_3, \delta_4, \delta_7, \delta_9, \delta_{10}$, and δ_{11} are all restricted to be zero, and $\delta_2 = \beta_2 \times \beta_5$.

A model in PcFiml is formulated by:

(1) which *variables* enter each equation, including identities;
(2) coefficients of identity equations need not be specified, as PcFiml automatically derives these by estimating the equation (provided $R^2 \geq .99$);
(3) *constraints*, if the model is to be estimated by constrained FIML.

6.2 Starting the tutorial

We resume this tutorial where we ended Chapter 5. The system has been mapped to a parsimonious VAR (PVAR) in I(0) space, with the yet unused information that *DYa* and *DYd* satisfy the necessary conditions for being weakly exogenous for the long-run parameters of interest in the *DYb* and *DYc* equations. It is convenient to reload the data, system and model using the batch file PCFTUT3.FL we saved previously. This creates the basic equation structure, even though we will now condition on *DYa* and *DYd* (replace loaddata("pcftut1.in7"); by usedata("pcftut1.in7"); if the data are already loaded). Notice how easy replication is using batch files, yet no complicated command language had to be learned to create them, since PcFiml writes the instructions from your menu-based selections. We have left on recursive estimation, and since FIML is being used, this may take some time to calculate: at the end of the file change the 26 in `estmodel("FIML", 26);` to 0 to switch off prior to running.

```
Batch loaded from C:\Program Files\GiveWin\PcFiml\PcfTut3.fl

module("PcFiml");
loaddata("pcftut1.in7");
algebra
{
  CIa = Ya - 1 * Yd - 0.004 * trend();
  CIb = Yb - 0.35 * Ya - Yc;
  CIc = Yc + 1.8 * Yd - Yb;
```

```
  DYa = diff(Ya, 1);
  DYb = diff(Yb, 1);
  DYc = diff(Yc, 1);
  DYd = diff(Yd, 1);
}
system
{
  Y = DYa, DYb, DYc, DYd;
  Z = DYa_1,DYb_1, DYc_1, DYd_1, CIc_1, CIa_1, CIb_1, Constant;
  I = CIc, CIa, CIb;
}
estsystem("OLS", 1974, 4, 1993, 12, 0, 0, 0);
model
{
  DYa = DYa_1,DYb_1,DYc_1,DYd_1, CIc_1,CIa_1,CIb_1, Constant;
  DYb = DYa_1,DYb_1,DYc_1,DYd_1, CIc_1,CIa_1,CIb_1, Constant;
  DYc = DYa_1,DYb_1,DYc_1,DYd_1, CIc_1,CIa_1,CIb_1, Constant;
  DYd = DYa_1,DYb_1,DYc_1,DYd_1, CIc_1,CIa_1,CIb_1, Constant;
  CIc = DYb, DYc, DYd, CIc_1;
  CIa = DYa, DYd, CIa_1, Constant;
  CIb = DYa, DYb, DYc, CIb_1;
}
estmodel("FIML", 0);
system
{
  Y = DYa, DYb, DYc, DYd;
  Z = DYb_1, DYc_1, CIc_1, CIa_1, CIb_1, Constant;
  I = CIc, CIa, CIb;
}
estsystem("OLS", 1974, 4, 1993, 12, 0, 0, 0);
model
{
  DYa = DYb_1, DYc_1, CIa_1, Constant;
  DYb = DYb_1, DYc_1, CIc_1, CIb_1, Constant;
  DYc = DYb_1, DYc_1, CIc_1, CIb_1, Constant;
  DYd = DYb_1, DYc_1, Constant;
  CIc = DYb, DYc, DYd, CIc_1;
  CIa = DYa, DYd, CIa_1, Constant;
  CIb = DYa, DYb, DYc, CIb_1;
}
estmodel("FIML", 0);

                    **** output from batch run deleted ****
```

6.3 A conditional system

Select Model, Formulate System (`Alt+m`, `s`; or click on the first 'building block' icon), and mark *DYa* and *DYd* in the system. Clear their status, so that they become non-modelled, and hence conditioning variables, and accept. Although *CIa* is then also a valid conditioning variable, leave its status unchanged at Identity, which remains true.

Estimate by recursive OLS, keeping the sample period as above, to produce the following two-equation system for 'consumption' and 'income' (*DYb* and *DYc*):

```
EQ( 5) Estimating the urf by OLS  (using pcftut1.in7)
The present sample is:  1974 (4) to 1993 (12)

URF Equation 1 for DYb
Variable   Coefficient    Std.Error  t-value  t-prob
DYb_1          0.27439     0.074796    3.669  0.0003
DYc_1          0.11791     0.063530    1.856  0.0648
CIc_1        -0.031184    0.0090861   -3.432  0.0007
CIa_1        -0.013049     0.013444   -0.971  0.3328
CIb_1         -0.13350     0.023798   -5.610  0.0000
DYa           0.045152     0.040056    1.127  0.2608
DYd           -0.16903     0.027665   -6.110  0.0000
Constant     0.0095873    0.0014603    6.565  0.0000

σ = 0.0160213    RSS = 0.05877994769

URF Equation 2 for DYc
Variable   Coefficient    Std.Error  t-value  t-prob
DYb_1        -0.064891     0.092715   -0.700  0.4847
DYc_1          0.35138     0.078750    4.462  0.0000
CIc_1        -0.071344     0.011263   -6.335  0.0000
CIa_1       -0.0070460     0.016665   -0.423  0.6728
CIb_1        -0.061337     0.029499   -2.079  0.0387
DYa          -0.070925     0.049652   -1.428  0.1545
DYd           -0.32075     0.034292   -9.353  0.0000
Constant     0.0081915    0.0018101    4.525  0.0000

σ = 0.0198594    RSS = 0.09031643733

correlation of URF residuals
                    DYb         DYc
DYb               1.000
DYc              0.6582       1.000

standard deviations of URF residuals
        DYb         DYc
    0.01602     0.01986

loglik=1983.9671  log|Ω|=-16.7423   |Ω|=5.35667e-008  T=237
log|Y'Y/T| = -14.5132
R²(LR) = 0.892375  R²(LM) = 0.587575

F-test against unrestricted regressors,
F(16, 456) = 58.374 [0.0000] **
No variables entered unrestricted.
```

```
F-tests on retained regressors, F(2, 228)
DYb_1    15.2203 [0.0000]**        DYc_1    10.9377 [0.0000]**
CIc_1    20.4530 [0.0000]**        CIa_1   0.509996 [0.6012]
CIb_1    17.9513 [0.0000]**          DYa    4.77019 [0.0093]**
  DYd    43.5543 [0.0000]**     Constant    21.4937 [0.0000]**

correlation of actual and fitted
        DYb         DYc
     0.8572      0.8329
```

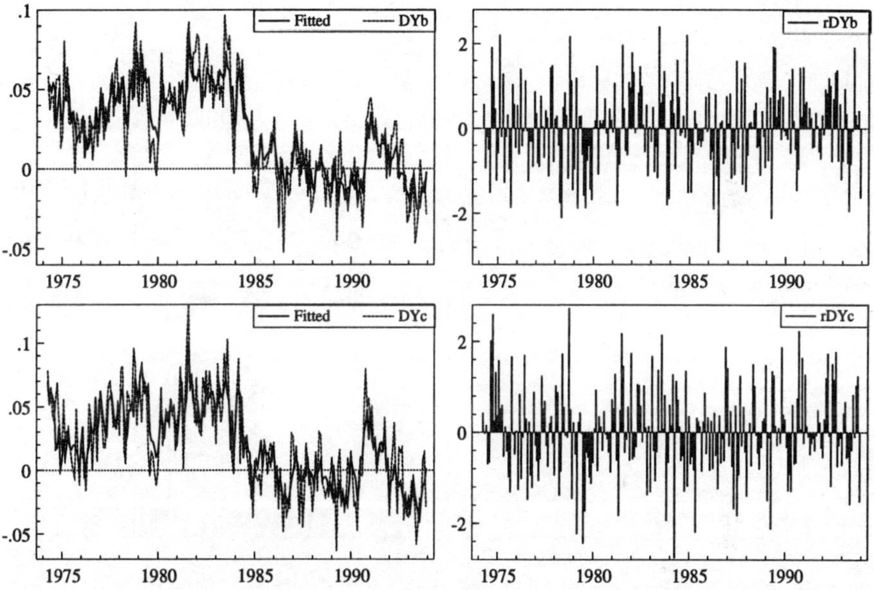

Figure 6.1 Fitted and actual values and scaled residuals for the conditional system.

Click on the graphics analysis icon , or select Test, Graphics, and mark Actual and fitted, and Residuals (scaled) to see Figure 6.1.

The variables are closely tracked, and the residuals seem well behaved. In particular, the reduction in the growth of consumption and income from 1984 appears to be owing to the rapid rise in the real exchange rate. Note its high level of significance with a negative coefficient in both equations. The test summary produces:

```
DYb      : Portmanteau 12 lags=   9.4434
DYc      : Portmanteau 12 lags=   13.096
DYb      : AR 1- 7F( 7,222) =    0.34103 [0.9344]
DYc      : AR 1- 7F( 7,222) =     0.6745 [0.6936]
DYb      : Normality Chi^2(2)=    0.6684 [0.7159]
DYc      : Normality Chi^2(2)=   0.72586 [0.6956]
DYb      : ARCH 7 F( 7,215) =     1.7636 [0.0960]
DYc      : ARCH 7 F( 7,215) =     1.7081 [0.1084]
DYb      : Xi^2     F(14,214) =   1.9378 [0.0241] *
DYc      : Xi^2     F(14,214) =    0.605 [0.8595]
```

```
DYb      : Xi*Xj    F(35,193) =    2.0607 [0.0011] **
DYc      : Xi*Xj    F(35,193) =   0.46606 [0.9956]

Vector portmanteau 12 lags=       58.098
Vector AR 1-7 F(28,428)    =      1.4381 [0.0712]
Vector normality Chi^2(4)   =     1.2841 [0.8641]
Vector Xi^2     F(42,629)   =    0.88578 [0.6780]
Vector Xi*Xj  F(105,572)   =      1.1075 [0.2352]
```

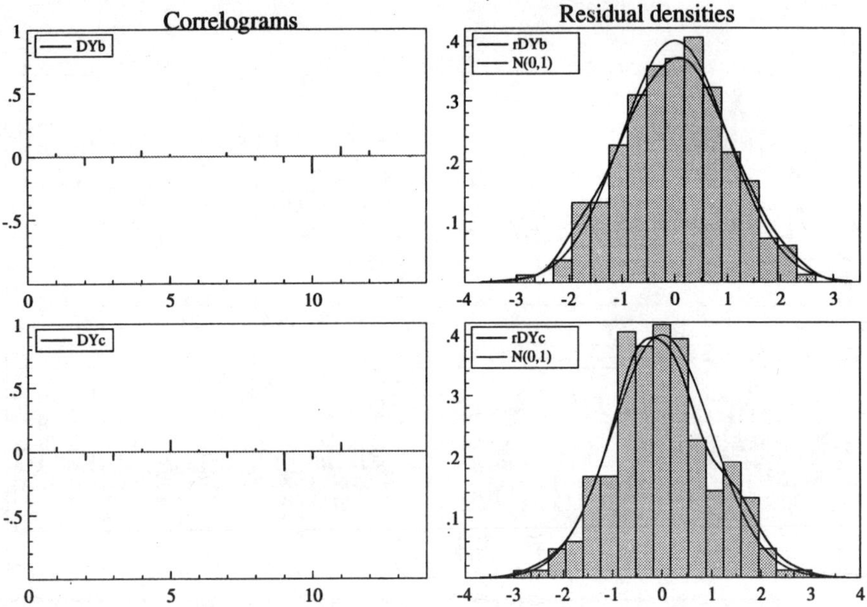

Figure 6.2 Residual correlogram, histogram and density for the conditional system.

There is slight evidence of residual heteroscedasticity which needs watching to see if reduction exacerbates or attenuates the statistic. The graphic diagnostics (`Alt+t`, g and mark the items for correlogram, histogram, density, and normal) show Figure 6.2. There are no signs of problems here, matching the numerical results for the single-equation diagnostics above. To investigate the vector error autocorrelation, compute the test for different lag lengths (`Alt+t`, t, `Alt+e`, `Tab`, `Tab` and type in 4 as the longest lag), which produces:

```
Testing for vector error autocorrelation from lags 1 to 4
Chi²(16) = 23.051 [0.1124]  and F-Form(16,440) = 1.4209 [0.1273]
```

The correlogram had a bump at 9 lags so we directly test for vector error autocorrelation there:

```
Testing for vector error autocorrelation from lags 9 to 9
Chi²(4) = 7.6119 [0.1069]  and F-Form(4,452) = 1.8486 [0.1185]
```

There are no evident problems from this outcome.

Next, select Recursive Graphics, mark 1-step residuals, likelihood, 1-step Chows, and break-point Chows, and set the significance level to 1%:

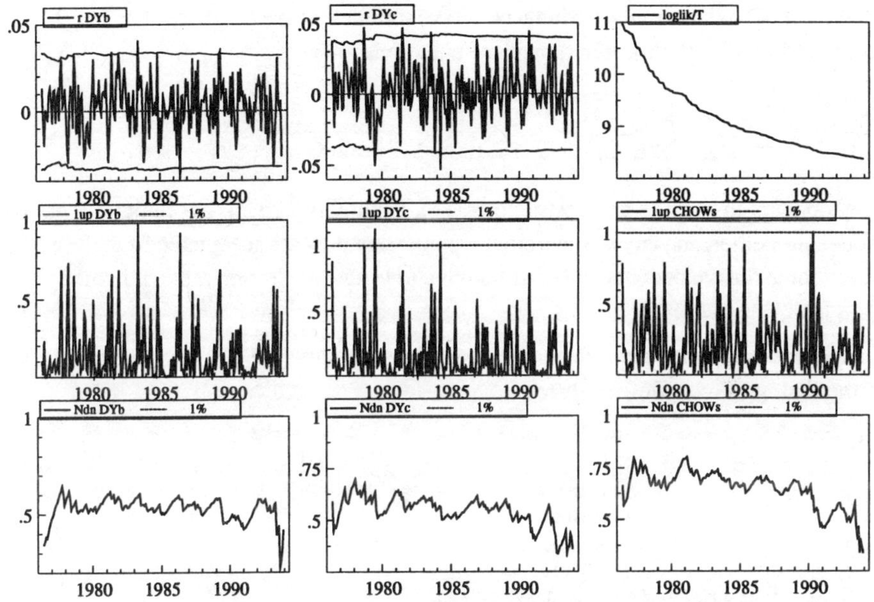

Figure 6.3 Constancy statistics for the conditional system.

Constancy is clearly accepted for this conditional model; unsurprisingly, given that the unconditional system was already found to be constant. The residual standard deviations are constant and the break-point tests never reject. Note that the large number of tests compared to one-off critical values should over-reject, so non-rejection is overly stringent. Thus, we turn to developing a model of the system.

6.4 Modelling the system

The main feature to be modelled is the correlation of 0.65 between the residuals, and this could derive from any of several factors in practice. First, *DYb* could depend on *DYc* (short-run marginal propensity to consume), or vice versa (an impact of expenditure on income, which seems less likely, though it has its proponents). Next, the 'shocks' may just be cross-correlated in nature. Finally, common omitted variables might induce the observed correlation.

The first possibility seems the most reasonable given the available information, so we restrict the system equations appropriately. We already know from the tests in Chapter 4 that *CIa_1* does not enter either equation. The coefficient of *DYd* in the *DYb* equation is about 0.6 of its value in the *DYc* equation, and hence might reflect having substituted the latter in the former. Restricting it to zero but including *DYc* in the first equation would map to a just-identified, and hence observationally equivalent, representation which might clarify the model's form.

Select Model, Formulate Model (`Alt+y`) (or click on the 'next-step building block' icon), and modify the formulation of the equations to be:

```
DYb = DYb_1, DYc_1, CIc_1, CIb_1, Constant, DYa, DYc;
DYc = DYb_1, DYc_1, CIc_1, CIb_1, Constant, DYa, DYd;
```

This appears to impose two restrictions (i.e., excluding *CIa*_1), but omits it from the model altogether, and anyway, we already know that they are acceptable from the earlier test of long-run weak exogeneity. Although *CIa* is now irrelevant, retain it in the system for a later illustration.

Accept the model, and select Two-stage least squares (2SLS, second from the top of the dialog). Accepting produces:

```
Identity for CIc
DYb              -1.0000
DYc               1.0000
DYd               1.8000
CIc_1             1.0000
R² = 1 over 1974 (4) to 1993 (12)
Identity for CIa
DYa               1.0000
DYd              -1.0000
CIa_1             1.0000
Constant      -0.0040000
R² = 1 over 1974 (4) to 1993 (12)
Identity for CIb
DYa             -0.35000
DYb               1.0000
DYc              -1.0000
CIb_1             1.0000
R² = 1 over 1974 (4) to 1993 (12)

EQ( 6) Estimating the model by 2SLS  (using pcftut1.in7)
The present sample is:  1974 (4) to 1993 (12)

Equation 1 for DYb
Variable     Coefficient    Std.Error  t-value  t-prob
DYb_1            0.31812     0.055484    5.734  0.0000
DYc_1          -0.078736     0.050883   -1.547  0.1231
CIc_1          0.0089459    0.0076948    1.163  0.2462
CIb_1           -0.10556     0.017702   -5.963  0.0000
Constant       0.0052040    0.0012052    4.318  0.0000
DYa             0.091125     0.028759    3.169  0.0017
DYc              0.52991     0.064833    8.173  0.0000

σ = 0.0120574
```

```
Equation 2 for DYc
Variable      Coefficient     Std.Error  t-value  t-prob
DYb_1           -0.057819      0.091030   -0.635  0.5260
DYc_1             0.34344      0.076340    4.499  0.0000
CIc_1           -0.069581      0.010443   -6.663  0.0000
CIb_1           -0.064791      0.028295   -2.290  0.0229
Constant        0.0081583     0.0018052    4.519  0.0000
DYa             -0.064524      0.047203   -1.367  0.1730
DYd              -0.32080      0.034231   -9.372  0.0000

σ = 0.0198239

loglik=1983.4373  log|Ω|=-16.7379  |Ω|=5.38067e-008  T=237
LR test of over-identifying restrictions:
Chi²(2) = 1.05967 [0.5887]

correlation of residuals
                   DYb          DYc
DYb             1.0000
DYc          0.0034938       1.0000
```

Thus, 2SLS is easy and fast to compute once a model has been formulated. The output is similar in structure and form to that produced for a system, although the layout can be reset in the Options dialog. The likelihood-ratio test of the over-identifying restrictions is only an approximation here, but is not significant (unsurprisingly). More usefully, the residual cross correlation has disappeared, so the model form is 'successful' in accounting for that feature.

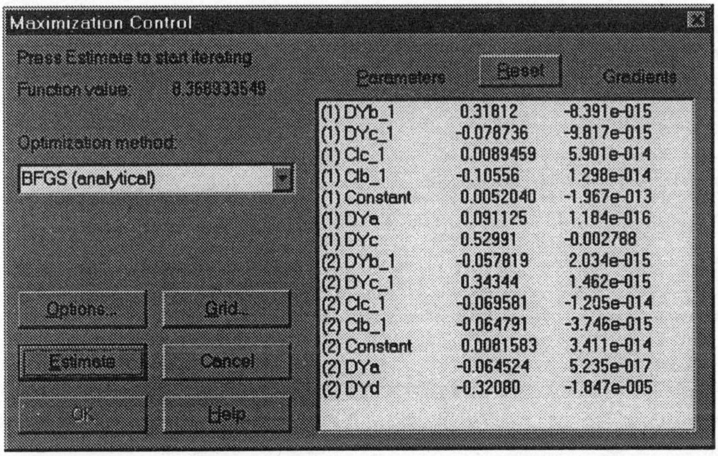

`Alt+1` to re-estimate, and this time, select Full information maximum likelihood (FIML) on the Estimation dialog. Make sure that recursive estimation is *not* ticked at this stage (or you may wait some time for the output to appear). Clicking OK (or tab to it and `Enter`) then brings up the FIML control dialog. If this does not appear, access the Options dialog to switch off the automatic maximization button.

This dialog allows the numerical optimization method to be selected, the choice being seen from clicking on the 'down-arrow' button beside BFGS (analytical).

The default is the recommended option. One-dimensional grids of the likelihood function may be plotted, initial values for optimization changed (or reset), and optimization commenced. Convergence criteria, and the maximum number of iterations may be tightened or loosened in the Options dialog, as may writing of iterative output.

For the present, press Estimate (or `Alt+e`) to estimate. The Message window monitors progress: this is on the PcFiml module icon itself, and you may need to move the maximization dialog to see the former (although PcFiml can be set to Always on Top on the File menu, this is over-ridden by its own dialogs – otherwise you may not be able to read them!). `Esc` will abort if, for example, divergence occurs or the process is taking too long – but then no estimates will be produced. On convergence, control reverts to this dialog (for example, to try other initial values or an alternative numerical method, graph the optimized likelihoods, or continue iterating). Here, accept the final values (click OK) to see (the identities have been omitted: the numbers may differ slightly depending on the number of iterations and convergence criteria set):

```
EQ( 7) Estimating the model by FIML  (using pcftut1.in7)
The present sample is:  1974 (4) to 1993 (12)

Equation 1 for DYb
Variable  Coefficient    Std.Error  t-value  t-prob       HCSE
DYb_1         0.31801     0.055485    5.731  0.0000   0.055406
DYc_1       -0.077880     0.050893   -1.530  0.1273   0.046387
CIc_1       0.0087657    0.0076975    1.139  0.2560  0.0083794
CIb_1        -0.10573     0.017703   -5.973  0.0000   0.019002
Constant    0.0052251    0.0012054    4.335  0.0000  0.0012786
DYa          0.091008     0.028760    3.164  0.0018   0.029262
DYc           0.52719     0.064899    8.123  0.0000   0.070844
σ = 0.0120576
Equation 2 for DYc
Variable  Coefficient    Std.Error  t-value  t-prob       HCSE
DYb_1       -0.057819     0.091030   -0.635  0.5260   0.099249
DYc_1         0.34343     0.076340    4.499  0.0000   0.078999
CIc_1       -0.069583     0.010443   -6.663  0.0000   0.010028
CIb_1       -0.064783     0.028295   -2.290  0.0230   0.028184
Constant    0.0081582    0.0018052    4.519  0.0000  0.0018184
DYa         -0.064525     0.047203   -1.367  0.1730   0.047072
DYd          -0.32081     0.034231   -9.372  0.0000   0.036527
σ = 0.0198239

loglik=1983.4381  log|Ω|=-16.7379   |Ω|=5.38063e-008  T=237
LR test of over-identifying restrictions:
Chi²(2)  = 1.05789 [0.5892]
```

```
correlation of residuals
                       DYb          DYc
DYb                 1.0000
DYc              0.0079630       1.0000
```

The one additional column is for HCSE, namely heteroscedastic-consistent standard errors. Otherwise, the results are close to 2SLS. *CIc_1* is insignificant in the first equation consistent with its being of importance in the corresponding system equation owing to eliminating *DYc*. Also, *DYa* and *DYb_1* seem irrelevant in the second equation. To reduce parameter dimensionality further, delete the above three variables from their respective equations and re-estimate the model.

This time, after convergence, and prior to accepting, select Grid on the FIML control dialog (`Alt+g`) which will bring up a dialog for grid parameters.

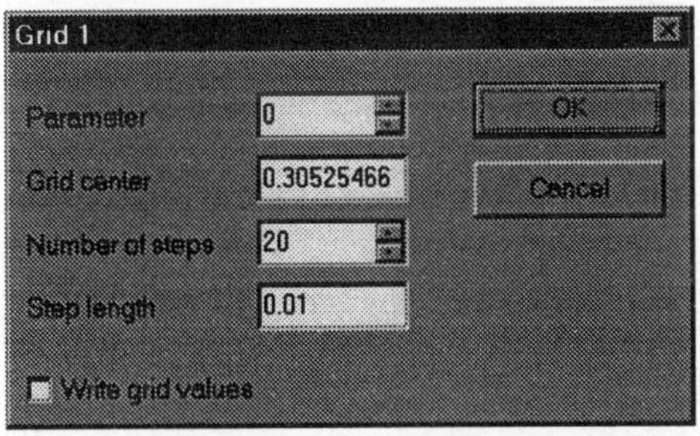

Set the number of steps to 50 (the default of 20 will work as well), and the step length to 0.005, then press `Enter` 11 times (once for each parameter) or click on the OK button with the mouse until parameter 0 recurs, then press `Esc`. The Message window will record the calculation of the one-dimensional projection of the likelihood function for each parameter in turn, holding the other parameters fixed at their optimum values. The graphics adjusts automatically to the number of plots (up to the maximum of 36) and on returning to GiveWin, you should see Figure 6.4.

There are no problems of multiple optima, or of flat likelihoods, so the likelihood function seems well behaved.

The grids can be used in many ways. For example, reselect Grid and parameter 0, selecting 25 steps. After clicking OK, reselect parameter 0 but with 50 steps – OK to accept them; then again parameter 0 with 200 steps, and finally again parameter 0 with (say) 800 and OK (or, for example, 25, 50, 100, 200 if you are using a slow PC). Pressing `Esc` (or Close) will portray the likelihood as you 'walk away' from it: see Figure 6.5.

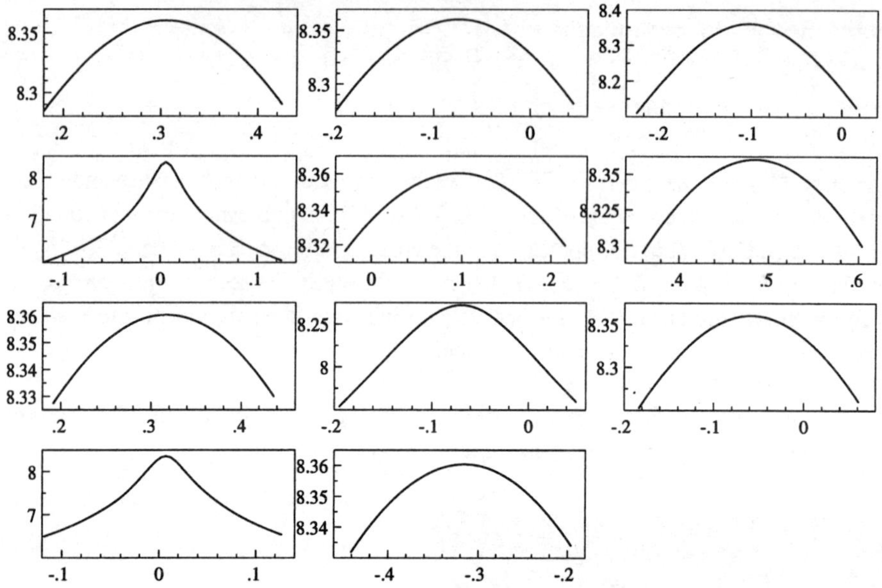

Figure 6.4 Likelihood function projections for the conditional model.

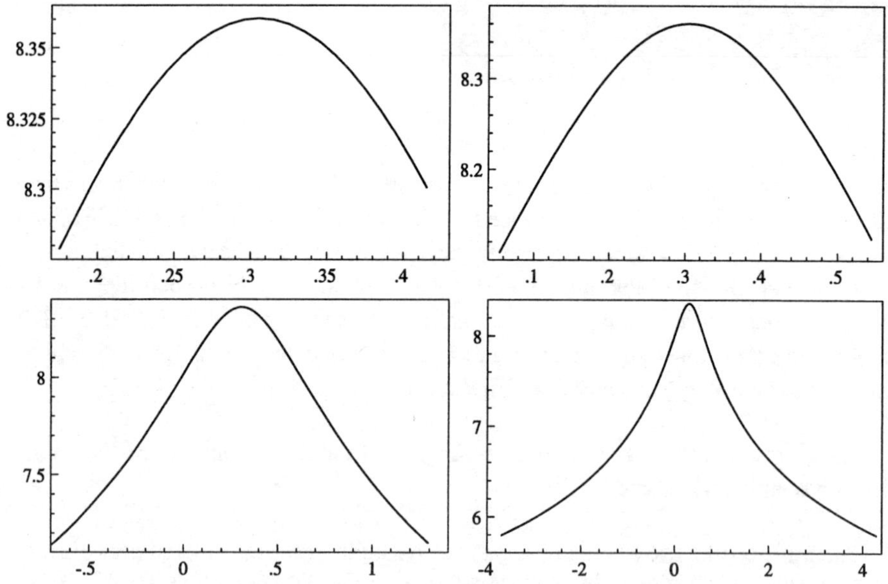

Figure 6.5 Likelihood function projections for the first parameter.

Now re-estimate (`Alt+e`) to obtain (ignoring the identities):

```
EQ( 8) Estimating the model by FIML  (using pcftut1.in7)
The present sample is:  1974 (4) to 1993 (12)

Equation 1 for DYb
Variable   Coefficient      Std.Error  t-value  t-prob        HCSE
DYb_1          0.30527       0.054077    5.645  0.0000    0.052742
DYc_1        -0.074508       0.050266   -1.482  0.1396    0.045777
CIb_1         -0.10320       0.017510   -5.894  0.0000    0.018938
Constant     0.0054800      0.0011563    4.739  0.0000   0.0012084
DYa           0.096026       0.028369    3.385  0.0008    0.029617
DYc            0.48438       0.054084    8.956  0.0000    0.056758

σ = 0.0120761

Equation 2 for DYc
Variable   Coefficient      Std.Error  t-value  t-prob        HCSE
DYc_1          0.31659       0.061259    5.168  0.0000    0.060634
CIc_1        -0.069951       0.010050   -6.961  0.0000   0.0093481
CIb_1        -0.058672       0.027505   -2.133  0.0340    0.027564
Constant     0.0069638      0.0015642    4.452  0.0000   0.0014976
DYd           -0.31579       0.034177   -9.240  0.0000    0.035781

σ = 0.0198522

loglik=1981.4188  log|Ω|=-16.7208  |Ω|=5.47311e-008  T=237
LR test of over-identifying restrictions:
Chi²(5)  = 5.09667 [0.4042]

correlation of residuals
                   DYb          DYc
DYb              1.000
DYc           0.078913        1.000
```

The likelihood-ratio test of over-identifying restrictions is again not significant, so the reduced model parsimoniously encompasses the system (see Hendry and Mizon, 1993).

Given the number of hypotheses tested, and the large sample relative to the model size, it seems sensible to use about a 1% (or even 0.1%) critical value rather than a 5%, in which case, delete *DYc_1* from the first equation and *CIb_1* from the second. Re-estimate by FIML to obtain:

```
EQ( 9) Estimating the model by FIML  (using pcftut1.in7)
The present sample is:  1974 (4) to 1993 (12)

Equation 1 for DYb
Variable   Coefficient  Std.Error  t-value  t-prob        HCSE
DYb_1          0.26842   0.046498    5.773  0.0000    0.046930
CIb_1        -0.097797   0.016553   -5.908  0.0000    0.017496
Constant     0.0055902  0.0011401    4.903  0.0000   0.0011964
DYa            0.10127   0.028153    3.597  0.0004    0.029089
DYc            0.44858   0.046300    9.689  0.0000    0.051573

σ = 0.0121825
```

```
Equation 2 for DYc
Variable    Coefficient   Std.Error   t-value   t-prob        HCSE
DYc_1           0.37486    0.056152     6.676   0.0000    0.054973
CIc_1         -0.077751   0.0092347    -8.419   0.0000   0.0089592
Constant      0.0059500   0.0015109     3.938   0.0001   0.0014262
DYd            -0.31166    0.034298    -9.087   0.0000    0.035802

σ = 0.020009

loglik=1978.1639   log|Ω|=-16.6934   |Ω|=5.62553e-008   T=237
LR test of over-identifying restrictions:
Chi^2(7)  = 11.6064 [0.1143]

correlation of residuals
                      DYb         DYc
DYb                1.0000
DYc               0.14304      1.0000
```

The final set of restrictions is acceptable over the full sample, and only 10 parameters are needed to characterize the system.

The batch code for this model is in PCFTUT4.FL. If you create one yourself, don't forget to copy the `Module("PcFiml");`, `loaddata` and `algebra` sections from the start of the Results window, if you want a stand-alone file.

6.5 Reduction progress

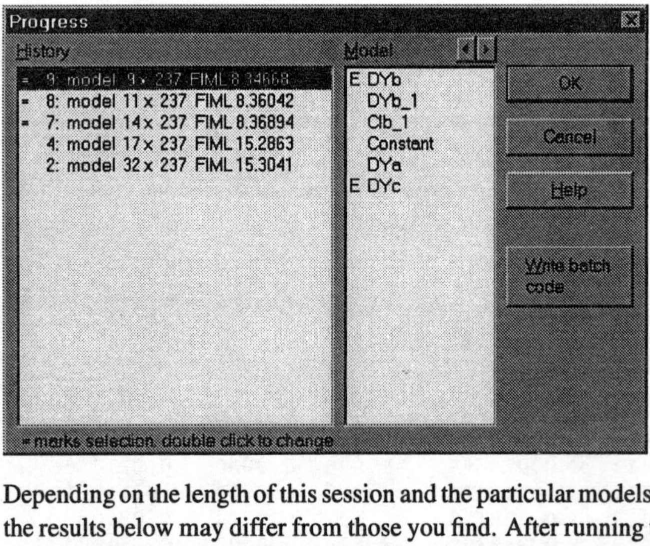

Depending on the length of this session and the particular models and systems estimated, the results below may differ from those you find. After running the initial batch file, we began by estimating an unrestricted first-order lag system. There were three models of this system, imposing two, five and seven restrictions respectively. Select Model, Progress (`Alt+m,p`) to see the progress selection dialog (this is slightly different if you did extra estimations in between). Unmark 2SLS if it is shown (since that is redundant given the FIML estimates) by highlighting and double clicking with the mouse; also unmark the first system as shown above. Accept and the output is (we dropped AIC):

```
Progress to date

model   T      p              log-likelihood           SC          HQ
  9    237     9   FIML          1978.1639         -16.49      -16.56
  8    237    11   FIML          1981.4188         -16.47      -16.56
  7    237    14   FIML          1983.4381         -16.41      -16.54
system T       p              log-likelihood           SC          HQ
  5    237    16   RLS           1983.9671         -16.37      -16.51

Tests of model reduction
Model  8 --> Model 9: Chi²(2) =    6.5097 [0.0386]  *
Model  7 --> Model 9: Chi²(5) =    10.548 [0.0611]

Model  7 --> Model 8: Chi²(3) =    4.0388 [0.2573]

System 5 --> Model 9: Chi²(7) =    11.606 [0.1143]
System 5 --> Model 8: Chi²(5) =    5.0967 [0.4042]
System 5 --> Model 7: Chi²(2) =    1.0579 [0.5892]
```

No test of reduction rejects at the 1% level and only the last is significant at the 5% level, as anticipated by deleting a variable with $|t| > 2$. However, several insignificant results were assured from our earlier knowledge. The final model here has nine parameters in total, and even had we considered a two-equation system from the outset, that would represent a reduction from 24. Hopefully, the final model is more interpretable, and more closely captures the structure underlying the artificial economy.

6.6 Forecasting with the model

Both static and dynamic forecasts can be calculated, but because the system is open, there are no post-sample observations on the stochastic conditioning variables (an analogous situation arises in practical forecast exercises where, for example, world trade is an important non-modelled explanatory variable and so has to be predicted 'off-line' by some extrapolative procedure). Thus, the forecast horizon has to be set within sample, by curtailing estimation h periods before the end of the database sample. Select System estimation, set the number of forecasts to 24 (two years), and estimate to obtain:

```
1-step (ex post) forecast analysis 1992 (1) to 1993 (12)
Parameter constancy forecast tests:
using Ω    Chi²(48)=43.28 [0.6663]    F(48,205)=0.90167 [0.6567]
using V[e] Chi²(48)=41.874 [0.7208]   F(48,205)=0.87236 [0.7072]
using V[E] Chi²(48)=42.445 [0.6990]   F(48,205)=0.88427 [0.6869]
```

Next, select Model, Formulate Model (`Alt+y`), accept (OK), FIML, `Enter` and `Alt+e` to commence FIML; on convergence OK leads to the general output plus the forecast statistics:

```
1-step (ex post) forecast analysis 1992 (1) to 1993 (12)
Parameter constancy forecast tests:
using Ω     Chi²(48)=41.447 [0.7366]  F(48,209)=0.86347 [0.7223]
using V[e] Chi²(48)=40.449 [0.7722]  F(48,209)=0.84268 [0.7560]
```

These statistics fail to reject constancy as expected. The degrees of freedom differ because the model has fewer estimated parameters, but the difference is small here.

Forecast outcomes can be considered in detail numerically: set the Options dialog accordingly, by marking Individual forecast statistics, and the output then comprises:

```
1-step (ex post) forecast analysis 1992 (1) to 1993 (12)
Parameter constancy forecast tests:
using Ω     Chi²(48)=41.447 [0.7366]  F(48,209)=0.86347 [0.7223]
using V[e] Chi²(48)=40.449 [0.7722]  F(48,209)=0.84268 [0.7560]

Descriptive statistics of forecast errors
Means
      DYb        DYc          CIc          CIa          CIb
0.0024155  0.0027916  0.00037603 -5.9784e-018 -0.00037603

Standard Deviations
     DYb         DYc          CIc          CIa          CIb
0.016803    0.019782     0.012573  6.8341e-017     0.012573

Correlation matrix
            DYb        DYc        CIc        CIa       CIb
DYb      1.0000
DYc     0.77558     1.0000
CIc    -0.11619    0.53686     1.0000
CIa     0.00000    0.00000    0.00000    0.00000
CIb     0.11619   -0.53686    -1.0000    0.00000    1.0000

matrix of forecast standard errors
               DYb         DYc         CIc         CIa         CIb
1992-1    0.016393    0.020449    0.015802    0.00000    0.015802
1992-2    0.016270    0.020290    0.015685    0.00000    0.015685
1992-3    0.016214    0.020172    0.015621    0.00000    0.015621
1992-4    0.016194    0.020209    0.015608    0.00000    0.015608
1992-5    0.016288    0.020366    0.015713    0.00000    0.015713
1992-6    0.016274    0.020199    0.015684    0.00000    0.015684
1992-7    0.016225    0.020249    0.015635    0.00000    0.015635
1992-8    0.016230    0.020278    0.015645    0.00000    0.015645
1992-9    0.016331    0.020364    0.015745    0.00000    0.015745
1992-10   0.016399    0.020508    0.015824    0.00000    0.015824
1992-11   0.016362    0.020350    0.015780    0.00000    0.015780
1992-12   0.016340    0.020296    0.015746    0.00000    0.015746
1993-1    0.016305    0.020313    0.015712    0.00000    0.015712
1993-2    0.016324    0.020327    0.015726    0.00000    0.015726
```

1993-3	0.016282	0.020304	0.015693	0.00000	0.015693
1993-4	0.016267	0.020322	0.015686	0.00000	0.015686
1993-5	0.016250	0.020235	0.015656	0.00000	0.015656
1993-6	0.016357	0.020294	0.015763	0.00000	0.015763
1993-7	0.016356	0.020388	0.015760	0.00000	0.015760
1993-8	0.016338	0.020350	0.015740	0.00000	0.015740
1993-9	0.016333	0.020291	0.015746	0.00000	0.015746
1993-10	0.016334	0.020283	0.015751	0.00000	0.015751
1993-11	0.016271	0.020299	0.015691	0.00000	0.015691
1993-12	0.016288	0.020400	0.015718	0.00000	0.015718

Forecast tests, single Chi^2(2)

	using Ω	using V[e]
1992-1	0.249411 [0.8828]	0.240044 [0.8869]
1992-2	1.47369 [0.4786]	1.44330 [0.4860]
1992-3	1.29522 [0.5233]	1.28101 [0.5270]
1992-4	2.83747 [0.2420]	2.79659 [0.2470]
1992-5	1.72941 [0.4212]	1.69174 [0.4292]
1992-6	1.48699 [0.4754]	1.46676 [0.4803]
1992-7	2.35856 [0.3075]	2.31527 [0.3142]
1992-8	1.70017 [0.4274]	1.66866 [0.4342]
1992-9	3.12359 [0.2098]	3.03271 [0.2195]
1992-10	0.965476 [0.6171]	0.926637 [0.6292]
1992-11	1.71550 [0.4241]	1.65363 [0.4374]
1992-12	2.13323 [0.3442]	2.06219 [0.3566]
1993-1	0.522222 [0.7702]	0.509388 [0.7752]
1993-2	1.14060 [0.5654]	1.10912 [0.5743]
1993-3	0.339913 [0.8437]	0.331842 [0.8471]
1993-4	0.772082 [0.6797]	0.755467 [0.6854]
1993-5	4.77017 [0.0921]	4.67805 [0.0964]
1993-6	1.93094 [0.3808]	1.88670 [0.3893]
1993-7	0.180941 [0.9135]	0.175232 [0.9161]
1993-8	3.75037 [0.1533]	3.64038 [0.1620]
1993-9	0.446258 [0.8000]	0.431421 [0.8060]
1993-10	1.42817 [0.4896]	1.39166 [0.4987]
1993-11	1.60585 [0.4480]	1.56794 [0.4566]
1993-12	3.49059 [0.1746]	3.39298 [0.1833]

Alternatively, for a graphical summary `Alt+t,g`, mark forecasts and forecast Chows, and accept to see Figure 6.6. We have drawn the graphs using Forecast bands as set in the Options dialog: error bars are the default.

The Chow tests are treated as χ^2 here, so are not scaled, although the approximate 5% significance line is shown. Should you wish a different critical value, use GiveWin's Algebra to compute it (e.g., here, `pp=quanchi(0.99,2);` adds 9.21 to the database as the 1% critical value of $\chi^2(2)$), then draw a line at that level (adjust the axes of the graphs first; then highlight the plot and click on Edit, Draw a line). No statistic rejects, unsurprisingly given that the system is constant and the model parsimoniously encompasses the system.

For dynamic forecasts, click on its icon (graph line with error bars) or `Alt+t,f`, and the procedure is just like that for a system. Mark all variables except *CIa*, and click

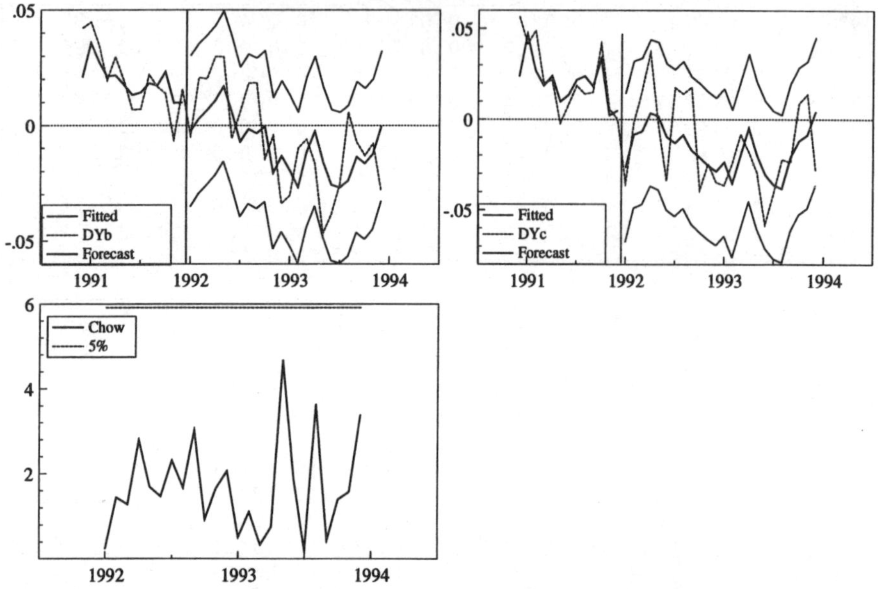

Figure 6.6 Constancy statistics for the parsimonious conditional model.

on With parameter uncertainty as shown in the following screen capture:

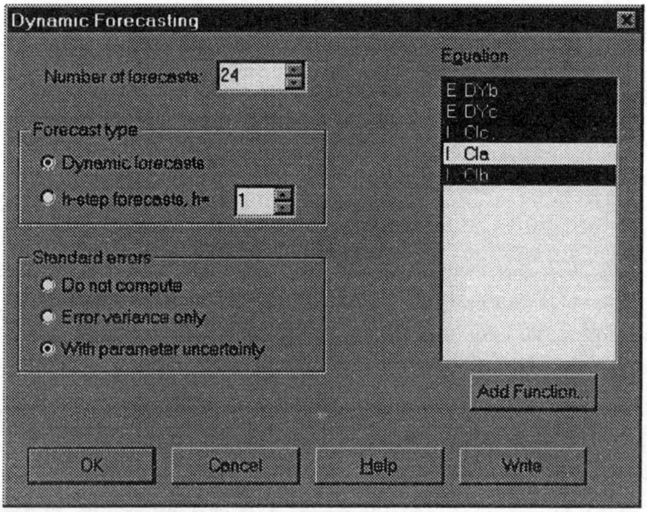

Figure 6.7 illustrates the outcome. If you marked all five variables for dynamic forecasts, the *CIa* graph has zero error bands (or bars): can you explain why it does so here when it had considerable uncertainty in earlier graphs? Figure 6.8 illustrates this phenomenon.

As pointed out at the beginning of this section, we cannot forecast beyond the data sample of the conditioning variables *DYa* and *DYd*. However, we could provide a scen-

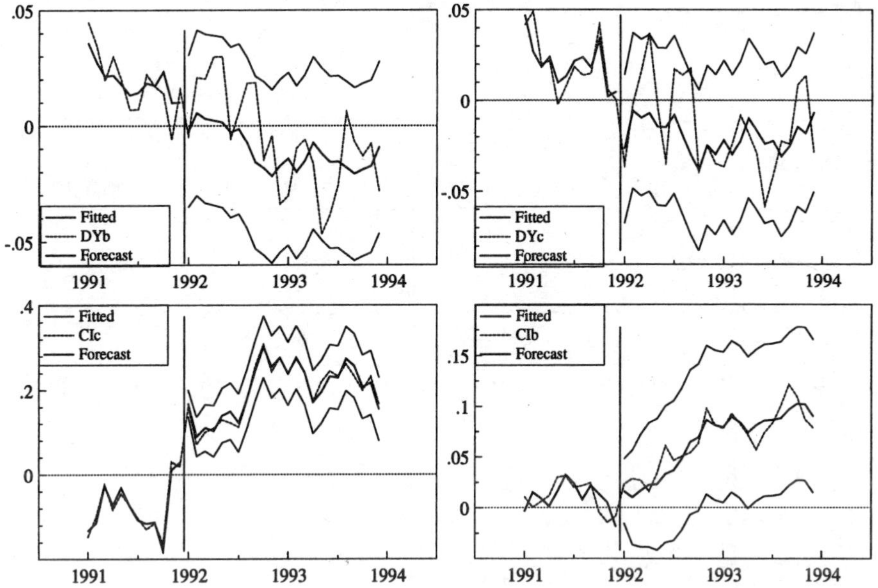

Figure 6.7 Dynamic forecasts from the parsimonious conditional model.

ario for these variables, and then forecast further ahead, conditional on the projected path of *DYa* and *DYd*. Access the Algebra editor and enter the following code:

```
DYa = insample(1994, 1, 1994, 12) ? .006;
DYd = insample(1994, 1, 1994, 12) ? .000;
```

This sets *DYa* to 0.006 for 1994, corresponding to an annual growth rate of 7.2%, which is just below the full-sample mean. *DYd* is kept at zero, compared to a historic monthly mean of 0.27%.

Note: Make sure that you do not overwrite any data used for estimation. In general for forecast experiments with perturbed variables, it is safer to use a copy of the original variables, and not save the data set afterwards.

To get PcFiml to use the new data *re-estimate both the system and the model.* The Dynamic forecasting dialog now allows us to create dynamic forecasts for three years so increase the Number of forecasts to 36: see Figure 6.8.

The selection of error bars or bands depends on the purposes of the exercise as well as the number of forecasts, and the extent of 'crossing' of the various lines on the graphs. Here, the fact that the actuals lie within the uncertainty bands around the forecast is clearer from bands; but as Figure 6.9 shows, the rapid increase in the width of the confidence interval as the horizon increases is clearer from bars (see the fourth plot for *CIb* in particular). Conversely, with bars so close together, the graphs are somewhat messy.

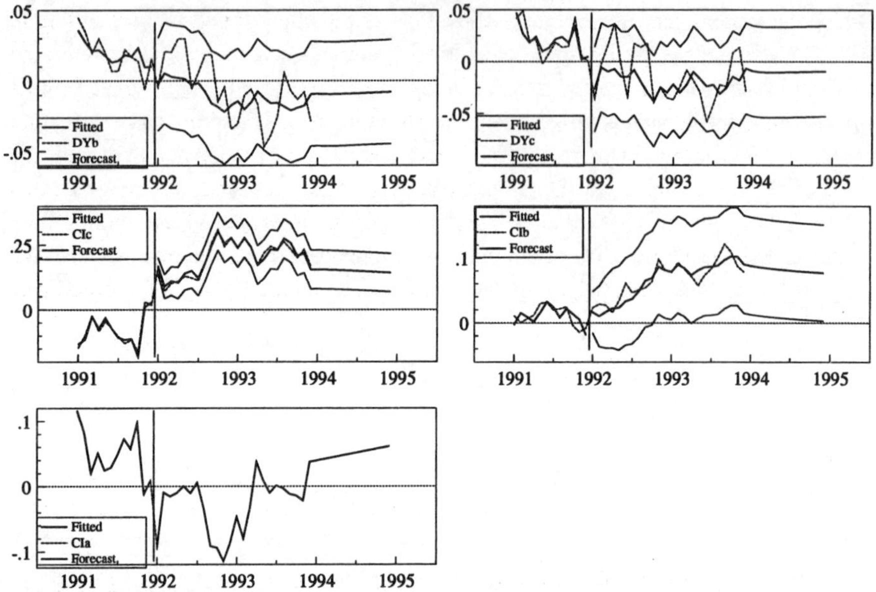

Figure 6.8 Dynamic forecasts with a scenario for the non-modelled variables.

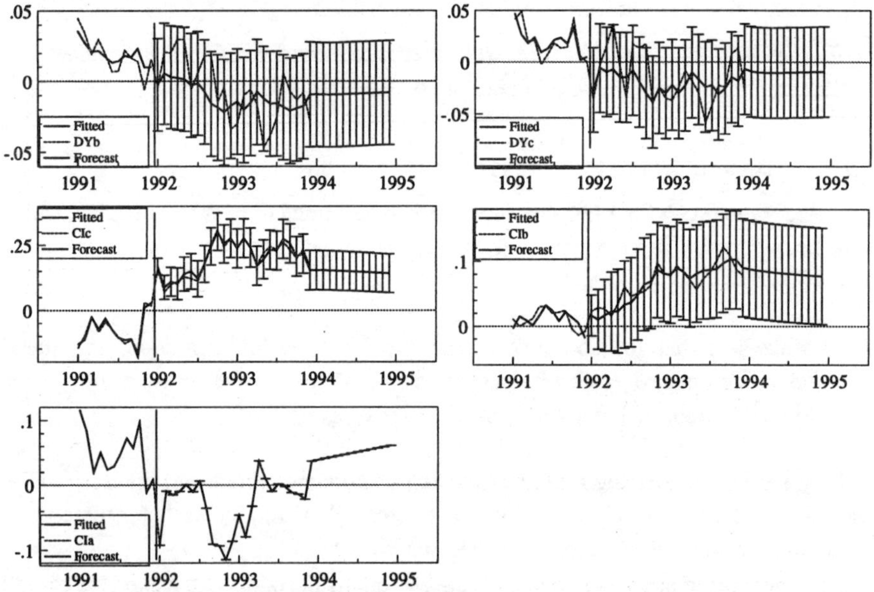

Figure 6.9 Dynamic scenario forecasts with error bars.

6.7 Recursive FIML

While we already know that the system is constant and that the model encompasses the system, it is of interest to estimate the model recursively by FIML. First select zero forecasts for the system and estimate it recursively over the unperturbed sample ending in 1993(12). Next, select Model, Formulate Model, mark Recursive estimation with the initialization set to 36), and estimate. The model is first estimated for the whole sample to acquire good initial values for the successive numerical optimization, and a good first estimate of the Hessian. Then the sample is reduced one observation at a time until the initialization period is reached. On a Pentium, despite the number of calculations, this complete set takes but a few seconds: the number of iterations per observation will be about 2–4. If you are using a slow computer, but are interested in trying recursive FIML, set the number of observations for initialization to 140, allowing 100 recursive outcomes.

The output must be viewed graphically: `Alt+t,r` and mark 1-step residuals, likelihood function, encompassing tests, 1-step, and $N\downarrow$ Chow tests at the 1% level, and accept to see Figure 6.10.

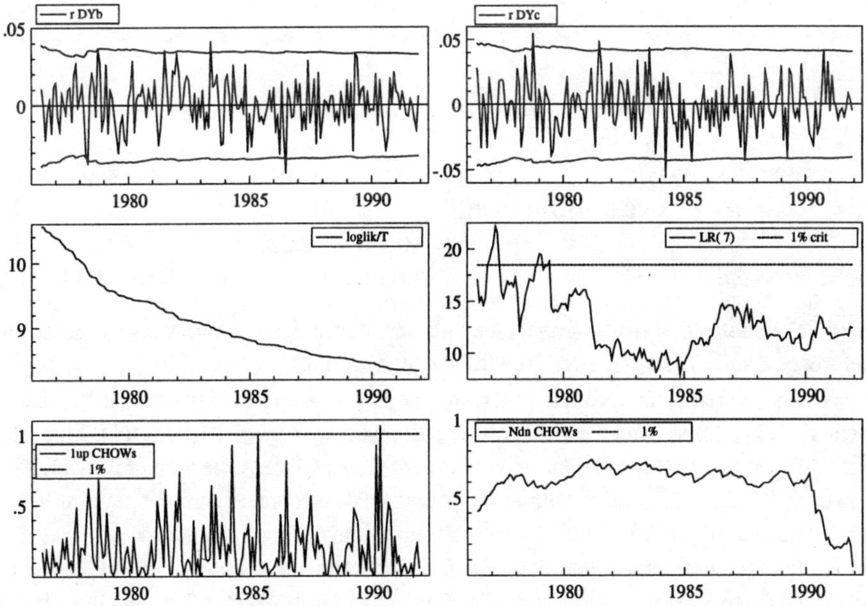

Figure 6.10 Recursive output from the parsimonious conditional model.

The 1-step residuals are well behaved, with constant standard error bands, the Chow tests behave as anticipated from the system results, but the likelihood-ratio parsimonious encompassing appears to reject early in the sample. The small-sample behaviour of this test is not known at present, and there may be a need for degrees-of-freedom corrections to offset over-rejection at small sample sizes (for example, we commenced here with only 26 initial observations).

6.8 How well did we do?

Since the data are generated artificially, we know the data generation process (DGP), so can check on the closeness of the selected model to the DGP. As will be seen, we ourselves learned from the tutorial modelling exercises that the chosen DGP created substantive problems relative to our intentions.

In fact the system was:

$$\begin{aligned}
\Delta Ya_t &= -0.1\,(Ya_{t-1} - Yd_{t-1} - 0.004t) + 0.001 + \epsilon_{1,t} \\
\Delta Yb_t &= 0.1\Delta Ya_t + 0.5\Delta Yc_t - 0.25\,(Yb_{t-1} - Yc_{t-1} - 0.4\,Ya_{t-1}) + 0.002 + u_{2,t} \\
\Delta Yc_t &= -0.3\Delta Yd_t - 0.20\,(Yc_{t-1} - Yb_{t-1} + 1.5\,Yd_{t-1}) + 0.002 + u_{3,t} \\
\Delta Yd_t &= 0.001 + \epsilon_{4,t}
\end{aligned} \tag{6.1}$$

where:

$$\begin{aligned}
u_{2,t} &= 0.5u_{2,t-1} + \epsilon_{2,t} \\
u_{3,t} &= 0.4u_{3,t-1} + \epsilon_{3,t}
\end{aligned} \tag{6.2}$$

and:

$$\epsilon_t \sim \mathsf{IN}_4\left[\mathbf{0}, \boldsymbol{\Omega}\right] \text{ where } \boldsymbol{\Omega}^* =$$

$$\begin{pmatrix}
0.0006 \approx (0.024)^2 & 0 & 0 & \mathit{0.6} \\
0 & 0.00015 \approx (0.012)^2 & 0 & 0 \\
0 & 0 & 0.0005 \approx (0.022)^2 & 0 \\
\mathit{0.6} & 0 & 0 & 0.0015 \approx (0.038)^2
\end{pmatrix}$$

when $\boldsymbol{\Omega}^*$ denotes that off-diagonal elements are correlations. There were no breaks in the process, and the slower later growth was 'endogenous'.

We discovered in the process of writing the tutorials that the system is I(2). This is because *Yd* is I(1), so from the third cointegration vector, $Yc_{t-1} - Yb_{t-1}$ is I(1). Since the first equation creates an I(0) relation between Ya_{t-1} and Yd_{t-1}, the former is again I(1). However, $Yc_{t-1} - Yb_{t-1}$ can be eliminated between the second and third equations, leaving a combination of ΔYb_t and ΔYc_t as a non-cointegrating I(1) function of Ya_{t-1} and Yd_{t-1}. For the parameter values in the DGP, the criterion for not being I(2) in Chapter 11 fails when there are three cointegration vectors. The long-run matrix has rank three in the DGP, but with *two* zero eigenvalues, also warning of the problem, although the empirical counterpart is less clearcut. The eigenvalues of the empirical dynamic companion form provide a hint of the problem (three near unity despite three cointegration relations): in the companion form derived from the DGP, there are two unit roots despite there being three cointegration relations. Further analysis of the DGP is in §6.10.

Nevertheless, we treated the data as if they were I(1). Technically, the system can be changed to I(1) by adding ΔYc_{t-1} with a small coefficient to the final equation, so its dynamics offset the tendency to I(2), although the generated data would be little altered. This issue affects the legitimacy of the critical values adopted, but by insisting on a congruent final representation, does not greatly alter the implications of the conditional model. On the other hand, for practical modelling, so long as the coefficient of *Trend* is not fixed but many other βs are, the various cointegration algorithms experience considerable difficulty in locating the optimum.

Given this issue, a comparison of the data representation in terms of observables with the above DGP shows that the selected model is a reasonable match, although it is overly simplified. Solving (6.1) given (6.2) yields for the two middle equations:

$$
\begin{aligned}
\Delta Yb_t = \; & 0.1\Delta Ya_t + 0.5\Delta Yc_t - 0.25 CIb_{t-1} + 0.002 + 0.5u_{2,t-1} + \epsilon_{2,t} \\
= \; & 0.1\Delta Ya_t + 0.5\Delta Yc_t - 0.125 CIb_{t-1} + 0.002 + 0.5\Delta Yb_{t-1} \\
& -0.05\Delta Ya_{t-1} - 0.25\Delta Yc_{t-1} - 0.125\Delta CIb_{t-1} - 0.001 + \epsilon_{2,t} \\
= \; & 0.1\Delta Ya_t + 0.5\Delta Yc_t - 0.125 CIb_{t-1} + 0.001 + 0.375\Delta Yb_{t-1} \\
& -0.125\Delta Yc_{t-1} + \epsilon_{2,t}
\end{aligned}
$$

and

$$
\begin{aligned}
\Delta Yc_t = \; & -0.3\Delta Yd_t - 0.20 CIc_{t-1} + 0.002 + 0.4u_{3,t-1} + \epsilon_{3,t} \\
= \; & -0.3\Delta Yd_t - 0.12 CIc_{t-1} + 0.002 + 0.4\Delta Yc_{t-1} \\
& +0.12\Delta Yd_{t-1} - 0.08\Delta CIc_{t-1} - 0.001 + \epsilon_{3,t} \\
= \; & -0.3\Delta Yd_t - 0.12 CIc_{t-1} + 0.32\Delta Yc_{t-1} + 0.001 + 0.08\Delta Yb_{t-1} + \epsilon_{3,t}
\end{aligned}
\tag{6.3}
$$

The smaller coefficients on differenced variables were not retained, but all other main effects were detected. The final reduction step in fact moved away from the DGP, but that must often be a consequence of stringent critical values. It certainly helped to know the approximate form of the DGP when developing the tutorials, especially on the choice between two and three cointegrating vectors, and the explanation for the residual correlation between equations two and three, but there were few 'strained' decisions other than to retain 3 long-run relations. The DGP was not a particularly simple one, with 21 non-zero coefficients in its VAR. Thus, it seems feasible to analyse linear dynamic systems of this size. Hendry and Doornik (1994) provide a 'real data' application.

6.9 Constrained FIML

The final aspect we will consider in these tutorials is that of testing and imposing parametric restrictions on the model. The first is implemented via the Test Restrictions test option. First re-estimate the system and model without forecasts (if you lost the model, you can run PCFTUT4.FL to recreate it). Then select Test, Test restrictions and in the general restrictions editortype the desired restrictions. For example, to assess the importance of the intercepts in the two equations, to illustrate the approach, enter:

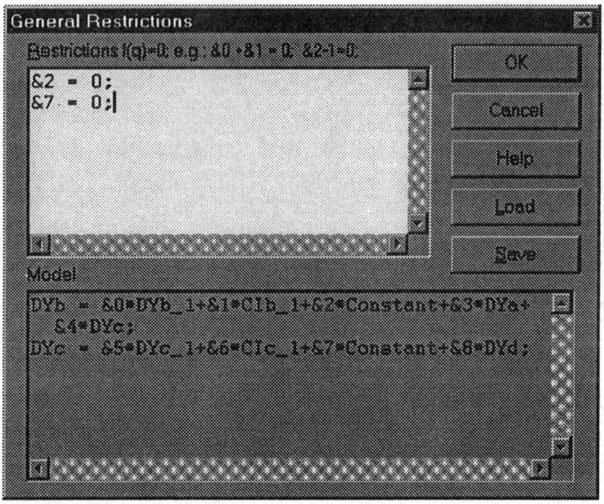

Accept and:

```
Restrictions for testing:
&2 = 0;
&7 = 0;
Wald test for general restrictions
GenRes Chi^2( 2) =     35.472 [0.0000] **
```

Clearly, the intercepts are important.

A more interesting set of constraints is to check the DGP autoregressive error form. This involves formulating a new system and model, and illustrates the strengths of PcFiml for system modelling. Start a new system (`Alt+s`, `Alt+n`), select the four differences and the three cointegration vectors using one lag on each (this is a previously considered system), clear the status on the constant, *DYa* and *DYd*, and set the three cointegration vectors to identities. Accept and estimate by OLS with no forecasts. Now select Model formulation (`Alt+y`) and setup the equations (make sure you have the same order for the regressors, otherwise the coefficients will have different numbers):

```
DYb = DYc, DYb_1, DYc_1, DYa, DYa_1, Constant, CIb_1;
DYc = DYc_1, CIc_1, Constant, DYd, DYd_1, DYb_1;
```

The identities should still be remembered by PcFiml. Estimate by FIML. Check the log-likelihood value, to see if the model was setup correctly: `loglik = 1979.5613.`

The restrictions for an autoregressive error are awkward when there exist variables which are redundant when lagged (as here), but (6.3) shows that we can at least impose the constraints that:

```
&2  = -(&1+&6)*&0;
&4  =   0.;
```

```
&11 =    0.;
```

First, to test the restrictions on FIML, access the general restrictions test (`Alt+t,n`), collect terms on the left-hand side to form:

```
&2 + (&1+&6)*&0 = 0;
&4  =   0.;
&11 =   0.;
```

Accept and:

```
Wald test for general restrictions
GenRes Chi^2( 3) =      1.2214 [0.7479]
```

The Wald test does not reject, correctly as the restrictions are valid, although we ignored the dependencies arising from the lagged equilibrium corrections (see the form of the DGP above).

To see the resulting restricted coefficient estimates, activate model estimation, select FIML with parameter restrictions and change the constraints to:

```
&2 = - (&1 + &6) * &0;
&4 = 0;
&11 = 0;
```

Accept, then `Alt+l,c` (for constrained FIML) `Alt+e` and optimize by BFGS using analytical derivatives (we clicked Estimate a few times to reduce the gradients):

```
Constraints for CFIML:
&2 = - (&1 + &6) * &0;
&4 = 0;
&11 = 0;

EQ(14) Estimating the model by CFIML  (using Pcftut1.in7)
The present sample is:  1974 (4) to 1993 (12)
Equation 1 for DYb
```

Variable	Coefficient	Std.Error	t-value	t-prob
DYc	0.49705	0.047165	10.538	0.0000
DYb_1	0.30457	0.054060	5.634	0.0000
DYc_1	-0.097898	---		
DYa	0.094312	0.028325	3.330	0.0010
DYa_1	0.00000	---		
Constant	0.0056629	0.0011005	5.146	0.0000
CIb_1	-0.10761	0.013443	-8.005	0.0000

σ = 0.0120674

```
Equation 2 for DYc
Variable  Coefficient     Std.Error  t-value  t-prob
DYc_1         0.38552      0.075202    5.126  0.0000
CIc_1       -0.079680     0.0099152   -8.036  0.0000
Constant    0.0062890     0.0016799    3.744  0.0002
DYd          -0.31670      0.034521   -9.174  0.0000
DYd_1         0.00000           ---
DYb_1       -0.030969      0.088017   -0.352  0.7253

σ = 0.0200458

loglik=1978.9454  log|Ω|=-16.7   |Ω|=5.58855e-008   T=237
LR test of over-identifying restrictions:
Chi²(10)  = 10.4896 [0.3986]

LR test of restrictions: Chi²(3)  = 1.23185 [0.7454]

correlation of residuals
                      DYb          DYc
 DYb                1.000
 DYc              0.05782        1.000
```

The choice between analytical and numerical derivatives is analogous to that for the switching algorithm as described in §4.8: analytical derivatives compute the Jacobian in (12.30) below numerically, whereas numerical derivatives compute $\partial \ell / \partial \phi_i$ numerically. The covariance matrix of the parameters in CFIML is computed numerically. The likelihood ratio test of the constraints ($\chi^2(3) = 1.23$) also fails to reject, with a value close to that of the Wald test above. Moreover, the augmented over-identifying restrictions statistic ($\chi^2(10) = 10.5$) also accepts. Constraints can be saved in a file for later use.

This concludes the tutorial on modelling a dynamic system. The final section of this chapter undertakes a theoretical analysis of the tutorial DGP.

6.10 Addendum: dynamic analysis of the DGP using Ox

It is easy to do a dynamic analysis of an estimated system or model in PcFiml: just press the toolbar button. However, the theoretical counterpart for the DGP used in these chapters is not so simple. Fortunately we have Ox at our disposal. Ox is a matrix language, which has object-oriented features. One of these is a class for generating data from a DGP of the type used here. That class, called `PcNaiveDgp`, can also do a dynamic analysis of the DGP. A Full description of Ox, as well as the `PcNaiveDgp` class, is provided in Doornik (1996).

The DGP has the general form:

$$\begin{aligned}\mathbf{y}_t &= \mathbf{A}_0\mathbf{y}_t + \mathbf{A}_1\mathbf{y}_{t-1} + \mathbf{A}_2\mathbf{z}_t + \mathbf{a}_3 + \mathbf{u}_t,\\ \mathbf{u}_t &= \mathbf{B}_0\mathbf{u}_{t-1} + \mathbf{e}_t + \mathbf{B}_1\mathbf{e}_{t-1},\\ \mathbf{z}_t &= \mathbf{C}_0\mathbf{z}_{t-1} + \mathbf{c}_1 + \mathbf{c}_2 t + \mathbf{v}_t.\end{aligned}$$

First, we need to map (6.1) to levels, which gives for the $\mathbf{y}$ equation:

$$\mathbf{A}_0 = \begin{pmatrix} 0 & 0 & 0 & 0 \\ 0.1 & 0 & 0.5 & 0 \\ 0 & 0 & 0 & -0.3 \\ 0 & 0 & 0 & 0 \end{pmatrix}, \quad \mathbf{A}_1 = \begin{pmatrix} 0.9 & 0 & 0 & 0.1 \\ 0 & 0.75 & -0.25 & 0 \\ 0 & 0.2 & 0.8 & 0 \\ 0 & 0 & 0 & 1 \end{pmatrix},$$

$\mathbf{A}_2 = \mathbf{I}_4$; and for the z-equation:

$$\mathbf{C}_0 = \mathbf{0}, \quad \mathbf{c}_1' = (0.001, 0.002, 0.002, 0.001), \quad \mathbf{c}_2' = (0.004, 0, 0, 0),$$

with $\mathbf{v}_t = \mathbf{0}$; and for the error distributions:

$$\mathbf{B}_0 = \begin{pmatrix} 0 & 0 & 0 & 0 \\ 0 & 0.5 & 0 & 0 \\ 0 & 0 & 0.4 & 0 \\ 0 & 0 & 0 & 0 \end{pmatrix}, \quad \mathbf{B}_1 = \mathbf{0}, \quad \mathbf{e}_t \sim \mathsf{N}_4\left[\mathbf{0}, \begin{pmatrix} 0.06 & 0 & 0 & 0.057 \\ 0 & 0.015 & 0 & 0 \\ 0 & 0 & 0.05 & 0 \\ 0.057 & 0 & 0 & 0.15 \end{pmatrix}\right].$$

The following program (called `PcfDgp.ox`) creates an object of the `PcNaiveDgp` class, and sets the parameters for the DGP. It then prints the DGP plus the asymptotic analysis.

```
#include <oxstd.h>
#include <pcnaive.h>

#pragma link("pcnaive.oxo")

main()
{
    decl dgp;                          // dgp container
    dgp = new PcNaiveDgp(4,4);         // create the DGP

    decl a0, a1, var, b0, c1, c2;      // create coefficients
    a0 = <0,0,0,0; 0.1,0,0.5,0; 0,0,0,-0.3; 0,0,0,0>;
    a1 = <0.9,0,0,0.1; 0,0.75,-0.25,0; 0,0.2,0.8,0; 0,0,0,1>;
    var = <0.6,0,0,0.57; 0,0.15,0,0; 0,0,0.5,0; 0.57,0,0,1.5>;
    b0 = <0,0,0,0; 0,0.5,0,0; 0,0,0.4,0; 0,0,0,0>;
    c1 = <0.001; 0.002; 0.002; 0.001>;
    c2 = <0.004; 0; 0; 0>;

    dgp->SetYParameter(a0, a1, unit(4), zeros(4,1));

    dgp->SetUParameter(b0, zeros(4,4));
    dgp->SetDistribution(U_DGP, MVNORMAL, zeros(4,1), var/10);
```

```
    dgp->SetZParameter(zeros(4,4), c1, c2);
    dgp->SetDistribution(Z_DGP, NO_DIST, zeros(4,1),zeros(4,4));

    dgp->Print();                           // print the DGP
    dgp->Asymp();                           // dynamic analysis
}
```

If Ox has been installed correctly, this program can be run using OxRun (this will present the results in a GiveWin text window; alternatively use OXL, the MS-DOS version, or OXLW, the Windows console version). The program cannot be used to recreate the actual dataset, because that was created with PC-NAIVE, which has a different random number generator.

The output shows that there are two unit roots in the companion matrix.

```
Ox version 1.11 (Windows) (C) J.A. Doornik, 1994-96.

----PcNaive DGP ----
y is (4 x 1), z is (4 x 1) and fixed.

y[t] = u[t] + a0 y[t] + a1 y[t-1] + a2 z[t]
a0 =
       0.00000      0.00000      0.00000      0.00000
       0.10000      0.00000      0.50000      0.00000
       0.00000      0.00000      0.00000     -0.30000
       0.00000      0.00000      0.00000      0.00000
a1 =
       0.90000      0.00000      0.00000      0.10000
       0.00000      0.75000     -0.25000      0.00000
       0.00000      0.20000      0.80000      0.00000
       0.00000      0.00000      0.00000       1.0000
a2 =
        1.0000      0.00000      0.00000      0.00000
       0.00000       1.0000      0.00000      0.00000
       0.00000      0.00000       1.0000      0.00000
       0.00000      0.00000      0.00000       1.0000

reduced form y[t] = p0 y[t-1] + p1 z[t] + p2 + w[t]
p0 =
       0.90000      0.00000      0.00000      0.10000
      0.090000      0.85000      0.15000     -0.14000
       0.00000      0.20000      0.80000     -0.30000
       0.00000      0.00000      0.00000       1.0000
p1 =
        1.0000      0.00000      0.00000      0.00000
       0.10000       1.0000      0.50000     -0.15000
       0.00000      0.00000       1.0000     -0.30000
       0.00000      0.00000      0.00000       1.0000
p2 =
       0.00000
       0.00000
       0.00000
       0.00000
```

```
u[t] = b0 u[t-1] + e[t] + b1 e[t-1]
b0 = 0 b1 = 0
e ~ MVN(0,sigma)
sigma=
     0.060000       0.00000       0.00000      0.057000
      0.00000      0.015000       0.00000       0.00000
      0.00000       0.00000      0.050000       0.00000
     0.057000       0.00000       0.00000       0.15000

z[t] = v[t] + c1 + c2 t
c1 =
    0.0010000
    0.0020000
    0.0020000
    0.0010000
c2 =
    0.0040000
      0.00000
      0.00000
      0.00000

v = 0

companion matrix:
 0.9    0    0   0.1  0      0      0  0  0    0    0  0
0.04 1.35  0.1 -0.08  0 -0.415 -0.035  0  0 -0.5 -0.2  0
   0  0.2  1.2 -0.18  0  -0.08  -0.32  0  0    0 -0.4  0
   0    0    0     1  0      0      0  0  0    0    0  0
   1    0    0     0  0      0      0  0  0    0    0  0
   0    1    0     0  0      0      0  0  0    0    0  0
   0    0    1     0  0      0      0  0  0    0    0  0
   0    0    0     1  0      0      0  0  0    0    0  0
   0    0    0     0  0      0      0  0  0    0    0  0
   0    0    0     0  0      0      0  0  0    0    0  0
   0    0    0     0  0      0      0  0  0    0    0  0
   0    0    0     0  0      0      0  0  0    0    0  0

eigenvalues of companion matrix:
         real          imag
       1.0000       0.00000
      0.65000       0.00000
      0.50000       0.00000
      0.40000       0.00000
      0.00000       0.00000
      0.90000       0.00000
      0.00000       0.00000
       1.0000       0.00000
      0.00000       0.00000
      0.00000       0.00000
      0.00000       0.00000
      0.00000       0.00000
```

By itself, two unit roots in the companion matrix are not problematic; but they are here as we created three cointegrating vectors linking the four variables. Thus, the system cannot be I(1).

We can write an additional small Ox program to further analyse the long-run matrix. In the next program (`PcfDgpP0.ox`), we define the long-run matrix $\mathbf{P}_0 = \pi(1) - \mathbf{I}$ as reported above, as well as the α and β' matrices for rank 3 (worked out by hand from the theoretical specification).

```
#include <oxstd.h>

decl mp0 = <   // I - Po
    -0.1,    0,       0,       0.1;
     0.09, -0.15,   0.15,  -0.14;
     0,      0.2,   -0.2,   -0.3;
     0,      0,       0,       0>;

decl ma = <    // alpha, rank = 3
    -0.1,    0,       0;
    -0.01, -0.25,  -0.1;
     0,      0,      -0.2;
     0,      0,       0>;

decl mbt = <   // beta', rank = 3
     1,      0,       0,      -1;
    -0.4,    1,      -1,       0;
     0, -    1,       1,       1.5>;

main()
{
    decl vev, vsv, mu, mv;

    eigen(mp0, &vev);
    decsvd(mp0, &mu, &vsv, &mv);
    print("Rank of long run matrix:", rank(mp0), "\n",
          "eigenvalues of long run matrix", vev,
          "sigular values of long run matrix", vsv);
    print("long-run matrix (alpha*beta')", ma*mbt,
          "alpha orthogonal", nullspace(ma),
          "beta orthogonal", nullspace(mbt'));

    print("alpha orthogonal", mu[][3],
          "beta orthogonal", mv[][3]);
}
```

The output from the program is listed below (with near zeros replaced by zero). The rank of the long-run matrix is reported as three, but as mentioned in §6.8, there are two eigenvalues of zero (the first row is the real part, the second the imaginary part). Next, $\alpha\beta'$ is printed to check if it equals $\mathbf{P}_0$. The `nullspace` function computes $\alpha_\perp$ and $\beta'_\perp$. We could also have factorized $\mathbf{P}_0$ directly using the singular value decomposition, and used the columns which are not part of α and β'. These are the same, as is shown in the output.

```
Rank of long run matrix: 3
eigenvalues of long run matrix
     -0.35000            0      -0.10000       0.00000
      0.00000      0.00000       0.00000       0.00000
sigular values of long run matrix
      0.42136      0.28452      0.064882       0.00000
long-run matrix (alpha*beta')
     -0.10000      0.00000       0.00000       0.10000
     0.090000     -0.15000       0.15000      -0.14000
      0.00000      0.20000      -0.20000      -0.30000
      0.00000      0.00000       0.00000       0.00000
alpha orthogonal
      0.00000
      0.00000
      0.00000
       1.0000
beta orthogonal
            0
      0.70711
      0.70711
            0
alpha orthogonal
      0.00000
      0.00000
      0.00000
       1.0000
beta orthogonal
            0
      0.70711
      0.70711
            0
```

Referring back to page 78, the condition in equation (4.5) has to hold for the DGP to be I(1). The crucial thing to note is that the mean-lag matrix is the identity matrix because there are no variables of lag two or longer. Hence, for the tutorial DGP, the condition becomes:

$$\mathrm{r}\left(\alpha'_{\perp}\beta_{\perp}\right) = n - p.$$

The output shows that $\alpha_{\perp}$ and $\beta_{\perp}$ are orthogonal to each other, so that $\mathrm{r}(\alpha'_{\perp}\beta_{\perp}) = 0$, and not $4 - 3 = 1$. Thus, the DGP is I(2). The claim made in §6.8, namely that adding a little bit of ΔYc_{t-1} to the final equation, can now be inferred easily. A value in the mean-lag matrix at the position of the $*$ would satisfy the I(2) rank condition:

$$\begin{pmatrix} 0 & 0 & 0 & 1 \end{pmatrix} \begin{pmatrix} \cdot & \cdot & \cdot & \cdot \\ \cdot & \cdot & \cdot & \cdot \\ \cdot & \cdot & \cdot & \cdot \\ \cdot & * & * & \cdot \end{pmatrix} \begin{pmatrix} 0 \\ \sqrt{1/2} \\ \sqrt{1/2} \\ 0 \end{pmatrix}.$$

Chapter 7

VAR Modelling: Some Advanced Features

7.1 Introduction

In Chapter 3 we formulated and estimated a system which was a vector autoregression. The modelling sequence progressed as:

VAR in I(1) space
↓
VAR in I(0) space
↓
Parsimonious VAR
↓
Structural model

This chapter discusses some of the features of PcFiml that were not addressed in the previous tutorials. It is assumed that you have some familiarity with the material in the preceding tutorials: required mouse actions or keystrokes are often not given here.

The basis for this chapter is Lütkepohl (1991) (in the remainder referred to as Lütkepohl). Using a data set listed there, we shall replicate many of the calculations and graphs. The purpose is to discuss remaining features of PcFiml, show its flexibility, and explain any differences in results. The emphasis will be on technique, rather than interpretation.

7.2 Loading the Lütkepohl data

The data are listed in Table E.1 of Appendix E in Lütkepohl, and are provided with PcFiml in the file PCFTUT5.IN7. Start GiveWin and load this file (if the default installation was used, the file will be in `\Program files\GiveWin\PcFiml` under Windows NT and 95, and in `\ProgramF\GiveWin\PcFiml` under Windows 3.1).

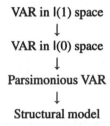

The data are quarterly, and have sample period 1960(1)–1979(4) (with one year used for forecasting):

- *I* investment,
- *Y* income,
- *C* consumption.

These are seasonally adjusted data for West Germany, the units are billions of DM. The levels are graphed in Figure 7.1.

The calculator was used to create logarithms of the variables: $i = \log(I)$, $y = \log(Y)$, $c = \log(C)$, as well as first differences: $Di = \Delta i$, $Dy = \Delta y$, $Dc = \Delta c$:

```
i = log(I);
y = log(Y);
c = log(C);
Di = diff(i, 1);
Dy = diff(y, 1);
Dc = diff(c, 1);
```

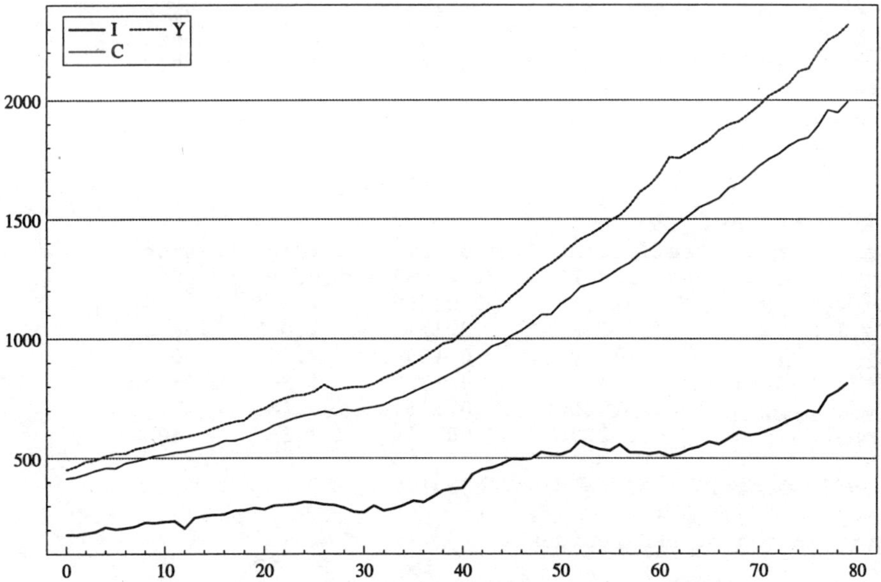

Figure 7.1 Levels of investment, income and consumption.

7.3 Estimating a VAR

Activate Model, Formulate System and set up a two-lag VAR with unrestricted constant. Reduce the estimation sample by one year (that is, estimate up to 1978 (4); estimation yields:

```
EQ( 1) Estimating the urf by OLS  (using PcfTut5.in7)
The present sample is:  1960 (4) to 1978 (4)

URF Equation 1 for Di
Variable       Coefficient     Std.Error  t-value  t-prob
Di_1             -0.31963       0.12546    -2.548  0.0132
Di_2             -0.16055       0.12491    -1.285  0.2032
Dy_1              0.14599       0.54567     0.268  0.7899
Dy_2              0.11460       0.53457     0.214  0.8309
Dc_1              0.96122       0.66431     1.447  0.1526
Dc_2              0.93439       0.66510     1.405  0.1647
Constant         -0.016722      0.017226   -0.971  0.3352

σ = 0.0461479    RSS = 0.1405555086

URF Equation 2 for Dy
Variable       Coefficient     Std.Error  t-value  t-prob
Di_1              0.043931      0.031859    1.379  0.1726
Di_2              0.050031      0.031720    1.577  0.1195
Dy_1             -0.15273       0.13857    -1.102  0.2744
Dy_2              0.019166      0.13575     0.141  0.8882
Dc_1              0.28850       0.16870     1.710  0.0919
Dc_2             -0.010205      0.16890    -0.060  0.9520
Constant          0.015767      0.0043746   3.604  0.0006

σ = 0.0117191    RSS = 0.009064290022

URF Equation 3 for Dc
Variable       Coefficient     Std.Error  t-value  t-prob
Di_1             -0.0024227     0.025676   -0.094  0.9251
Di_2              0.033880      0.025564    1.325  0.1896
Dy_1              0.22481       0.11168     2.013  0.0482
Dy_2              0.35491       0.10941     3.244  0.0019
Dc_1             -0.26397       0.13596    -1.942  0.0565
Dc_2             -0.022230      0.13612    -0.163  0.8708
Constant          0.012926      0.0035256   3.666  0.0005

σ = 0.00944476    RSS = 0.00588743192

correlation of URF residuals
                      Di            Dy            Dc
Di                1.0000
Dy                0.13242       1.0000
Dc                0.28275       0.55526       1.0000

standard deviations of URF residuals
           Di            Dy            Dc
     0.046148      0.011719     0.0094448

loglik=917.05451  log|Ω|=-25.1248   |Ω|=1.22588e-011 T=73
log|Y'Y/T| = -24.425
R^2(LR) = 0.503318  R^2(LM) = 0.198829
```

```
F-test against unrestricted regressors,
  F(18,181) = 2.8306 [0.0002] **
variables entered unrestricted:   Constant

F-tests on retained regressors, F(3, 64)
  Di_1   3.10599 [0.0326] *         Di_2    1.83313 [0.1500]
  Dy_1   3.66382 [0.0168] *         Dy_2    4.89344 [0.0040] **
  Dc_1   6.39472 [0.0007] **        Dc_2   0.750599 [0.5260]

correlation of actual and fitted
             Di           Dy           Dc
      0.35855      0.33793      0.50128
```

Here we have $T = 73$, $k = 7$, so that the t-probabilities come from a Student-t distribution with 66 degrees of freedom. Most statistics (such as the standard errors, standard deviations of URF residuals and correlation of URF residuals) are based on $\widetilde{\Omega}$. To compute σ without degrees-of-freedom correction for the first equation, for example:

$$\widehat{\sigma} = \sqrt{\frac{T-k}{T}}\widetilde{\sigma} = 0.9508 * 0.04615 = 0.0439.$$

7.4 Dynamic analysis

Select Test, Dynamic analysis (the 'rolling cart' icon) to see:

```
Dynamic analysis of the system
Mean lag matrix
                     Di          Dy          Dc
Di              0.64073    -0.37520     -2.8300
Dy             -0.14399     0.11440    -0.26809
Dc            -0.065338    -0.93464     0.30843

Long-run matrix π(1)-I = Po
                     Di          Dy          Dc
Di              -1.4802     0.26059      1.8956
Dy             0.093962     -1.1336     0.27830
Dc             0.031458     0.57973     -1.2862

Long-run covariance
                     Di          Dy          Dc
Di            0.0019289
Dy           0.00049528  0.00024515
Dc           0.00047269  0.00020511  0.00020007

Eigenvalues of π(1)-I
       real     complex     modulus
     -1.639      0.2614       1.659
     -1.639     -0.2614       1.659
    -0.6228      0.0000      0.6228
```

Eigenvalues of companion matrix

λ_i real	complex	modulus	z_i real	complex	modulus
0.5705	0.0000	0.5705	1.75	0.00	1.75
-0.07725	0.4856	0.4917	-0.320	-2.01	2.03
-0.07725	-0.4856	0.4917	-0.320	2.01	2.03
-0.3712	0.0000	0.3712	-2.69	0.00	2.69
-0.3906	0.3891	0.5513	-1.29	-1.28	1.81
-0.3906	-0.3891	0.5513	-1.29	1.28	1.81

The companion matrix for the VAR(2) model $\mathbf{y}_t = \boldsymbol{\pi}_1 \mathbf{y}_{t-1} + \boldsymbol{\pi}_2 \mathbf{y}_{t-2} + \mathbf{v}_t$ is:

$$\begin{pmatrix} \widehat{\boldsymbol{\pi}}_1 & \widehat{\boldsymbol{\pi}}_2 \\ \mathbf{I}_3 & \mathbf{0} \end{pmatrix} = \begin{pmatrix} -0.320 & 0.044 & -0.0024 & -0.161 & 0.0500 & 0.034 \\ 0.146 & -0.153 & 0.225 & 0.115 & 0.0192 & 0.355 \\ 0.961 & 0.289 & -0.264 & 0.934 & -0.0102 & -0.022 \\ 1 & 0 & 0 & 0 & 0 & 0 \\ 0 & 1 & 0 & 0 & 0 & 0 \\ 0 & 0 & 1 & 0 & 0 & 0 \end{pmatrix}$$

All the roots, λ_i, of the companion matrix are inside the unit circle (modulus[1] is less than 1). Or in terms of $z_i = 1/\lambda_i$, all roots are outside the unit circle. The numbers for z_i have been added to the output.

7.5 Forecasting

Static forecasting is possible only if we retain observations for that purpose, so is not feasible given our present selection (if you selected the data sample as described above). However, it is easy to re-estimate the system reserving some observations for static forecasting. Dynamic forecasting requires data over the forecast period on any non-modelled, stochastic variables. When the system is closed, it is feasible computationally to dynamically forecast well beyond the available data period, but the practical value of such an exercise is doubtful for long horizons.

Change the Options dialog to printing of individual forecast statistics. Now re-estimate the VAR on the sample to 1979(4), withholding the four new observations for forecasting, by requiring 4 forecasts. The dialog becomes:

[1]Modulus is defined as: $|a + ib| = \sqrt{(a^2 + b^2)}$. If $x.z = (a + ib)(c + id) = 1$ then $c = a/|x|^2$ and $d = -b/|x|^2$.

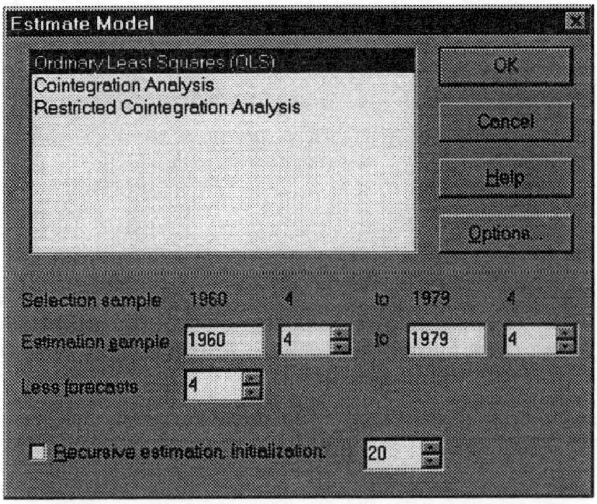

The extra information in the results window is:

```
1-step (ex post) forecast analysis 1979 (1) to 1979 (4)
Parameter constancy forecast tests:
using Ω     Chi^2(12)=16.366 [0.1750]   F(12,66)=1.3638 [0.2059]
using V[e]  Chi^2(12)=15.113 [0.2353]   F(12,66)=1.2594 [0.2638]
using V[E]  Chi^2(12)=15.155 [0.2331]   F(12,66)=1.2629 [0.2616]

Descriptive statistics of forecast errors
Means
               Di            Dy            Dc
         0.033911 -0.00023377  -0.0011706

Standard Deviations
               Di            Dy            Dc
         0.035924     0.011472     0.018025

Correlation matrix
               Di            Dy            Dc
Di         1.0000
Dy        0.15380       1.0000
Dc        0.61229      0.82748        1.0000

matrix of forecast standard errors
               Di            Dy            Dc
1979-1   0.048054     0.012203    0.0098349
1979-2   0.047793     0.012137    0.0097814
1979-3   0.047830     0.012146    0.0097889
1979-4   0.049567     0.012588     0.010145

Forecast tests, single Chi^2(3)
              using Ω                        using V[e]
    1979-1      0.911299 [0.8227]           0.840431 [0.8398]
    1979-2       6.17238 [0.1035]            5.75482 [0.1242]
```

```
    1979-3        7.35949 [0.0613]               6.85109 [0.0768]
    1979-4        1.92292 [0.5886]               1.66676 [0.6443]
```

The Graphics analysis dialog can be used to plot the outcomes: mark forecasts and forecast chow tests – use Zoom sample to extend the pre-forecast period plotted if desired. Figure 7.2 shows the outcomes.

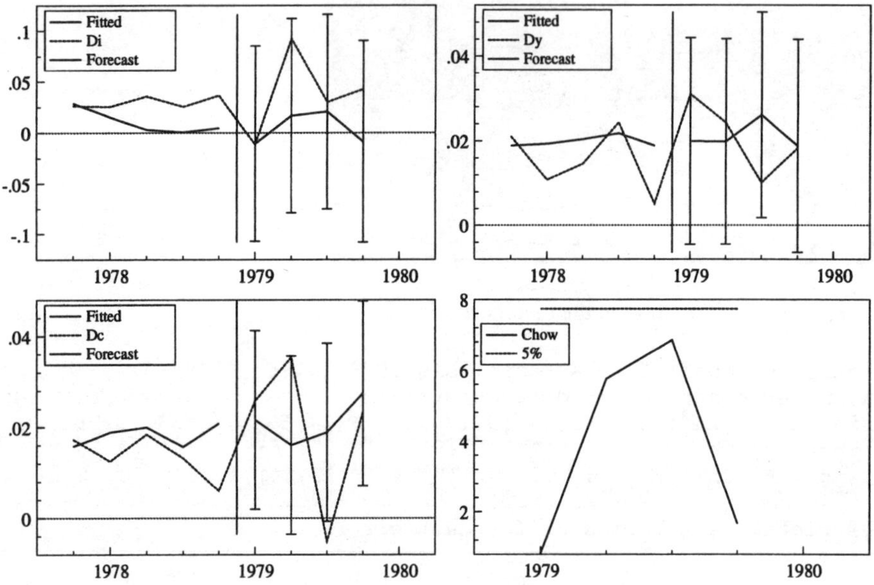

Figure 7.2 1-step forecasts with parameter-variance based error bars.

We can compare these results to the output from dynamic forecasting. Access its dialog, select four 1-step forecasts, and press the write button to obtain the second set of 1-step forecast standard errors. Next, select four dynamic forecasts in the Dynamic forecast dialog and write:

```
1-step forecast (S.E. using Ω) for Di
     1979-1    -0.01081094  (   0.046148)
     1979-2     0.01654712  (   0.046148)
     1979-3     0.02068541  (   0.046148)
     1979-4   -0.008732301  (   0.046148)

1-step forecast (S.E. using Ω) for Dy
     1979-1     0.01991084  (   0.011719)
     1979-2     0.01981556  (   0.011719)
     1979-3     0.02607487  (   0.011719)
     1979-4     0.01877805  (   0.011719)

1-step forecast (S.E. using Ω) for Dc
     1979-1     0.02162873  (  0.0094448)
     1979-2     0.01605427  (  0.0094448)
```

```
        1979-3      0.01884599   (   0.0094448)
        1979-4      0.02744401   (   0.0094448)

Dynamic (ex ante) forecast (S.E. using Ω) for Di
        1979-1     -0.01081094   (    0.046148)
        1979-2      0.01078091   (    0.048656)
        1979-3      0.02111570   (    0.049033)
        1979-4      0.01235830   (    0.049424)

Dynamic (ex ante) forecast (S.E. using Ω) for Dy
        1979-1      0.01991084   (    0.011719)
        1979-2      0.02034868   (    0.012199)
        1979-3      0.01698059   (    0.012314)
        1979-4      0.02060094   (    0.012430)

Dynamic (ex ante) forecast (S.E. using Ω) for Dc
        1979-1      0.02162873   (   0.0094448)
        1979-2      0.01465388   (   0.0097549)
        1979-3      0.01982574   (    0.010787)
        1979-4      0.01872030   (    0.010832)
```

The first set of 1-step forecast standard errors (under the heading 'matrix of forecast standard errors') takes parameter uncertainty into account, the second set (created with the Dynamic forecasting dialog) does not. Hence in the second set, the standard errors remain constant (at $\tilde{\sigma}$), and are smaller than the full forecast standard errors. Figure 7.3 gives four dynamic forecasts with these constant error bands, together with some pre-forecast data. Compared to Figure 7.2, the error bars are noticeably smaller only for *Dc*.

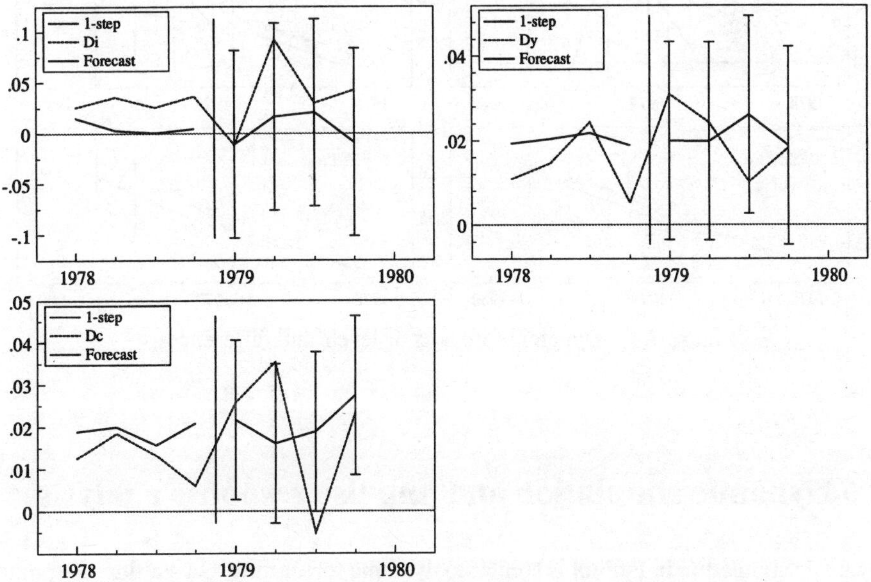

Figure 7.3 1-step forecasts with error-variance based bars.

It is often interesting to have forecasts of both the levels and the differences. This can be achieved using identities. Add *i, y, c* with one lag to the system, and mark the current-dated levels as I(dentities). Re-estimate keeping four forecasts. Activate Model, Formulate Model, and define the three identities as:

$$i = i\_1, Di,$$
$$y = y\_1, Dy,$$
$$c = c\_1, Dc.$$

Also delete any lagged levels from the stochastic equations, so these remain in differences. Estimate by FIML. The results should be as before. Figure 7.4 shows four dynamic forecasts, with error bars, both for the differences and the levels (the identities have to be marked in the dialog). Note the rapid increase in the height of the error bars for the levels.

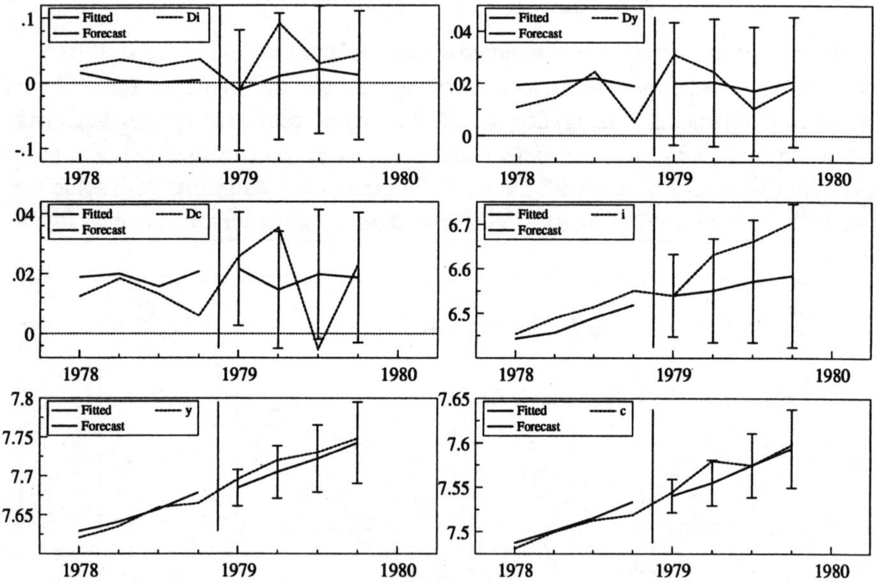

Figure 7.4 Dynamic forecasts of levels and differences.

7.6 Dynamic simulation and impulse response analysis

Dynamic simulation in PcFiml is similar to dynamic forecasting, but starting at a point inside the estimation sample. Select Simulation and Impulses:

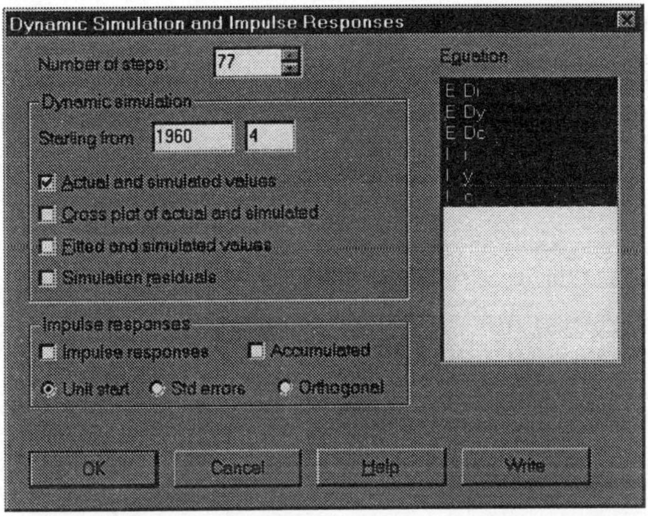

Marking identities and checking 'Actual and simulated values' gives Figure 7.5.

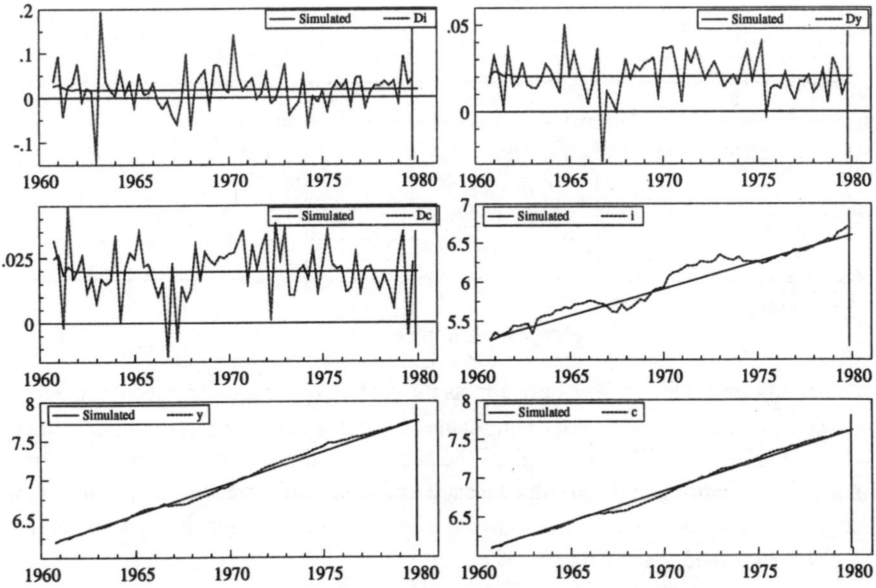

Figure 7.5 Dynamic simulation for levels and differences.

Notice the complete lack of explanatory power for simulated differences after the first couple of data points, apart from the mean. That the levels appear to track well is therefore essentially an artefact due to the residuals summing to zero (see Pagan, 1989).

7.6.1 Impulse response analysis

Impulse response analysis amounts to dynamic simulation from an initial value of zero, where a shock at $t = 1$ in a variable is traced through. This amounts to graphing powers of the companion matrix. As with dynamic simulation, for linear systems, most information is given in the dynamic analysis, but graphs might be easier to interpret than numbers.

Re-estimate the previous system without the identities. Select Simulation and Impulses, unmark the actual and simulated value check box, set eight impulse responses with standard error initial values. This gives Figure 7.6.

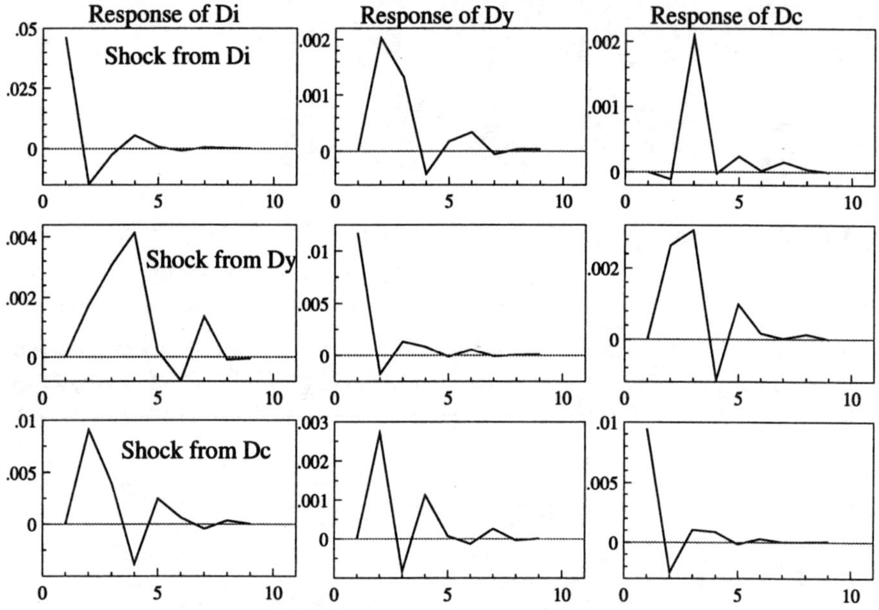

Figure 7.6 Impulse responses.

Selecting unit initial values only affects the scaling of the graphs. Accumulated responses are also available. Mark Accumulated responses and unmark *Di* and *Dy* in the list box. The resulting Figure 7.7 gives the accumulated responses to a standard error impulse in *Dc*. Orthogonalized responses are available, but these alter the conditioning assumptions, and care is required to avoid violating weak exogeneity conditions (see e.g., Ericsson, Hendry and Mizon, 1997).

7.7 Sequential reduction and information criteria

Re-estimate an initial VAR in differences with four lags and U(nrestricted) *Constant*, using 1978(4) as the last observation for estimation. Remove one lag of all variables

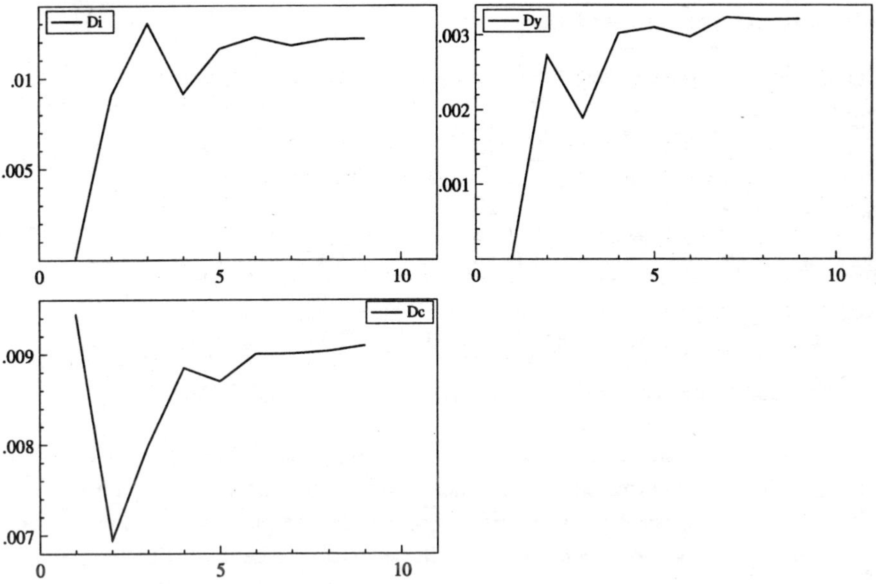

Figure 7.7 Accumulated responses to an impulse in *Dc*.

at a time, and re-estimate over the same sample (which is automatic, and necessary for Progress to work). Clear the status of the *Constant* for the 'VAR' without any lags, so at least one regressor remains. Preserving only the line with the likelihood for each model gives ($T = 71$ in each case):

```
4 lags: loglik=900.6904 log|Ω|=-25.371  |Ω|=9.57792e-012
3 lags: loglik=893.4712 log|Ω|=-25.168  |Ω|=1.17378e-011
2 lags: loglik=891.0930 log|Ω|=-25.101  |Ω|=1.25511e-011
1 lag:  loglik=878.6425 log|Ω|=-24.750  |Ω|=1.78236e-011
0 lags: loglik=867.0181 log|Ω|=-24.423  |Ω|=2.4729e-011
```

Remember that these are based on $\widehat{\mathbf{\Omega}} = \frac{1}{T}\widehat{\mathbf{V}}'\widehat{\mathbf{V}}$, whereas most other statistics use $\widetilde{\mathbf{\Omega}} = \frac{1}{T-k}\widehat{\mathbf{V}}'\widehat{\mathbf{V}}$ ($\widehat{\Sigma}_u$ in Lütkepohl). Conversion for an n-dimensional VAR is:

$$\log\left|\widetilde{\mathbf{\Omega}}\right| = \log\left|\widehat{\mathbf{\Omega}}\right| + n\log\left(\frac{T}{T-k}\right).$$

Model/Progress lists the log-likelihoods, Schwarz, Hannan-Quinn and Akaike information criteria, and F-tests for the model reduction.

system	T	p		log-likelihood	SC	HQ	AIC
5	71	3	OLS	867.01815	-24.243	-24.301	-24.423
4	71	12	OLS	878.64257	-24.030	-24.260	-24.750
3	71	21	OLS	891.09302	-23.840	-24.244	-25.101
2	71	30	OLS	893.47122	-23.367	-23.943	-25.168
1	71	39	OLS	900.69040	-23.030	-23.779	-24.372

```
Tests of system reduction
System 4 --> System 5: F( 9,158) =    2.5338 [0.0097]**
System 3 --> System 5: F(18,175) =    2.6470 [0.0006]**
System 2 --> System 5: F(27,172) =    1.8618 [0.0094]**
System 1 --> System 5: F(36,166) =    1.7475 [0.0101]*

System 3 --> System 4: F( 9,151) =    2.6014 [0.0081]**
System 2 --> System 4: F(18,167) =    1.4797 [0.1028]
System 1 --> System 4: F(27,164) =    1.4410 [0.0863]

System 2 --> System 3: F( 9,143) =   0.44573 [0.9079]
System 1 --> System 3: F(18,158) =   0.88530 [0.5970]

System 1 --> System 2: F( 9,136) =    1.3212 [0.2314]
```

The F-form of the likelihood ratio test (see §10.8) is expected to have better small-sample behaviour than the uncorrected χ^2 form (these can be easily computed by hand, then use GiveWin's Data, Tail probability to check significance). Sequential reduction based on the F-tests would accept system $1 \to 2 \to 3$, but reject further reduction to system 4. A direct reduction from system $1 \to 4$ only has a p-value of 8.6%; the large number of restrictions somewhat hides the significance of the second lags. Thus, we began with an appropriate reduction when using 2 lags.

PcFiml includes all parameters (including coefficient of the constant) in the computation of the information criteria. The outcomes are easily verified, using the equations in (14.66) and the T and k as listed. Here both SC and HQ have a minimum for system 5, which only has a constant term: that seems an excessive simplification, and would certainly fail on diagnostic testing (try and see: Vector AR 1-2 $\mathsf{F}(18, 175) =$ 2.4318[0.0016]** for example).

7.8 Diagnostic checking

Re-estimate the VAR using two lags (use Recall to find it on the System formulation), and the estimation sample 1960(4)–1978(4).

Residual correlograms, see Figure 7.8, are obtained through the graphic analysis, here shown up to lag 12 (residual-based vector tests featured in the tutorial sections 3.2 and 5.1). Activate Test, Test (multivariate)..., and mark Vector portmanteau selecting 12 lags, and Vector normality.

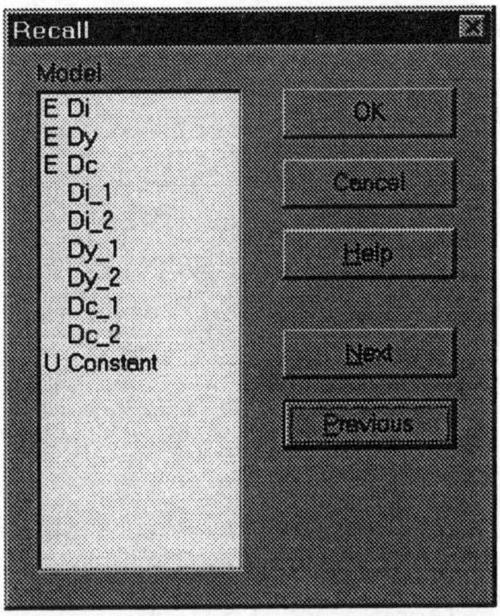

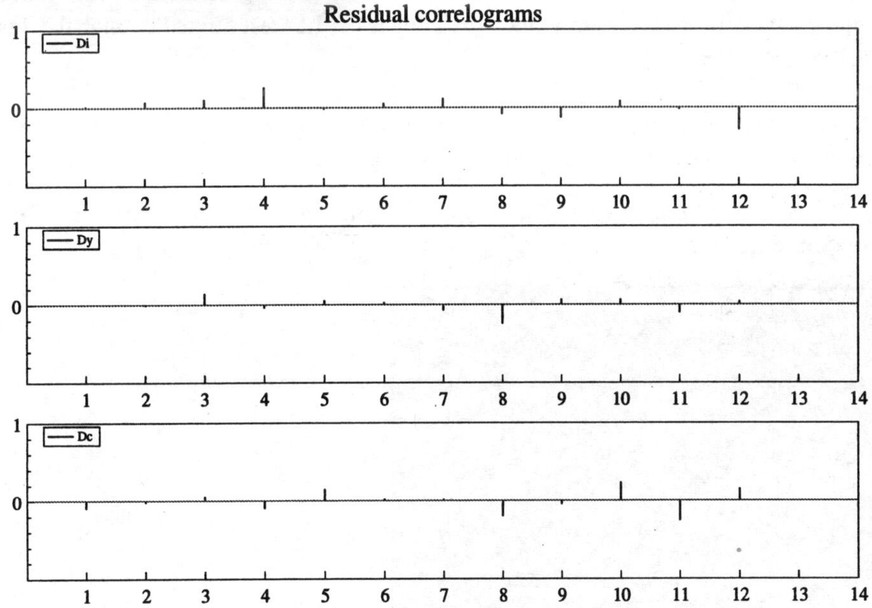

Figure 7.8 Residual correlograms.

```
Vector portmanteau statistic for 12 lags, 73 observations: 81.93

Vector normality test for residuals
The present sample is:  1960 (4) to 1978 (4)
Skewness
       1.0479     -0.96504      -2.7431
Excess kurtosis
       3.3502      0.93428      0.18474

Vector normality Chi^2( 6)=     21.685 [0.0014] **
```

These tests are discussed in §10.9.2.1 and §10.9.2.3 respectively. The reported skewness and excess kurtosis are not of the individual residuals, but of the transformed residuals. They are approximately standard normally distributed; here one of each is significant. Overall, normality is clearly rejected. More detail on the vector normality test is provided in Doornik and Hansen (1994). It is preferred to the test in Lütkepohl for two reasons. First, the test reported by PcFiml employs a small-sample correction. Second, Lütkepohl's test uses Choleski decomposition, resulting in a test which is not invariant to reordering the dependent variables, for example:

$$\begin{aligned} &Di,\ Dy,\ Dc: \chi^2(6) = 7.84\ \ [0.2501] \\ &Dc,\ Dy,\ Di: \chi^2(6) = 25.6\ \ [0.0003] **\end{aligned}$$

The reported portmanteau statistic is already corrected for degrees of freedom. A more appropriate test for vector error autocorrelation is the LM test offered through the Test dialog. Select three lags:

```
Testing for vector error autocorrelation from lags 1 to 3
Chi^2(27)=32.807 [0.2035] and F-Form(27,161)=1.1448 [0.2962]
```

We shall try to replicate this manually. First save the residuals of the VAR: Test, Store in database.

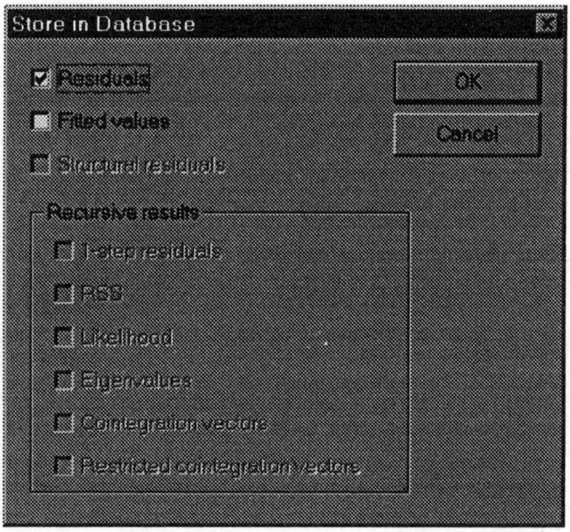

Select Residuals and accept the default names *VDi, VDy, VDc* (remember to return to GiveWin to accept names). Access the database and replace the initial three missing values of these residuals by 0. We wish to label the lagged dependent variables as unrestricted. However, PcFiml does not allow this. To bypass this restriction, create lags in the Calculator, removing the underscore from the name (the code is in PCFTUT5.ALG):

```
Di1 = lag(Di, 1);
Di2 = lag(Di, 2);
Dy1 = lag(Dy, 1);
Dy2 = lag(Dy, 2);
Dc1 = lag(Dc, 1);
Dc2 = lag(Dc, 2);
```

Access Formulate System, remove the lagged dependent variables and add the newly created variables. Change the classification from endogenous to unrestricted. Also classify the *Constant* as unrestricted. Add three lags of the residuals, removing the current variables. Estimate this system:

```
R² (LR) = 0.40077   R² (LM) = 0.149802

F-test against unrestricted regressors,
F(27, 161) = 1.1448 [0.2962]
variables entered unrestricted:
 Constant        Di1        Di2        Dy1        Dy2        Dc1
      Dc2

F-tests on retained regressors, F(3, 55)
   VDi_1  0.119026 [0.9485]          VDi_2    3.20095 [0.0302] *
   VDi_3   1.72735 [0.1720]          VDy_1    3.04572 [0.0363] *
   VDy_2   1.32545 [0.2754]          VDy_3    4.54787 [0.0064] **
   VDc_1   3.17154 [0.0313] *        VDc_2  0.131043 [0.9412]
   VDc_3   2.03838 [0.1191]
```

Now remove the lagged residuals, clear the status of some unrestricted variables (to allow estimation), and ask for a progress, keeping only the two most recent systems marked:

```
Progress to date

system    T    p           log-likelihood      Schwarz Hannan-Quinn
   16    73   21  OLS           917.05451       -23.89        -24.29
   15    73   48  OLS           935.74650       -22.82        -23.72

Tests of model reduction
System 15 --> System 16: F(27, 161) =    1.1448 [0.2962]
```

The original F-form has been replicated twice, and is computed as in (10.111)–(10.113), here:

$$\frac{1-(1-\mathrm{R}^2(\mathrm{LR}))^{1/2.92}}{\mathrm{R}^2(\mathrm{LR})^{1/2.92}} * \frac{59.5 * 2.92 - 12.5}{3 * 9}.$$

The LM test follows from (10.133):

$$73 * 3 * \mathrm{R}^2(\mathrm{LM}).$$

7.9 Parameter constancy

Chow tests for constancy are readily computed and graphed following recursive estimation. For a system, both single equation and system tests are computed, whereas for a model only the system tests are available. Estimate the original VAR(2) over 1960(4)–1978(4) by RLS using 40 observations for initialization. Don't use any unrestricted variables (which would have their coefficients fixed at the full sample values). Then estimate the same system by recursive FIML. The single-equation Chow tests are not graphed, and we may obtain Figure 7.9.

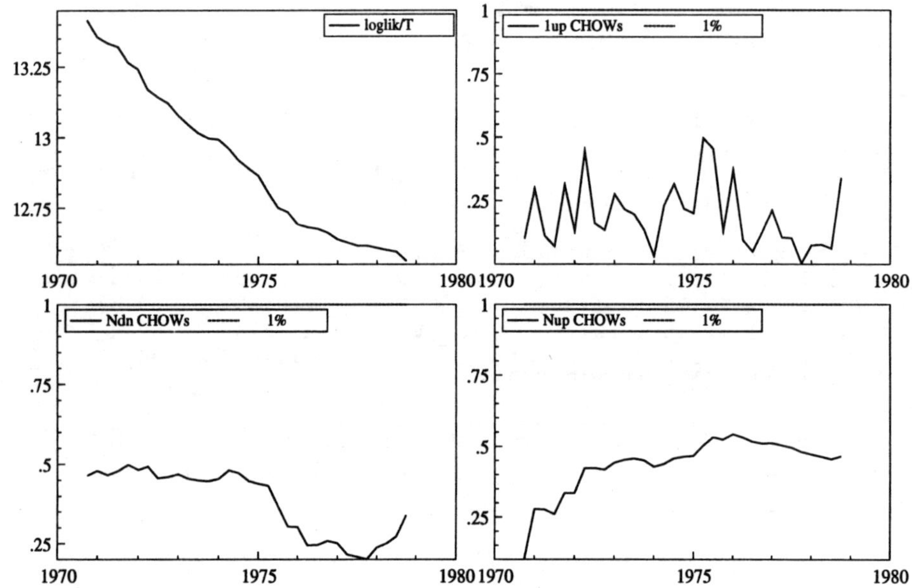

Figure 7.9 Log-likelihood/T and system Chow tests.

The values in these graphs can be written to the results editor. To make the amount of data more manageable, estimate up to 1974(2) with 51 observations for initialization. This gives four recursive estimates. Again: make sure that there are no unrestricted variables. Activate the Recursive graphics dialog, mark loglik/T and the three Chow tests and press the Write button:

```
               loglik/T, (t),          loglik
1973-3         12.5913 (  52)         692.523
1973-4         12.5720 (  53)         691.462
1974-1         12.5686 (  54)         691.218
1974-2         12.5369 (  55)         689.474

System:   1 step Chow tests
1973-3    F(  3, 42) =        0.83707 [0.4812]
1973-4    F(  3, 43) =        0.56380 [0.6418]
```

```
1974-1    F(  3, 44) =        0.13087 [0.9412]
1974-2    F(  3, 45) =        0.98173 [0.4098]

System:   N↑ step Chow tests
1973-3    F(  3, 42) =        0.83707 [0.4812]
1973-4    F(  6, 84) =        0.69318 [0.6557]
1974-1    F(  9,102) =        0.50407 [0.8686]
1974-2    F( 12,111) =        0.61214 [0.8281]

System:   N↓ step Chow tests
1973-3    F( 12,111) =        0.61214 [0.8281]
1973-4    F(  9,104) =        0.54269 [0.8402]
1974-1    F(  6, 88) =        0.53974 [0.7766]
1974-2    F(  3, 45) =        0.98173 [0.4098]
```

These results can be replicated using dummy variables. Use the calculator to create four impulse dummy variables (in the calculator, click the Dummy button, then enter period of the impulse, accept and name as shown below, copied from our results file, and usable in the algebra, or use PCFTUT5A.ALG):

```
i1973p3 = dummy(1973,3, 1973,3);
i1973p4 = dummy(1973,4, 1973,4);
i1974p1 = dummy(1974,1, 1974,1);
i1974p2 = dummy(1974,2, 1974,2);
```

Add the four dummies to the VAR, no lags, and clear their status. Estimate by OLS up to 1974(2). This effectively removes the last four observations. The 1-step Chow test amounts to adding one observation at a time, and testing its significance.

Towards the end of the output, you will see:

```
F-tests on retained regressors, F(3, 42)
   i1973p3      0.837065 [0.4812]
```

similarly for the other three dummies. Deleting that dummy, re-estimating gives the same result in the progress:

```
Tests of model reduction
System  1 --> System  2: F( 3, 42) = 0.83707 [0.4812]
```

Similarly for the second 1-step Chow test: estimate up to 1973(4), adding the dummy for the last observation, then delete the dummy:

```
F-tests on retained regressors, F(3, 43)
   i1973p4      0.563801 [0.6418]

Tests of system reduction
System  3 --> System  4: F( 3, 43) = 0.56380 [0.6418]
```

Next estimate the system up to 1974(2) with all four dummies. Then delete one dummy at a time, starting with *i1973p3*:

```
system
     9 :  no dummies, constant only;
     8 :  constant,                               i1974p2;
     7 :  constant,                     i1974p1, i1974p2;
     6 :  constant,           i1973p4, i1974p1, i1974p2;
     5 :  constant, i1973p3, i1973p4, i1974p1, i1974p2.
```

The progress report, after some reordering of the F-tests is:

```
Progress to date
system    T    p          log-likelihood      Schwarz Hannan-Quinn
     9   55   21   OLS         689.47425       -23.54        -24.01
     8   55   24   OLS         691.21763       -23.39        -23.92
     7   55   27   OLS         691.46192       -23.18        -23.78
     6   55   30   OLS         692.52290       -23.00        -23.67
     5   55   33   OLS         694.11985       -22.84        -23.57

Tests of system reduction
System  5 --> System  9: F(12, 111) =   0.61214 [0.8281]
System  6 --> System  9: F( 9, 104) =   0.54269 [0.8402]
System  7 --> System  9: F( 6,   88) =   0.53974 [0.7766]
System  8 --> System  9: F( 3,   45) =   0.98173 [0.4098]

System  5 --> System  6: F( 3,   42) =   0.83707 [0.4812]
System  5 --> System  7: F( 6,   84) =   0.69318 [0.6557]
System  5 --> System  8: F( 9, 102) =   0.50407 [0.8686]
System  5 --> System  9: F(12, 111) =   0.61214 [0.8281]
```

The forecast Chow tests correspond to testing the significance of *i1973p3* in the system with all the dummies, then of both *i1973p3* and *i1973p4*, then of the first three dummies etc. In other words, the first statistic tests stability for one period, the next for two periods, then for three periods, etc. (the forecast horizon increases). The break-point Chow tests have a shrinking forecast horizon: four from 1973(2), three from 1973(3), etc.

Estimation up to 1973(2) is equivalent to estimation up to 1974(2) with four dummies. However, we cannot do a likelihood ratio test for constancy by comparing reported log-likelihood values for the different periods, as these are based on different Ts. For example:

$$1960(4) - 1973(2): \ \widehat{\ell}_1 = 637.86208 \ \ T_1 = 51,$$
$$1960(4) - 1973(3): \ \widehat{\ell}_1 = 650.37394 \ \ T_1 = 52,$$

would give a negative likelihood-ratio test. To 'rebase' $\widehat{\ell}_1$ to T_2, compute:

$$\left(\frac{-2}{T_1}\widehat{\ell}_1 + n\log\left(\frac{T_1}{T_2}\right)\right)\frac{T_2}{-2}.$$

Using $T_2 = 55$ yields the log-likelihood values as given in the progress report.

The parameter constancy tests that are reported when observations are withheld for forecasting test the same hypothesis as the $N\uparrow$ system Chow test, but are based on the Wald principle. Estimation with 1973(3) and 1973(3)–1973(4) as forecasts respectively yields:

```
1-step (ex post) forecast analysis 1973 (3) to 1973 (3)
Parameter constancy forecast tests:
using Ω     Chi²(3)=2.9742 [0.3956]   F(3,44)=0.9914 [0.4057]
using V[e] Chi²(3)=2.6308 [0.4521]   F(3,44)=0.87693 [0.4603]
using V[E] Chi²(3)=2.6308 [0.4521]   F(3,44)=0.87693 [0.4603]

1-step (ex post) forecast analysis 1973 (3) to 1973 (4)
Parameter constancy forecast tests:
using Ω     Chi²(6)=4.8958 [0.5573]   F(6,44)=0.81596 [0.5634]
using V[e] Chi²(6)=4.3874 [0.6244]   F(6,44)=0.73123 [0.6270]
using V[E] Chi²(6)=4.3903 [0.6240]   F(6,44)=0.73172 [0.6266]
```

Estimation with *i1973p3* up to 1973(3), and both *i1973p3* and *i1973p4* estimated up to 1973(4), allows us to test the significance of the dummies through the general restrictions test option:

```
Wald test for general restrictions
GenRes Chi²( 3) =      2.6308 [0.4521]

Wald test for general restrictions
GenRes Chi²( 6) =      4.3903 [0.6240]
```

Finally, note that the small sample correction to obtain the F-test in PcFiml is different from that in Lütkepohl. The test statistic ξ_1 of (10.46) is identical to $\widehat{\lambda}_h$ of equation (4.6.13) in Lütkepohl. PcFiml computes (ξ_1 already has a degrees of freedom correction)

$$\eta_1 = \frac{\xi_1}{nH}$$

in contrast to

$$\bar{\lambda}_h = \widehat{\lambda}_h \frac{T}{nH\,(T+k)}.$$

The F-tests from recursive estimation and progress use Rao's approximation, see (10.111)–(10.113).

7.10 Non-linear parameter constraints

Reduced-rank VAR models can be estimated through CFIML, which is FIML with non-linear parameter constraints. Consider the two-lag VAR $\mathbf{y}_t = \boldsymbol{\pi}_1\mathbf{y}_{t-1} + \boldsymbol{\pi}_2\mathbf{y}_{t-2} + \mathbf{v}_t$ imposing rank-one restrictions on $\boldsymbol{\pi}_1$ and $\boldsymbol{\pi}_2$:

$$\boldsymbol{\pi}_1 = \mathbf{bc}' = \begin{pmatrix} b_1c_1 & b_1c_2 & b_1c_3 \\ b_2c_1 & b_2c_2 & b_2c_3 \\ b_3c_1 & b_3c_2 & b_3c_3 \end{pmatrix}, \quad \boldsymbol{\pi}_2 = \mathbf{bd}' = \begin{pmatrix} b_1d_1 & b_1d_2 & b_1d_3 \\ b_2d_1 & b_2d_2 & b_2d_3 \\ b_3d_1 & b_3d_2 & b_3d_3 \end{pmatrix}.$$

Note that this is different from the cointegration analysis, which is reduced rank estimation of the long-run matrix (Chapter 4). Numbering the coefficients as

$$(\pi_1 \; \pi_2) = \begin{pmatrix} \&0 & \&1 & \&2 & \&3 & \&4 & \&5 \\ \&6 & \&7 & \&8 & \&9 & \&10 & \&11 \\ \&12 & \&13 & \&14 & \&15 & \&16 & \&17 \end{pmatrix}$$

this corresponds to the following restrictions (in PCFTUT5.RES):

```
&0=&6*&1/&7;   &2=&8*&1/&7;    &12=&6*&13/&7;  &14=&8*&13/&7;
&3=&9*&1/&7;   &5=&11*&1/&7;   &15=&9*&13/&7;  &17=&11*&13/&7;
&4=&10*&1/&7;  &16=&10*&13/&7;
```

For the computations we follow Lütkepohl, and first remove the means from the variables. Setup a system which regresses *Di, Dy, Dc* on a *Constant* (clear status) over 1960(2)–1978(4):

```
EQ( 1) Estimating the unrestricted reduced form by OLS
The present sample is:  1960 (2) to 1978 (4)

URF Equation 1 for Di
Variable      Coefficient     Std.Error  t-value  t-prob
Constant         0.018108     0.0054039    3.351  0.0013

URF Equation 2 for Dy
Variable      Coefficient     Std.Error  t-value  t-prob
Constant         0.020711     0.0013951   14.846  0.0000

URF Equation 3 for Dc
Variable      Coefficient     Std.Error  t-value  t-prob
Constant         0.019871     0.0012010   16.546  0.0000
```

Then save the residuals as *VDi, VDy, VDc*; remember to switch to GiveWin to name them – you may choose overwrite if these already exist in the database. Setup the two-lag VAR in *VDi* etc., but without a constant and estimate over 1960(4)–1978(4), the URF will have loglik=916.96685. In the Options dialog, switch automatic maximization off. Next, formulate this VAR as a model, but reorder the regressors as *VDi_1, VDy_1, VDc_1, VDi_2, VDy_2, VDc_2*. Estimate by FIML, which, of course, gives the same results. Activate Model, Constrained FIML (or CFIML) which will lead to the Constraints editor, and enter the above restrictions (or load them from the file PCFTUT5.RES, supplied with PcFiml). Estimate the model (strong convergence is quickly reached).

The restrictions involve division by &7, and a grid reveals the singularity when parameter 3 (&7) is zero: see Figure 7.10. The grid computations could fail if the third parameter gets too close to zero. Unlike version 8 of PcFiml, the current version uses analytical differentiation throughout, and the maximization procedure works better: the area of numerical singularity around &7 has been reduced considerably. To experiment, you could try setting &7 to a small negative or positive number and see what happens. When too close to zero, the algorithm results in very large parameters, with failure to improve in the line search.

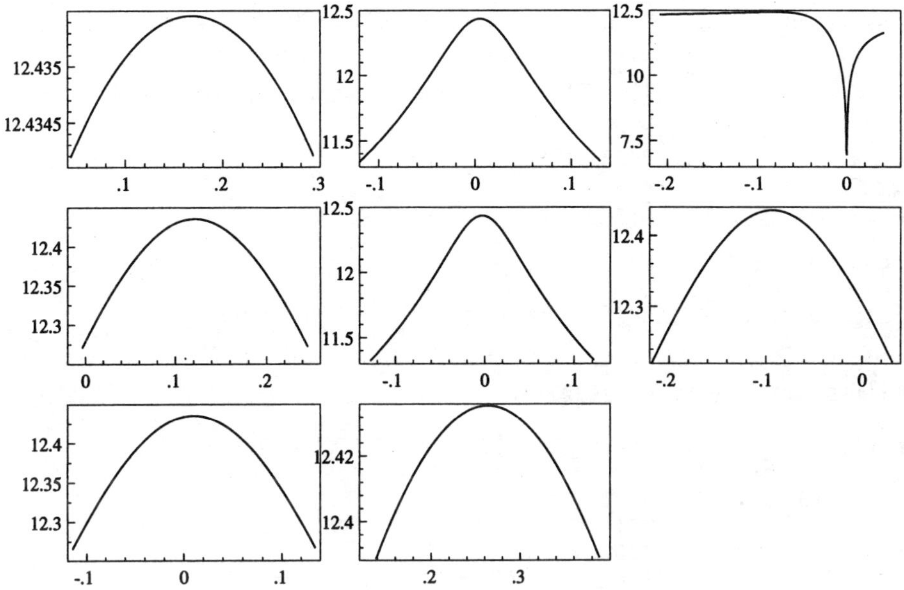

Figure 7.10 Grid of reduced rank VAR.

The output is:

```
EQ(11) Estimating the model by CFIML
       The present sample is:  1960 (4) to 1978 (4)

Equation 1 for VDi
Variable      Coefficient     Std.Error  t-value  t-prob
VDi_1           -0.010653           ---
VDy_1             0.16832       0.30891    0.545  0.5875
VDc_1            -0.24531           ---
VDi_2           0.0054104           ---
VDy_2             0.18793           ---
VDc_2           -0.020656           ---

σ = 0.0475615

Equation 2 for VDy
Variable      Coefficient     Std.Error  t-value  t-prob
VDi_1           0.0052701     0.0073303    0.719  0.4745
VDy_1           -0.083272      0.079334   -1.050  0.2974
VDc_1             0.12136       0.11398    1.065  0.2906
VDi_2          -0.0026767     0.0060408   -0.443  0.6590
VDy_2           -0.092973      0.087626   -1.061  0.2923
VDc_2            0.010219      0.030861    0.331  0.7415

σ = 0.0119145
```

```
Equation 3 for VDc
Variable       Coefficient      Std.Error  t-value  t-prob
VDi_1            -0.016678            ---
VDy_1              0.26353       0.087897     2.998  0.0037
VDc_1             -0.38407            ---
VDi_2            0.0084710            ---
VDy_2              0.29423            ---
VDc_2            -0.032339            ---

σ = 0.00933563

loglik=907.78816  log|Ω|=-24.8709  |Ω|=1.58016e-011
T=73
LR test of over-identifying restrictions:
chi²(10) = 18.3574 [0.0492] *

LR test of restrictions: Chi²(10) = 18.3574 [0.0492] *

correlation of residuals
                    VDi          VDy          VDc
VDi              1.0000
VDy             0.10106       1.0000
VDc             0.26111      0.58193       1.0000
```

This model can be further explored. For example, eigenvalues of the companion matrix reveal that it is rank 2:

```
Dynamic analysis of the model
Mean lag matrix
                      VDi          VDy          VDc
 VDi          -0.00016823     -0.54419      0.28662
 VDy          8.3228e-005      0.26922     -0.14180
 VDc          -0.00026339     -0.85200      0.44875

Long-run matrix π(1)-I = Po
                     VDi          VDy          VDc
 VDi              -1.005       0.3563      -0.2660
 VDy            0.002594       -1.176       0.1316
 VDc           -0.008202       0.5573       -1.416

Long-run covariance
                     VDi          VDy          VDc
 VDi            0.002239
 VDy          0.00008252   0.0001226
 VDc           0.0001011 0.00009366 0.00009732

Eigenvalues of π(1)-I
           real       complex      modulus
        -1.0000        0.0000       1.0000
         -1.598        0.0000        1.598
        -1.0000        0.0000       1.0000
```

```
Eigenvalues of companion matrix
              real        complex       modulus
           -0.2389         0.2507        0.3462
           -0.2389        -0.2507        0.3462
                 0         0.0000             0
                 0         0.0000             0
                 0         0.0000             0
                 0         0.0000             0
```

Another option is recursive estimation. The recursive tests for over-identifying restrictions and Chow tests are shown in Figure 7.11. Many possibilities remain, but we leave you now to explore on your own.

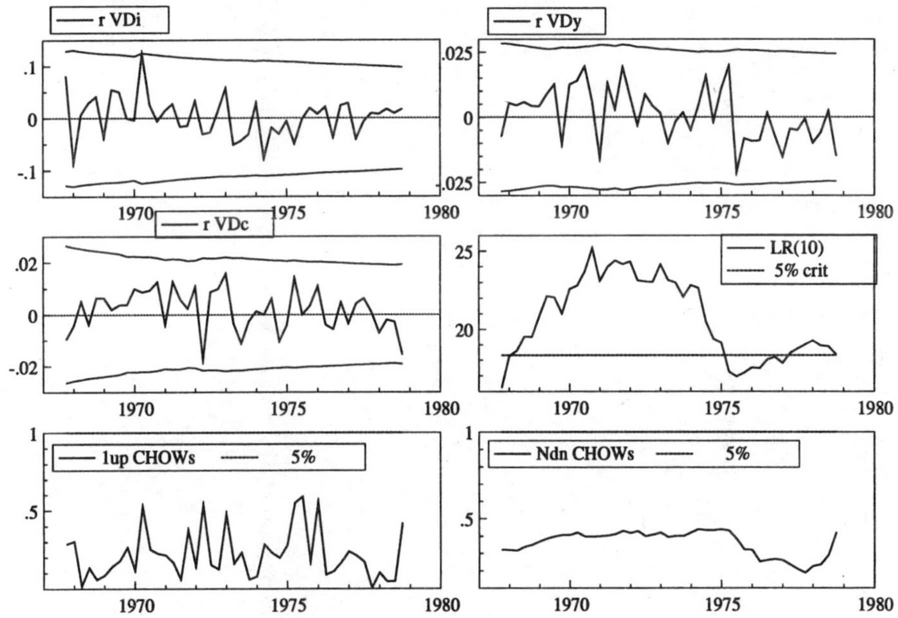

Figure 7.11 Recursive tests of VAR with reduced rank coefficients.

Part III

The Econometrics of PcFiml

Chapter 8

An Introduction to the Econometrics of PcFiml

8.1 Summary of Part III

Linear system modelling is structured from the general to the specific. The general model is a dynamic statistical system. This is the maintained model, defined by the variables of interest, their distributions, whether they are modelled or non-modelled, and their lag polynomials. Thus, for example, four variables may be modelled as linearly dependent on another two, intercept and linear deterministic trend, with a maximum of three lags. System formulation, the status of the variables therein, dynamic specification, estimation, and evaluation are all discussed. Because of their central role, integration and cointegration are analysed in a separate chapter. Once a congruent system is available, a postulated econometric model can be evaluated against it, or a model of the system developed.

An econometric model is usually a simultaneous equations structure, which is treated as a model of the system. It is intended to isolate autonomous, parsimonious relationships based on economic theory. The system must adequately characterize the data evidence, and the model must account for the results obtained by the system. Model formulation and identification, estimation (using an estimator generating equation), encompassing, and model evaluation are considered. Numerical optimization is considered separately.

All these issues are addressed at various levels in Part III. Chapter 8 provides an introduction, with a more rigorous review in Chapter 10 (system modelling), Chapter 11 (cointegration analysis), and Chapter 12 (simultaneous equations modelling). Chapter 9 presents a brief summary of the matrix algebra required to understand the derivations in Chapters 10–12. Chapter 13 discusses numerical optimization and numerical accuracy. Although separate subjects, these are fundamental to a computer program such as PcFiml. Finally, Chapter 14, which is in Part IV, lists all the output (both numerical and graphical) generated by PcFiml. That chapter also repeats the econometric notation, and is to a large extent self-contained (if preceded by this chapter).

8.2 Introduction

Simultaneous equations models have been criticized from a number of viewpoints (see Sims, 1980, and Hendry, Neale and Srba, 1988, among others). Such criticisms arise in part because dynamic system modelling usually commences from (an assumed known) structural form of the process generating the data, from which the reduced form is derived (see, Judge, Griffiths, Hill, Lütkepohl and Lee, 1985, Chapter 14, for example). Such an approach raises numerous difficulties: in particular, by not first testing the validity of the reduced form, which constitutes the baseline for the test of over-identifying restrictions, the credibility of the structural parameter estimates is unclear. A more methodical and ordered approach to linear dynamic system modelling circumvents most of the extant criticisms (see Hendry and Mizon, 1993, and Hendry and Doornik, 1994).

The dynamic system is the maintained statistical model. Its initial specification is crucial to the success of the entire analysis since a simultaneous equations structure is a model of that system (see, for example, Spanos, 1986). Given linearity, the system is defined by the variables of interest, their distributions, their classification into modelled and non-modelled variables (although the latter may be absent, as in a vector autoregressive representation or VAR), and the lag polynomials applicable to every variable. Section 8.3 describes the theoretical formulation; §8.4 discusses the statistical system and the status of its variables; §8.5 considers the specification of the system dynamics to ensure that the residuals are innovation processes; then §8.6 considers system evaluation. At that stage, a congruent system is available against which any postulated econometric model can be evaluated. The step of mapping to a stationary, or non-integrated (I(0)) representation would follow §8.5 and is discussed in §8.7.

An econometric model imposes a structure on a statistical system to isolate autonomous relationships with parsimonious interpretations based on economic theory. Necessary conditions for a valid model are that the system adequately characterizes the data evidence (congruency), that its parameters are uniquely identified, and that the model accounts for the results obtained by the system (parsimonious encompassing). System congruency conditions are the focus of §8.3–§8.7 as just described; the latter are the subject of §8.8–§8.9. Thus, §8.8 considers model formulation and identification; §8.9 considers model evaluation by testing its parsimonious encompassing of the system.

This sequence of stages aims to structure the empirical modelling of small linear dynamic systems, and represents the steps needed to ensure valid parsimonious representations of the data generation process (DGP) within a general-to-specific modelling methodology: see Mizon (1977), Hendry (1987) and Pagan (1987). Moreover, the same stages are inherent in the working of PcFiml. The statistical system must be formulated first (the selection of variables, their classification into modelled and non-modelled, the choice of lag polynomials, and any deterministic components such as constants and seasonals etc.). Then the system must be estimated, and evaluated for congruency (homoscedastic innovation errors; valid weak exogeneity of any conditioning variables for the parameters of interest; I(0) regressors, and constant parameters). Only then can a model of the system be formulated, checked for identification, estimated, and its parsimonious encompassing of the system investigated. The process of specification is in fact straightforward and quick, and is designed to avoid endless and directionless revisions of postulated models in the light of adverse diagnostic test findings.

8.3 Economic theoretical formulation

Starting from a general economic theoretical framework of intertemporal optimizing behaviour by rational agents, empirical research in economics is often faced with the issue of jointly modelling a number of potentially interdependent variables (denoted $\mathbf{y}_t$) as a function of a second set not to be modelled (denoted $\mathbf{z}_t$). The subject-matter theory specifies systems of relationships of the form:

$$\mathbf{B}(L)\,\boldsymbol{\xi}_t = \mathsf{E}\left[\boldsymbol{\Gamma}(L)\,\boldsymbol{\zeta}_t \mid \mathcal{I}_t\right] \tag{8.1}$$

where $(\boldsymbol{\xi}_t, \boldsymbol{\zeta}_t)$ are $(n \times 1)$ and $(q \times 1)$ vectors of the theoretical variables of interest for which $(\mathbf{y}_t, \mathbf{z}_t)$ will be taken as the observable correspondences, $\mathsf{E}[\cdot|\mathcal{I}_t]$ is the conditional expectations operator, and $\mathcal{I}_t$ denotes the information set available to agents at the start of decision time-period t. Also, L denotes the lag operator such that $L^h x_t = x_{t-h}$. The lag polynomial matrices $\mathbf{B}(\cdot)$ and $\boldsymbol{\Gamma}(\cdot)$ may involve leads (L^{-1} etc.), in which case the latent constructs become expectations of future variables. If only finite lags are involved, then $\mathbf{B}(L)$ and $\boldsymbol{\Gamma}(L)$ can be written as:

$$\mathbf{B}(L) = \sum_{j=0}^{h} \mathbf{B}_j L^j \quad \text{and} \quad \boldsymbol{\Gamma}(L) = \sum_{j=0}^{h} \boldsymbol{\Gamma}_j L^j$$

where h is the maximum lag length (some of the elements of $\{\mathbf{B}_j, \boldsymbol{\Gamma}_j\}$ may be zero). It is often assumed that there are sufficient restrictions to identify the $\{\mathbf{B}_j, \boldsymbol{\Gamma}_j\}$, some of which may be zero with others normalized, and that these parameters are constant.

While the economic theory may appear to offer a complete specification of the elements of the system determining $\boldsymbol{\xi}_t$, its practical implementation confronts a number of serious difficulties as follows:

(1) Decision time and observation time-periods need not coincide, such that one decision period may equal N observation periods (N could be greater than or less than unity). Thus $\mathbf{B}(L)$ and $\boldsymbol{\Gamma}(L)$ may not correspond to the relevant empirical lag polynomials characterizing the agents' responses.

(2) The theory may be incomplete (for example, involve *ceteris paribus* conditions) and variables other than $(\boldsymbol{\xi}_t, \boldsymbol{\zeta}_t)$ may in fact be directly involved in the decision process. Thus, the theory system must be reinterpreted as marginalized with respect to such variables so that apparent cross restrictions on $\mathbf{B}(\cdot)$, $\boldsymbol{\Gamma}(\cdot)$ may be invalid, and even identification (in the sense of uniqueness) could fail.

(3) The contents of $\mathcal{I}_t$ could be empirically mis-specified since the economists' perception of the information set selected by agents need not coincide one-to-one with that actually used: it could be both over- and under-inclusive in important aspects.
(4) How $\mathcal{I}_t$ enters the joint density (and thereby determines $\mathsf{E}[\cdot|\mathcal{I}_t]$) may not be as postulated, and hence the formulation may fail to characterize the actual behaviour of the agents.
(5) The assumption that $\boldsymbol{\xi}_t$ can be explained as a function of $\boldsymbol{\zeta}_t$ without modelling the latter may be inappropriate, and doubtless would be seen as such in a larger model. Even if the assumption is correct, it is insufficient to ensure that $\mathbf{z}_t$ need not be modelled empirically: an example is multi-step forecasting when past values of $\boldsymbol{\xi}_t$ influence $\boldsymbol{\zeta}_t$.
(6) The correspondence of $(\boldsymbol{\xi}_t, \boldsymbol{\zeta}_t)$ to $(\mathbf{y}_t, \mathbf{z}_t)$ may be tenuous and may itself be dynamic (for example, permanent income; choice of a 'money' magnitude etc.).
(7) Evolution, innovation, learning, regime shifts, and other forms of non-stationarity are not yet easily incorporated into intertemporal theoretical analyses but are crucial elements to model in any empirical study.

Thus, while any given economic theory potentially offers a useful initial framework, theory is not so much definitive as guiding. Hence, theory should not constitute a strait-jacket to empirical research in the sense that theory models should not simply be imposed on data. If an empirical counterpart to a theory is imposed on data, it will exclude many phenomena: it is valid to test such restrictions under the assumption that the theory is correct. However, for any inferences concerning $\mathbf{B}(\cdot)$ and $\mathbf{\Gamma}(\cdot)$ (and hence the underlying theory) to be sustainable, accurate estimates of the inferential uncertainty are required. This necessitates establishing both the innovation variance for $\mathbf{y}_t$ given the available information, and a set of constants or invariants $\boldsymbol{\theta}$ characterizing the data density, on which $\mathbf{B}(\cdot)$ and $\mathbf{\Gamma}(\cdot)$ therefore depend. In the present state of knowledge, modelling is inevitable if such objectives are to be achieved (see Hendry *et al.*, 1988).

First, consider the case where $(\mathbf{y}_t, \mathbf{z}_t)$ are accurate measures of $(\boldsymbol{\xi}_t, \boldsymbol{\zeta}_t)$ respectively and $\mathbf{z}_t \in \mathcal{I}_t$ so that a conditional analysis is valid, and future expectations do not affect outcomes (this is a convenient simplification here, but is not necessary and may not coincide with agent behaviour in some markets). Thus, the counterpart of (8.1) in terms of observable variables becomes:

$$\mathsf{E}\left[\mathbf{y}_t \mid \mathbf{z}_t, \mathbf{X}_0, \mathbf{x}_1, \ldots, \mathbf{x}_{t-1}\right] = \mathbf{p}_0 \mathbf{z}_t + \sum_{i=1}^{h} \mathbf{p}_i \mathbf{x}_{t-i} \tag{8.2}$$

where $\mathbf{x}_t' = (\mathbf{y}_t' : \mathbf{z}_t')$, and $\mathbf{X}_0$ denotes the set of initial conditions, with h being the longest lag. Only current and lagged values of observable variables enter this formulation, so that if it is a solved-out version of the theory system (for example, eliminating future values) its parameters $\boldsymbol{\phi}$ will be functions of the parameters in the marginal model for $\mathbf{z}_t$. Thus the constancy of ϕ will depend on the constancy of that marginal model; this point applies even more forcefully to closed (or VAR) representations. Of course, the marginal model for $\mathbf{z}_t$ may itself be studied for constancy, but any conclusions about its behaviour depend on precisely the same considerations as those currently being discussed. Equally, the constancy of the $\{\mathbf{p}_i\}$ could be ascertained directly, and if failure results (that is, the $\{\mathbf{p}_i\}$ are non-constant), a revised specification is clearly needed. The recursive procedures incorporated in PcFiml offer a powerful tool for this task.

In the present setting, the observable system in (8.2) comprises the most unrestricted model to be entertained. If the $\{\mathbf{p}_i\}$ are empirically constant, then:

$$\mathbf{v}_t = \mathbf{y}_t - \mathsf{E}\left[\mathbf{y}_t \mid \mathbf{z}_t, \mathbf{x}_{t-1}, \ldots, \mathbf{x}_{t-h}\right] \tag{8.3}$$

is an innovation process against the available information, with variance $\mathsf{E}[\mathbf{v}_t\mathbf{v}_t'] = \boldsymbol{\Omega}_t$. Direct tests for $\{\mathbf{v}_t\}$ being homoscedastic and white noise are feasible, and the value of continued modelling requires both that such tests are applied and that satisfactory outcomes result. If so, the system is data-congruent and it seems worth developing a parsimonious model: Spanos (1986) refers to (8.3) as the statistical model, and a parsimonious, interpretable representation thereof as the econometric model. The main advantage of first formulating the statistical model is that later tests (for example, tests of over-identifying restrictions) can be conducted against a valid background, so awkward circles of the kind arising in simple-to-general searches are avoided (see Hendry, 1979).

When writing a computer program like PcFiml, the dichotomy of a system versus a model thereof (or of a statistical versus an econometric model) is essential, since every so-called structural model entails a reduced form which is a restriction of the system. If the former is deemed valid, the latter must be also, so tests of it are valid. As noted above, prior to specifying structural models, the program requires the specification of the data set $\mathbf{X}_T^1 = (\mathbf{x}_1 \ldots \mathbf{x}_T)$, the maximum lag h, and the status of modelled or non-modelled for the elements of $\mathbf{x}_t$. Together, these define the system. Estimators of the parameters of interest ϕ correspond to minimizing $|\boldsymbol{\Omega}|$ with respect to ϕ subject to various restrictions (that is, parsimonious interpretations of the $\{\mathbf{p}_i\}$).

In this framework, a test of over-identifying restrictions is equivalent to a test of whether the restricted reduced form (RRF) parsimoniously encompasses the unrestricted reduced form (URF) (see Hendry and Mizon, 1993). If this hypothesis is not rejected, the model constitutes a valid reduction of the system and as such is more interpretable, more robust and (being lower-dimensional) allows more powerful tests for mis-specification. The next issue is whether the theoretical model is consistent with the empirical model: this is testable in principle, but the practical difficulties are great for forward-looking or non-linear models and incomplete specifications of $\mathcal{I}_t$. Some considerations for expectations models versus feedback representations are discussed in Hendry (1988) and Favero and Hendry (1992).

Next, consider the case where $\mathbf{z}_t \notin \mathcal{I}_t$. Either a lag formulation could be used or, when a set $\mathbf{z}_t^*$ is available ($\mathbf{Z}_{t-h}^{t-k^*}$ in general), the system should be extended to incorporate these additional variables as instruments. Such variables could enter (8.1) directly, in which case the initial system needs reformulating, or enter only through affecting the marginal process for $\mathbf{z}_t$. It is a testable restriction that they matter only via the marginal model for $\mathbf{z}_t$, but to do so requires modelling $\{\mathbf{z}_t\}$.

Particular economic theory implementations cannot be discussed in the abstract, but readers doubtless have examplars in mind when consulting this book. Standard cases include highly aggregate macro-models; models of sectors (such as the monetary or labour sector); or small systems that commence by endogenizing all variables to allow tests of conditioning assumptions (such as when modelling consumers' expenditure).

8.4 The statistical system

The statistical system is the Haavelmo distribution defined by specifying the variables of interest, their status (modelled or not), their degree of integration, data transformations, the retained history of the process, and the sample period. As above, $\{\mathbf{x}_t\}$ denotes the complete vector of observable variables of interest suggested by previous research, economic theory and the objectives of the analysis, available over a sample period of size T. The statistical generating mechanism is denoted by $\mathsf{D_X}\left(\mathbf{X}_T^1|\mathbf{X}_0,\boldsymbol{\theta}\right)$, where $\mathbf{X}_0$ is the set of initial conditions and $\boldsymbol{\theta} \in \Theta \subseteq \mathbb{R}^N$ is the parameter vector in an N-dimensional parameter space Θ. Writing $\mathbf{X}_{t-1} = (\mathbf{X}_0\mathbf{x}_1\ldots\mathbf{x}_{t-1}) = \left(\mathbf{X}_0 : \mathbf{X}_{t-1}^1\right)$, $\mathsf{D_X}(\cdot)$ is sequentially factorized as:

$$\mathsf{D_X}\left(\mathbf{X}_T^1 \mid \mathbf{X}_0,\boldsymbol{\theta}\right) = \prod_{t=1}^{T} \mathsf{D_x}\left(\mathbf{x}_t \mid \mathbf{X}_{t-1},\boldsymbol{\theta}\right), \tag{8.4}$$

where $\boldsymbol{\theta}$ allows for any necessary transient parameters.

Since $\mathbf{x}_t' = (\mathbf{y}_t' : \mathbf{z}_t')$, then $\mathbf{X}_T^{1\prime} = \left(\mathbf{Y}_T^{1\prime} : \mathbf{Z}_T^{1\prime}\right)$ where $\mathbf{y}_t$ is the $n \times 1$ vector of endogenous variables and $\mathbf{z}_t$ is the $q \times 1$ vector of variables which will not be modelled.[1] To treat $\mathbf{z}_t$ as a valid conditioning vector requires that $\mathbf{z}_t$ be weakly exogenous for the parameters of interest $\boldsymbol{\phi}$ (see Engle, Hendry and Richard, 1983). If so, inference in the conditional distribution of $\mathbf{y}_t$, given $\mathbf{z}_t$ and the history of the process, involves no loss of information relative to analysing the joint distribution of $\mathbf{x}_t$. Map from $\boldsymbol{\theta} \mapsto \boldsymbol{\lambda} = \mathbf{f}(\boldsymbol{\theta}) \in \boldsymbol{\Lambda}$ where $\mathbf{f}(\cdot)$ is 1–1, then from (8.4):

$$\prod_{t=1}^{T} \mathsf{D_x}\left(\mathbf{x}_t|\mathbf{X}_{t-1},\boldsymbol{\theta}\right) = \prod_{t=1}^{T} \mathsf{D_{y|z}}\left(\mathbf{y}_t|\mathbf{z}_t,\mathbf{X}_{t-1},\boldsymbol{\lambda}_1\right) \mathsf{D_z}\left(\mathbf{z}_t,|\mathbf{X}_{t-1},\boldsymbol{\lambda}_2\right). \tag{8.5}$$

Thus, if $\boldsymbol{\phi}$ is a function of $\boldsymbol{\lambda}_1$ alone, and $\boldsymbol{\lambda}_1$ and $\boldsymbol{\lambda}_2$ are variation free, so that $(\boldsymbol{\lambda}_1 : \boldsymbol{\lambda}_2) \in \boldsymbol{\Lambda}_1 \times \boldsymbol{\Lambda}_2$, then $\mathbf{z}_t$ is weakly exogenous for $\boldsymbol{\phi}$. When the same parameters enter both $\boldsymbol{\lambda}_1$

[1] The system may be closed as in a VAR, in which case there are no non-modelled variables $\mathbf{z}_t$, except possibly deterministic variables such as a constant, trend or seasonals.

and $\boldsymbol{\lambda}_2$, as with cross-equation restrictions linking the conditional and marginal models, then weak exogeneity is liable to be violated, leading to a loss of information from analysing only the conditional distribution. Such information loss could entail just inefficiency, but could also entail a loss of structurality. This formulation is a direct application of the principles for reducing a process to a model thereof, and clarifies when reduction is valid.

If, in addition, $\mathbf{y}$ does not Granger cause $\mathbf{z}$ (see Granger, 1969), then the marginal distribution $\mathsf{D}_{\mathbf{z}}(\mathbf{z}_t|\mathbf{X}_{t-1}, \boldsymbol{\lambda}_2)$ can be simplified without loss to $\mathsf{D}_{\mathbf{z}}(\mathbf{z}_t|\ \mathbf{Z}_{t-1}, \boldsymbol{\lambda}_2)$, so that $\mathbf{z}_t$ is strongly exogenous for $\boldsymbol{\phi}$. This condition is needed to sustain conditional dynamic, or multi-period, forecasts and conditional dynamic simulation.

Finally, if $\mathbf{z}_t$ is weakly exogenous for $\boldsymbol{\phi}$, and $\boldsymbol{\lambda}_1$ is invariant to changes in $\boldsymbol{\lambda}_2$, then $\mathbf{z}_t$ is super exogenous for $\boldsymbol{\phi}$ (see Engle and Hendry, 1993).

Since we restrict attention to linear systems, the $\{\mathbf{x}_t\}$ will generally have been transformed from the original raw data such that linearity is a reasonable approximation. Consequently, we commence by selecting $\mathbf{y}_t$ and $\mathbf{z}_t$ and specifying the statistical structure as in (8.5). The econometric model then seeks to isolate the autonomous relationships with interpretable parameters, having an economic theory basis, while still remaining statistically consistent with the system.

8.5 System dynamics

Having assumed linearity, specified the menu comprising $\{\mathbf{x}_t\}$, and classified the variables into $\{\mathbf{y}_t\}$ and $\{\mathbf{z}_t\}$, the system formulation is complete when the degrees and roots of every lag polynomial are specified.[2] Let:

$$\mathbf{y}_t \mid \mathbf{z}_t, \mathbf{X}_{t-1} \sim \mathsf{N}_n \left[\mathbf{p}_0 \mathbf{z}_t + \sum_{i=1}^{h} \mathbf{p}_i \mathbf{x}_{t-i}, \boldsymbol{\Omega} \right], \tag{8.6}$$

so that the longest lag is h periods and the conditional distribution is normal. Then the conditional system of n linear equations for $t = 1, \ldots, T$ is:

$$\mathbf{y}_t = \sum_{i=1}^{m} \boldsymbol{\pi}_{1i} \mathbf{y}_{t-i} + \sum_{j=0}^{r} \boldsymbol{\pi}_{2j} \mathbf{z}_{t-j} + \mathbf{v}_t \text{ where } \mathbf{v}_t \sim \mathsf{N}_n \left[\mathbf{0}, \boldsymbol{\Omega} \right], \tag{8.7}$$

and $h = \max(r, m)$, noting that $\mathbf{p}_0 = \boldsymbol{\pi}_{20}$ and $\mathbf{p}_i = (\boldsymbol{\pi}_{1i} : \boldsymbol{\pi}_{2i})$ for $i = 1, \ldots, h$. A subset of the variables in $\mathbf{y}_t$ can be linked by identities but otherwise $\boldsymbol{\Omega}$ is symmetric, positive definite and unrestricted. Then (8.7) is the general, unrestricted, conditional dynamic system once r and m are specified. Let $\boldsymbol{\Pi} = (\boldsymbol{\pi}_{11} \ldots \boldsymbol{\pi}_{1m} \boldsymbol{\pi}_{20} \ldots \boldsymbol{\pi}_{2r})$, then $\boldsymbol{\Pi}$

[2] For estimation, models of the system need not be complete but must be fully specified (see Richard, 1984).

and $\mathbf{\Omega}$ are variation-free and are the parameters of interest in the sequential conditional distribution, though not necessarily the parameters of interest in the overall analysis.

At this stage, the main requirement is that the system in (8.7) should be a congruent representation of the data, since it will be the specification against which all other simplifications are tested, and hence is the baseline for encompassing: see Hendry and Richard (1982, 1989) and Mizon and Richard (1986). Congruency requires that:

(1) $\{\mathbf{v}_t\}$ is a homoscedastic innovation process against $\mathbf{X}_{t-1}$, which depends on the adequate specification of the lag structure (see Hendry, Pagan and Sargan, 1984);
(2) $\mathbf{z}_t$ is weakly exogenous for $(\mathbf{\Pi}, \mathbf{\Omega})$ (see Engle *et al.*, 1983); and:
(3) $(\mathbf{\Pi}, \mathbf{\Omega})$ is constant $\forall t$ (see Hendry and Richard, 1983).

Once the system is congruent, a structural model of that system can be developed. Although the system (8.7) corresponds to what is often called the unrestricted reduced form (URF), it is the initial formulation and not a derived representation based on a prior structural specification. This is an important difference, since if the system is mis-specified, owing to residual autocorrelation, parameter non-constancy, and so on, further restrictions on it will be invalid, and tests thereof will be against an invalid baseline. In the conventional approach, where the structural model is estimated first, tests of the structural over-identifying restrictions against the URF are conditional on untested assumptions about the validity of the latter. When the URF is itself a parsimonious specification, assumptions about its validity are less than fully plausible.

The selection of r and m is usually data-based, given a prior maximum lag length. Since (8.7) is a statistical model, parsimony is not essential at this stage, whereas ensuring that the $\{\mathbf{v}_t\}$ are innovations is crucial for later inferences. This argument supports commencing with an over-parameterized representation. Although the context is multivariate, lag selection is susceptible to the usual approaches (see, for example, Hendry *et al.*, 1984).

The next issue for valid inference concerns the degree of integratability of the time series in $\{\mathbf{x}_t\}$ since the correct critical values of tests are different between I(0) and I(1) or higher orders of integration (for an overview, see Banerjee, Dolado, Galbraith and Hendry, 1993, Hendry, 1995, and Johansen, 1995b). Moreover, equilibrium correction mechanisms (ECMs) – which are isomorphic to cointegration in linear models – play a fundamental role in stabilizing economic behaviour and attaining long-run targets, as well as implementing insights from economic theory into dynamic statistical analyses, see §8.7.

8.6 System evaluation

If system residuals are not innovations, or parameters are statistically non-constant over time, then the distributions of likelihood ratio tests will not correspond to those conventionally assumed even after the transformation to I(0) variables. Restricting the parameterization by structural formulations of the system, without changing the conditioning or lag assumptions, cannot remove, but could camouflage, such problems. System evaluation seeks to reduce the chances of imposing restrictions on a system only to discover at a later stage that the framework cannot provide an adequate representation of the data.

There is a wide range of hypotheses to be investigated corresponding to the three basic information sets of past, present and future data, applied to the system as a whole rather than to single equations isolated from it (as in PcGive). The modelling procedures and tests are vector analogues of those arising for single equations albeit that modelling a system is more difficult than modelling a single conditional relationship. System tests of congruency can be constructed for vector residual autocorrelation (for example, Lagrange Multiplier tests for dependence between $\mathbf{v}_t$ and $\mathbf{v}_{t-1}$), vector heteroscedasticity (for example, testing whether squared residuals depend on squared functions of conditioning variables), dynamic mis-specification (the significance of a longer lag $(\mathbf{y}_{t-m-1}, \mathbf{z}_{t-r-1})$), weak exogeneity (modelling $\mathbf{z}_t$ as a function of $(\mathbf{y}_{t-i}, \mathbf{z}_{t-i};\ i = 1, \ldots, h)$ and perhaps further lagged non-modelled variables, and testing cross-equation independence from the $\mathbf{y}_t$ system), and constancy (using recursive procedures). Weak exogeneity is also indirectly testable via super exogeneity tests which include tests of $(\mathbf{\Pi}, \mathbf{\Omega})$ being constant. Some of the $\mathbf{z}_t$ could be dummy variables so that the corresponding parameters are transients. Normality is useful but not essential in a linear formulation, and is also testable. For example, the various constancy statistics from multivariate RLS match those from univariate RLS closely, so the analysis of PcGive applies to, for example, break-point tests of one equation from the system or the system as a whole. The formulae for forecast statistics are also similar. Details of all the available tests in PcFiml are presented in Chapter 10 for the system.

The weak exogeneity of $\mathbf{z}_t$ for the parameters of interest in the system remains important. Subject to a correct specification of the marginal system for $\mathbf{z}_t$, the errors on the conditional system could be tested for being uncorrelated with those in the marginal system. The difficulty lies in appropriately formulating the marginal system, especially when conditioning is desired because of anticipated non-constancy in the marginal process. Direct tests on the common presence of the cointegrating vectors in both marginal and conditional systems at least check for weak exogeneity of $\mathbf{z}_t$ for the long-run parameters (see Chapter 11).

8.7 The impact of I(1) on econometric modelling

At first sight, unit-root econometrics seems wholly different from stationary econometrics. On the statistical side, the limiting distributions of estimators and tests are functionals of Brownian motions, so the forms of analysis, the resulting distributions and the associated critical values of tests are usually different. On the conceptual side, the treatment of many 'problems' differs for integrated data. For example, collinearity problems may be owing to including in a relationship all the elements in a cointegrating combination (a 'problem' which cannot be solved by deleting variables); and measurement errors may be irrelevant (if I(0)) or even more serious than usual (if I(1) and not cointegrated). Parameter change may lead to confusing an I(1) process with an I(0) subject to shifts (see Hendry and Neale, 1991) and so on.

However, both the statistical and conceptual differences seem less marked on second sight. Many functionals of Brownian motions in fact have normal distributions (for a summary, see Banerjee and Hendry, 1992). Moreover, even with I(1) data, many tests have conventional distributions; and conditioning later tests on the I(1) decision for the number of cointegrating combinations allows them to be treated as having conventional distributions once variables are reduced to I(0) (see e.g. Johansen, 1992a). Further, I(0) and I(1) are more like the ends of a continuum than discrete entities (see Molinas, 1986): a root of nearly -1 on a moving-average error in a unit-root autoregression essentially cancels the latter, leaving a process which is empirically similar to white noise. Conversely, a stationary process with a root near unity may be better treated as if it were I(1) in samples of the size common in economics (see, for example, Campbell and Perron, 1991, for a survey). In practice, therefore, modelling decisions may sensibly be conditioned on the outcome of unit-root tests, even if theory tests remain open to question (as with tests for 'persistence' of shocks).

In cointegrated processes, weak exogeneity of the conditioning variables for the parameters of interest remains as vital as it has proved to be in stationary processes – even for the long-run parameters (see Johansen, 1992b, and Hendry, 1995). One necessary condition is the absence of cointegrating vectors in other equations, and system modelling seems advisable until weak exogeneity has been ascertained (see Hendry and Doornik, 1994, for further details).

On the positive side, a number of benefits are clear. The Granger representation theorem links cointegration to equilibrium correction mechanisms (ECMs), so that ECMs do not necessarily violate rationality in an I(1) world. Thus, the links between economic theory or long-run equilibrium reasoning and data modelling have been placed on a sounder footing. Other problems appear in a new light. For example, a linear system is invariant under non-singular linear transforms, but usually its parameters are altered by such transforms. However, in I(1) processes, the cointegrating vector β is an invariant of a linear system. Further, β is also invariant to seasonal adjustment by a diagonal scale-preserving seasonal filter (like X-11: see Ericsson, Hendry and Tran, 1994).

Conditional models of I(1) data essentially complete the circle to reinstate structural dynamic models as a viable research vehicle. Now it is possible to test for the existence of a long-run relation before devoting resources to modelling it. Weak exogeneity of a subset of the variables for the long-run parameters simplifies doing so by allowing contemporaneous conditioning. Once a long-run relation is established, then conditional on a reduction from I(1) to I(0), the analysis can proceed as a reduction of the system to a parsimonious and interpretable econometric model thereof. The tutorials in Part II follow this approach through all the steps of an empirical application.

8.8 The econometric model and its identification

The main criterion for the validity of the system is its congruence, since that is a necessary condition for efficient statistical estimation and inference. An econometric model is a restricted version of a congruent system which sustains an economic interpretation, consistent with the associated theory. All linear structural models of (8.7) can be obtained by premultiplying (8.7) by a non-singular matrix $\mathbf{B}$ which generates:

$$\mathbf{B}\mathbf{y}_t = \sum_{i=1}^{m} \mathbf{B}\boldsymbol{\pi}_{1i}\mathbf{y}_{t-i} + \sum_{j=0}^{r} \mathbf{B}\boldsymbol{\pi}_{2j}\mathbf{z}_{t-j} + \mathbf{B}\mathbf{v}_t. \quad (8.8)$$

Let $\mathbf{B}_i = -\mathbf{B}\boldsymbol{\pi}_{1i}$ for $i = 1, \ldots, m$ and $\mathbf{C}_j = -\mathbf{B}\boldsymbol{\pi}_{2j}$ for $j = 0, \ldots, r$ with $\mathbf{u}_t = \mathbf{B}\mathbf{v}_t$, then:

$$\sum_{i=0}^{m} \mathbf{B}_i\mathbf{y}_{t-i} + \sum_{j=0}^{r} \mathbf{C}_j\mathbf{z}_{t-j} = \mathbf{u}_t \quad \text{where } \mathbf{u}_t \sim \mathsf{IN}_n[\mathbf{0}, \boldsymbol{\Sigma}], \quad (8.9)$$

with $\boldsymbol{\Sigma} = \mathbf{B}\boldsymbol{\Omega}\mathbf{B}'$ and $\mathbf{B}_0 = \mathbf{B}$. Let $\mathbf{C} = (\mathbf{B}_1 \ldots \mathbf{B}_m\mathbf{C}_0 \ldots \mathbf{C}_r)$, with $\mathbf{A} = (\mathbf{B} : \mathbf{C})$ and $\mathbf{X} = (\mathbf{Y} : \mathbf{W})$ being the matrices of all the coefficients and all the observations respectively, partitioned by current endogenous and all other variables. We drop the sample subscripts on data matrices, and implicitly assume that the diagonal of $\mathbf{B}_0$ is normalized at unity to ensure a unique scaling in every equation: other normalizations are feasible. Further, the reformulation in $\mathsf{I}(0)$ space would have the same form, but in terms of $\mathsf{I}(0)$ variables: the notation $\mathbf{W}$ is intended to highlight that reformulation. Then (8.9) can be written in compact notation as:

$$\mathbf{B}\mathbf{Y}' + \mathbf{C}\mathbf{W}' = \mathbf{A}\mathbf{X}' = \mathbf{U}'. \quad (8.10)$$

When identities are present, the corresponding elements of $\{\mathbf{u}_t\}$ are precisely zero, so the model can be written as:

$$\mathbf{A}\mathbf{X}' = \begin{pmatrix} \mathbf{A}_1 \\ \mathbf{A}_2 \end{pmatrix} \mathbf{X}' = \begin{pmatrix} \mathbf{U}_1' \\ \mathbf{0} \end{pmatrix}, \quad (8.11)$$

where $n = n_1 + n_2$, for n_1 stochastic equations and n_2 identities. The elements of $\mathbf{A}_2$ must be known and do not need estimation. In what follows, we set $n_2 = 0$ for simplicity: the program handles identities as required.

However, without some restrictions, the coefficients in $\mathbf{A}$ in (8.11) will not be identified. The matrix $\mathbf{B}$ used to multiply the system to obtain the model could in turn be multiplied by an arbitrary non-singular matrix, $\mathbf{D}$ say, and still produce a linear model, but with different coefficients. To resolve such arbitrariness, we need to know the form of $\mathbf{A}$ in advance (or perhaps of $\boldsymbol{\Sigma}$), and it must be sufficiently restricted that the only admissible $\mathbf{D}$ matrix is $\mathbf{I}_{n_1}$. This issue of unique parameterization is further discussed in Chapter 12.

8.9 Simultaneous equations modelling

So far, we have assumed that the structural form of the DGP was known. Textbook presentations of simultaneous equations estimation usually treat $\mathbf{A}(\phi)$ as given, then derive the reduced form from this structure (for example, Judge *et al.*, 1985, Chapter 14). However, since the reduced form has many more parameters than there are ϕs in the structure, such an approach is simple to general and so is open to all the difficulties discussed in Hendry *et al.* (1988). Moreover, by not first testing the validity of the reduced form, which is the basis of the test of over-identifying restrictions used to validate the structural form, all inferences are doubtful (see Sims, 1980, and Hendry, 1987). Thus, in practice, the statistical system should be modelled from the data to determine its congruency before any structural interpretation can be attempted in terms of an econometric model of that system (as discussed in, for example, Spanos, 1986, 1989). Our approach, therefore, remains within the general → specific modelling methodology, extended to allow for the complications of multi-equations, cointegration and identification.

For the model to be a valid, congruent representation of the data, given that the system already is, the model must parsimoniously encompass the system (see Hendry and Richard, 1989). In the present context, that can be checked by a likelihood ratio test for over-identifying restrictions. Denote the concentrated likelihood function for the system with n_1 stochastic equations by ℓ and that for the complete model by ℓ_0. The test is computed by:

$$\xi\left(M - n_1^2\right) = 2\left(\widehat{\ell}_0 - \widehat{\ell}\right) \underset{a}{\sim} \chi^2\left(M - n_1^2\right)$$

for M *a priori* restrictions on $\mathbf{A}$. If $\xi\,(.)$ is significant, the model fails to encompass the system, so that particular implementation of the underlying theory should be rejected. To ensure that appropriate critical values are selected, the system must first be mapped to $\mathsf{I}(0)$ space.

There may be several models consistent with the identification restrictions, even if all are highly over-identified. In particular, this is true for just-identified models when $M = n_1^2$, so that $\xi\,(\cdot)$ is not computable. More generally, however, satisfying the test is insufficient to justify a model, especially if the system is itself not rigorously tested for congruency.

Consequently, the modelling approach described in detail in the tutorials first specifies the statistical dynamic system, assesses its congruency against the past (homoscedastic innovation errors), thereby ensuring an adequate lag length, then tests constancy. At present, such tests are only approximate when the data are $\mathsf{I}(1)$ but seem to provide reasonable guides in practice. Next, cointegration is investigated, thereby determining the degree of integration of the system *en route*. Once the cointegration rank and the number of unit roots have been determined, identified cointegration vectors can be considered, allowing useful tests of necessary conditions for weak exogeneity of some of the potential conditioning variables for the parameters of interest. The roles of deterministic variables and their presence/absence from the long run also can be investigated.

Given that information, the system can be reduced to $\mathsf{I}(0)$ space in terms of differences and cointegrating combinations of the levels data using tests based on appropriate critical values.

Next, that system can be modelled. Depending on the outcomes of the weak exogeneity tests, conditional representations in terms of open systems may be feasible. These are unique by construction, but need not always represent agent behaviour. Simultaneous equations offer the possibility of jointly obtaining parsimonious and structural representations, so these merit careful consideration given the underlying theory. The final model can be checked for unique identification (which does not by itself preclude other observationally-equivalent representations, although regime shifts tend to make such an outcome unlikely). If dummies are needed to make any marginal processes constant, then super-exogeneity tests are feasible. Finally, the model can be tested for parsimonious encompassing of the system and its parsimony may allow more powerful tests of some hypothesis of interest, especially constancy. Forecasting exercises are then feasible and have some credibility (see Clements and Hendry, 1997, for a more detailed analysis).

8.10 General to specific modelling of systems

Enforcing a system approach to simultaneous equations modelling necessitates a large modelling burden, primarily determined by the 'infoglut' of handling large numbers of variables, equations, and parameters. While PcFiml is specifically designed to help attenuate that burden by its graphical presentation of information and its support of simplification procedures, it behoves us to consider the potential advantages of commencing from the unrestricted joint density of all the stochastic variables.

We presented a number of arguments for general to specific methods in Hendry and Doornik (1996b), including developing directed search strategies; validly interpreting intermediate test outcomes by avoiding later potential contradictions; escaping the *non sequitur* of accepting the alternative hypothesis when a test rejects a null; determining the baseline innovation-error process on the available information; and circumventing the drawbacks of correcting flaws only to have to alter their interpretation later. These are powerful arguments for commencing an empirical econometric study from the most general model it is feasible to consider at the outset. Certainly, it is difficult to specify that general system when the sample may be small and heterogeneous, or the potential model class includes non-linear specifications. Nevertheless, tracking deliberate simplifying assumptions made at the commencement of an analysis can clarify later problems and potential directions for their resolution. This advice remains applicable even if a complete economic theory specification is available, since it can be embedded in a extended dynamic system that it should encompass when its claimed completeness is indeed correct.

In the limit, the joint density should comprise all relevant economic variables, but an important source of an investigator's value added is appropriate specifications of the sets of variables which necessitate joint modelling. We now develop some further, interrelated, reasons for commencing econometric analyses of economic time series from the joint density (see Hendry and Doornik, 1994).

8.10.1 The economy is a system

This is the most obvious reason for joint modelling, and was the basis for the advances in econometrics precipitated by Haavelmo (1944). Potentially all variables are endogenously determined by the economic mechanism, and these interact in many ways. In a Walrasian general-equilibrium setting, all variables influence each other in the long run (like a waterbed, which oscillates in all directions when disturbed anywhere). It may happen that some sectors or variables can be decoupled (i.e., the system is block decomposable), but that is an empirical matter. However, to make progress some simplifying assumptions will be essential, depending on the numbers of variables involved and the available sample size. Implicitly, all empirical analyses are based on reductions of the DGP from marginalizing with respect to all variables omitted from the system under study: the crucial issue is to retain as informative a set as possible.

8.10.2 To test marginalization

To check the validity of marginalizing with respect to any set of variates, their joint density must be modelled. Let $\mathbf{w}_t$ denote the vector of possibly relevant variables, and $\mathsf{D}_{\mathsf{W,X}}(\cdot)$ the joint density of all the variables characterized by the parameter $\psi \in \Psi$, then since:

$$\mathsf{D}_{\mathsf{W,X}}\left(\mathbf{W}_T^1, \mathbf{X}_T^1 \mid \mathbf{W}_0, \mathbf{X}_0, \psi\right) = \mathsf{D}_{\mathsf{W|X}}\left(\mathbf{W}_T^1 \mid \mathbf{X}_T^1, \mathbf{W}_0, \psi_1\right) \mathsf{D}_{\mathsf{X}}\left(\mathbf{X}_T^1 \mid \mathbf{X}_0, \psi_2\right) \tag{8.12}$$

the conditions for a fully efficient analysis from $\mathsf{D}_{\mathsf{X}}(\cdot)$ alone mirror those of weak exogeneity (see Engle *et al.*, 1983, and Ericsson, 1992) namely:

- the parameters of interest ϕ are a function of ψ_2 alone; and
- $(\psi_1, \psi_2) \in \Psi_1 \times \Psi_2$ (variation free).

In such a case, $\psi_2 = \boldsymbol{\theta}$ in (8.4), and there is no loss of relevant information about ϕ from analysing the marginal density only. A necessary condition for the validity of such a reduction is that $\mathbf{W}_{t-1}^1$ does not Granger cause $\mathbf{x}_t$: this can only be tested from either $\mathsf{D}_{\mathsf{W,X}}(\cdot)$ or $\mathsf{D}_{\mathsf{W|X}}(\cdot)$.

8.10.3 Simultaneity

Simultaneity is a system property. Although individual-equation (limited information) methods exist, and the curse of dimensionality relative to data availability remains a serious limitation, computational problems no longer provide an excuse for avoiding system methods. Simultaneity is also a long-standing reason, dating from Haavelmo (1943), but a much disputed formulation in the history of econometrics (see Hendry and Morgan, 1995).

8.10.4 To test weak exogeneity

To test conditioning on a subset of stochastic variables (denoted $\{\mathbf{z}_t\} \subset \{\mathbf{x}_t\}$) rather paradoxically first requires modelling $\mathbf{z}_t$, then testing that the marginal density does not contain information relevant to the parameters of interest. For example, elements of ϕ (such as cointegration vectors) could occur in λ_2 which would violate weak exogeneity, and could induce serious distortions of inference in $\mathsf{I}(1)$ systems (see below).

8.10.5 To check identification

The necessary and sufficient criterion for identification (in the sense of uniqueness) under linear restrictions on simultaneous systems is given by the rank condition (see Koopmans, 1950), which depends on the (unknown) values of the parameters in all equations. These other equations need to be specified to ensure the condition is met. PcFiml checks generic identification within the system being modelled, by using non-zero random values for parameters, so global unidentification does not occur when that condition is satisfied.

8.10.6 Cointegration is a system property

The rank of the long-run system matrix can only be determined by considering the complete vector of variables $\mathbf{x}_t$, which necessitates modelling the joint density either explicitly (as in Johansen, 1988) or implicitly (as in Phillips, 1991). Similarly, determining the matrix of cointegrating vectors involves a system analysis. This requirement interacts with the issue of testing weak exogeneity, since if elements of the cointegrating vectors from the ith equation enter any other equation weak exogeneity for parameters of interest which include cointegrating vectors is violated. Tests on the structure of the feedback matrix provide information about cointegration links, are easily conducted, and have conventional (χ^2) distributions asymptotically when cointegration rank is preserved (see Johansen, 1992b, and Boswijk, 1992).

8.10.7 To test cross-equation dependencies

Cross-equation links include many forms of restrictions, cross-equation serial correlation and so on. Any test for system mis-specification logically requires system analysis. One important test is that of over-identifying restrictions, and is equivalent to a test of whether the restricted model parsimoniously encompasses the VAR (see Hendry and Mizon, 1993).

8.10.8 To test super exogeneity and invariance

In many economic processes, a VAR will not manifest constant parameters. This is because it is a derived, rather than a structural, representation so every equation involves functions of the more basic parameters of agents' decision rules. When one of the agents is a policy maker, or an agency of the central government, regime shifts are liable to have occurred, so a constant linear parameterization will be insufficient to capture the data behaviour. Thus, some dummy variables may be needed to make the system approximately constant in practice, especially in equations for policy variables (which the investigator may not wish to model). Conditioning on such variables without first testing for weak and super exogeneity runs the risk that the resulting model will not sustain policy analysis, and may be inadequate as a forecasting device when economic policy change occurs. Engle and Hendry (1993) develop constant-parameter representations of the policy processes, then test the irrelevance of the newly-created variables in the equations of interest. This is most usefully conducted in a system context, and a natural generalization of their test is the significance of the additional variables from the joint marginal model in the joint conditional model under analysis.

8.10.9 To conduct h-step forecasts

The system context has no effect on 1-step forecasts, and each equation could be used in isolation from the others. However, for h-step forecasting when $h \geq 2$ and the system is dynamic, then to predict $\Delta \mathbf{x}_{T+2}$, $\Delta \widehat{\mathbf{x}}_{T+1}$ must first be forecast, so the system context is of the essence.

We believe that any of these reasons by itself is sufficient justification for commencing an econometric analysis from the joint density to allow a sustainable analysis of any proposed empirical models. Together, they constitute a strong case for joint modelling, without resolving how general the starting point must be. Data limitations alone preclude beginning with more than a relatively small number of variables, and the illustration in the tutorials only involves 4 variables, but the issue is one of modelling principles. In particular, knowledge acquisition tends to be progressive and partial, rather than once-for-all crucial discoveries that permanently resolve a modelling problem by forging an empirical 'law'.

Chapter 9

Some Matrix Algebra

An essential element of multivariate analysis is concise notation using matrix algebra. In this section we shall summarize the matrix algebra required to understand Part III of this book. No proofs will be given. For a more thorough overview consult Magnus and Neudecker (1988), Dhrymes (1984), Rao (1973, Chapter 1) or Anderson (1984, Appendix A), among others.

First consider the four-equation model which generated the artificial data set as used in PcGive:

$$\begin{aligned}
\Delta c_t &= -0.9 + 0.4\,\Delta y_t + 0.15\,(y-c)_{t-1} - 0.9\,\Delta p_t + \epsilon_{1t} && (9.1)\\
\Delta y_t &= -75.0 + 0.3\,\Delta c_t + 0.25\,(q-y)_{t-1} + 0.25\,\Delta q_t + \epsilon_{2t} && (9.2)\\
\Delta p_t &= 0.3 + 0.7\,\Delta p_{t-1} + 0.08\,(q-1200)_{t-1} + \epsilon_{3t} && (9.3)\\
\Delta q_t &= 121.3 - 0.1\,q_{t-1} - 1.30\,\Delta p_{t-1} + \epsilon_{4t} && (9.4)
\end{aligned}$$

The relevant matrices are:

$$\begin{pmatrix} 1 & -0.4 & 0.9 & 0 \\ -0.3 & 1 & 0 & -0.25 \\ 0 & 0 & 1 & 0 \\ 0 & 0 & 0 & 1 \end{pmatrix} \begin{pmatrix} \Delta c_t \\ \Delta y_t \\ \Delta p_t \\ \Delta q_t \end{pmatrix} +$$

$$\begin{pmatrix} 0.9 & -0.15 & 0 & 0 & 0 \\ 75 & 0 & -0.25 & 0 & 0 \\ 95.7 & 0 & 0 & -0.08 & -0.7 \\ -121.3 & 0 & 0 & 0.1 & 1.3 \end{pmatrix} \begin{pmatrix} 1 \\ (y-c)_{t-1} \\ (q-y)_{t-1} \\ q_{t-1} \\ \Delta p_{t-1} \end{pmatrix} = \begin{pmatrix} u_{1t} \\ u_{2t} \\ u_{3t} \\ u_{4t} \end{pmatrix}. \qquad (9.5)$$

In matrix form the model can be expressed as:

$$\mathbf{B}\mathbf{y}_t + \mathbf{C}\mathbf{w}_t = \mathbf{u}_t,\ t = 1, \ldots, T, \qquad (9.6)$$

in which the matrices are written in bold face upper case and the vectors in bold face lower case. $\mathbf{B}$ is a (4×4) matrix, $\mathbf{C}$ is (4×5), $\mathbf{y}_t$ and $\mathbf{u}_t$ are (4×1) and $\mathbf{w}_t$ is (5×1). The simultaneous system (9.6) can be expressed more concisely by merging all T equations. Take $\mathbf{y}_t$ for example:

$$\mathbf{Y}' = (\mathbf{y}_1 \cdots\cdots \mathbf{y}_T) = \begin{pmatrix} \Delta c_1 \cdots\cdots \Delta c_T \\ \Delta y_1 \cdots\cdots \Delta y_T \\ \Delta p_1 \cdots\cdots \Delta p_T \\ \Delta q_1 \cdots\cdots \Delta q_T \end{pmatrix}.$$

Using this notation the model becomes:

$$\mathbf{BY}' + \mathbf{CW}' = \mathbf{U}',$$

in which $\mathbf{Y}$ and $\mathbf{U}$ are $(T \times 4)$ and $\mathbf{W}$ is $(T \times 5)$. The matrices $\mathbf{B}$ and $\mathbf{C}$ are unchanged. Of course this is identical to:

$$\mathbf{YB}' + \mathbf{WC}' = \mathbf{U}.$$

To define the elementary operators on matrices we shall write $(a_{ij})_{m,n}$ for the $(m \times n)$ matrix $\mathbf{A}$ when this is convenient:

$$\mathbf{A} = (a_{ij})_{m,n} = \begin{pmatrix} a_{11} & \cdots & a_{1n} \\ \vdots & \ddots & \vdots \\ a_{m1} & \cdots & a_{mn} \end{pmatrix}.$$

- *addition,* $\mathbf{A}$ is $(m \times n)$, $\mathbf{B}$ is $(m \times n)$:

$$\mathbf{A} + \mathbf{B} = (a_{ij} + b_{ij})_{m,n}.$$

- *multiplication,* $\mathbf{A}$ is $(m \times n)$, $\mathbf{B}$ is $(n \times p)$, c is a scalar:

$$\mathbf{AB} = \left(\sum_{k=1}^{n} a_{ik} b_{kj} \right)_{m,p}, \quad c\mathbf{A} = (c a_{ij})_{m,n}.$$

- *Kronecker product,* $\mathbf{A}$ is $(m \times n)$, $\mathbf{B}$ is $(p \times q)$:

$$\mathbf{A} \otimes \mathbf{B} = (a_{ij}\mathbf{B})_{mp,nq}.$$

For example, with $\mathbf{\Omega} = (\omega_{ij})_{2,2}$, $\mathbf{S} = (s_{ij})_{2,2}$:

$$\mathbf{\Omega} \otimes \mathbf{S} = \begin{pmatrix} \omega_{11}s_{11} & \omega_{11}s_{12} & \omega_{12}s_{11} & \omega_{12}s_{12} \\ \omega_{11}s_{21} & \omega_{11}s_{22} & \omega_{12}s_{21} & \omega_{12}s_{22} \\ \omega_{21}s_{11} & \omega_{21}s_{12} & \omega_{22}s_{11} & \omega_{22}s_{12} \\ \omega_{21}s_{21} & \omega_{21}s_{22} & \omega_{22}s_{21} & \omega_{22}s_{22} \end{pmatrix}.$$

- *Hadamard product,* $\mathbf{A}$ is $(m \times n)$, $\mathbf{B}$ is $(m \times n)$:

$$\mathbf{A} \odot \mathbf{B} = (a_{ij} b_{ij})_{m,n}.$$

For example:

$$\mathbf{\Omega} \odot \mathbf{S} = \begin{pmatrix} \omega_{11} s_{11} & \omega_{12} s_{12} \\ \omega_{21} s_{21} & \omega_{22} s_{22} \end{pmatrix}.$$

- *transpose,* $\mathbf{A}$ is $(m \times n)$:

$$\mathbf{A}' = (a_{ji})_{n,m}.$$

- *determinant,* $\mathbf{A}$ is $(n \times n)$:

$$|\mathbf{A}| = \sum (-1)^{c(j_1,\ldots,j_n)} \prod_{i=1}^{n} a_{ij_i}$$

where the summation is over all permutations $(j_1, \ldots, j_n)$ of the set of integers $(1, \ldots, n)$, and $c(j_1, \ldots, j_n)$ is the number of transpositions required to change $(1, \ldots, n)$ into $(j_1, \ldots, j_n)$. In the 2×2 case, the set $(1, 2)$ can be transposed once into $(2, 1)$, so $|\mathbf{\Omega}| = (-1)^0 \omega_{11}\omega_{22} + (-1)^1 \omega_{12}\omega_{21}$.
- *trace,* $\mathbf{A}$ is $(n \times n)$:

$$\mathrm{tr}\mathbf{A} = \sum_{i=1}^{n} a_{ii}.$$

- *rank,* $\mathbf{A}$ is $(m \times n)$: the rank of $\mathbf{A}$ is the number of linearly independent columns (or rows, row rank always equals column rank) in $\mathbf{A}$, $\mathrm{r}(\mathbf{A}) \leq \min(m, n)$. If $\mathbf{A}$ is $(n \times n)$ and of full rank then:

$$\mathrm{r}(\mathbf{A}) = n.$$

- *symmetric matrix,* $\mathbf{A}$ is $(n \times n)$: $\mathbf{A}$ is symmetric if:

$$\mathbf{A}' = \mathbf{A}.$$

- *matrix inverse,* $\mathbf{A}$ is $(n \times n)$ and of full rank (non-singular, which is equivalent to $|\mathbf{A}| \neq 0$) then $\mathbf{A}^{-1}$ is the unique $(n \times n)$ matrix such that:

$$\mathbf{A}\mathbf{A}^{-1} = \mathbf{I}_n.$$

This implies that $\mathbf{A}^{-1}\mathbf{A} = \mathbf{I}_n$; $\mathbf{I}_n$ is the $(n \times n)$ identity matrix:

$$\mathbf{I}_n = \begin{pmatrix} 1 & 0 & \cdots & 0 \\ 0 & 1 & \cdots & 0 \\ \vdots & \vdots & \ddots & \vdots \\ 0 & 0 & \cdots & 1 \end{pmatrix}.$$

- *orthogonal matrix*, $\mathbf{A}$ is $(n \times n)$: $\mathbf{A}$ is orthogonal if:

$$\mathbf{A}'\mathbf{A} = \mathbf{I}_n.$$

Then also $\mathbf{A}\mathbf{A}' = \mathbf{I}_n$; further: $\mathrm{r}(\mathbf{A}) = n$, $\mathbf{A}' = \mathbf{A}^{-1}$.
- *orthogonal complement*, $\mathbf{A}$ is $(m \times n)$, $m > n$ and $\mathrm{r}(\mathbf{A}) = n$, define the orthogonal complement $\mathbf{A}_\perp$ as the $(m \times (m-n))$ matrix such that: $\mathbf{A}'\mathbf{A}_\perp = \mathbf{0}$ with $\mathrm{r}(\mathbf{A}_\perp) = m - n$ and $\mathrm{r}(\mathbf{A} : \mathbf{A}_\perp) = m$. $\mathbf{A}_\perp$ spans the *null space* of $\mathbf{A}$; $\mathrm{r}(\mathbf{A}_\perp)$ is called the *nullity* of $\mathbf{A}$.
- *idempotent matrix*, $\mathbf{A}$ is $(n \times n)$: $\mathbf{A}$ is idempotent if:

$$\mathbf{A}\mathbf{A} = \mathbf{A}.$$

An example is the projection matrix $\mathbf{M}_X = \mathbf{I}_T - \mathbf{X}\left(\mathbf{X}'\mathbf{X}\right)^{-1}\mathbf{X}'$.
- *vectorization*, $\mathbf{A}$ is $(m \times n)$:

$$\mathrm{vec}\mathbf{A} = \begin{pmatrix} a_{11} \\ \vdots \\ a_{m1} \\ \vdots \\ a_{1n} \\ \vdots \\ a_{mn} \end{pmatrix},$$

which is an $(mn \times 1)$ vector consisting of the stacked columns of $\mathbf{A}$. Transposing the vectorized form of the $\mathbf{B}'$ matrix of (9.5) gives:

$$(\mathrm{vec}\,(\mathbf{B}'))' = (1\ \ -0.4\ 0.9\ 0\ \ -0.3\ 1\ 0\ \ -0.25\ 0\ 0\ 1\ 0\ 0\ 0\ 0\ 1).$$

This is the order we wish to have the model coefficients in: stacked by equation. We use $\mathrm{vec}(\mathbf{B}') \equiv \mathrm{vec}\mathbf{B}'$. With $\mathbf{a}$ an $(n \times 1)$ vector: $\mathrm{vec}(\mathbf{a}) = \mathbf{a}$.

If $\mathbf{A}$ is $(n \times n)$ and symmetric, we can use the vech operator to vectorize the unique elements, thus ignoring the elements above the diagonal:

$$\mathrm{vech}\mathbf{A} = \begin{pmatrix} a_{11} \\ \vdots \\ a_{n1} \\ a_{22} \\ \vdots \\ a_{n2} \\ \vdots \\ a_{nn} \end{pmatrix},$$

which is a $(\frac{1}{2}n(n+1) \times 1)$ vector.

- *unrestricted elements,* when deriving simultaneous equations estimators, it is often convenient to restrict attention to the parameters that are to be estimated and ignore the remaining parameters. $(\cdot)^u$ selects the unrestricted elements of a vector, or crosses out rows and columns of a matrix, thus reducing the dimensionality. $(\cdot)^{v_u}$ transposes and vectorizes a matrix, stores the elements in a column vector, and selects the unrestricted elements. In the $\mathbf{B}$ matrix of (9.5), the 0s and 1s are restrictions, the remainder are parameters, so:

$$\mathbf{B}^{v_u} = (\mathrm{vec}\,(\mathbf{B}'))^u = \begin{pmatrix} -0.4 \\ 0.9 \\ -0.3 \\ -0.25 \end{pmatrix}.$$

- *diagonalization,* $\mathbf{A}$ is $(n \times n)$:

$$\mathrm{dg}\mathbf{A} = \begin{pmatrix} a_{11} & 0 & \cdots & 0 \\ 0 & a_{22} & \cdots & 0 \\ \vdots & \vdots & \ddots & \vdots \\ 0 & 0 & \cdots & a_{nn} \end{pmatrix} = \mathrm{diag}\,(a_{11}, a_{22}, \ldots, a_{nn}).$$

- *positive definite,* $\mathbf{A}$ is $(n \times n)$ and symmetric: $\mathbf{A}$ is positive definite if $\mathbf{x}'\mathbf{A}\mathbf{x} > 0$ for all $(n \times 1)$ vectors $\mathbf{x} \neq \mathbf{0}$, positive semi-definite if $\mathbf{x}'\mathbf{A}\mathbf{x} \geq 0$ for all $\mathbf{x} \neq \mathbf{0}$, and negative definite if $\mathbf{x}'\mathbf{A}\mathbf{x} < 0$ for all $\mathbf{x} \neq \mathbf{0}$.
- *eigenvalues and eigenvectors,* $\mathbf{A}$ is $(n \times n)$: the eigenvalues of $\mathbf{A}$ are the roots of the characteristic equation:

$$|\mathbf{A} - \lambda \mathbf{I}_n| = 0.$$

  If λ_i is an eigenvalue of $\mathbf{A}$, then $\mathbf{x}_i \neq \mathbf{0}$ is an eigenvector of $\mathbf{A}$ if it satisfies:

$$(\mathbf{A} - \lambda_i \mathbf{I}_n)\,\mathbf{x}_i = \mathbf{0}.$$

- *Choleski decomposition,* $\mathbf{A}$ is $(n \times n)$ and positive definite, then:

$$\mathbf{A} = \mathbf{L}\mathbf{L}',$$

  where $\mathbf{L}$ is a unique lower-triangular matrix with positive diagonal elements.
- *singular value decomposition,* decomposes an $(m \times n)$ matrix $\mathbf{A}$, $m \geq n$ and $\mathrm{r}(\mathbf{A}) = r > 0$, into:

$$\mathbf{A} = \mathbf{U}\mathbf{W}\mathbf{V}',$$

  with:

  $\mathbf{U}$ is $(m \times r)$ and $\mathbf{U}'\mathbf{U} = \mathbf{I}_r$,
  $\mathbf{W}$ is $(r \times r)$ and diagonal, with non-negative diagonal elements,
  $\mathbf{V}$ is $(n \times r)$ and $\mathbf{V}'\mathbf{V} = \mathbf{I}_r$.

This can be used to find the orthogonal complement of $\mathbf{A}$. Assume $\mathrm{r}(\mathbf{A}) = n$ and compute the singular value decomposition of the $(m \times m)$ matrix $\mathbf{B} = (\mathbf{A} : \mathbf{0})$. The last $m - n$ diagonal elements of $\mathbf{W}$ will be zero. Corresponding to that are the last $m - n$ columns of $\mathbf{U}$ which form $\mathbf{A}_\perp$:

$$\mathbf{B} = (\mathbf{A} : \mathbf{0}) = \mathbf{U}\mathbf{W}\mathbf{V}' = (\mathbf{U}_1 : \mathbf{U}_2) \begin{pmatrix} \mathbf{W}_1 & \mathbf{0} \\ \mathbf{0} & \mathbf{0} \end{pmatrix} \begin{pmatrix} \mathbf{V}_1' \\ \mathbf{V}_2' \end{pmatrix}.$$

Here $\mathbf{U}$, $\mathbf{V}$ and $\mathbf{W}$ are $(m \times m)$ matrices; $\mathbf{U}_2'\mathbf{U}_1 = \mathbf{0}$ so that $\mathbf{U}_2'\mathbf{A} = \mathbf{U}_2'\mathbf{U}_1\mathbf{W}_1\mathbf{V}_1' = \mathbf{0}$ and $\mathrm{r}(\mathbf{A} : \mathbf{U}_2) = m$ as $\mathbf{U}_2'\mathbf{U}_2 = \mathbf{I}_{(m-n)}$.

- *differentiation*, define $f(\cdot) : \mathbb{R}^m \mapsto \mathbb{R}$ then:

$$\nabla f = \frac{\partial f(\mathbf{a})}{\partial \mathbf{a}} = \begin{pmatrix} \frac{\partial f(\mathbf{a})}{\partial a_1} \\ \vdots \\ \frac{\partial f(\mathbf{a})}{\partial a_m} \end{pmatrix}, \quad \nabla^2 f = \frac{\partial^2 f(\mathbf{a})}{\partial \mathbf{a} \partial \mathbf{a}'} = \left(\frac{\partial^2 f(\mathbf{a})}{\partial a_i \partial a_j} \right)_{m,m}.$$

If $f(\cdot)$ is a log-likelihood function we shall write $\mathbf{q}(\cdot)$ for the first derivative (or score), and $\mathbf{H}(\cdot)$ for the second derivative (or Hessian) matrix.
For $f(\cdot) : \mathbb{R}^{m \times n} \mapsto \mathbb{R}$ we define:

$$\frac{\partial f(\mathbf{A})}{\partial \mathbf{A}} = \left(\frac{\partial f(\mathbf{A})}{\partial a_{ij}} \right)_{m,n}.$$

- *Jacobian matrix*, for a vector function $\mathbf{f}(\cdot) : \mathbb{R}^m \mapsto \mathbb{R}^n$ we define the $(n \times m)$ Jacobian matrix $\mathbf{J}$:

$$\frac{\partial \mathbf{f}(\mathbf{a})}{\partial \mathbf{a}'} = \begin{pmatrix} \frac{\partial f_1(\mathbf{a})}{\partial a_1} & \cdots & \frac{\partial f_1(\mathbf{a})}{\partial a_m} \\ \vdots & & \vdots \\ \frac{\partial f_n(\mathbf{a})}{\partial a_1} & \cdots & \frac{\partial f_n(\mathbf{a})}{\partial a_m} \end{pmatrix} = \begin{pmatrix} (\nabla f_1)' \\ \vdots \\ (\nabla f_m)' \end{pmatrix} = (\nabla \mathbf{f})'.$$

The transpose of the Jacobian is called the gradient, and corresponds to the $\mathbf{q}(\cdot)$ above for $n = 1$ (so in that case the Jacobian is $(1 \times m)$ and the score $(n \times 1)$). The Jacobian is the absolute value of the determinant of $\mathbf{J}$ when $m = n$: $||\mathbf{J}||$. Normally we wish to compute the Jacobian matrix for a transformation of a coefficient matrix: $\boldsymbol{\Psi} = \mathbf{F}(\boldsymbol{\Pi}')$ where $\mathbf{F}$ is a matrix function $\mathbf{F}(\cdot) : \mathbb{R}^{m \times n} \mapsto \mathbb{R}^{p \times q}$:

$$\mathbf{J} = \frac{\partial \mathrm{vec}\boldsymbol{\Psi}}{\partial (\mathrm{vec}\boldsymbol{\Pi}')'},$$

with $\boldsymbol{\Pi}$ $(n \times m)$ and $\boldsymbol{\Psi}$ $(p \times q)$ so that $\mathbf{J}$ is $(pq \times mn)$.

Some useful relations (c is scalar, λ_i are eigenvalues of $\mathbf{A}$):

- product, determinant, trace, rank

$$
\begin{aligned}
&(\mathbf{AB})' = \mathbf{B}'\mathbf{A}' \\
&(\mathbf{AB})^{-1} = \mathbf{B}^{-1}\mathbf{A}^{-1}, \text{ if } \mathbf{A}, \mathbf{B} \text{ non-singular} \\
&(\mathbf{A}^{-1})' = (\mathbf{A}')^{-1} \\
&|\mathbf{AB}| = |\mathbf{A}|\,|\mathbf{B}|\,, \mathbf{A}, \mathbf{B} \text{ are } (n \times n) \\
&|\mathbf{A}'| = |\mathbf{A}| \\
&|c\mathbf{A}| = c^n\,|\mathbf{A}|\,, \mathbf{A} \text{ is } (n \times n) \\
&\left|\mathbf{A}^{-1}\right| = |\mathbf{A}|^{-1} \\
&\text{tr}(\mathbf{AB}) = \text{tr}(\mathbf{BA}) \\
&\text{tr}(\mathbf{A} + \mathbf{B}) = \text{tr}\mathbf{A} + \text{tr}\mathbf{B} \\
&\text{tr}\mathbf{A} = \textstyle\sum \lambda_i, \mathbf{A} \text{ is } (n \times n) \\
&|\mathbf{A}| = \textstyle\prod \lambda_i, \mathbf{A} \text{ is } (n \times n) \\
&\text{if } \mathbf{A}\ (n \times n), \text{ symmetric with } p \text{ roots } \lambda_i \neq 0 \text{ and } n - p \text{ roots } \lambda_i = 0, \\
&\quad \text{then r}(\mathbf{A}) = p.
\end{aligned}
$$

- Kronecker, vec

$$
\begin{aligned}
&(\mathbf{A} \otimes \mathbf{B})' = \mathbf{A}' \otimes \mathbf{B}' \\
&(\mathbf{A} \otimes \mathbf{B})^{-1} = \mathbf{A}^{-1} \otimes \mathbf{B}^{-1}, \text{ if } \mathbf{A}, \mathbf{B} \text{ non-singular} \\
&|\mathbf{A} \otimes \mathbf{B}| = |\mathbf{A}|^m\,|\mathbf{B}|^n\,, \mathbf{A} \text{ is } (n \times n) \text{ and } \mathbf{B} \text{ is } (m \times m) \\
&(\mathbf{A} \otimes \mathbf{B})(\mathbf{C} \otimes \mathbf{D}) = \mathbf{AC} \otimes \mathbf{BD} \\
&c \otimes \mathbf{A} = c\mathbf{A} = \mathbf{A}c = \mathbf{A} \otimes c \\
&\text{tr}(\mathbf{A} \otimes \mathbf{B}) = \text{tr}\mathbf{A}\text{tr}\mathbf{B} \\
&(\text{vec}\mathbf{A})'\text{vec}\mathbf{B} = \text{tr}(\mathbf{A}'\mathbf{B}), \mathbf{A}, \mathbf{B} \text{ both } (m \times n) \\
&\text{vec}(\mathbf{a}') = \text{vec}(\mathbf{a}) = \mathbf{a}, \mathbf{a} \text{ is } (n \times 1) \\
&\text{vec}(\mathbf{ABC}) = (\mathbf{C}' \otimes \mathbf{A})\text{vec}\mathbf{B}, \text{ if } \mathbf{ABC} \text{ defined} \\
&\text{tr}(\mathbf{ABCD}) = (\text{vec}\mathbf{D}')'(\mathbf{C}' \otimes \mathbf{A})\text{vec}\mathbf{B} = (\text{vec}\mathbf{D})'(\mathbf{A} \otimes \mathbf{C}')\text{vec}\mathbf{B}' \\
&\quad \text{since vec}\mathbf{B}' \equiv \text{vec}(\mathbf{B}')
\end{aligned}
$$

- differentiation

$$
\begin{aligned}
\frac{\partial \log|\mathbf{A}|}{\partial \mathbf{A}} &= \mathbf{A}'^{-1} \text{ if } \mathbf{A} \text{ asymmetric} \\
\frac{\partial \log|\mathbf{A}|}{\partial \mathbf{A}} &= 2\mathbf{A}^{-1} - \text{dg}\left(\mathbf{A}^{-1}\right) \text{ if } \mathbf{A} \text{ symmetric} \\
\frac{\partial \text{tr}(\mathbf{BA})}{\partial \mathbf{B}} &= \mathbf{A}' \text{ if } \mathbf{B} \text{ asymmetric} \\
\frac{\partial \text{tr}(\mathbf{BA})}{\partial \mathbf{B}} &= \mathbf{A} + \mathbf{A}' - \text{dg}\mathbf{A} \text{ if } \mathbf{B} \text{ symmetric}
\end{aligned}
$$

$$
\frac{\partial \mathbf{g}(\mathbf{f}(\mathbf{a}))}{\partial \mathbf{a}'} = \frac{\partial \mathbf{g}(\mathbf{b})}{\partial \mathbf{b}'}\frac{\partial \mathbf{f}(\mathbf{a})}{\partial \mathbf{a}'}
$$

$$\text{with } \mathbf{f}(\cdot):\mathbb{R}^m \mapsto \mathbb{R}^n,\ \mathbf{g}(\cdot):\mathbb{R}^n \mapsto \mathbb{R}^p,\ \mathbf{b}=\mathbf{f}(\mathbf{a})$$

$$\frac{\partial \text{vec}(\mathbf{ABC})}{\partial (\text{vec}\mathbf{B})'} = \mathbf{C}' \otimes \mathbf{A}$$

$$\frac{\partial \text{vec}\left(\mathbf{A}^{-1}\right)}{\partial (\text{vec}\mathbf{A})'} = -\mathbf{A}^{-1\prime} \otimes \mathbf{A}^{-1}$$

- Jacobian matrix

$$\mathsf{V}\left[\text{vec}\,\mathbf{F}\left(\widehat{\mathbf{\Pi}}'\right)\right] = \mathbf{J}\mathsf{V}\left[\text{vec}\widehat{\mathbf{\Pi}}'\right]\mathbf{J}',$$

where $\mathbf{J}$ is the Jacobian matrix. This relation is only approximately valid, unless $\mathbf{F}(\cdot)$ is linear. Here $\mathsf{V}[\mathbf{x}]$ denotes the (co)variance matrix of the vector $\mathbf{x}$:

$$\mathsf{V}[\mathbf{x}] = \mathsf{E}\left[(\mathbf{x}-\mathsf{E}[\mathbf{x}])(\mathbf{x}-\mathsf{E}[\mathbf{x}])'\right],$$

and $\mathsf{E}[\cdot]$ is the expected value.

- partitioned matrices

Let $\mathbf{F} = \begin{pmatrix} \mathbf{A} & \mathbf{C} \\ \mathbf{B} & \mathbf{D} \end{pmatrix}$ be non-singular. If $\mathbf{A}$ and $\mathbf{H} = \mathbf{D} - \mathbf{BA}^{-1}\mathbf{C}$ are non-singular then:

$$\mathbf{F}^{-1} = \begin{pmatrix} \mathbf{A}^{-1} + \mathbf{A}^{-1}\mathbf{CH}^{-1}\mathbf{BA}^{-1} & -\mathbf{A}^{-1}\mathbf{CH}^{-1} \\ -\mathbf{H}^{-1}\mathbf{BA}^{-1} & \mathbf{H}^{-1} \end{pmatrix}.$$

If $\mathbf{D}$ and $\mathbf{G} = \mathbf{A} - \mathbf{CD}^{-1}\mathbf{B}$ are non-singular then:

$$\mathbf{F}^{-1} = \begin{pmatrix} \mathbf{G}^{-1} & -\mathbf{G}^{-1}\mathbf{CD}^{-1} \\ -\mathbf{D}^{-1}\mathbf{BG}^{-1} & \mathbf{D}^{-1} + \mathbf{D}^{-1}\mathbf{BG}^{-1}\mathbf{CD}^{-1} \end{pmatrix}.$$

If $\mathbf{A}$ is non-singular:

$$|\mathbf{F}| = \left|\mathbf{D} - \mathbf{BA}^{-1}\mathbf{C}\right| |\mathbf{A}|.$$

If $\mathbf{D}$ is non-singular:

$$|\mathbf{F}| = \left|\mathbf{A} - \mathbf{CD}^{-1}\mathbf{B}\right| |\mathbf{D}|.$$

Chapter 10

Econometric Analysis of the System

10.1 System estimation

As discussed in Chapter 8, the modelling process in PcFiml starts with the statistical system, which is the maintained hypothesis against which further reductions can be tested. We assume in this chapter that all the variables in the system have been reduced to I(0), that the conditions for valid weak exogeneity of the $\mathbf{z}_t$ for the parameters of interest in the conditional system are satisfied, and write the system as:

$$\mathbf{y}_t = \mathbf{\Pi}\mathbf{w}_t + \mathbf{v}_t, \quad t = 1, \ldots, T, \tag{10.1}$$

with

$$\mathsf{E}\left[\mathbf{v}_t\right] = \mathbf{0} \text{ and } \mathsf{E}\left[\mathbf{v}_t\mathbf{v}_t'\right] = \mathbf{\Omega}, \tag{10.2}$$

where $\mathbf{w}$ here contains $\mathbf{z}$, r lags of $\mathbf{z}$ and m lags of $\mathbf{y}$:

$$\mathbf{w}_t' = \left(\mathbf{y}_{t-1}', \ldots, \mathbf{y}_{t-m}', \mathbf{z}_t', \ldots, \mathbf{z}_{t-r}'\right).$$

As in Chapter 8, we take $\mathbf{y}_t$ as an $(n \times 1)$ vector and $\mathbf{z}_t$ as $(q \times 1)$.

As an example of a system, consider the parsimonious unrestricted reduced form corresponding to the model which generated the artificial data set (see Chapter 9):

$$\begin{pmatrix} \Delta c_t \\ \Delta y_t \\ \Delta p_t \\ \Delta q_t \end{pmatrix} = \begin{pmatrix} \pi_{11} & \pi_{12} & \pi_{13} & \pi_{14} & \pi_{15} \\ \pi_{21} & \pi_{22} & \pi_{23} & \pi_{24} & \pi_{25} \\ \pi_{31} & \pi_{32} & \pi_{33} & \pi_{34} & \pi_{35} \\ \pi_{41} & \pi_{42} & \pi_{43} & \pi_{44} & \pi_{45} \end{pmatrix} \begin{pmatrix} \Delta p_{t-1} \\ 1 \\ (y-c)_{t-1} \\ (q-y)_{t-1} \\ q_{t-1} \end{pmatrix} + \begin{pmatrix} v_{1t} \\ v_{2t} \\ v_{3t} \\ v_{4t} \end{pmatrix}. \tag{10.3}$$

The system (10.1) can be written more compactly by using $\mathbf{Y}' = (\mathbf{y}_1\, \mathbf{y}_2 \ldots \mathbf{y}_T)$, and $\mathbf{W}'$, $\mathbf{V}'$ correspondingly:

$$\mathbf{Y}' = \mathbf{\Pi}\mathbf{W}' + \mathbf{V}', \tag{10.4}$$

in which $\mathbf{Y}'$ is $(n \times T)$, $\mathbf{W}'$ is $(k \times T)$ and $\mathbf{\Pi}$ is $(n \times k)$, with $k = nm + (r+1)q$ (assuming no lags have been dropped altogether, as in the example of equation (10.3)). This is simply the multivariate linear regression model since there is a common set of regressors in each equation. Formulae for parameter and equation standard errors, test statistics etc. are generalized analogues of those in ordinary least squares (OLS), as in PcGive. Anderson (1984) contains an extensive discussion of the multivariate linear regression model, also see Spanos (1986). If $q = 0$ (no zs) the system is a vector autoregression (VAR): see, for example, Lütkepohl (1991) or Ooms (1994).

The multivariate least squares estimates of the coefficients and residual covariance are:

$$\widehat{\mathbf{\Pi}}' = (\mathbf{W}'\mathbf{W})^{-1}\mathbf{W}'\mathbf{Y} \text{ and } \widetilde{\mathbf{\Omega}} = \widehat{\mathbf{V}}'\widehat{\mathbf{V}}/(T-k), \tag{10.5}$$

where the residuals are defined by:

$$\widehat{\mathbf{V}} = \mathbf{Y} - \mathbf{W}\widehat{\mathbf{\Pi}}' = \mathbf{M}_W\mathbf{Y}. \tag{10.6}$$

$\mathbf{M}_W$ is the symmetric idempotent projection matrix which annihilates $\mathbf{W}$:

$$\mathbf{M}_W = \mathbf{I}_T - \mathbf{W}(\mathbf{W}'\mathbf{W})^{-1}\mathbf{W}' = \mathbf{I}_T - \mathbf{Q}_W, \tag{10.7}$$

$\mathbf{M}_W\mathbf{W} = \mathbf{0}$, and $\mathbf{M}_W\mathbf{M}_W = \mathbf{M}_W$.

To derive the variance of the estimated coefficients, we need:

$$\mathsf{V}\left[\text{vec}\widehat{\mathbf{\Pi}}'\right] = \mathsf{E}\left[\text{vec}\left(\widehat{\mathbf{\Pi}}' - \mathbf{\Pi}'\right)\left(\text{vec}\left(\widehat{\mathbf{\Pi}}' - \mathbf{\Pi}'\right)\right)'\right]. \tag{10.8}$$

Note that $\text{vec}\mathbf{\Pi}'$ is an $(nk \times 1)$ column vector of coefficients, stacked by equation. In dynamic models, this calculation is intractable, and an asymptotic approximation is used as follows. It is convenient to consider the transpose of (10.4) in vectorized form, with $\boldsymbol{\pi} = \text{vec}\mathbf{\Pi}'$, $\mathbf{y} = \text{vec}\mathbf{Y}$ and $\mathbf{v} = \text{vec}\mathbf{V}$:

$$\mathbf{y} = (\mathbf{I}_n \otimes \mathbf{W})\boldsymbol{\pi} + \mathbf{v}. \tag{10.9}$$

So:

$$\widehat{\boldsymbol{\pi}} = \left((\mathbf{I}_n \otimes \mathbf{W})'(\mathbf{I}_n \otimes \mathbf{W})\right)^{-1}(\mathbf{I}_n \otimes \mathbf{W})'\mathbf{y} = \left(\mathbf{I}_n \otimes (\mathbf{W}'\mathbf{W})^{-1}\mathbf{W}'\right)\mathbf{y} \tag{10.10}$$

and:

$$\widehat{\boldsymbol{\pi}} - \boldsymbol{\pi} = \left(\mathbf{I}_n \otimes (\mathbf{W}'\mathbf{W})^{-1}\mathbf{W}'\right)\mathbf{v}. \tag{10.11}$$

In the case of fixed $\mathbf{W}$, direct evaluation yield:

$$\begin{aligned}\mathsf{E}\left[(\widehat{\boldsymbol{\pi}} - \boldsymbol{\pi})(\widehat{\boldsymbol{\pi}} - \boldsymbol{\pi})'\right] &= \left(\mathbf{I}_n \otimes (\mathbf{W}'\mathbf{W})^{-1}\mathbf{W}'\right)(\mathbf{\Omega} \otimes \mathbf{I}_n)\left(\mathbf{I}_n \otimes \mathbf{W}(\mathbf{W}'\mathbf{W})^{-1}\right) \\ &= \mathbf{\Omega} \otimes (\mathbf{W}'\mathbf{W})^{-1}.\end{aligned} \tag{10.12}$$

A corresponding formula holds asymptotically (when suitably scaled by T) in $\mathsf{I}(0)$ dynamic processes:

$$\sqrt{T}\left(\widehat{\boldsymbol{\pi}}-\boldsymbol{\pi}\right) \xrightarrow{D} \mathsf{N}_{n^2}\left[\mathbf{0}, \boldsymbol{\Omega} \otimes \mathbf{S}_W^{-1}\right] \quad \text{where } \mathbf{S}_W = \underset{T\to\infty}{\operatorname{plim}}\, T^{-1}\mathbf{W}'\mathbf{W}. \tag{10.13}$$

The estimated variance matrix of the coefficients is:

$$\widetilde{\mathsf{V}\left[\text{vec}\widehat{\boldsymbol{\Pi}}'\right]} = \widetilde{\boldsymbol{\Omega}} \otimes \left(\mathbf{W}'\mathbf{W}\right)^{-1} \tag{10.14}$$

The variance matrix of coefficients derived from $\boldsymbol{\Pi}$, $\boldsymbol{\Psi} = \mathbf{f}\left(\boldsymbol{\Pi}'\right)$, has the general form:

$$\mathsf{V}\left[\text{vec}\,\mathbf{f}\left(\widehat{\boldsymbol{\Pi}}'\right)\right] = \mathsf{V}\left[\text{vec}\widehat{\boldsymbol{\Psi}}\right] \simeq \mathbf{J}'\mathsf{V}\left[\text{vec}\widehat{\boldsymbol{\Pi}}'\right]\mathbf{J} \tag{10.15}$$

where $\mathbf{J}$ is the Jacobian matrix of the transformation $\boldsymbol{\Psi} = \mathbf{f}\left(\boldsymbol{\Pi}'\right)$:

$$\mathbf{J} = \frac{\partial \text{vec}\boldsymbol{\Psi}}{\partial\left(\text{vec}\boldsymbol{\Pi}'\right)'}. \tag{10.16}$$

This approximation is asymptotically valid in that from (10.13), when $\boldsymbol{\psi} = \text{vec}\boldsymbol{\Psi}$:

$$\sqrt{T}\left(\widehat{\boldsymbol{\psi}}-\boldsymbol{\psi}\right) \xrightarrow{D} \mathsf{N}_{ns}\left[\mathbf{0}, \mathbf{J}\left(\boldsymbol{\Omega} \otimes \mathbf{S}_W^{-1}\right)\mathbf{J}'\right].$$

With $\widehat{\boldsymbol{\Pi}}$ an $(n \times k)$ matrix and $\widehat{\boldsymbol{\Psi}}$ an $(s \times n)$ matrix, $\mathbf{J}$ will be $(ns \times nk)$.

10.2 Maximum likelihood estimation

Under the assumptions that (10.1) is the DGP, $\mathbf{v}_t \sim \mathsf{IN}_n[\mathbf{0}, \boldsymbol{\Omega}]$, and that all the coefficient matrices are constant, the log-likelihood function $\ell\left(\boldsymbol{\Pi}, \boldsymbol{\Omega}|\mathbf{Y}, \mathbf{W}\right)$ depends on the multivariate normal distribution:

$$\begin{aligned} \ell\left(\boldsymbol{\Pi}, \boldsymbol{\Omega} \mid \mathbf{Y}, \mathbf{W}\right) &= -\tfrac{Tn}{2}\log 2\pi - \tfrac{T}{2}\log|\boldsymbol{\Omega}| - \tfrac{1}{2}\sum_{t=1}^{T}\mathbf{v}_t'\boldsymbol{\Omega}^{-1}\mathbf{v}_t \\ &= K - \tfrac{T}{2}\log|\boldsymbol{\Omega}| - \tfrac{1}{2}\text{tr}\left(\boldsymbol{\Omega}^{-1}\mathbf{V}'\mathbf{V}\right) \\ &= K + \tfrac{T}{2}\log\left|\boldsymbol{\Omega}^{-1}\right| - \tfrac{1}{2}\text{tr}\left(\boldsymbol{\Omega}^{-1}\mathbf{V}'\mathbf{V}\right). \end{aligned} \tag{10.17}$$

The sample is denoted $t = 1, \ldots, T$ after creating all necessary lags.

We first concentrate $\ell(\cdot)$ with respect to $\boldsymbol{\Omega}$, which involves differentiating (10.17) with respect to $\boldsymbol{\Omega}^{-1}$ and equating that to $\mathbf{0}$. Taking account of its symmetry (that is, $\omega_{ij} = \omega_{ji}$) we find:

$$2\mathbf{V}'\mathbf{V} - \text{dg}\left(\mathbf{V}'\mathbf{V}\right) = 2T\boldsymbol{\Omega} - T\text{dg}\left(\boldsymbol{\Omega}\right), \tag{10.18}$$

evaluated at $\boldsymbol{\Omega} = \boldsymbol{\Omega}_c$, yielding:

$$\boldsymbol{\Omega}_c = T^{-1} \sum_{t=1}^{T} \mathbf{v}_t \mathbf{v}_t' = T^{-1} \mathbf{V}'\mathbf{V}. \tag{10.19}$$

This is a rather natural result, given that $\mathsf{E}[T^{-1}\mathbf{V}'\mathbf{V}] = \boldsymbol{\Omega}$. The resulting concentrated log-likelihood function (CLF) $\ell_c(\boldsymbol{\Pi}|\mathbf{Y}, \mathbf{W}; \boldsymbol{\Omega})$ is:

$$\begin{aligned} \ell_c(\boldsymbol{\Pi} \mid \mathbf{Y}, \mathbf{W}; \boldsymbol{\Omega}) &= K - \tfrac{T}{2} \log |\mathbf{V}'\mathbf{V}| + \tfrac{Tn \log T}{2} - \tfrac{Tn}{2} \\ &= K^* - \tfrac{T}{2} \log \left| \left(\mathbf{Y}' - \boldsymbol{\Pi}\mathbf{W}'\right) \left(\mathbf{Y} - \mathbf{W}\boldsymbol{\Pi}'\right) \right|. \end{aligned} \tag{10.20}$$

We know the minimizer of $\left(\mathbf{Y}' - \boldsymbol{\Pi}\mathbf{W}'\right)\left(\mathbf{Y} - \mathbf{W}\boldsymbol{\Pi}'\right)$ from least-squares theory, and find the maximum likelihood estimates:

$$\widehat{\boldsymbol{\Pi}}' = \left(\mathbf{W}'\mathbf{W}\right)^{-1} \mathbf{W}'\mathbf{Y} \ \text{ and } \ \widehat{\boldsymbol{\Omega}} = T^{-1}\widehat{\mathbf{V}}'\widehat{\mathbf{V}}, \tag{10.21}$$

The attained maximum of $\ell(\cdot)$ is:

$$\widehat{\ell} = K_c - \frac{T}{2} \log \left| \widehat{\boldsymbol{\Omega}} \right| \tag{10.22}$$

with:

$$K_c = \frac{-Tn}{2} \left(1 + \log 2\pi\right). \tag{10.23}$$

Note that $\widehat{\boldsymbol{\Omega}}$ is scaled by T, whereas $\widetilde{\boldsymbol{\Omega}}$ is scaled by $T - k$. This convention is adopted throughout the book.

10.3 Recursive estimation

Recursive least squares (RLS) is OLS where coefficients are estimated sequentially, and is a powerful tool for investigating parameter constancy. The sample starts from a minimal number of observations, and statistics are recalculated adding observations one at a time. The multivariate version of RLS is analogous to univariate RLS, and involves little additional computation since the formulae for updating the regressor second-moment matrix are identical owing to the common regressors. Write $\mathbf{W}_t' = (\mathbf{w}_1 \ldots \mathbf{w}_t)$. The parameter estimates up to t are:

$$\widehat{\boldsymbol{\Pi}}_t' = \left(\mathbf{W}_t'\mathbf{W}_t\right)^{-1} \mathbf{W}_t'\mathbf{Y}_t \ \text{ and } \ \widetilde{\boldsymbol{\Omega}}_t = \widehat{\mathbf{V}}_t'\widehat{\mathbf{V}}_t / \left(t - k\right). \tag{10.24}$$

If the sample is increased by one observation, we can avoid inverting the second moment matrix by using the following rank-one updating formula for the inverse:

$$\left(\mathbf{W}_{t+1}'\mathbf{W}_{t+1}\right)^{-1} = \left(\mathbf{W}_t'\mathbf{W}_t\right)^{-1} - \frac{\boldsymbol{\lambda}_{t+1}\boldsymbol{\lambda}_{t+1}'}{1 + \mathbf{w}_{t+1}'\boldsymbol{\lambda}_{t+1}} \tag{10.25}$$

where:

$$\boldsymbol{\lambda}_{t+1} = \left(\mathbf{W}_t'\mathbf{W}_t\right)^{-1}\mathbf{w}_{t+1}.$$

From this, $\widehat{\boldsymbol{\Pi}}_{t+1}$ can be calculated by application of (10.24). To update $\widetilde{\boldsymbol{\Omega}}_t$, we define the innovations $\boldsymbol{\nu}_t$ and the standardized innovations (or recursive residuals, see Harvey, 1990) $\mathbf{s}_t$:

$$\boldsymbol{\nu}_t = \mathbf{y}_t - \widehat{\boldsymbol{\Pi}}_{t-1}\mathbf{w}_t,\ \ \mathbf{s}_t = \frac{\boldsymbol{\nu}_t}{\sqrt{1+\mathbf{w}_t'\boldsymbol{\lambda}_t}}. \tag{10.26}$$

Successive innovations are independent, $\mathsf{E}[\boldsymbol{\nu}_t\boldsymbol{\nu}_{t+1}'] = 0$. Now (see, for example, Hendry, 1995):

$$\widehat{\mathbf{V}}_{t+1}'\widehat{\mathbf{V}}_{t+1} = \widehat{\mathbf{V}}_t'\widehat{\mathbf{V}}_t + \mathbf{s}_{t+1}\mathbf{s}_{t+1}', \tag{10.27}$$

from which $\widetilde{\boldsymbol{\Omega}}_{t+1}$ and $\widehat{\boldsymbol{\Omega}}_{t+1}$ can be derived. The 1-step residuals at $t+1$ are $\mathbf{y}_{t+1} - \widehat{\boldsymbol{\Pi}}_{t+1}\mathbf{w}_{t+1}$. Sequences of parameter constancy tests are readily computed and their use for investigating parameter constancy is discussed in §10.8.1.

10.4 Unrestricted variables

If any variables (such as, for example, the constant, seasonal shift factors or trend) are included unrestrictedly in all equations, the likelihood function can be concentrated with respect to these. The stochastic part of the system is then rewritten as:

$$\mathbf{Y}' = \boldsymbol{\Pi}\mathbf{W}' + \mathbf{D}\mathbf{S}' + \mathbf{V}' \tag{10.28}$$

where $\mathbf{D}$ is the $(n \times s)$ of coefficients of the unrestricted variables, and $\mathbf{S}$ is the $T \times s$ matrix of observations on these variables (where, for example, $s = 1$ if only a constant term is partialled out). The log-likelihood for (10.28) is:

$$\begin{aligned}
&\ell\left(\boldsymbol{\Pi}, \mathbf{D}, \boldsymbol{\Omega} \mid \mathbf{Y}, \mathbf{W}, \mathbf{S}\right) \\
&= K + \tfrac{T}{2}\log\left|\boldsymbol{\Omega}^{-1}\right| - \tfrac{1}{2}\mathrm{tr}\left(\boldsymbol{\Omega}^{-1}(\mathbf{Y}' - \boldsymbol{\Pi}\mathbf{W}' - \mathbf{D}\mathbf{S}')\left(\mathbf{Y} - \mathbf{W}\boldsymbol{\Pi}' - \mathbf{S}\mathbf{D}'\right)\right) \\
&= K + \tfrac{T}{2}\log\left|\boldsymbol{\Omega}^{-1}\right| \\
&\quad -\tfrac{1}{2}\mathrm{tr}\left(\boldsymbol{\Omega}^{-1}\left\{(\mathbf{Y}' - \boldsymbol{\Pi}\mathbf{W}')(\mathbf{Y} - \mathbf{W}\boldsymbol{\Pi}') - 2\mathbf{Y}'\mathbf{S}\mathbf{D}' + 2\boldsymbol{\Pi}\mathbf{W}'\mathbf{S}\mathbf{D}' + \mathbf{D}\mathbf{S}'\mathbf{S}\mathbf{D}'\right\}\right).
\end{aligned} \tag{10.29}$$

Therefore, since $\mathbf{D}$ is unrestricted:

$$\frac{\partial\ell(\cdot)}{\partial\mathbf{D}} = \tfrac{1}{2}\,\boldsymbol{\Omega}^{-1}\left(2\mathbf{Y}'\mathbf{S} - 2\boldsymbol{\Pi}\mathbf{W}'\mathbf{S} - 2\mathbf{D}\mathbf{S}'\mathbf{S}\right). \tag{10.30}$$

Equating the derivative to zero yields the solution $\mathbf{D}_c'$ as a function of $\boldsymbol{\Pi}'$:

$$\mathbf{D}_c' = \left(\mathbf{S}'\mathbf{S}\right)^{-1}\mathbf{S}'\left(\mathbf{Y} - \mathbf{W}\boldsymbol{\Pi}'\right) = \mathbf{P}_Y' - \mathbf{P}_W'\boldsymbol{\Pi}'. \tag{10.31}$$

and in turn the maximum likelihood estimator of $\mathbf{D}'$ is:

$$\widehat{\mathbf{D}}' = \mathbf{P}_Y' - \mathbf{P}_W'\widehat{\mathbf{\Pi}}'. \tag{10.32}$$

$\mathbf{P}_W'$, $\mathbf{P}_Y'$ are the 'prior coefficients' from regressing $\mathbf{W}$ on $\mathbf{S}$ and $\mathbf{Y}$ on $\mathbf{S}$ respectively. Although $\mathbf{\Pi}$ is not known at the time $\mathbf{D}$ is eliminated, the effect of (10.31) is to remove $\mathbf{S}$ from (10.28) and replace the original data by deviations from the 'seasonal' means. Using (10.7), we let $\check{\mathbf{Y}} = \mathbf{M}_S\mathbf{Y}$ and $\check{\mathbf{W}} = \mathbf{M}_S\mathbf{W}$ denote the 'deseasonalized' data (that is, the residuals from the least-squares regressions of $\mathbf{Y}$ and $\mathbf{W}$ on $\mathbf{S}$; we shall also refer to these as the data after 'partialling out' $\mathbf{S}$).

The CLF is:

$$\ell_c(\mathbf{\Pi}, \mathbf{\Omega} \mid \mathbf{Y}, \mathbf{W}, \mathbf{S}; \mathbf{D}) = K + \frac{T}{2}\log\left|\mathbf{\Omega}^{-1}\right| - \tfrac{1}{2}\mathrm{tr}\left(\mathbf{\Omega}^{-1}\left(\check{\mathbf{Y}}' - \mathbf{\Pi}\check{\mathbf{W}}'\right)\left(\check{\mathbf{Y}} - \check{\mathbf{W}}\mathbf{\Pi}'\right)\right) \tag{10.33}$$

Now $\mathbf{\Pi}$ can be estimated using:

$$\check{\mathbf{Y}}' = \mathbf{\Pi}\check{\mathbf{W}}' + \check{\mathbf{V}}'. \tag{10.34}$$

The formula for the variance matrix of $\widehat{\mathbf{D}}$ after obtaining $\widehat{\mathbf{\Pi}}$ is derived in Hendry (1971). Using the Jacobian matrix:

$$\mathbf{J}_S = -\left(\mathbf{I}_n \otimes \mathbf{P}_W'\right), \tag{10.35}$$

it is given as:

$$\mathsf{V}\left[\widetilde{\mathrm{vec}\widehat{\mathbf{D}}'}\right] = \widetilde{\mathbf{\Omega}} \otimes \left(\mathbf{S}'\mathbf{S}\right)^{-1} + \widehat{\mathbf{J}}_S\mathsf{V}\left[\widetilde{\mathrm{vec}\widehat{\mathbf{\Pi}}'}\right]\widehat{\mathbf{J}}_S' \tag{10.36}$$

with:

$$\mathsf{V}\left[\widetilde{\mathrm{vec}\widehat{\mathbf{\Pi}}'}\right] = \widetilde{\mathbf{\Omega}} \otimes \left(\check{\mathbf{W}}'\check{\mathbf{W}}\right)^{-1}. \tag{10.37}$$

Thus, the model can be stated throughout in terms of deseasonalized data $\check{\mathbf{Y}}$, $\check{\mathbf{W}}$, and multivariate least squares applied to the smaller specification.

10.5 Forecasting

Forecasting may be done 1-step ahead or h-steps ahead. The former are *ex post* (or static): any lagged information required to form forecasts is based on observed values. The latter are *ex ante* (or dynamic) and will reuse forecasts from previous period(s) if required. Consider the simple 1-equation system:

$$y_t = \pi_1 y_{t-1} + \pi_2 y_{t-2} + \pi_3 z_t + v_t$$

estimated over $t = 1, \ldots, T$; z_t is not modelled. Assuming a forecast horizon of $H = 3$, we find:

$$\begin{array}{lll} & \text{static forecast} & \text{dynamic forecast} \\ T+1 & \widehat{y}_{T+1} = \widehat{\pi}_1 y_T + \widehat{\pi}_2 y_{T-1} + \widehat{\pi}_3 z_{T+1} & \widehat{y}_{T+1} = \widehat{\pi}_1 y_T + \widehat{\pi}_2 y_{T-1} + \widehat{\pi}_3 z_{T+1} \\ T+2 & \widehat{y}_{T+2} = \widehat{\pi}_1 y_{T+1} + \widehat{\pi}_2 y_T + \widehat{\pi}_3 z_{T+2} & \widehat{y}_{T+2} = \widehat{\pi}_1 \widehat{y}_{T+1} + \widehat{\pi}_2 y_T + \widehat{\pi}_3 z_{T+2} \\ T+3 & \widehat{y}_{T+3} = \widehat{\pi}_1 y_{T+2} + \widehat{\pi}_2 y_{T+1} + \widehat{\pi}_3 z_{T+3} & \widehat{y}_{T+3} = \widehat{\pi}_1 \widehat{y}_{T+2} + \widehat{\pi}_2 \widehat{y}_{T+1} \\ & & \quad + \widehat{\pi}_3 z_{T+3} \end{array} \tag{10.38}$$

Both types of forecast require data for $t = 1, \ldots, T$ to obtain the coefficient estimates. Beyond that, static forecasts require z for $t = T + 1, \ldots, T + H$ and y up to $T + H - 1$, whereas dynamic forecasts only need z for $t = T + 1, \ldots, T + H$. In both types of forecast, the parameter estimates in PcFiml are not updated over the forecast period. This would be possible in principle for static forecasts, and would then mimic an operational procedure where a system was re-estimated each period on the maximum data prior to forecasting. However, given the unrealistic assumption that the future z are known, we prefer to think of static forecasts as delivering information about parameter constancy, and therefore use the usual (rather than the recursive) residuals.

To distinguish the two types of forecast we let $\widehat{y}_{T+i,h}$ denote the h-step forecast made for period $T+i$ ($i \geq h$) and based on parameter estimation up to T. The h-step forecasts use actual values for lagged ys which go further back than h periods. An extreme case is 1-step forecasts, $\widehat{y}_{T+h,1}$ ($h = 1, \ldots, H$), which always use actual values for lagged ys. Dynamic forecasts, $\widehat{y}_{T+h,h}$ ($h = 1, \ldots, H$), are at the other end of the spectrum: they never use actual values beyond T. In addition to these two cases it is possible to define intermediate (h) step forecasts. Using the new notation and dropping the zs:

$$\begin{array}{llll} & \text{1-step} & \text{2-step} & \text{3-step} \\ T+1 & \widehat{y}_{T+1,1} & - & - \\ T+2 & \widehat{y}_{T+2,1} & \widehat{y}_{T+2,2} = \widehat{\pi}_1 \widehat{y}_{T+1,1} + \widehat{\pi}_2 y_T & - \\ T+3 & \widehat{y}_{T+3,1} & \widehat{y}_{T+3,2} = \widehat{\pi}_1 \widehat{y}_{T+2,1} + \widehat{\pi}_2 y_{T+1} & \widehat{y}_{T+3,3} = \widehat{\pi}_1 \widehat{y}_{T+2,2} \\ & & & \quad + \widehat{\pi}_2 \widehat{y}_{T+1,1} \\ \vdots & \vdots & \vdots & \vdots \\ T+i & \widehat{y}_{T+i,1} & \widehat{y}_{T+i,2} = \widehat{\pi}_1 \widehat{y}_{T+i-1,1} + \widehat{\pi}_2 y_{T+i-2} & \widehat{y}_{T+i,3} = \widehat{\pi}_1 \widehat{y}_{T+i-1,2} \\ & & & \quad + \widehat{\pi}_2 \widehat{y}_{T+i-2,1} \end{array} \tag{10.39}$$

In this terminology, the static forecasts are equivalent to the 1-step forecasts, whereas the dynamic forecasts are the sequence of $1, 2, \ldots, H$ step forecasts.

The innovations defined in (10.26) can be seen as 1-step forecast errors, where the parameter estimates are updated after each step. From (10.41) below, the variance matrix of the 1-step forecast error vector in the notation of (10.26) is $\boldsymbol{\Omega}\,(1 + \mathbf{w}_t' \boldsymbol{\lambda}_t)$.

10.5.1 Static forecasting

To test for predictive failure, 1-step forecast errors $\mathbf{e}_{T+i,1} = \mathbf{y}_{T+i} - \widehat{\mathbf{y}}_{T+i,1}$ are calculated as:

$$
\begin{aligned}
\mathbf{e}_{T+i,1} &= \mathbf{\Pi w}_{T+i} + \mathbf{v}_{T+i} - \widehat{\mathbf{\Pi}}\mathbf{w}_{T+i} \\
&= \left(\mathbf{\Pi} - \widehat{\mathbf{\Pi}}\right)\mathbf{w}_{T+i} + \mathbf{v}_{T+i} \\
\mathbf{e}'_{T+i,1} &= \mathbf{w}'_{T+i}\left(\mathbf{\Pi} - \widehat{\mathbf{\Pi}}\right)' + \mathbf{v}'_{T+i} \\
\text{vec}\left(\mathbf{e}'_{T+i,1}\right) = \mathbf{e}_{T+i,1} &= \left(\mathbf{I}_n \otimes \mathbf{w}'_{T+i}\right)\text{vec}\left(\mathbf{\Pi}' - \widehat{\mathbf{\Pi}}'\right) + \mathbf{v}_{T+i}
\end{aligned}
\tag{10.40}
$$

Note that $\mathbf{e}_t$ is $(n \times 1)$ and that $\mathbf{I}_n \otimes \mathbf{w}'_{T+i}$ is $(n \times nk)$. To a first approximation, $\widehat{\mathbf{\Pi}}$ is an unbiased estimator of $\mathbf{\Pi}$ for forecasting purposes (see Clements and Hendry, 1997), so $\mathsf{E}[\mathbf{e}_{T+i,1}] \simeq \mathbf{0}$ and:

$$
\begin{aligned}
\mathsf{V}\left[\mathbf{e}_{T+i,1}\right] &= \mathbf{\Omega} + \left(\mathbf{I}_n \otimes \mathbf{w}'_{T+i}\right)\mathsf{V}\left[\text{vec}\widehat{\mathbf{\Pi}}'\right]\left(\mathbf{I}_n \otimes \mathbf{w}_{T+i}\right) \\
&= \mathbf{\Omega} + \mathbf{\Omega} \otimes \mathbf{w}'_{T+i}\left(\mathbf{W}'\mathbf{W}\right)^{-1}\mathbf{w}_{T+i} \\
&= \mathbf{\Omega}\left(1 + \mathbf{w}'_{T+i}\left(\mathbf{W}'\mathbf{W}\right)^{-1}\mathbf{w}_{T+i}\right) \\
&= \mathbf{\Psi}_{T+i},
\end{aligned}
\tag{10.41}
$$

so that:

$$
\mathbf{e}_{T+i,1} \underset{app}{\sim} \mathsf{IN}_n\left[\mathbf{0}, \mathbf{\Psi}_{T+i}\right], \tag{10.42}
$$

where $\mathbf{\Psi}_{T+i}$ reflects both innovation and parameter uncertainty (also see Chong and Hendry, 1986 and Clements and Hendry, 1994). The parameter uncertainty is of order T^{-1} and tends to be small relative to $\mathbf{\Omega}$. However, the derivation assumes constant parameters and homoscedastic innovation errors over the forecast period, which may be invalid assumptions in practice – see Clements and Hendry (1997) on the general issue of forecasting under conditions of parameter change.

To derive forecast accuracy and constancy tests we require the full variance matrix of all forecast errors. Transposing the error vector of (10.40), and stacking the H rows on top of each other we may write (10.40) as:

$$
\mathbf{E} = \mathbf{W}_H\left(\mathbf{\Pi} - \widehat{\mathbf{\Pi}}\right)' + \mathbf{V}_H. \tag{10.43}
$$

$\mathbf{E}$ is the $(H \times n)$ matrix of 1-step forecast errors, $\mathbf{W}_H$ is the $(H \times k)$ matrix of data for the forecast period $T+1, \ldots, T+H$. Proceeding in similar fashion:

$$
\mathbf{e} = \text{vec}\mathbf{E} = \left(\mathbf{I}_H \otimes \mathbf{W}_H\right)\text{vec}\left(\mathbf{\Pi}' - \widehat{\mathbf{\Pi}}'\right) + \text{vec}\mathbf{V}_H. \tag{10.44}
$$

So again $\mathsf{E}[\mathbf{e}] = \mathbf{0}$, and:

$$\mathsf{E}[\mathbf{e}\mathbf{e}'] = \boldsymbol{\Omega} \otimes \left(\mathbf{I}_H + \mathbf{W}_H \left(\mathbf{W}'\mathbf{W}\right)^{-1} \mathbf{W}_H'\right) = \boldsymbol{\Psi}. \tag{10.45}$$

Under the null of no parameter change, tests can be based on the following approximate test statistics over a forecast horizon of H periods:

$$\begin{array}{llll}
\xi_1 = & \mathbf{e}'\left(\widetilde{\boldsymbol{\Omega}} \otimes \mathbf{I}_H\right)^{-1}\mathbf{e} = & \sum_{i=1}^H \mathbf{e}_{T+i}'\widetilde{\boldsymbol{\Omega}}^{-1}\mathbf{e}_{T+i} & \widetilde{_{app}}\ \chi^2(nH) \\
\xi_2 = & & \sum_{i=1}^H \mathbf{e}_{T+i}'\widetilde{\boldsymbol{\Psi}}_{T+i}^{-1}\mathbf{e}_{T+i} & \widetilde{_{app}}\ \chi^2(nH) \\
\xi_3 = & & \mathbf{e}'\widetilde{\boldsymbol{\Psi}}^{-1}\mathbf{e} & \widetilde{_{app}}\ \chi^2(nH) \\
\eta_i = & & (nH)^{-1}\xi_i,\ i = 1,2,3 & \widetilde{_{app}}\ \mathsf{F}(nH, T-k)
\end{array} \tag{10.46}$$

The first test arises from ξ_2 when $\widetilde{\boldsymbol{\Psi}}_{T+i} = \widetilde{\boldsymbol{\Omega}}_H$ is used, thus ignoring the parameter uncertainty. This implies $\xi_1 \geq \xi_2$. The η_i are the F equivalents of ξ_i and are expected to have better small-sample properties. The form of ξ_3 as given in (10.46) requires an $(nH \times nH)$ matrix, and is computationally inconvenient. Analogous to the procedure used in PcGive, the test may be rewritten as:

$$\begin{aligned}
\xi_3 &= \mathrm{tr}\left(\widetilde{\boldsymbol{\Omega}}^{-1}\mathbf{E}'\left(\mathbf{I}_H + \mathbf{W}_H\left(\mathbf{W}'\mathbf{W}\right)^{-1}\mathbf{W}_H'\right)^{-1}\mathbf{E}\right) \\
&= \mathrm{tr}\left(\widetilde{\boldsymbol{\Omega}}^{-1}\mathbf{E}'\left(\mathbf{I}_H - \mathbf{W}_H\left(\mathbf{W}'\mathbf{W} + \mathbf{W}_H'\mathbf{W}_H\right)^{-1}\mathbf{W}_H'\right)\mathbf{E}\right)
\end{aligned} \tag{10.47}$$

The first line involves inversion of an $(H \times H)$ matrix, whereas the inversion in the second expression is $(k \times k)$. PcGive, which has $n = 1$, reports ξ_1 and η_3.

10.5.2 Dynamic forecasting

To derive expressions for dynamic forecasts, we need to take the lag structure of $\mathbf{y}$ into account. Consider a simple system with one lag of the dependent variable:

$$\mathbf{y}_t = \boldsymbol{\pi}_1\mathbf{y}_{t-1} + \boldsymbol{\pi}_2\mathbf{z}_t + \mathbf{v}_t \tag{10.48}$$

Using backward substitution for any h $(h = 1, \ldots, H)$ commencing at T we find:

$$\begin{aligned}
\mathbf{y}_{T+h} &= \boldsymbol{\pi}_1\mathbf{y}_{T+h-1} + \boldsymbol{\pi}_2\mathbf{z}_{T+h} + \mathbf{v}_{T+h} \\
&= \boldsymbol{\pi}_1\left(\mathbf{y}_{T+h-2} + \boldsymbol{\pi}_2\mathbf{z}_{T+h-1} + \mathbf{v}_{T+h-1}\right) + \boldsymbol{\pi}_2\mathbf{z}_{T+h} + \mathbf{v}_{T+h} \\
&= \boldsymbol{\pi}_1^h\mathbf{y}_T + \sum_{j=0}^{h-1}\boldsymbol{\pi}_1^j\boldsymbol{\pi}_2\mathbf{z}_{T+h-j} + \sum_{j=0}^{h-1}\boldsymbol{\pi}_1^j\mathbf{v}_{T+h-j}.
\end{aligned} \tag{10.49}$$

The forecast at h is:

$$\widehat{\mathbf{y}}_{T+h,h} = \widehat{\boldsymbol{\pi}}_1^h \mathbf{y}_T + \sum_{j=0}^{h-1} \widehat{\boldsymbol{\pi}}_1^j \widehat{\boldsymbol{\pi}}_2 \mathbf{z}_{T+h-j}, \tag{10.50}$$

so that the forecast error at h is:

$$\begin{aligned}\mathbf{e}_{T+h,h} &= \mathbf{y}_{T+h} - \widehat{\mathbf{y}}_{T+h,h} \\ &= (\boldsymbol{\pi}_1^h - \widehat{\boldsymbol{\pi}}_1^h)\mathbf{y}_T + \sum_{j=0}^{h-1}(\boldsymbol{\pi}_1^j \boldsymbol{\pi}_2 - \widehat{\boldsymbol{\pi}}_1^j \widehat{\boldsymbol{\pi}}_2)\mathbf{z}_{T+h-j} + \sum_{j=0}^{h-1} \boldsymbol{\pi}_1^j \mathbf{v}_{T+h-j}.\end{aligned} \tag{10.51}$$

When the parameter uncertainty is negligible, the forecast error is:

$$\mathbf{e}_{T+h,h} = \sum_{j=0}^{h-1} \boldsymbol{\pi}_1^j \mathbf{v}_{T+h-j} \tag{10.52}$$

with variance:

$$\mathsf{V}\left[\mathbf{e}_{T+h,h}\right] = \mathsf{E}\left[\sum_{i=0}^{h-1}\sum_{j=0}^{h-1} \boldsymbol{\pi}_1^i \mathbf{v}_{T+h-i} \mathbf{v}_{T+h-j}' \boldsymbol{\pi}_1^{j\prime}\right] = \sum_{j=0}^{h-1} \boldsymbol{\pi}_1^j \boldsymbol{\Omega} \boldsymbol{\pi}_1^{j\prime} \tag{10.53}$$

since $\mathsf{E}\left[\mathbf{v}_i \mathbf{v}_j'\right] = \mathbf{0}$ for $i \neq j$; $\mathsf{E}\left[\mathbf{v}_i \mathbf{v}_i'\right] = \boldsymbol{\Omega}$. The next section takes parameter uncertainty into account.

With m lags of the dependent variable we may still use expression (10.53) by writing the system:

$$\mathbf{y}_t = \sum_{i=1}^{m} \boldsymbol{\pi}_i \mathbf{y}_{t-i} + \sum_{j=0}^{r} \boldsymbol{\pi}_{m+1+j} \mathbf{z}_{t-j} + \mathbf{v}_t \tag{10.54}$$

in *companion form*:

$$\begin{pmatrix} \mathbf{y}_t \\ \mathbf{y}_{t-1} \\ \vdots \\ \mathbf{y}_{t-m+1} \end{pmatrix} = \begin{pmatrix} \boldsymbol{\pi}_1 & \boldsymbol{\pi}_2 & \cdots & \boldsymbol{\pi}_{m-1} & \boldsymbol{\pi}_m \\ \mathbf{I}_n & \mathbf{0} & \cdots & \mathbf{0} & \mathbf{0} \\ \mathbf{0} & \mathbf{I}_n & \cdots & \mathbf{0} & \mathbf{0} \\ \vdots & \vdots & \ddots & \vdots & \vdots \\ \mathbf{0} & \mathbf{0} & \cdots & \mathbf{I}_n & \mathbf{0} \end{pmatrix} \begin{pmatrix} \mathbf{y}_{t-1} \\ \mathbf{y}_{t-2} \\ \vdots \\ \mathbf{y}_{t-m} \end{pmatrix}$$

$$+ \begin{pmatrix} \boldsymbol{\pi}_{m+1} & \cdots & \boldsymbol{\pi}_{m+1+r} \\ \mathbf{0} & \cdots & \mathbf{0} \\ \vdots & \ddots & \vdots \\ \mathbf{0} & \cdots & \mathbf{0} \end{pmatrix} \begin{pmatrix} \mathbf{z}_t \\ \vdots \\ \mathbf{z}_{t-r} \end{pmatrix} + \begin{pmatrix} \mathbf{v}_t \\ \mathbf{0} \\ \vdots \\ \mathbf{0} \end{pmatrix}$$

or more briefly:

$$\mathbf{y}_t^* = \mathbf{D}\mathbf{y}_{t-1}^* + \mathbf{E}\mathbf{z}_t^* + \mathbf{v}_t^*. \tag{10.55}$$

With the companion matrix, $\mathbf{D}$, of dimension $(nm \times nm)$, taking the place of $\boldsymbol{\pi}_1$ in (10.53), the variance of the forecast error $\mathbf{e}_{T+h,h}^* = \mathbf{y}_{T+h}^* - \widehat{\mathbf{y}}_{T+h,h}^*$ becomes:

$$\mathsf{V}\left[\mathbf{e}_{T+h,h}^*\right] = \sum_{j=0}^{h-1} \mathbf{D}^j \mho \mathbf{D}^{j\prime}, \quad \mho = \begin{pmatrix} \boldsymbol{\Omega} & \mathbf{0} & \cdots \\ \mathbf{0} & \mathbf{0} & \cdots \\ \vdots & \vdots & \ddots \end{pmatrix}. \tag{10.56}$$

The relevant part of this expression is the $(n \times n)$ top-left block.

The system must characterize the economy as accurately in the forecast period as it did over the estimation sample if the forecast errors are to be from the same distribution as that assumed in (10.55) (ignoring the sampling variation owing to estimating $\mathbf{D}$). This is a strong requirement, and seems unlikely to be met unless $\mathbf{D}$ is constant within sample: the further condition that $\mathbf{D}$ is invariant to any regime changes out-of-sample is not considered here. Even if $\mathbf{D}$ is both constant and invariant, $\mathsf{V}[\mathbf{y}_{T+h,h}^* - \widehat{\mathbf{y}}_{T+h,h}^*]$ will generally increase with h, often quite rapidly, and the forecast errors will be heteroscedastic and serially correlated, so care is required in interpreting forecast errors. Clements and Hendry (1994) give forecast error variances for the whole sequence of forecasts.

Finally, we may wish to compute h-step forecasts, where $h \leq H$ is a fixed number, rather than running from 1 to H as in dynamic forecasting. Using the companion form (10.55):

$$\begin{aligned} \widehat{\mathbf{y}}_{T+i,h}^* &= \widehat{\mathbf{D}}\widehat{\mathbf{y}}_{T+i-1,h-1}^* + \widehat{\mathbf{E}}\mathbf{z}_{T+i}^* \\ &= \widehat{\mathbf{D}}^h \mathbf{y}_{T+i-h}^* + \sum_{j=0}^{h-1} \widehat{\mathbf{D}}^j \widehat{\mathbf{E}} \mathbf{z}_{T+i-j}^*, \quad i = h, \ldots, H. \end{aligned} \tag{10.57}$$

Again we ignore the parameter uncertainty in computing the error variance of the h-step forecast errors, so that we may use (10.56): when h is fixed the variance is constant.

10.5.3 Dynamic forecasting: parameter uncertainty

Equation (10.53) ignored the parameter uncertainty in forming dynamic forecasts. The static forecast standard errors of (10.41) take this into account, and we shall now derive this component for dynamic forecasts in a similar way, which corresponds to Schmidt (1974). It is assumed that the system has been mapped to an I(0) representation, and there are no unrestricted variables.

Rewrite the dynamic forecast at $T+h$ as:

$$\widehat{\mathbf{y}}_{T+h,h} = \widehat{\boldsymbol{\pi}}_1^h \mathbf{y}_T + \sum_{j=1}^{h} \widehat{\boldsymbol{\pi}}_1^{h-j} \widehat{\boldsymbol{\pi}}_2 \mathbf{z}_{T+j} = \widehat{\mathbf{A}}_h \mathbf{W}_h, \tag{10.58}$$

where

$$\widehat{\mathbf{A}}_h = \left(\widehat{\pi}_1^h, \widehat{\pi}_1^{h-1}\widehat{\pi}_2, \widehat{\pi}_1^{h-2}\widehat{\pi}_2, \ldots, \widehat{\pi}_2\right), \tag{10.59}$$

and

$$\mathbf{W}_h = \left(\mathbf{y}_T', \mathbf{z}_{T+1}', \mathbf{z}_{T+2}', \ldots, \mathbf{z}_{T+h}'\right)'. \tag{10.60}$$

The matrix $\widehat{\mathbf{A}}_h$ is $(n \times r)$ and $\mathbf{W}_h$ is $(r \times 1)$ where $r = n + hq$ when $\mathbf{z}$ is $(q \times 1)$. Note that $\mathbf{y}_T$ still belongs to the estimation sample, and is known when forecasting. Write $\mathbf{y}_{T+h,h}$ for the forecasts when the parameters are known:

$$\mathbf{y}_{T+h,h} = \pi_1^h \mathbf{y}_T + \sum_{j=1}^{h} \pi_1^{h-j} \pi_2 \mathbf{z}_{T+j} = \mathbf{A}_h \mathbf{W}_h. \tag{10.61}$$

Then the parameter uncertainty component of the forecast errors is:

$$\mathbf{p} = \mathbf{y}_{T+h,h} - \widehat{\mathbf{y}}_{T+h,h} = \left(\mathbf{A}_h - \widehat{\mathbf{A}}_h\right) \mathbf{W}_h, \tag{10.62}$$

from which we can derive:

$$\text{vec}(\mathbf{p}) = \mathbf{p} = (\mathbf{W}_h' \otimes \mathbf{I}_n) \, \text{vec}\left(\mathbf{A}_h - \widehat{\mathbf{A}}_h\right), \tag{10.63}$$

so that

$$\widetilde{\mathsf{V}[\mathbf{p}]} \approx (\mathbf{W}_h' \otimes \mathbf{I}_n) \widehat{\mathbf{J}} \mathsf{V}\left[\widetilde{\text{vec}\widehat{\mathbf{\Pi}}}\right] \widehat{\mathbf{J}}' (\mathbf{W}_h \otimes \mathbf{I}_n), \tag{10.64}$$

where

$$\mathbf{J} = \frac{\partial \text{vec}\mathbf{A}_h}{\partial (\text{vec}\mathbf{\Pi})'}. \tag{10.65}$$

Using

$$\frac{\partial \text{vec}\left(\pi^h\right)}{\partial (\text{vec}\pi)'} = \sum_{i=0}^{h-1} (\pi')^{h-1-i} \otimes \pi^i \tag{10.66}$$

the $(nr \times nk)$ Jacobian matrix can be found:

$$\mathbf{J} = \begin{pmatrix} \left(\dfrac{\partial \text{vec}\pi_1^h}{\partial (\text{vec}\pi_1)'}\right)_{n^2 \times n^2} & \left(\dfrac{\partial \text{vec}\pi_1^h}{\partial (\text{vec}\pi_2)'}\right)_{n^2 \times nq} \\ \left(\dfrac{\partial \text{vec}\pi_1^{h-1}\pi_2}{\partial (\text{vec}\pi_1)'}\right)_{nq \times n^2} & \left(\dfrac{\partial \text{vec}\pi_1^{h-1}\pi_2}{\partial (\text{vec}\pi_2)'}\right)_{nq \times nq} \\ \vdots & \vdots \\ \left(\dfrac{\partial \text{vec}\pi_2}{\partial (\text{vec}\pi_1)'}\right)_{nq \times n^2} & \left(\dfrac{\partial \text{vec}\pi_2}{\partial (\text{vec}\pi_2)'}\right)_{nq \times nq} \end{pmatrix}, \tag{10.67}$$

$$\mathbf{J} = (\mathbf{J}_1 : \mathbf{J}_2) = \begin{pmatrix} \sum_{i=0}^{h-1} (\boldsymbol{\pi}_1')^{h-1-i} \otimes \boldsymbol{\pi}_1^i & \mathbf{0} \\ \sum_{i=0}^{h-2} \boldsymbol{\pi}_2' (\boldsymbol{\pi}_1')^{h-2-i} \otimes \boldsymbol{\pi}_1^i & \mathbf{I}_q \otimes \boldsymbol{\pi}_1^{h-1} \\ \vdots & \vdots \\ \boldsymbol{\pi}_2' \otimes \mathbf{I}_n & \mathbf{I}_q \otimes \boldsymbol{\pi}_1 \\ \mathbf{0} & \mathbf{I}_q \otimes \mathbf{I}_n \end{pmatrix}. \tag{10.68}$$

As Calzolari (1987) points out, the $\mathbf{J}$ matrix can be quite massive, for example for $n = 5$, $q = 20$, $h = 10$ the matrix is (1025×125). However, we are not interested in $\mathbf{J}$ per se, but in $(\mathbf{W}_h' \otimes \mathbf{I}_n)\mathbf{J}$ and find using:

$$(\mathbf{W}_h' \otimes \mathbf{I}_n) = \left(\mathbf{y}_T' \otimes \mathbf{I}_n : \mathbf{z}_{T+1}' \otimes \mathbf{I}_n : \cdots : \mathbf{z}_{T+h}' \otimes \mathbf{I}_n\right) \tag{10.69}$$

the following expression:

$$\begin{aligned} (\mathbf{W}_h' \otimes \mathbf{I}_n)\mathbf{J}_1 &= \sum_{i=0}^{h-1} \mathbf{y}_T' (\boldsymbol{\pi}_1')^{h-1-i} \otimes \boldsymbol{\pi}_1^i + \sum_{j=1}^{h-1} \sum_{i=0}^{h-1-j} \mathbf{z}_{T+j}' \boldsymbol{\pi}_2' (\boldsymbol{\pi}_1')^{h-1-j-i} \otimes \boldsymbol{\pi}_1^i, \\ (\mathbf{W}_h' \otimes \mathbf{I}_n)\mathbf{J}_2 &= \sum_{j=1}^{h} \mathbf{z}_{T+j}' \otimes \boldsymbol{\pi}_1^{h-j} = \sum_{i=0}^{h-1} \mathbf{z}_{T+h-i}' \otimes \boldsymbol{\pi}_1^i. \end{aligned} \tag{10.70}$$

Hence, we see that the results in Schmidt (1974) do not require computation of $\mathbf{J}$.

Reordering the double summation and using (10.61) yields for the first part of (10.70):

$$\begin{aligned} (\mathbf{W}_h' \otimes \mathbf{I}_n)\mathbf{J}_1 &= \sum_{i=0}^{h-1} \mathbf{y}_T' (\boldsymbol{\pi}_1')^{h-1-i} \otimes \boldsymbol{\pi}_1^i + \sum_{i=0}^{h-2} \sum_{j=1}^{h-1-i} \mathbf{z}_{T+j}' \boldsymbol{\pi}_2' (\boldsymbol{\pi}_1')^{h-1-j-i} \otimes \boldsymbol{\pi}_1^i \\ &= \sum_{i=0}^{h-1} \mathbf{y}_{T+h-1-i,h-1-i}' \otimes \boldsymbol{\pi}_1^i \end{aligned} \tag{10.71}$$

Combining $\mathbf{J}_1$ and $\mathbf{J}_2$, and writing $\mathbf{b}_{T+h-i}' = \left(\mathbf{y}_{T+h-1-i,h-1-i}' : \mathbf{z}_{T+h-i}'\right)$, $\mathbf{b}_T' = \left(\mathbf{y}_T' : \mathbf{z}_{T+1}'\right)$:

$$(\mathbf{W}_h' \otimes \mathbf{I}_n)\mathbf{J} = \sum_{i=0}^{h-1} \mathbf{b}_{T+h-i}' \otimes \boldsymbol{\pi}_1^i. \tag{10.72}$$

This is computationally more convenient than (10.70).

To express the Jacobian in terms of $\mathsf{V}[\mathrm{vec}\widehat{\mathbf{\Pi}}']$, rather than $\mathsf{V}[\mathrm{vec}\widehat{\mathbf{\Pi}}]$, requires column reordering. The asymptotic variance of $\mathbf{p}$ is then estimated by:

$$\widehat{\mathsf{V}[\mathbf{p}]} \approx \left(\sum_{i=0}^{h-1} \widehat{\boldsymbol{\pi}}_1^i \otimes \widehat{\mathbf{b}}_{T+h-i}'\right) \widetilde{\mathsf{V}\left[\mathrm{vec}\widehat{\mathbf{\Pi}}'\right]} \left(\sum_{i=0}^{h-1} \widehat{\boldsymbol{\pi}}_1^i \otimes \widehat{\mathbf{b}}_{T+h-i}'\right)', \tag{10.73}$$

which corresponds to the result in Calzolari (1987). When more than one lag of the dependent variable is used, $\boldsymbol{\pi}_1$ should be replaced by the companion matrix $\mathbf{D}$, but $\widehat{\mathbf{b}}_{T+h-i}$ remains unchanged.

The formulae can be derived somewhat differently, bringing out more clearly the terms which are omitted in the approximation. Write:

$$\widehat{\boldsymbol{\pi}}_1 = \boldsymbol{\pi}_1 + \boldsymbol{\delta}, \tag{10.74}$$

so that, ignoring higher order terms in $\boldsymbol{\delta}$:

$$\begin{aligned} \widehat{\boldsymbol{\pi}}_1^h &= (\boldsymbol{\pi}_1 + \boldsymbol{\delta})^h \\ &\approx \boldsymbol{\pi}_1^h + \sum_{i=0}^{h-1} \boldsymbol{\pi}_1^i \boldsymbol{\delta} \boldsymbol{\pi}_1^{h-1-i} \\ &= \boldsymbol{\pi}_1^h + \sum_{i=0}^{h-1} \boldsymbol{\pi}_1^i (\widehat{\boldsymbol{\pi}}_1 - \boldsymbol{\pi}_1) \boldsymbol{\pi}_1^{h-1-i}. \end{aligned} \tag{10.75}$$

In a closed system, this would lead to:

$$\widetilde{\mathsf{V}[\mathbf{p}]} \approx \left(\sum_{i=0}^{h-1} \mathbf{y}_T' (\widehat{\boldsymbol{\pi}}_1')^{h-1-i} \otimes \widehat{\boldsymbol{\pi}}_1^i \right) \widetilde{\mathsf{V}\left[\mathrm{vec}\widehat{\boldsymbol{\Pi}}\right]} \left(\sum_{i=0}^{h-1} \mathbf{y}_T' (\widehat{\boldsymbol{\pi}}_1')^{h-1-i} \otimes \widehat{\boldsymbol{\pi}}_1^i \right)', \tag{10.76}$$

which corresponds to the first component in (10.70).

Next, consider the part arising from non-modelled variables, for $j = 1, \ldots, h-1$:

$$\begin{aligned} \widehat{\boldsymbol{\pi}}_1^j \widehat{\boldsymbol{\pi}}_2 - \boldsymbol{\pi}_1^j \boldsymbol{\pi}_2 &= \boldsymbol{\pi}_1^j (\widehat{\boldsymbol{\pi}}_2 - \boldsymbol{\pi}_2) + \left(\widehat{\boldsymbol{\pi}}_1^j - \boldsymbol{\pi}_1^j\right) \boldsymbol{\pi}_2 - \left(\boldsymbol{\pi}_1^j - \widehat{\boldsymbol{\pi}}_1^j\right) (\widehat{\boldsymbol{\pi}}_2 - \boldsymbol{\pi}_2) \\ &\approx \boldsymbol{\pi}_1^j (\widehat{\boldsymbol{\pi}}_2 - \boldsymbol{\pi}_2) + \left(\widehat{\boldsymbol{\pi}}_1^j - \boldsymbol{\pi}_1^j\right) \boldsymbol{\pi}_2 \\ &\approx \boldsymbol{\pi}_1^j (\widehat{\boldsymbol{\pi}}_2 - \boldsymbol{\pi}_2) + \sum_{i=0}^{j-1} \boldsymbol{\pi}_1^i (\widehat{\boldsymbol{\pi}}_1 - \boldsymbol{\pi}_1) \boldsymbol{\pi}_1^{j-1-i} \boldsymbol{\pi}_2. \end{aligned} \tag{10.77}$$

The first approximation ignores $(\boldsymbol{\pi}_1^j - \widehat{\boldsymbol{\pi}}_1^j)(\widehat{\boldsymbol{\pi}}_2 - \boldsymbol{\pi}_2)$, then (10.75) is used. Combining (10.75) and (10.77) gives:

$$\begin{aligned} \mathbf{p} &= \left(\boldsymbol{\pi}_1^h - \widehat{\boldsymbol{\pi}}_1^h\right) \mathbf{y}_T + \sum_{j=1}^{h} \left(\boldsymbol{\pi}_1^{h-j} \boldsymbol{\pi}_2 - \widehat{\boldsymbol{\pi}}_1^{h-j} \widehat{\boldsymbol{\pi}}_2\right) \mathbf{z}_{T+j} \\ &\approx \sum_{i=0}^{h-1} \boldsymbol{\pi}_1^i (\boldsymbol{\pi}_1 - \widehat{\boldsymbol{\pi}}_1) \boldsymbol{\pi}_1^{h-1-i} \mathbf{y}_T + (\boldsymbol{\pi}_2 - \widehat{\boldsymbol{\pi}}_2) \mathbf{z}_{T+h} + \\ &\quad \sum_{j=1}^{h} \left(\boldsymbol{\pi}_1^{h-j} (\boldsymbol{\pi}_2 - \widehat{\boldsymbol{\pi}}_2) + \sum_{i=0}^{h-j-1} \boldsymbol{\pi}_1^i (\boldsymbol{\pi}_1 - \widehat{\boldsymbol{\pi}}_1) \boldsymbol{\pi}_1^{h-j-1-i} \boldsymbol{\pi}_2 \right) \mathbf{z}_{T+j} \\ &= \sum_{i=0}^{h-1} \boldsymbol{\pi}_1^i (\boldsymbol{\pi}_1 - \widehat{\boldsymbol{\pi}}_1) \boldsymbol{\pi}_1^{h-1-i} \mathbf{y}_T + \sum_{i=0}^{h-1} \boldsymbol{\pi}_1^i (\boldsymbol{\pi}_2 - \widehat{\boldsymbol{\pi}}_2) \mathbf{z}_{T+h-i} \\ &\quad + \sum_{j=1}^{h-1} \sum_{i=0}^{h-j-1} \boldsymbol{\pi}_1^i (\boldsymbol{\pi}_1 - \widehat{\boldsymbol{\pi}}_1) \boldsymbol{\pi}_1^{h-j-1-i} \boldsymbol{\pi}_2 \mathbf{z}_{T+j}, \end{aligned}$$

which leads directly to (10.70).

When the system is in I(1) space, it can be expressed as an I(0) model augmented with I(1) linear combinations of variables (essentially 'nonsense regressions'). The standard errors of the latter are not well defined (see, for example, Phillips, 1986, and Banerjee, Dolado, Galbraith and Hendry, 1993). Moreover, the approximation in (10.75) may be poor, in that unit roots are generally underestimated. When the system is properly estimated in I(0) space, forecasts and their standard errors for levels can be obtained by augmenting the system with identities of the form

$$\mathbf{y}_T \equiv \mathbf{y}_{T-1} + \Delta\mathbf{y}_T.$$

Unit roots are estimated, and the resulting (explosive) confidence bands reflect the cumulative uncertainty.

10.5.4 Dynamic simulation and impulse response analysis

A concept closely related to dynamic forecasting is dynamic simulation. Dynamic simulation values are obtained by computing dynamic forecasts from a starting point within the estimation sample. Commencing from period M as initial conditions:

$$\widehat{\mathbf{s}}_t = \sum_{i=1}^{m} \widehat{\boldsymbol{\pi}}_i \widehat{\mathbf{s}}_{t-i} + \sum_{j=0}^{r} \widehat{\boldsymbol{\pi}}_{j+m+1} \mathbf{z}_{t-j} \quad \text{for } t = M+1, \ldots, M+H \leq T, \tag{10.78}$$

where $\widehat{\mathbf{s}}_{t-i} = \mathbf{y}_{t-i}$ for $t - i \leq M$.

Dynamic simulation uses actual values of the non-modelled variables, but the simulated values of the ys. It can be seen as conditional dynamic forecasting within the estimation sample. However, the forecast error-variance formulae do not apply. As Chong and Hendry (1986) argue, dynamic simulation is not a valid method of model selection or model evaluation. To quote: 'In fact, what dynamic simulation tracking accuracy mainly reflects is the extent to which the *explanation of the data is attributed to non-modelled variables*.' However, dynamic simulation could be useful to investigate theory consistency or data admissibility. In addition, it can help elucidate the dynamic properties of the model. This information is also available through the eigenvalues of the companion matrix: roots outside or on the unit circle entail an unstable system with explosive behaviour. In that case, (10.56) will diverge as the forecast horizon increases towards infinity.

Impulse response analysis is similar to dynamic simulation, but focuses on the dynamics of the endogenous variables only:

$$\widehat{\boldsymbol{\imath}}_t = \sum_{i=1}^{m} \widehat{\boldsymbol{\pi}}_i \widehat{\boldsymbol{\imath}}_{t-i} \quad \text{for } t = 2, \ldots, H < \infty, \tag{10.79}$$

where $\widehat{\boldsymbol{\imath}}_t = \mathbf{0}$ for $t \leq 0$ and $\widehat{\boldsymbol{\imath}}_1 = \mathbf{i}_1$. Various forms are commonly used for the initial values $\mathbf{i}_1$. A simple form is to take all but one values zero, which can be set to unity, or the residual standard error of that equation. This effectively gives powers of the companion matrix. Then the matrix of $\{\widehat{\imath}_t\}$ with $\mathbf{I}_n$ as a basis shows the system equivalent of the moving-average representation. Alternatively, initial values can be taken from the orthogonalized system: see Lütkepohl (1991).

10.6 Dynamic analysis

Consider the system (10.1), and rewrite it slightly as (cf. equation 10.54):

$$\mathbf{y}_t = \sum_{i=1}^{m} \boldsymbol{\pi}_i \mathbf{y}_{t-i} + \sum_{j=0}^{r} \boldsymbol{\Gamma}_j \mathbf{z}_{t-j} + \mathbf{v}_t, \quad \mathbf{v}_t \sim \mathsf{IN}_n\left[\mathbf{0}, \boldsymbol{\Omega}\right], \tag{10.80}$$

with $\mathbf{y}_t$ $(n \times 1)$ and $\mathbf{z}_t$ $(q \times 1)$, $\boldsymbol{\Pi} = (\boldsymbol{\pi}_1 \cdots \boldsymbol{\pi}_m, \boldsymbol{\Gamma}_0 \cdots \boldsymbol{\Gamma}_r)$. Write this as:

$$\left(\mathbf{I} - \boldsymbol{\pi}\left(L\right)\right) \mathbf{y}_t = \mathbf{B}(L)\mathbf{y}_t = \boldsymbol{\Gamma}\left(L\right) \mathbf{z}_t + \mathbf{v}_t, \tag{10.81}$$

where $\mathbf{B}\left(L\right)$ and $\boldsymbol{\Gamma}\left(L\right)$ are matrix lag polynomials of order m and r respectively.[1] L is the lag operator:

$$L^i \mathbf{x}_t = \mathbf{x}_{t-i},$$

and a matrix lag polynomial of order m is:

$$\mathbf{B}\left(L\right) = \mathbf{B}_0 + \mathbf{B}_1 L^1 + \cdots + \mathbf{B}_m L^m.$$

So $\mathbf{B}_0 = \mathbf{I}_n$, $\mathbf{B}_1 = -\boldsymbol{\pi}_1$, $\mathbf{B}_2 = -\boldsymbol{\pi}_2$, etc. Also $\boldsymbol{\pi}(1) = \boldsymbol{\pi}_1 + \cdots + \boldsymbol{\pi}_m$, with m the longest lag on the endogenous variable(s), and $\boldsymbol{\Gamma}(1) = \boldsymbol{\Gamma}_0 + \cdots + \boldsymbol{\Gamma}_r$, with r the longest lag on any non-modelled variable. The lag polynomial $\mathbf{B}\left(L\right)$ is invertible if all solutions z_i to $|\mathbf{B}\left(z\right)| = 0$ lie outside the unit circle (the modulus of all $\lambda_i = 1/z_i$ is less than unity), in which case, the inverse can be written as:

$$\mathbf{B}\left(L\right)^{-1} = \sum_{i=0}^{\infty} \mathbf{G}_i L^i.$$

$\mathbf{P}_0 = -\mathbf{B}(1) = \boldsymbol{\pi}(1) - \mathbf{I}_n$ can be inverted only if it is of rank $p = n$, in which case, for $q > 0$, $\mathbf{y}$ and $\mathbf{z}$ are cointegrated. If $p < n$, only a subset of the ys and zs are cointegrated: see Chapter 11. If $\mathbf{P}_0$ is invertible, and the variables are I(0), we can write the static long-run solution as:

$$\mathsf{E}\left[\mathbf{y}_t\right] = -\mathbf{P}_0^{-1}\boldsymbol{\Gamma}\left(1\right)\mathsf{E}\left[\mathbf{z}_t\right]. \tag{10.82}$$

Let $\mathbf{u}_t = -\mathbf{P}_0^{-1}\mathbf{v}_t$, then the covariance matrix of $\{\mathbf{u}_t\}$ is the long-run covariance matrix of $\{\mathbf{y}_t\}$, namely:

$$\mathsf{V}\left[\mathbf{u}_t\right] = \mathbf{P}_0^{-1}\boldsymbol{\Omega}\mathbf{P}_0^{-1\prime} \tag{10.83}$$

[1]Note that this use of $\mathbf{B}$ and $\boldsymbol{\Gamma}$ is different from that in §8.3.

If $q = 0$, the system is closed (that is, a VAR), and (10.82) is not defined. However, $\mathbf{P}_0$ can still be calculated, in which case, p characterizes the number of cointegrating vectors linking the ys (again see Chapter 11).

The unconditional covariance matrix $\mathbf{\Phi}_y$ of $\mathbf{y}_t$ can be derived from the companion form (10.55):

$$\begin{aligned}\mathbf{\Phi}_y^* &= \mathsf{V}\left[\mathbf{y}_t^*\right] \\ &= \mathsf{E}\left[\left(\mathbf{D}\mathbf{y}_{t-1}^* + \mathbf{v}_t^*\right)\left(\mathbf{y}_{t-1}^{*\prime}\mathbf{D}' + \mathbf{v}_t^{*\prime}\right)\right] \\ &= \mathbf{D}\mathsf{E}\left[\mathbf{y}_{t-1}^*\mathbf{y}_{t-1}^{*\prime}\right]\mathbf{D}' + \mathsf{E}\left[\mathbf{v}_t^*\mathbf{v}_t^{*\prime}\right] \\ &= \mathbf{D}\mathbf{\Phi}_y^*\mathbf{D}' + \mho\end{aligned} \tag{10.84}$$

using the stationarity of $\mathbf{v}_t$, and with $\mho$ as in (10.56). $\mathbf{\Phi}_y$ is the $(n \times n)$ top left block of $\mathbf{\Phi}_y^*$:

$$\mathbf{\Phi}_y = \boldsymbol{\pi}(1)\mathbf{\Phi}_y\boldsymbol{\pi}(1)' + \mathbf{\Omega}. \tag{10.85}$$

Then, using vectorization:

$$\text{vec}\mathbf{\Phi}_y = \left(\boldsymbol{\pi}(1) \otimes \boldsymbol{\pi}(1)\right)\text{vec}\mathbf{\Phi}_y + \text{vec}\mathbf{\Omega}, \tag{10.86}$$

so that:

$$\text{vec}\mathbf{\Phi}_y = \left(\mathbf{I} - \boldsymbol{\pi}(1) \otimes \boldsymbol{\pi}(1)\right)^{-1}\text{vec}\mathbf{\Omega}. \tag{10.87}$$

The estimated static long-run solution is:

$$\widehat{\mathbf{y}} = -\widehat{\mathbf{P}}_0^{-1}\widehat{\mathbf{\Gamma}}(1)\,\mathbf{z}. \tag{10.88}$$

The variance of $\widehat{\mathbf{P}} = -\widehat{\mathbf{P}}_0^{-1}\widehat{\mathbf{\Gamma}}(1)$ is most easily derived in two steps. Changing notation slightly, we write $\mathbf{P} = -\mathbf{B}^{-1}\mathbf{C}$, $\mathbf{A} = (\mathbf{B} : \mathbf{C}) = (\mathbf{P}_0 : \mathbf{\Gamma}(1))$.[2] With $\mathbf{R}$ summing the two parts of $\mathbf{\Pi}$ (defined below equation (10.80)), so $\mathbf{A} = \mathbf{\Pi}\mathbf{R}$, we have:

$$\mathsf{V}\left[\text{vec}\widehat{\mathbf{A}}'\right] = \mathbf{H}\mathsf{V}\left[\text{vec}\widehat{\mathbf{\Pi}}'\right]\mathbf{H}' \quad \text{where} \quad \mathbf{H} = (\mathbf{I}_n \otimes \mathbf{R}') \tag{10.89}$$

$\mathbf{R}$ is $(k \times (n+q))$ so that $\mathbf{H}$ is $(n(n+q) \times nk)$; remember that $\mathbf{P}$ is $(n \times q)$. The Jacobian matrix of the transformation in (10.88) based on $\mathbf{A}$ can now be written as:

$$\begin{aligned}\mathbf{J} = \frac{\partial \text{vec}\mathbf{P}'}{\partial\left(\text{vec}\mathbf{A}'\right)'} &= \left(\frac{\partial \text{vec}\mathbf{P}'}{\partial\left(\text{vec}\mathbf{B}'\right)'} : \frac{\partial \text{vec}\mathbf{P}'}{\partial\left(\text{vec}\mathbf{C}'\right)'}\right)\mathbf{K}' \\ &= \left(\left(\mathbf{I}_q \otimes -\mathbf{C}'\right)\left(-\mathbf{B}^{-1} \otimes \mathbf{B}^{-1\prime}\right) : -\mathbf{B}^{-1} \otimes \mathbf{I}_q\right)\mathbf{K}' \\ &= \left(-\mathbf{B}^{-1} \otimes \mathbf{P}' : -\mathbf{B}^{-1} \otimes \mathbf{I}_q\right)\mathbf{K}' \\ &= -\mathbf{B}^{-1} \otimes \left(\mathbf{P}' : \mathbf{I}_n\right).\end{aligned} \tag{10.90}$$

[2]Here the use of $\mathbf{B}$ and $\mathbf{C}$ is different from, but analogous to, that in Chapter 12.

The $(nq \times n(n+q))$ matrix $\mathbf{J}$ does not have its elements in the right order to allow partitioning. However, $\mathbf{JK}$ does, when $\mathbf{K}$ is the $(n(n+q) \times n(n+q))$ matrix which permutes columns of $\mathbf{J}$, so that for each row, we first take the derivatives with respect to elements of $\mathbf{B}$, and then with respect to elements of $\mathbf{C}$. As $\mathbf{K}$ is orthogonal, $\mathbf{K}^{-1} = \mathbf{K}'$. When moving from line 3 to line 4 in (10.90), $\mathbf{K}'$ drops out again, as the same column reordering is required to collect the partitioned component on the right-hand side.

The variance of the static long-run coefficients may now be computed as:

$$\widetilde{\mathsf{V}\left[\mathrm{vec}\widehat{\mathbf{P}}'\right]} = \widehat{\mathbf{J}}\widehat{\mathbf{H}}\widetilde{\mathsf{V}\left[\mathrm{vec}\widehat{\mathbf{\Pi}}'\right]}\widehat{\mathbf{H}}'\widehat{\mathbf{J}}'. \tag{10.91}$$

This improves on PcGive, which computes the variance numerically, and is a multivariate extension of the results derived by Bårdsen (1989).

Returning to the companion form (10.55), we find by back substitution that $\mathbf{y}_t$ consists of the accumulation of past zs and errors:

$$\mathbf{y}_t^* = \sum_{i=0}^{\infty} \mathbf{D}^i \mathbf{E} \mathbf{z}_{t-i}^* + \sum_{i=0}^{\infty} \mathbf{D}^i \mathbf{v}_{t-i}^*. \tag{10.92}$$

A dynamically stable system requires $\mathbf{D}^i \to \mathbf{0}$ as $i \to \infty$, which implies that all eigenvalues of $\mathbf{D}$ must lie inside the unit circle. When the system is closed ($q = 0$), under stationarity, the unconditional variance of $\mathbf{y}_t^*$ is also given by:

$$\mathsf{V}\left[\mathbf{y}_t^*\right] = \sum_{i=0}^{\infty} \mathbf{D}^i \mho \mathbf{D}^{i\prime}. \tag{10.93}$$

When $\{\mathbf{z}_t\}$ is strongly exogenous and stationary, (10.93) applies to the variance of $\mathbf{y}_t^*$ around its long-run mean.

10.7 Test types

Various test principles are commonly used in econometrics and the three main ones are Wald (W), Lagrange multiplier (LM, also called score test) and likelihood ratio (LR) tests (for a thorough discussion of these tests, and testing in general, see Hendry, 1995, and Godfrey, 1988, and the references cited therein). For example, the Chow (1960) test for parameter constancy in a single equation is derivable from all three principles, whereas the test of over-identifying restrictions is LR, most of the mis-specification tests are LM, and tests for non-linear parameter restrictions are Wald tests. In each instance, the choice of test type tends to reflect computational ease. Under the relevant null hypothesis and for local alternatives, the three test types are asymptotically equivalent in stationary systems; however, if equations are mis-specified in other ways than that under test, or the sample size is small, different inferences can result.

With a k vector of parameters $\boldsymbol{\theta} \in \Theta \subset \mathbb{R}^k$ and corresponding likelihood function $\mathsf{L}(\boldsymbol{\theta}|\cdot)$ we assume that the regularity conditions hold, so that the limiting distribution of the MLE $\widehat{\boldsymbol{\theta}}$ is:

$$\sqrt{T}\left(\widehat{\boldsymbol{\theta}} - \boldsymbol{\theta}_p\right) \xrightarrow{D} \mathsf{N}_k\left[\mathbf{0}, \boldsymbol{\Sigma}\right], \tag{10.94}$$

where $\boldsymbol{\theta}_p$ denotes the population value of $\boldsymbol{\theta}$, and $\boldsymbol{\Sigma}$ is the variance-covariance matrix of the limiting distribution. In finite samples, we approximate the distribution in (10.94) by:

$$\widehat{\boldsymbol{\theta}} \underset{app}{\sim} \mathsf{N}_k\left[\boldsymbol{\theta}_p, T^{-1}\boldsymbol{\Sigma}\right]. \tag{10.95}$$

The general problem is formulated as follows. The maintained hypothesis H_m: $\boldsymbol{\theta} \in \Theta$ defines the statistical model within which all testing will take place. We wish to know which of two hypotheses holds within H_m, the null hypothesis denoted by H_0 or the alternative hypothesis H_1. Thus, we wish to test the r restrictions imposed by H_0:

$$\mathsf{H}_0\colon \boldsymbol{\theta} = \boldsymbol{\theta}_0 \text{ or } \boldsymbol{\theta} \in \Theta_0 \quad \text{versus} \quad \mathsf{H}_1\colon \boldsymbol{\theta} \neq \boldsymbol{\theta}_0 \text{ or } \boldsymbol{\theta} \notin \Theta_0.$$

The likelihood ratio λ is given by:

$$0 \leq \lambda = \frac{\max_{\boldsymbol{\theta} \in \Theta_0} \mathsf{L}(\boldsymbol{\theta})}{\max_{\boldsymbol{\theta} \in \Theta} \mathsf{L}(\boldsymbol{\theta})} \leq 1. \tag{10.96}$$

If H_m is true and the regularity conditions hold, the likelihood ratio test is:

$$-2\log\widehat{\lambda} = 2\ell\left(\widehat{\boldsymbol{\theta}}\right) - 2\ell\left(\widehat{\boldsymbol{\theta}}_0\right) \xrightarrow{D} \chi^2(r) \tag{10.97}$$

when H_0 holds and imposes r restrictions and $\ell(\cdot) = \log \mathsf{L}(\cdot)$.

Writing the r restrictions implied by the null hypothesis as:

$$\mathsf{H}_0\colon \mathbf{f}(\boldsymbol{\theta}) = \mathbf{0} \tag{10.98}$$

where $\mathbf{f}\colon \Theta \mapsto \Theta_0$, the Wald test of hypothesis (10.98) is expressed as:

$$\widehat{\mathsf{w}} = \mathbf{f}(\widehat{\boldsymbol{\theta}})'\left(\mathbf{J}(\widehat{\boldsymbol{\theta}})\widehat{\mathsf{V}[\boldsymbol{\theta}]}\mathbf{J}'(\widehat{\boldsymbol{\theta}})\right)^{-1}\mathbf{f}(\widehat{\boldsymbol{\theta}}) \underset{\mathsf{H}_0}{\xrightarrow{D}} \chi^2(r) \tag{10.99}$$

where $\mathbf{J}$ is the Jacobian matrix of the transformation: $\mathbf{J}(\boldsymbol{\theta}) = \partial\mathbf{f}(\boldsymbol{\theta})/\partial\boldsymbol{\theta}'$.

The Lagrange multiplier (or efficient score) test may be expressed as:

$$\mathbf{q}\left(\widehat{\boldsymbol{\theta}}_0\right)\widehat{\mathsf{V}[\boldsymbol{\theta}_0]}\mathbf{q}'\left(\widehat{\boldsymbol{\theta}}_0\right) \underset{\mathsf{H}_0}{\xrightarrow{D}} \chi^2(r), \tag{10.100}$$

in which the score and variance of the unrestricted model are evaluated at the restricted parameters. With respect to the last two expressions, we may point out three consistent estimators of the asymptotic variance of the MLEs under the maintained being a congruent model:

$$
\begin{aligned}
\mathsf{V}_1\widehat{[\widehat{\boldsymbol{\theta}}]} &= \mathcal{I}\left(\widehat{\boldsymbol{\theta}}\right)^{-1}, \\
\mathsf{V}_2\widehat{[\widehat{\boldsymbol{\theta}}]} &= -\mathbf{H}\left(\widehat{\boldsymbol{\theta}}\right)^{-1}, \\
\mathsf{V}_3\widehat{[\widehat{\boldsymbol{\theta}}]} &= \left(\sum_{t=1}^{T} \mathbf{q}_t\left(\widehat{\boldsymbol{\theta}}\right)\mathbf{q}_t'\left(\widehat{\boldsymbol{\theta}}\right)\right)^{-1}.
\end{aligned}
\tag{10.101}
$$

$\mathcal{I}$ is the information matrix, $\mathsf{E}[\sum_{t=1}^{T} \mathbf{q}_t(\boldsymbol{\theta})\mathbf{q}_t'(\boldsymbol{\theta})]$; the second form involves the Hessian matrix $\mathbf{H}$, $\partial^2\ell/\partial\boldsymbol{\theta}\partial\boldsymbol{\theta}'$; the third form is based on the sample outer product of the gradients (OPG).

The LR test requires estimation of both the unrestricted and the restricted model; the W test requires estimation of the unrestricted model, whereas the LM test only requires estimation of the restricted model.

10.8 Specification tests

The objective of specification testing in PcFiml is to simplify the specification of the system at hand. As the unrestricted system has already been estimated, the most convenient candidates for test types are LR and W.

An obvious example of a specification test is testing whether a group of variables can be omitted from the system, that is, testing whether columns of $\mathbf{\Pi}$ are significantly different from zero. With the system expressed as in (10.4) and taken to be congruent,

$$
\mathbf{Y}' = \mathbf{\Pi}\mathbf{W}' + \mathbf{V}', \tag{10.102}
$$

and partitioning the coefficients as $\mathbf{\Pi} = (\mathbf{\Pi}_1 : \mathbf{\Pi}_2)$ and $\mathbf{W}$ accordingly, we may write this test as:

$$
\mathsf{H}_0 : \mathbf{\Pi}_2 = \mathbf{0} \text{ versus } \mathsf{H}_1 : \mathbf{\Pi}_2 \neq \mathbf{0} \text{ with } \mathsf{H}_m \text{ as in (10.102).} \tag{10.103}
$$

$\mathbf{\Pi}$ is $(n \times k)$, $\mathbf{\Pi}_i$ is $(n \times k_i)$, so that $k = k_1 + k_2$. The likelihood ratio follows from Section [10.2]:

$$
\widehat{\lambda} = \frac{\mathsf{L}_0\left(\widehat{\mathbf{\Pi}}_1 : \mathbf{0}\right)}{\mathsf{L}\left(\widehat{\mathbf{\Pi}}\right)} = \frac{K_c\left|\widehat{\mathbf{\Omega}}_0\right|^{-T/2}}{K_c\left|\widehat{\mathbf{\Omega}}\right|^{-T/2}} = \left(\left|\widehat{\mathbf{\Omega}}\right|\left|\widehat{\mathbf{\Omega}}_0\right|^{-1}\right)^{T/2}. \tag{10.104}
$$

$T\widehat{\mathbf{\Omega}}_0 = \widehat{\mathbf{V}}_0'\widehat{\mathbf{V}}_0 = \mathbf{Y}'\mathbf{M}_{W_1}\mathbf{Y}$, $\widehat{\mathbf{V}}_0$ are the residuals from regressing $\mathbf{Y}$ on $\mathbf{W}_1$, whereas $\widehat{\mathbf{\Omega}}$ comes from the unrestricted system (10.102). Minus twice the logarithm of (10.104) is asymptotically $\chi^2(nk_2)$ distributed under the null hypothesis. Anderson (1984, Section 8.4) and Rao (1973, Section 8b.2) derive the exact distribution of $\lambda^{2/T}$ for fixed $\mathbf{W}$; Anderson gives small-sample correction factors for the χ^2 test.

The restriction imposed by H_0 in (10.103) may be expressed as:

$$\mathbf{\Pi R} = (\mathbf{\Pi}_1 : \mathbf{\Pi}_2)\begin{pmatrix} \mathbf{0} \\ \mathbf{I}_{k_2} \end{pmatrix} = \mathbf{0}, \tag{10.105}$$

in which $\mathbf{R}$ is $(k \times k_2)$. The Jacobian matrix of this transformation is $\mathbf{J} = \mathbf{I}_n \otimes \mathbf{R}'$, so that the Wald test may be written as:

$$\begin{aligned} \widehat{\mathsf{w}} &= \left(\text{vec}\left(\widehat{\mathbf{\Pi}}\mathbf{R}\right)\right)' \left\{\widehat{\mathbf{\Omega}}^{-1} \otimes \left(\mathbf{R}'\left(\mathbf{W}'\mathbf{W}\right)^{-1}\mathbf{R}\right)^{-1}\right\} \text{vec}\left(\widehat{\mathbf{\Pi}}\mathbf{R}\right) \\ &= \text{tr}\left\{\left(\left(\mathbf{W}'\mathbf{W}\right)^{22}\right)^{-1} \widehat{\mathbf{\Pi}}_2'\widehat{\mathbf{\Omega}}^{-1}\widehat{\mathbf{\Pi}}_2\right\}, \end{aligned} \tag{10.106}$$

where $(\mathbf{W}'\mathbf{W})^{22}$ is the relevant block of $(\mathbf{W}'\mathbf{W})^{-1}$. $\widehat{\mathsf{w}}$ has an asymptotic $\chi^2(nk_2)$ distribution. When testing one column of $\mathbf{\Pi}$ (that is, the significance of one variable), the trace is taken of a scalar expression. In this case, the test statistic $\widehat{\mathsf{w}}$ is an instance of the Hotelling T^2 statistic, and is distributed as (assuming normality and fixed regressors):

$$\widehat{\mathsf{w}}\frac{T-k}{Tn} \sim \mathsf{F}(n, T-k). \tag{10.107}$$

Expressions (10.104) and (10.106) are more similar than they might seem at first sight. From §10.4, we know that $\widehat{\mathbf{V}}' = \mathbf{Y}'\mathbf{M}_{W_1} - \widehat{\mathbf{\Pi}}_2\mathbf{W}_2'\mathbf{M}_{W_1}$, so:

$$\widehat{\mathbf{V}}'\widehat{\mathbf{V}} = \mathbf{Y}'\mathbf{M}_{W_1}\mathbf{Y} - \widehat{\mathbf{\Pi}}_2\mathbf{W}_2'\mathbf{M}_{W_1}\mathbf{W}_2\widehat{\mathbf{\Pi}}_2'$$

follows. Using partitioned inversion, (10.106) can be written as:

$$\widehat{\mathsf{w}}/T = \text{tr}\left(\widehat{\mathbf{\Pi}}_2\mathbf{W}_2'\mathbf{M}_{W_1}\mathbf{W}_2\widehat{\mathbf{\Pi}}_2'\widehat{\mathbf{\Omega}}^{-1}/T\right) = \text{tr}\left(\left(\widehat{\mathbf{\Omega}}_0 - \widehat{\mathbf{\Omega}}\right)\widehat{\mathbf{\Omega}}^{-1}\right). \tag{10.108}$$

$\widehat{\mathsf{w}}/T$ is known as the Lawley–Hotelling trace criterion.

R^2-type measures of goodness of fit, as reported by PcFiml, are based on LM and LR. The LM-test of (10.103) is:

$$\widehat{\mathsf{lm}}/T = \text{tr}\left(\left(\widehat{\mathbf{\Omega}}_0 - \widehat{\mathbf{\Omega}}\right)\widehat{\mathbf{\Omega}}_0^{-1}\right), \tag{10.109}$$

(Anderson calls this the Bartlett–Nanda–Pillai trace criterion), so that we may define:

$$\begin{aligned} \mathsf{R}_r^2 &= 1 - \left|\widehat{\mathbf{\Omega}}\right|\left|\widehat{\mathbf{\Omega}}_0\right|^{-1} \\ \mathsf{R}_m^2 &= 1 - \tfrac{1}{n}\text{tr}\left(\widehat{\mathbf{\Omega}}\widehat{\mathbf{\Omega}}_0^{-1}\right). \end{aligned} \tag{10.110}$$

In a one-equation system ($n = 1$), these two measures are identical, but they only correspond to the traditional R^2 if the constant term is the only variable excluded in the specification test.

Following Rao (1952), as described in Rao (1973, Section 8c.5) or Anderson (1984, Section 8.5.4), we may define an F-approximation for likelihood-ratio based tests of (10.103) as:

$$\frac{1-\left(1-\mathsf{R}_r^2\right)^{1/s}}{\left(1-\mathsf{R}_r^2\right)^{1/s}}\cdot\frac{Ns-q}{nk_2} \underset{app}{\sim} \mathsf{F}\left(nk_2, Ns-q\right), \qquad (10.111)$$

with:

$$s=\sqrt{\frac{n^2k_2^2-4}{n^2+k_2^2-5}},\ q=\ \tfrac{1}{2}\ nk_2-1,\ N=T-k_1-k_2-\ \tfrac{1}{2}\ (n-k_2+1) \qquad (10.112)$$

and:

k_1	number of regressors in restricted system	
k_2	number of regressors involved in test	
n	dimension of unrestricted system	(10.113)
T	number of observations in unrestricted system	
$T-k_1-k_2$	degrees of freedom in unrestricted system	

This F-approximation is exact for fixed regressors when $k_2 \leq 2$ or $n \leq 2$.

The following table gives the degrees of freedom of Rao's F-approximation for $T = 100$, $k = 20$:

k_2	$n=1$	$n=2$	$n=3$	$n=4$
1	1, 80	2, 79	3, 78	4, 77
2	2, 80	4, 158	6, 156	8, 154
3	3, 80	6, 158	9, 189.98	12, 204.01
4	4, 80	8, 158	12, 206.66	16, 235.88
5	5, 80	10, 158	15, 215.73	20, 256.33
6	6, 80	12, 158	18, 221.10	24, 269.83
7	7, 80	14, 158	21, 224.52	28, 279.05
8	8, 80	16, 158	24, 226.82	32, 285.56
9	9, 80	18, 158	27, 228.44	36, 290.29
10	10, 80	20, 158	30, 229.62	40, 293.83

The first two columns and the first two rows correspond to exact F-distributions (assuming fixed regressors and stationarity). Testing the significance of k_2 regressors in a single equation system is $\mathsf{F}(k_2, T-k)$; (10.114) below does not follow from Rao's F-approximation, although it is the same distribution. Testing the significance of one regressor in an n-equation system is $\mathsf{F}(n, T-k+1-n)$.

Testing for significance within a single equation of the n equation system proceeds as in the univariate case. This derives from the fact that $T\widehat{\Omega}$ and $\mathbf{\Pi}$ are independent with respectively a Wishart and a normal distribution. To test whether k_2 coefficients in equation i are zero:

$$\frac{RSS_0 - RSS}{RSS} . \frac{T-k}{k_2} \sim \mathsf{F}\left(k_2, T-k\right), \tag{10.114}$$

where RSS and RSS_0 are the ith diagonal element of $T\widehat{\Omega}$ and $T\widehat{\Omega}_0$ respectively. Also, the t-test may be used to test the significance of a single coefficient in an equation:

$$\frac{\widehat{\Pi}_{ij} - 0}{\sqrt{\widetilde{\sigma}^2 \left(\mathbf{W}'\mathbf{W}\right)^{-1}_{jj}}} \sim \mathsf{t}\left(T-k\right), \tag{10.115}$$

where $\widetilde{\sigma}^2$ is the ith diagonal element of $\widetilde{\Omega}$.

10.8.1 Parameter constancy tests

Parameter constancy tests for a one-off break at T_1, $T = T_1 + T_2$, as introduced by Chow (1960), may be described within the framework of this section. First, consider the prediction test where T_2 observations are added to the T_1 we already have. The Chow test may be expressed as a test for significance of $\mathbf{D}$ in:

$$\mathbf{Y}' = \mathbf{\Pi W}' + \mathbf{DS}' + \mathbf{V}', \tag{10.116}$$

where $\mathbf{S}$ consists of dummies removing the influence of the last T_2 observations (see Salkever, 1976). The parameter constancy test is H_0: $\mathbf{D} = \mathbf{0}$. This test is more conveniently done through two separate regressions: for the first T_1 observations (yielding $\widehat{\Omega}_{T_1}$; this is the unrestricted system, as it has all the dummies in it); and for all observations, yielding $\widehat{\Omega}_T$. The first term has to be corrected for the sample size, so that the F-test may be based on:

$$\mathsf{R}^2_r = 1 - \left(\frac{T_1}{T}\right)^n \left|\widehat{\Omega}_{T_1}\right| \left(\left|\widehat{\Omega}_T\right|\right)^{-1}. \tag{10.117}$$

The Wald test of H_0: $\mathbf{D} = \mathbf{0}$ is identical to the parameter-constancy test ξ_3 of (10.46). That equation gives an F-version with a degrees-of-freedom correction which is different from the LR-derived F-test based on (10.117).

When testing within a single equation (a row of $\mathbf{D}$), the familiar F-test arises:

$$\frac{RSS_T - RSS_{T_1}}{RSS_{T_1}} . \frac{T_1 - k}{T_2} \sim \mathsf{F}\left(T_2, T_1 - k\right). \tag{10.118}$$

Now RSS_T and RSS_{T_1} are the ith diagonal element of $T\widehat{\Omega}_T$ and $T_1\widehat{\Omega}_{T_1}$. This is approximate in dynamic models. After recursive estimation, these tests are computed for every possible break-point (although the distribution only holds for a one-off, known break-point). If T_2 is large enough, an analysis-of-covariance type test may be computed, by fitting the system three times, over T_1, T_2 and T, and performing a likelihood ratio test (see, for example, Pesaran, Smith and Yeo, 1985):

$$2\left(\widehat{\ell}_{T_1}+\widehat{\ell}_{T_2}-\widehat{\ell}_{T}\right) \underset{app}{\sim} \chi^2\left(nk-\ \tfrac{1}{2}\ n\left(n+1\right)\right). \qquad (10.119)$$

10.9 Mis-specification tests

Mis-specification tests check whether the system is deficient in the direction of more general specifications, such as systems incorporating heteroscedasticity, serial correlation, etc. The model should have constant parameters and residuals which are homoscedastic innovations, in order to allow us to perform specification tests. Note that rejection of the null hypothesis should not lead to automatic acceptance of the alternative hypothesis, as the tests could have power against other deficiencies. Hendry (1995) discusses these issues and the issue of multiple testing.

Mis-specification testing starts after system specification and estimation, so it can be no surprise that most tests encountered are derived as LM tests.

Diagnostic testing in PcFiml is performed at two levels: individual equations and the system as a whole. Individual-equation diagnostics take the residuals of each equation of the system in turn, and treat them as if they are from a single equation. Usually this means that they are only valid if the remaining equations are problem-free. We first consider single equation statistics.

10.9.1 Single equation tests

To simplify notation, write a single equation of the system (10.1) as:

$$y_t = \boldsymbol{\pi}'\mathbf{w}_t + v_t. \qquad (10.120)$$

In (10.120), the $(k \times 1)$ vector $\boldsymbol{\pi}$ is the transpose of a row of $\boldsymbol{\Pi}$ of (10.1) and $\mathsf{E}[v_t^2] = \sigma^2$. Many tests take the form of:

$$T\mathsf{R}^2 \qquad (10.121)$$

for an auxiliary regression, so that they are asymptotically distributed as $\chi^2(s)$ under their nulls, and hence have the usual additive property for independent $\chi^2 s$. In addition, following Harvey (1990) and Kiviet (1986), F-approximations of the form

$$\frac{\mathsf{R}^2}{1-\mathsf{R}^2}\cdot\frac{T-k-s}{s} \sim \mathsf{F}\left(s, T-k-s\right) \qquad (10.122)$$

are calculated because they may be better behaved in small samples. We can relate these to the Lagrange multiplier and Wald tests of (10.109) and (10.108) by writing $\widehat{\sigma}^2 =$

$\sum \widehat{v}_t^2/T$ and $\widehat{\sigma}_0^2 = \sum (y_t - \bar{y})^2/T$, giving:

$$\mathsf{R}^2 = \left(\widehat{\sigma}_0^2\right)^{-1}\left(\widehat{\sigma}_0^2 - \widehat{\sigma}^2\right) \text{ and } \frac{\mathsf{R}^2}{1-\mathsf{R}^2} = \left(\widehat{\sigma}^2\right)^{-1}\left(\widehat{\sigma}_0^2 - \widehat{\sigma}^2\right). \tag{10.123}$$

10.9.1.1 Portmanteau statistic

This is a degrees-of-freedom corrected version of the Box and Pierce (1970) statistic (it is sometimes called Ljung–Box or Q*-statistic), designed as a goodness-of-fit test in stationary autoregressive moving-average models. It is only a valid test in a single equation with no exogenous variables. An appropriate test for residual autocorrelation is provided by the LM test below. The statistic calculated is:

$$\mathsf{LB}(s) = T^2 \sum_{j=1}^{s} \frac{\mathsf{r}_j^2}{T-j}, \tag{10.124}$$

where s is the length of the correlogram and r_j is the jth coefficient of residual autocorrelation:

$$\mathsf{r}_j = \frac{\sum_{t=j+1}^{T}\left(\widehat{v}_t - \bar{v}_0\right)\left(\widehat{v}_{t-j} - \bar{v}_j\right)}{\sqrt{\sum_{t=j+1}^{T}\left(\widehat{v}_t - \bar{v}_0\right)^2 \sum_{t=j+1}^{T}\left(\widehat{v}_{t-j} - \bar{v}_j\right)^2}}. \tag{10.125}$$

Here $\bar{v}_0 = \frac{1}{T-j}\sum_{t=j+1}^{T}\widehat{v}_t$ is the sample mean of $\widehat{v}_t$, $t = j+1,\ldots,T$, and $\bar{v}_j = \frac{1}{T-j}\sum_{t=j+1}^{T}\widehat{v}_{t-j}$ is the sample mean of $\widehat{v}_{t-j}$, so that r_j corresponds to a sample correlation coefficient proper. Under the assumptions of the test, $\mathsf{LB}(s)$ is asymptotically distributed as $\chi^2(s-k)$, with k being the lag length in an autoregressive model. The degrees-of-freedom correction in (10.124) is not exactly identical to that in Ljung and Box (1978), who use $T(T+2)$ instead of T^2, but chosen to coincide with the vector analogue below. They also use $\{\mathsf{r}_j^*\}$ instead of $\{\mathsf{r}_j\}$:

$$\mathsf{r}_j^* = \frac{\sum_{t=j+1}^{T}\widehat{v}_t\widehat{v}_{t-j}}{\sum_{t=1}^{T}\widehat{v}_t^2}. \tag{10.126}$$

10.9.1.2 LM test for autocorrelated residuals

A Lagrange-multiplier test for serial correlation uses the formulation:

$$v_t = \sum_{i=r}^{s}\alpha_i v_{t-i} + \epsilon_t, \quad 1 \le r \le s \tag{10.127}$$

with $\epsilon_t \sim \mathsf{IID}[0, \sigma^2]$. This test is done through the auxiliary regression of the residuals on the original variables and lagged residuals (missing lagged residuals at the start of the sample are replaced by zero, so no observations are lost). Then the significance of all regressors in this regression is tested through the $\chi^2(s-r+1)$ and F-statistic, based on R^2. The null hypothesis is no autocorrelation, which would be rejected if the test statistic is too high. This LM test is valid for systems with lagged dependent variables, whereas neither the Durbin–Watson nor residual correlogram based tests are valid in that case.

10.9.1.3 LM test for autocorrelated squared residuals

In the linear ARCH model (autoregressive conditional heteroscedasticity, see Engle, 1982) the variance is specified as:

$$\sigma_t^2 = \mathsf{E}\left[v_t^2 \mid v_{t-1}, \ldots, v_{t-s}\right] = c + \sum_{i=1}^{s} \gamma_i v_{t-i}^2. \tag{10.128}$$

An LM-test for the hypothesis $\boldsymbol{\gamma} = (\gamma_1, \ldots, \gamma_s)' = \mathbf{0}$, called the ARCH test, may be obtained as $T\mathsf{R}^2$ from the regression of $\widehat{v}_t^2$ on a constant and $\widehat{v}_{t-1}^2$ to $\widehat{v}_{t-s}^2$. This test is asymptotically distributed as $\chi^2(s)$ on H_0: $\boldsymbol{\gamma} = \mathbf{0}$. The F-form (10.122) may also be computed. Engle, Hendry and Trumbull (1985) investigate the small-sample properties of this test.

10.9.1.4 Test for normality

Let μ, σ^2 denote the mean and variance of v, and write $\mu_i = \mathsf{E}[v-\mu]^i$, so that $\sigma^2 = \mu_2$. The skewness and kurtosis are defined as:

$$\sqrt{\beta_1} = \frac{\mu_3}{\mu_2^{3/2}} \text{ and } \beta_2 = \frac{\mu_4}{\mu_2^2}. \tag{10.129}$$

Sample counterparts are defined by:

$$\bar{v} = \frac{1}{T}\sum_{i=1}^{T} v_i,\ m_i = \frac{1}{T}\sum_{i=1}^{T}\left(v_i - \bar{v}\right)^i,\ \sqrt{b_1} = \frac{m_3}{m_2^{3/2}} \text{ and } b_2 = \frac{m_4}{m_2^2}. \tag{10.130}$$

A normal variate will have $\sqrt{\beta_1} = 0$ and $\beta_2 = 3$. Bowman and Shenton (1975) consider the test:

$$\frac{T\left(\sqrt{b_1}\right)^2}{6} + \frac{T\left(b_2-3\right)^2}{24} \underset{a}{\sim} \chi^2(2) \tag{10.131}$$

unsuitable unless used in very large samples. The statistics $\sqrt{b_1}$ and b_2 are not independently distributed, and the sample kurtosis especially approaches normality very slowly. The test reported by PcFiml is fully described in Doornik and Hansen (1994). It derives from Shenton and Bowman (1977), who give b_2 (conditional on $b_2 > 1 + b_1$) a gamma distribution, and D'Agostino (1970), who approximates the distribution of $\sqrt{b_1}$ by the Johnson S_u system. Let z_1 and z_2 denote the transformed skewness and kurtosis, where the transformation creates statistics which are much closer to standard normal. The test statistic is:

$$\mathsf{e}_2 = z_1^2 + z_2^2 \underset{app}{\sim} \chi^2(2). \qquad (10.132)$$

Table 10.1 compares (10.132) with its asymptotic form (10.131). It gives the rejection frequencies under the null of normality, using $\chi^2(2)$ critical values. The experiments are based on 10 000 replications and common random numbers.

Table 10.1 Empirical size of normality tests.

	nominal probabilities of e_2				nominal probabilities of (10.131)			
T	20%	10%	5%	1%	20%	10%	5%	1%
50	0.1734	0.0869	0.0450	0.0113	0.0939	0.0547	0.0346	0.0175
100	0.1771	0.0922	0.0484	0.0111	0.1258	0.0637	0.0391	0.0183
150	0.1845	0.0937	0.0495	0.0131	0.1456	0.0703	0.0449	0.0188
250	0.1889	0.0948	0.0498	0.0133	0.1583	0.0788	0.0460	0.0180

10.9.1.5 Test for heteroscedasticity

This test is based on White (1980), and involves an auxiliary regression of $\{\widehat{v}_t^2\}$ on a constant, the original regressors $\{w_{it}\}$, and all their squares $\{w_{it}^2\}$. The null is unconditional homoscedasticity, and the alternative is that the variance of the $\{v_t\}$ process depends on $\mathbf{w}_t$ and on the $\{w_{it}^2\}$. Assuming that the auxiliary regression has $1 + s$ regressors, the two statistics are distributed as $\chi^2(s)$ and $\mathsf{F}(s, T - s - 1 - k)$. If one of the $\{w_{it}\}$ is the constant term, and no other variables are redundant when squared, $s = (k-1)^2$. Redundant variables are automatically omitted from the regression, and s is adjusted accordingly.

10.9.2 Vector tests

During development of PcFiml 8 (in 1992) tests were implemented which operate on the system as a whole. Whenever the vector tests are implemented through an auxiliary multivariate regression, we define extensions of the χ^2 and F-statistics of (10.121) and (10.122). The first is an LM test in the auxiliary system, defined in terms of (10.110):

$$Tn\mathsf{R}_m^2 \underset{app}{\sim} \chi^2(sn). \qquad (10.133)$$

The second uses the F-approximation of (10.111). In addition to computational simplicity, this gives the vector tests of PcFiml the attractive property of reducing to the single equation tests in a one-equation system.

10.9.2.1 Vector portmanteau statistic

This is the multivariate equivalent of the single equation portmanteau statistic, and is a valid asymptotic test only in a VAR. The portmanteau statistic uses a small-sample correction. Define:

$$\widehat{\mathbf{C}}_{rs} = \frac{1}{T}\sum_{t=1}^{T} \widehat{\mathbf{v}}_{t-r}\widehat{\mathbf{v}}_{t-s}', \quad \text{with } \widehat{\mathbf{v}}_i = \mathbf{0} \text{ for } i \leq 0. \tag{10.134}$$

Then $\widehat{\mathbf{C}}_{00} = \widehat{\mathbf{\Omega}}$. The vector Box–Pierce statistic is:

$$\mathsf{BP}\left(s\right) = T\sum_{j=1}^{s} \operatorname{tr}\left(\widehat{\mathbf{C}}_{0j}'\widehat{\mathbf{C}}_{00}^{-1}\widehat{\mathbf{C}}_{0j}\widehat{\mathbf{C}}_{00}^{-1}\right), \tag{10.135}$$

whereas the vector portmanteau equals:

$$\mathsf{LB}\left(s\right) = T^2\sum_{j=1}^{s} \frac{1}{T-j}\operatorname{tr}\left(\widehat{\mathbf{C}}_{0j}'\widehat{\mathbf{C}}_{00}^{-1}\widehat{\mathbf{C}}_{0j}\widehat{\mathbf{C}}_{00}^{-1}\right). \tag{10.136}$$

See Hosking (1980) or Lütkepohl (1991). Under the assumptions of the test (one of them being that s is large: $s = O(T^{1/2})$), with s the chosen lag length and m the lag length of the n dependent variables, both statistics are asymptotically $\chi^2(n^2(s-m))$. The multivariate LB statistic is the only statistic in PcFiml that does not reduce to its univariate counterpart in a one-equation system. This would require $\widehat{\mathbf{C}}_{jj}^{-1}$ instead of $\widehat{\mathbf{C}}_{00}^{-1}$ as the last term in (10.136). The actual implementation is computationally simpler.

10.9.2.2 Vector error autocorrelation test

For lags $r \ldots s$ with $1 \leq r \leq s$, this tests the null hypothesis:

$$\mathsf{H}_0\colon \mathbf{R}_r = \cdots = \mathbf{R}_s = \mathbf{0} \tag{10.137}$$

in the augmented system with vector autoregressive errors:

$$\mathbf{Y}' = \mathbf{\Pi}\mathbf{W}' + \mathbf{V}' \quad \text{where} \quad \mathbf{V}' = \sum_{i=r}^{s}\mathbf{R}_i\mathbf{V}_i' + \mathbf{E}'. \tag{10.138}$$

It is implemented through the auxiliary system:

$$\mathbf{Y}' = \mathbf{\Pi}\mathbf{W}' + \mathbf{R}_r\widehat{\mathbf{V}}_r' + \cdots + \mathbf{R}_s\widehat{\mathbf{V}}_s' + \mathbf{E}'. \tag{10.139}$$

Lagged residuals are partialled out from the original regressors, and the original system is re-estimated using the new regressors, providing a Lagrange-multiplier test based on comparing the likelihoods for H_0 and H_1: $\mathbf{R}_r \neq \mathbf{0}, \ldots, \mathbf{R}_s \neq \mathbf{0}$. The LM form of the χ^2 test will be asymptotically $\chi^2\left((s-r+1)\,n^2\right)$ distributed. For a discussion, see Godfrey (1988). The F-approximation is also computed. Simulations on this test are reported in Doornik (1995c), showing that the F-approximation behaves considerably better in small samples than the χ^2 form, without loss of power.

10.9.2.3 Vector normality test

First standardize the residuals of each equation. Call the new residuals $\mathbf{r}_t$, with $\mathbf{R}' = (\mathbf{r}_1 \dots \mathbf{r}_T)$. So $\mathbf{C} = T^{-1}\mathbf{R}'\mathbf{R}$ is the correlation matrix. Following Doornik and Hansen (1994), we define the transformed residuals:

$$\mathbf{e}_t = \mathbf{E}\mathbf{\Lambda}^{-1/2}\mathbf{E}' (\mathbf{r}_t - \bar{\mathbf{r}}) \tag{10.140}$$

with $\mathbf{\Lambda} = \text{diag}(\lambda_1, \dots, \lambda_n)$ the matrix with the eigenvalues of $\mathbf{C}$ on the diagonal. The columns of $\mathbf{E}$ are the corresponding eigenvectors, such that $\mathbf{E}'\mathbf{E} = \mathbf{I}_n$ and $\mathbf{\Lambda} = \mathbf{E}'\mathbf{C}\mathbf{E}$. Equation (10.140) transforms residuals $\mathbf{r}_t \sim \mathsf{IN}_n[\mathbf{0}, \mathbf{C}]$ into independent normal: $\mathbf{e}_t \sim \mathsf{IN}_n[\mathbf{0}, \mathbf{I}]$. We may now compute univariate skewness and kurtosis of each transformed residual. Defining $\mathbf{b}_1' = (\sqrt{b_{11}}, \dots, \sqrt{b_{1n}})$, $\mathbf{b}_2' = (b_{21}, \dots, b_{2n})$, the test statistic:

$$\frac{T\mathbf{b}_1'\mathbf{b}_1}{6} + \frac{T(\mathbf{b}_2 - 3\iota)'(\mathbf{b}_2 - 3\iota)}{24} \underset{a}{\sim} \chi^2(2n). \tag{10.141}$$

will again require large samples. The reported statistic is:

$$e_{2n} = \mathbf{z}_1'\mathbf{z}_1 + \mathbf{z}_2'\mathbf{z}_2 \underset{app}{\sim} \chi^2(2n), \tag{10.142}$$

where $\mathbf{z}_1' = (z_{11}, \dots, z_{1p})$ and $\mathbf{z}_2' = (z_{21}, \dots, z_{2p})$ are determined as in (10.132). So, after transformation to standard normals, the univariate test is applied to each dimension. The transformation involved in (10.140) is the square root of $\mathbf{C}$. An alternative would be to use Choleski decomposition, but then the subsequent test would not be invariant to reordering of equations.

10.9.2.4 Vector heteroscedasticity test (using squares)

The test implemented by PcFiml amounts to a multivariate regression of all error variances and covariances on the original regressors and their squares. Consider, for example, a two-equation system with a constant and z_t as regressors. In this case the auxiliary regression would be:

$$\begin{pmatrix} \widehat{v}_{11}^2 & \cdots & \widehat{v}_{T1}^2 \\ \widehat{v}_{12}^2 & \cdots & \widehat{v}_{T2}^2 \\ \widehat{v}_{11}\widehat{v}_{12} & \cdots & \widehat{v}_{T1}\widehat{v}_{T2} \end{pmatrix} = \begin{pmatrix} \omega_1^2 \\ \omega_2^2 \\ \omega_{12} \end{pmatrix} + \begin{pmatrix} \beta_{11} & \beta_{12} \\ \beta_{21} & \beta_{22} \\ \beta_{31} & \beta_{32} \end{pmatrix} \begin{pmatrix} z_1 & \cdots & z_T \\ z_1^2 & \cdots & z_T^2 \end{pmatrix} + \epsilon. \tag{10.143}$$

The vector heteroscedasticity test checks the significance of the βs in the auxiliary system (10.143). Two statistics may be computed. The first is the LM test for $\boldsymbol{\beta} = \mathbf{0}$, which is $\chi^2(sn(n+1)/2)$, where s is the number of non-redundant added regressors (collinear regressors are automatically removed). Doornik (1995c) shows that this test is identical to the Kelejian (1982) procedure using a common regressor set. The second statistic is the F-approximation. Unlike the vector autocorrelation test, there is not so much benefit of using the F-approximation. In general, this test tends to underreject.

10.9.2.5 Vector heteroscedasticity test (using squares and cross-products)

This test is similar to the heteroscedasticity test, but now both squares and cross-products of the regressors are included in the auxiliary regression. Again, the null hypothesis is no heteroscedasticity (the name 'functional form' was used in version 8 of PcGive and PcFiml).

This concludes the discussion of the system statistics based on assuming that the data are I(0). We now consider the issues of unit roots and cointegration.

Chapter 11

Cointegration Analysis

11.1 Introduction

In the dynamic analysis of the system (see §10.6), we referred to the rank of the long-run matrix as determining the number of cointegrating vectors. In this chapter, we shall discuss how to estimate this rank. The original system contains n endogenous variables $\mathbf{y}$ and q non-modelled variables $\mathbf{z}$:

$$\mathbf{y}_t = \sum_{i=1}^{m} \boldsymbol{\pi}_i \mathbf{y}_{t-i} + \sum_{j=0}^{r} \boldsymbol{\Gamma}_j \mathbf{z}_{t-j} + \mathbf{v}_t, \mathbf{v}_t \sim \mathsf{IN}_n \left[\mathbf{0}, \boldsymbol{\Omega}\right], \tag{11.1}$$

so $\mathbf{y}_t$ is $n \times 1$ and $\mathbf{z}_t$ is $q \times 1$. Introducing lag-polynomials, this system is written as:

$$\left(\mathbf{I}_n - \boldsymbol{\pi}\left(L\right)\right) \mathbf{y}_t = \boldsymbol{\Gamma}\left(L\right) \mathbf{z}_t + \mathbf{v}_t, \tag{11.2}$$

with $\mathbf{P}_0 = \boldsymbol{\pi}\left(1\right) - \mathbf{I}_n$, the matrix of long-run responses.

In much of this chapter, we shall assume that no variables are known to be weakly exogenous for $(\boldsymbol{\Pi}, \boldsymbol{\Omega})$, and work with a fully endogenized system ($q = 0$, that is, the VAR):

$$\mathbf{y}_t = \sum_{i=1}^{m} \boldsymbol{\pi}_i \mathbf{y}_{t-i} + \mathbf{v}_t \ \text{ where } \ \mathbf{v}_t \sim \mathsf{IN}_n \left[\mathbf{0}, \boldsymbol{\Omega}\right]. \tag{11.3}$$

All non-singular, scale-preserving transformations of (11.3) are isomorphic, and in particular retain the same basic innovation process $\{\mathbf{v}_t\}$. When the data $\{\mathbf{y}_t\}$ are I(1), a useful reformulation of the system is to *equilibrium-correction form* (see Hendry, Pagan and Sargan, 1984, Engle and Granger, 1987, Johansen, 1988, Boswijk, 1992 and Banerjee, Dolado, Galbraith and Hendry, 1993):

$$\Delta \mathbf{y}_t = \sum_{i=1}^{m-1} \gamma_i \Delta \mathbf{y}_{t-i} + \mathbf{P}_0 \mathbf{y}_{t-m} + \mathbf{v}_t. \tag{11.4}$$

Note that this may also be written as:

$$\Delta \mathbf{y}_t = \sum_{i=1}^{m-1} \delta_i \Delta \mathbf{y}_{t-i} + \mathbf{P}_0 \mathbf{y}_{t-1} + \mathbf{v}_t, \tag{11.5}$$

and (11.5) is the convention adopted in PcFiml.[1] No restrictions are imposed by this transform. However, when $\mathbf{y}_t$ is I(1), then $\Delta\mathbf{y}_t$ is I(0) and the system specification is balanced only if $\mathbf{P}_0\mathbf{y}_{t-1}$ is I(0). Clearly $\mathbf{P}_0$ cannot be full rank in such a state of nature since that would contradict the assumption that $\mathbf{y}_t$ was I(1), so let rank($\mathbf{P}_0$) $= p < n$. Then $\mathbf{P}_0 = \boldsymbol{\alpha\beta}'$ where $\boldsymbol{\alpha}$ and $\boldsymbol{\beta}$ are $n \times p$ matrices of rank p, and $\boldsymbol{\beta}'\mathbf{y}_t$ must comprise p cointegrating I(0) relations inducing the restricted I(0) representation:

$$\Delta\mathbf{y}_t = \sum_{i=1}^{m-1} \boldsymbol{\delta}_i \Delta\mathbf{y}_{t-i} + \boldsymbol{\alpha}\left(\boldsymbol{\beta}'\mathbf{y}_{t-1}\right) + \mathbf{v}_t. \tag{11.6}$$

To ensure that $\mathbf{y}_t$ is not I(2), a further requirement is that:[2]

$$\text{rank}\left(\boldsymbol{\alpha}'_\perp \boldsymbol{\Upsilon} \boldsymbol{\beta}_\perp\right) = n - p \text{ when } \boldsymbol{\Upsilon} = -\sum_{i=1}^{m} i\boldsymbol{\pi}_i$$

where $\boldsymbol{\Upsilon}$ is the mean-lag matrix, $\boldsymbol{\alpha}_\perp$ and $\boldsymbol{\beta}_\perp$ are orthogonal complements of $\boldsymbol{\alpha}$ and $\boldsymbol{\beta}$ respectively (see Chapter 9, which also shows how to compute the orthogonal complement). Should the analysis commence in I(2) space, then $\boldsymbol{\alpha}'_\perp \boldsymbol{\Upsilon} \boldsymbol{\beta}_\perp = \boldsymbol{\mu\rho}'$ is also reduced rank, so some linear combinations first cointegrate from I(2) to I(1), and then p others (perhaps with I(1) differences of I(2) variables) cointegrate to I(0). Thus, both I(2) and I(1) impose reduced-rank restrictions on the initial formulation in (11.3), and the former imposes restrictions on (11.6).

The rank of $\mathbf{P}_0$ is estimated using the maximum likelihood method proposed by Johansen (1988), described in the next section.

The representation of a cointegrated process in (11.3) above is via an autoregression. There is also a moving-average representation of $\mathbf{y}_t$, obtained by inverting the VAR (see Banerjee *et al.*, 1993, and Johansen, 1995b):

$$\mathbf{y}_t = \mathbf{y}_0 + \mathbf{C}(1)\boldsymbol{\mu}t + \mathbf{C}(1)\sum_{i=1}^{t} \mathbf{v}_i + \mathbf{C}(L)\mathbf{v}_t.$$

Then $\mathbf{C}(1)$ is the moving-average impact matrix. It is computed from:

$$\mathbf{C}(1) = \boldsymbol{\beta}_\perp \left(\boldsymbol{\alpha}'_\perp \boldsymbol{\Upsilon} \boldsymbol{\beta}_\perp\right)^{-1} \boldsymbol{\alpha}'_\perp$$

where

$$\text{rank}\left(\boldsymbol{\alpha}'_\perp \boldsymbol{\Upsilon} \boldsymbol{\beta}_\perp\right) = n - p$$

as above.

[1] It may be verified that $(\boldsymbol{\pi}_1, \boldsymbol{\pi}_2, \boldsymbol{\pi}_3, \ldots, \boldsymbol{\pi}_m) = (\mathbf{P}_0 + \boldsymbol{\delta}_1 + \mathbf{I}_n, \boldsymbol{\delta}_2 - \boldsymbol{\delta}_1, \boldsymbol{\delta}_3 - \boldsymbol{\delta}_2, \ldots, -\boldsymbol{\delta}_{m-1})$ $= (\boldsymbol{\gamma}_1 + \mathbf{I}_n, \boldsymbol{\gamma}_2 - \boldsymbol{\gamma}_1, \boldsymbol{\gamma}_3 - \boldsymbol{\gamma}_2, \ldots, \mathbf{P}_0 - \boldsymbol{\gamma}_{m-1})$.

[2] This condition can also be written as rank$(\boldsymbol{\alpha}'_\perp \boldsymbol{\Gamma} \boldsymbol{\beta}_\perp) = n - p$, where $\boldsymbol{\Gamma} = \mathbf{I}_n - \Sigma_{i=1}^{m-1} \boldsymbol{\delta}_i$. To derive this result, use the previous footnote, and the fact that $\boldsymbol{\alpha}'_\perp \mathbf{P}_0 = \mathbf{0}$.

11.2 Estimating the cointegrating rank

Since the $\{\Delta\mathbf{y}_{t-i}\}$ on the left-hand side of (11.5) enter with unrestricted coefficients, we may concentrate these out as in §10.4: regress $\Delta\mathbf{y}_t$ and $\mathbf{y}_{t-1}$ on $\{\Delta\mathbf{y}_{t-i}\}$, giving residuals $\mathbf{r}_{0t}$, $\mathbf{r}_{1t}$ respectively (both $(n \times 1)$ vectors) for $t = 1, \ldots, T$. Writing $\mathbf{R}_i' = (\mathbf{r}_{i1}\ \mathbf{r}_{i2} \cdots \mathbf{r}_{iT})$ for $i = 0, 1$, the concentrated system is:

$$\mathbf{R}_0' = \mathbf{P}_0\mathbf{R}_1' + \mathbf{V}'. \tag{11.7}$$

From §10.2, we may find the concentrated likelihood function of the system (11.7) as:

$$\begin{aligned} \ell_c(\mathbf{P}_0) &= K_c - \tfrac{T}{2}\log\left|T^{-1}(\mathbf{R}_0' - \mathbf{P}_0\mathbf{R}_1')(\mathbf{R}_0 - \mathbf{R}_1\mathbf{P}_0')\right| \\ &= K_c - \tfrac{T}{2}\log\left|\mathbf{S}_{00} - \mathbf{P}_0\mathbf{S}_{10} - \mathbf{S}_{01}\mathbf{P}_0' + \mathbf{P}_0\mathbf{S}_{11}\mathbf{P}_0'\right|. \end{aligned} \tag{11.8}$$

In the last line, we introduced $\mathbf{S}_{ij} = T^{-1}\mathbf{R}_i'\mathbf{R}_j$ for $i, j = 0, 1$. If $\mathbf{P}_0$ were unrestricted, we would maximize the CLF by minimizing the sum of squares, and find:

$$\widehat{\mathbf{P}}_0 = \mathbf{S}_{01}(\mathbf{S}_{11})^{-1}. \tag{11.9}$$

We may impose the reduced-rank restriction by writing $\mathbf{P}_0 = \boldsymbol{\alpha}\boldsymbol{\beta}'$, where $\boldsymbol{\alpha}$ is an $(n \times p)$ and $\boldsymbol{\beta}'$ is a $(p \times n)$ matrix, and concentrate $\ell_c(\boldsymbol{\alpha}, \boldsymbol{\beta})$ with respect to $\boldsymbol{\alpha}$:

$$\frac{\partial \ell_c(\boldsymbol{\alpha}, \boldsymbol{\beta})}{\partial \boldsymbol{\alpha}}\Big\rfloor_{\boldsymbol{\alpha}_c} = \mathbf{0}, \tag{11.10}$$

which implies that:

$$\boldsymbol{\alpha}_c(\boldsymbol{\beta}) = \mathbf{S}_{01}\boldsymbol{\beta}(\boldsymbol{\beta}'\mathbf{S}_{11}\boldsymbol{\beta})^{-1}. \tag{11.11}$$

Substituting the expression for $\boldsymbol{\alpha}$ back into (11.8) yields the final CLF $\ell_c^*(\boldsymbol{\beta})$:

$$\ell_c^*(\boldsymbol{\beta}) = K_c - \frac{T}{2}\log\left|\mathbf{S}_{00} - \mathbf{S}_{01}\boldsymbol{\beta}(\boldsymbol{\beta}'\mathbf{S}_{11}\boldsymbol{\beta})^{-1}\boldsymbol{\beta}'\mathbf{S}_{10}\right|. \tag{11.12}$$

Differentiating $\ell_c^*(\boldsymbol{\beta})$ with respect to $\boldsymbol{\beta}$ uses the same algebra as the limited-information maximum likelihood estimator for simultaneous equations (LIML). The determinant in (11.12) is (using the determinantal relation for partitioned matrices):

$$|\mathbf{S}_{00}|\,|\boldsymbol{\beta}'\mathbf{S}_{11}\boldsymbol{\beta}|^{-1}\,\left|\boldsymbol{\beta}'(\mathbf{S}_{11} - \mathbf{S}_{10}\mathbf{S}_{00}^{-1}\mathbf{S}_{01})\boldsymbol{\beta}\right|. \tag{11.13}$$

Since $|\mathbf{S}_{00}|$ is a constant relative to $\boldsymbol{\beta}$, maximizing $\ell_c^*(\boldsymbol{\beta})$ with respect to $\boldsymbol{\beta}$ entails minimizing the generalized variance ratio, which is:

$$\frac{\left|\boldsymbol{\beta}'(\mathbf{S}_{11} - \mathbf{S}_{10}\mathbf{S}_{00}^{-1}\mathbf{S}_{01})\boldsymbol{\beta}\right|}{|\boldsymbol{\beta}'\mathbf{S}_{11}\boldsymbol{\beta}|}. \tag{11.14}$$

This is a ratio of determinants of quadratic forms, such that the denominator matrix exceeds the numerator by a non-negative definite matrix. A normalization is needed on $\boldsymbol{\beta}$

to select a unique outcome, and we use $\beta' \mathbf{S}_{11} \beta = \mathbf{I}_p$. The MLE therefore requires minimizing:

$$\left|\beta' \left(\mathbf{S}_{11} - \mathbf{S}_{10}\mathbf{S}_{00}^{-1}\mathbf{S}_{01}\right) \beta\right| \quad \text{subject to} \quad \beta' \mathbf{S}_{11} \beta = \mathbf{I}_p, \tag{11.15}$$

so we must solve:[3]

$$\left|\lambda \mathbf{S}_{11} - \mathbf{S}_{10}\mathbf{S}_{00}^{-1}\mathbf{S}_{01}\right| = 0 \tag{11.16}$$

for the p largest eigenvalues $1 > \widehat{\lambda}_1 > \cdots > \widehat{\lambda}_p > \cdots > \widehat{\lambda}_n > 0$. The corresponding eigenvectors are found from:

$$\left(\widehat{\lambda}_i \mathbf{S}_{11} - \mathbf{S}_{10}\mathbf{S}_{00}^{-1}\mathbf{S}_{01}\right) \widehat{\beta}_i = \mathbf{0}, \tag{11.17}$$

subject to $\widehat{\beta}_i' \mathbf{S}_{11} \widehat{\beta}_i = 1$ and $\widehat{\beta}_i' \mathbf{S}_{11} \widehat{\beta}_j = 0$ for $i \neq j$. Selecting the p largest eigenvalues, with corresponding eigenvector matrix $\widehat{\beta}$, corresponds to imposing a cointegrating rank of p. From (11.15) and (11.17) we find the restricted likelihood to be proportional to:

$$\left|\widehat{\beta}' \left(\mathbf{S}_{11} - \mathbf{S}_{10}\mathbf{S}_{00}^{-1}\mathbf{S}_{01}\right) \widehat{\beta}\right| = \left|\mathbf{I}_p - \widehat{\mathbf{\Lambda}}_p\right| = \prod_{i=1}^{p} \left(1 - \widehat{\lambda}_i\right), \tag{11.18}$$

where $\widehat{\mathbf{\Lambda}}_p$ is the $(p \times p)$ diagonal matrix of eigenvalues. Consequently, from (11.12) and (11.13):

$$\ell_c^* \left(\widehat{\beta}\right) = K_c - \frac{T}{2} \log |\mathbf{S}_{00}| - \frac{T}{2} \sum_{i=1}^{p} \log \left(1 - \widehat{\lambda}_i\right) \tag{11.19}$$

corresponding to the p largest eigenvalues.

When $\mathbf{P}_0$ is estimated unrestrictedly, the maximum of the likelihood is:

$$\ell_c^* \left(\widehat{\beta}_0\right) = K_c - \frac{T}{2} \log |\mathbf{S}_{00}| - \frac{T}{2} \sum_{i=1}^{n} \log \left(1 - \widehat{\lambda}_i\right), \tag{11.20}$$

where $\widehat{\beta}_0$ denotes the $(n \times n)$ matrix of eigenvectors.

The hypothesis that there are $0 \leq p < n$ cointegrating vectors yields (11.19), so tests can be based on twice the difference of (11.19) and (11.20):

$$\eta_p = -T \sum_{i=p+1}^{n} \log \left(1 - \widehat{\lambda}_i\right) \quad \text{for} \quad p = 0, 1, \ldots, n-1. \tag{11.21}$$

The distribution of the η_p test, derived under the hypothesis that there are p cointegrating vectors, is a functional of $n - p$ dimensional Brownian motion. Testing proceeds by the sequence $\eta_0, \eta_1, \ldots, \eta_{n-1}$. Then p is selected as the last significant statistic η_p, or

[3] This is a generalized eigenvalue problem which can be transformed to the standard eigenvalue problem by writing $\mathbf{S}_{11} = \mathbf{L}\mathbf{L}'$. Let $\gamma = \mathbf{L}'\beta$, then (11.15) may be written as: $\left|\gamma' (\mathbf{I}_p - \mathbf{L}^{-1}\mathbf{S}_{10}\mathbf{S}_{00}^{-1}\mathbf{S}_{01}\mathbf{L}'^{-1})\gamma\right|$ subject to $\gamma'\gamma = \mathbf{I}_p$.

zero if η_0 is not significant. This is the *trace statistic* for H_p within H_n, akin to a vector Dickey–Fuller test.

Tests of the hypothesis of p cointegrating vectors within H_{p+1} (that is, testing if there are p when at most $p+1$ exist) can be based on the $(p+1)^{st}$ eigenvalue using:

$$\xi_p = -T \log \left(1 - \widehat{\lambda}_{p+1}\right), \tag{11.22}$$

called the *maximum eigenvalue statistic.* Again ξ_p has a distribution that is a functional of vector Brownian motion.

Critical values for the trace and maximum eigenvalue tests have been tabulated by *inter alia* Johansen (1988), Johansen and Juselius (1990) and Osterwald-Lenum (1992). A simple small-sample correction, replacing T by $T - nm$ in (11.21) and (11.22), was discussed by Reimers (1992). It is unclear yet whether this is the preferred correction.

The solution to the unrestricted system is (11.20), with coefficient estimates $\widehat{\alpha}_0, \widehat{\beta}_0$ where $\widehat{\beta}_0$ is the full $(n \times n)$ matrix of orthogonalized eigenvectors (the coefficients in the equilibrium-correction mechanisms), and $\widehat{\alpha}_0$ the $(n \times n)$ matrix of feedback coefficients on the ECMs (the 'loadings') which may be found from (11.11): $\widehat{\alpha}_0 = \mathbf{S}_{01}\widehat{\beta}_0$. The unrestricted long-run matrix is $\widehat{\mathbf{P}}_0 = \widehat{\alpha}_0\widehat{\beta}_0'$. If, on the basis of the test procedure, it is decided to accept a rank of p, $0 < p < n$, the solution is (11.19), with loadings $\widehat{\alpha}$ (the first p columns of $\widehat{\alpha}$) and coefficients $\widehat{\beta}$ (the first p columns of $\widehat{\beta}_0$). The reduced rank long-run matrix will be $\widehat{\alpha}\widehat{\beta}'$, and $\widehat{\beta}'\mathbf{y}_{t-1}$ are the equilibrium-correction terms (this follows from Granger's representation theorem: see, for example, Banerjee *et al.*, 1993).

11.3 Numerically stable estimation

From the perspective of numerical analysis, it is not recommended to use equation (11.16) as it stands. The computations can become numerically unstable, and we have seen instances where the eigenvalues are far outside the $(0, 1)$ interval (in which they should fall theoretically). Although such cases are rare, we have implemented the stable computational method suggested by Doornik (1995a).

A first requirement is that the initial regression to obtain $\mathbf{R}_0$ and $\mathbf{R}_1$ in (11.7) should be done using a stable method. Next, we can apply the singular value decomposition (Chapter 9) to these:

$$\mathbf{R}_i = \mathbf{U}_i\mathbf{W}_i\mathbf{V}_i'.$$

Since both $\mathbf{U}$ and $\mathbf{V}$ are orthogonal, the eigenvalue problem reduces to

$$|\lambda\mathbf{I}_n - \mathbf{U}_1'\mathbf{U}_0\mathbf{U}_0'\mathbf{U}_1| = 0.$$

The required eigenvalues correspond to the squared singular values of $\mathbf{U}_1'\mathbf{U}_0$. This approach avoids multiplying two matrices with very large numbers by one with small numbers and subtracting the result from a matrix with large numbers.

11.4 Recursive estimation

Recursive estimation of the cointegrating space requires solving the eigenvalue problem (11.16) for each sample size $t = M, \ldots, T$. A choice has to be made between doing the whole procedure recursively, or fixing the short-run dynamics at their full sample values (hence recursively solving from (11.7) onwards). Hansen and Johansen (1992) call the former the Z-representation and the latter the R-representation. Both representations have been implemented in PcFiml.

11.5 Restricted variables

The above results are presented for the simplest model to clarify the analysis. One natural extension is the presence of intercepts in equations. Under the null of no cointegrating vectors, non-zero intercepts would generate trends. However, in equations with equilibrium corrections, two possibilities arise, namely, the intercept only enters the equilibrium correction (to adjust its mean value), or it enters as an autonomous growth factor in the equation.

Let us reintroduce the $(q \times 1)$ variable $\mathbf{z}_t$ to indicate the additional variables in the system. Usually $\mathbf{z}_t$ contains variables such as the constant, trend or centred seasonals, so we shall drop the subscript t. The second possibility implies that $\mathbf{z}$ enters unrestricted, and it is concentrated out together with the $\{\Delta \mathbf{y}_{t-i}\}$, leaving the procedure otherwise unaltered; denote these q_u variables by $\mathbf{z}_u$. The first possibility means that some zs are restricted to enter the cointegrating space, which now becomes $\beta'(\mathbf{y}_{t-1} : \mathbf{z}_r)$, so that β' is now $(p \times (n + q_r))$. Then $\mathbf{S}_{01}$ and $\mathbf{S}_{11}$ change accordingly, but otherwise the analysis of the previous section goes through unaltered, adding q_r eigenvalues of zero.

The distributions of the tests are affected by the presence of (un)restricted $\mathbf{z}$. Critical values of the tests in the presence of constant, centred seasonals, or trend were considered by Johansen and Juselius (1990) and Osterwald-Lenum (1992).

In practice, how the deterministic components are treated has an important impact on the statistics and careful thought should be given at the outset as to whether or not z_t can be restricted to the cointegrating space. If one component is a trend, such restriction is essential when there are unit roots unless a quadratic trend in levels is anticipated (although the inclusion may be an attempt to induce similarity in the associated tests: see Kiviet and Phillips, 1992).

11.6 Testing restrictions on α and β

11.6.1 Introduction

Having accepted H_p: cointegrating rank $= p$, we may test further restrictions on α and β. Over time, we have seen the development of procedures for testing a range of hypotheses. Initially, these were imposing the same restrictions on each vector, but now they are primarily concerned with identifying cointegrating vectors and testing for long-run weak exogeneity. Table 11.1 gives a summary of various hypotheses on the cointegrating space with references to their development and application. As one moves down the table, the complexity of the implementation increases.

H_g, which allows for general restrictions is the richest and encompasses the other test statistics. However, it is also the hardest to compute. Computation of H_a to H_c involves a modified eigenproblem, whereas the other test procedures use iterative methods. The hypothesis on α of type H_a can be combined with restrictions on β without substantial change to the methods; but often it is more interesting to test exclusion restrictions on the α matrix.

Table 11.1 Summary of restrictions on cointegrating space.

	hypothesis	reference
H_a	$\alpha = \mathbf{B}_1\boldsymbol{\theta}_1$	Johansen (1991), Johansen and Juselius (1990)
H_b	$\beta_2 = \mathbf{H}_2\boldsymbol{\phi}_2$	Johansen (1988, 1991) Johansen and Juselius (1990)
H_c	$\beta_3 = (\mathbf{H}_3 : \boldsymbol{\phi}_3)$	Johansen and Juselius (1992)
H_d	$\beta_4 = (\mathbf{H}_4\boldsymbol{\varphi} : \boldsymbol{\psi})$	Johansen and Juselius (1992)
H_e	$\beta_5 = (\mathbf{H}_1\boldsymbol{\varphi}_1 \ldots \mathbf{H}_p\boldsymbol{\varphi}_p)$	Johansen (1995a), Johansen and Juselius (1994)
H_f	$\text{vec}\beta_6 = \mathbf{H}\boldsymbol{\varphi} + h$, $\text{vec}\alpha_6' = \mathbf{G}\boldsymbol{\theta}$	Boswijk (1994)
H_g	$\beta_7 = \mathbf{f}_\beta(\boldsymbol{\theta}), \alpha = \mathbf{f}_\alpha(\boldsymbol{\theta})$	Doornik (1995b), Doornik and Hendry (1994a), Hendry and Doornik (1994)

In the remainder, we shall first discuss several types of restriction separately, and then combine the tests on α and β. Finally the more general procedures are discussed. Because all tests in this section are conditional on H_p, they are in I(0) space, and likelihood ratio test statistics have conventional χ^2 distributions (asymptotically). Detailed descriptions of the mathematics of the tests have been omitted.

11.6.2 Restrictions on α, H_a: $\alpha_1 = \mathbf{A}\boldsymbol{\theta}$

Suppose that we have a VAR of three equations, $\mathbf{y} = (y_1, y_2, y_3)'$, α_0 is (3×3) and β_0 is (3×3). Then we could (for example) test that none of the cointegrating vectors enters the first equation (believing that the cointegrating rank is 2: α and β are (3×2)).

This restricts the α matrix and is expressed as $\alpha_r = \mathbf{A}\theta$:

$$\mathbf{A} = \begin{pmatrix} 0 & 0 \\ 1 & 0 \\ 0 & 1 \end{pmatrix}, \quad \theta = \begin{pmatrix} \theta_{11} & \theta_{12} \\ \theta_{21} & \theta_{22} \end{pmatrix}, \quad \mathbf{A}\theta = \begin{pmatrix} 0 & 0 \\ \theta_{11} & \theta_{12} \\ \theta_{21} & \theta_{22} \end{pmatrix}. \tag{11.23}$$

This choice of **A** implies a selected cointegrating rank ≤ 2. If this restriction is rejected, Δy_1 is not weakly exogenous for α and β (the distribution of Δy_1 given lagged $\Delta y_1, \Delta y_2, \Delta y_3$ contains elements of α and β).

11.6.3 Restrictions on β, H_b: $\beta_2 = \mathbf{H}_2\phi_2$

The first test on β, $\beta = \mathbf{H}\phi$, allows us to impose linear restrictions linking coefficients in the cointegrating vectors. Suppose we wish to test that the first two variables enter the cointegrating vector with opposite sign. Assuming $p = 2$, the unrestricted vectors are:

$$\beta'\mathbf{y} = \begin{pmatrix} \beta_{11}y_1 + \beta_{21}y_2 + \beta_{31}y_3 \\ \beta_{12}y_1 + \beta_{22}y_2 + \beta_{32}y_3 \end{pmatrix}. \tag{11.24}$$

We can impose $\beta_{21} = -\beta_{11}$, $\beta_{22} = -\beta_{12}$:

$$\mathbf{H} = \begin{pmatrix} 1 & 0 \\ -1 & 0 \\ 0 & 1 \end{pmatrix}, \quad \phi = \begin{pmatrix} \phi_{11} & \phi_{12} \\ \phi_{21} & \phi_{22} \end{pmatrix}, \quad \phi'\mathbf{H}' = \begin{pmatrix} \phi_{11} & -\phi_{11} & \phi_{21} \\ \phi_{12} & -\phi_{12} & \phi_{22} \end{pmatrix}. \tag{11.25}$$

This **H** implies a selected cointegrating rank ≤ 2.

11.6.4 Restrictions on β, H_c: $\beta_3 = (\mathbf{H}_3 : \phi_3)$

The second test on β allows us to impose known cointegrating vectors. Consider that the first vector is $y_1 - y_2 - y_3$. Again assuming $p = 2$, the **H** matrix is:

$$\mathbf{H} = \begin{pmatrix} 1 \\ -1 \\ -1 \end{pmatrix}, \quad \phi = \begin{pmatrix} \phi_{11} \\ \phi_{21} \\ \phi_{31} \end{pmatrix}, \quad (\mathbf{H} : \phi)' = \begin{pmatrix} 1 & -1 & -1 \\ \phi_{11} & \phi_{21} & \phi_{31} \end{pmatrix}. \tag{11.26}$$

11.6.5 Combining restrictions on α and β

The combination of tests on α and β is explained more easily if we see that all tests start with a second moment matrix, which is transformed:

$$\begin{pmatrix} \mathbf{S}_{11} & \mathbf{S}_{12} \\ \mathbf{S}_{21} & \mathbf{S}_{22} \end{pmatrix} \longrightarrow \begin{pmatrix} \mathbf{S}_{11.1} & \mathbf{S}_{12.1} \\ \mathbf{S}_{21.1} & \mathbf{S}_{22.1} \end{pmatrix}, \tag{11.27}$$

and then solve the eigenproblem:

$$\left|\lambda \mathbf{S}_{22.1} - \mathbf{S}_{21.1}\mathbf{S}_{11.1}^{-1}\mathbf{S}_{12.1}\right| = 0. \tag{11.28}$$

The test on α effectively reduces the dimension of the $\mathbf{S}_{11}$ part, the test on β that of the $\mathbf{S}_{22}$ part. So combining H_a with either H_b or H_c works by first transforming according to H_a, then replacing $\mathbf{S}_{00}, \mathbf{S}_{01}, \mathbf{S}_{11}, \mathbf{S}_{10}$ by $\mathbf{S}_{aa.b}, \mathbf{S}_{a1.b}, \mathbf{S}_{1a.b}, \mathbf{S}_{11.b}$. Next H_b or H_c are implemented, and the resulting eigenvalue problem may be solved. From this $\widehat{\beta}$ may be derived as in the previous two sections.

11.6.6 Testing more general restrictions

The appeal of the aforementioned tests is that they all have a general eigenproblem as their solution. The drawback, however, is that the tests require separate implementation, while not exhausting all interesting hypotheses. The primary interest here is in restrictions of the form $\beta_i = \mathbf{H}_i\phi_i$, $i = 1, \ldots, p$, perhaps combined with restrictions on α: $\alpha_i = \mathbf{A}_i\psi_i$. It is crucial to check that the set of restrictions yields uniquely identified β_i: see Johansen (1995a). These tests are all in I(0) space and correspond to LR tests, so the easiest implementation is direct maximization of the likelihood function allowing for general restrictions (possibly non-linear). This is done sequentially using a numerical optimization procedure outlined below.

Again assume a cointegrating rank p. The test is expressed as:

$$\mathsf{H}_g\colon \ \{\alpha = \mathbf{f}(\alpha^u)\} \cap \{\beta = \mathbf{f}(\beta^u)\}, \tag{11.29}$$

where α and β are expressed as a function of the unrestricted elements α^u, β^u. The likelihood to maximize is:

$$\ell_c(\alpha^u, \beta^u) \propto -\log\left|(\mathbf{I}_n : -\alpha\beta')\begin{pmatrix} \mathbf{S}_{00} & \mathbf{S}_{01} \\ \mathbf{S}_{10} & \mathbf{S}_{11} \end{pmatrix}\begin{pmatrix} \mathbf{I}_n \\ -\beta\alpha' \end{pmatrix}\right|.$$

The function in (11.29) may be non-linear, and even link α and β. Consider an example with $n = 4$, $p = 2$:

$$\alpha = \begin{pmatrix} \theta_0 & \theta_1 \\ \theta_2 & \theta_3 \\ \theta_4 & \theta_5 \\ \theta_6 & \theta_7 \end{pmatrix}, \quad \beta' = \begin{pmatrix} \theta_8 & \theta_9 & \theta_{10} & \theta_{11} \\ \theta_{12} & \theta_{13} & \theta_{14} & \theta_{15} \end{pmatrix}. \tag{11.30}$$

A possible restriction we may wish to test is $\theta_6 = 0, \theta_7 = 0, \theta_{10} = \theta_{11}, \theta_{14} = \theta_{15}$. Another could be $\theta_6\theta_{11} + \theta_7\theta_{15} = 0$; this type of restriction is considered by Hunter (1992) and Mosconi and Giannini (1992) (also see Toda and Phillips, 1993, who note the need for care in testing when some parameters vanish from the hypothesis when others are zero).

11.7 Estimation under general restrictions

PcFiml implements a large set of techniques to estimate restrictions of the type H_e, H_f and H_g. One reason is that it happens occasionally that a method does not converge (for example, the α parameters go to zero, and the β to infinity). Unfortunately, no method is uniformly superior, and some experimentation is required at times.

Input of restrictions is not in the form of H matrices, but in the form of explicit relations. These restrictions are then analysed as follows:

(1) Analytical differentiation at two random points is used to check for linearity. If linear this yields the **F** and **f** matrices:

$$\left[(\text{vec}\alpha')' : (\text{vec}\beta)'\right]' = \mathbf{F}\phi + \mathbf{f}.$$

(2) Next, it is checked whether the restrictions on α and β are variation free, i.e. whether **F** is block diagonal. If so, this yields the **G**, **g**, **H** and **h** matrices:

$$\text{vec}\beta = \mathbf{H}\varphi + \mathbf{h}, \quad \text{vec}\alpha' = \mathbf{G}\theta + \mathbf{g}.$$

(3) The restrictions are homogenous when **h** or **g** are zero.

(4) The absence of cross-equation restrictions on β implies that **H** is block diagonal.

(5) The restrictions on α are simple if they consist of exclusion restrictions only.

One additional feature is implemented. When a normalizing restriction is imposed on each equation, the restrictions can be written in various ways. For example, the restriction $\beta' = (1, 0, -1, 1)$ can be written as:

$$(\beta_1 = 1, \ \beta_2 = 0, \ \beta_3 = -1, \ \beta_4 = 1),$$

or as:

$$(\beta_1 = \phi, \ \beta_2 = 0, \ \beta_3 = -\phi, \ \beta_4 = \phi),$$

in combination with the normalization $\phi = 1$. Thus, PcFiml is able to rewrite the equality restrictions on β, which makes additional estimation methods available.

The currently available implemented estimation methods are as follows:

- beta switching

  This method switches between restricted cointegrating vectors, keeping all but one fixed. At each step, this requires solution of a generalized eigenproblem, after the matrices have been deflated using the fixed vectors. Beta switching was suggested by Johansen (1995a), and is available when α is unrestricted, and the β restrictions are linear, within equation, and homogenous (after the normalization has been removed).

- linear switching (scaled)
  This method alternates between $\alpha|\beta$ and $\beta|\alpha$. Each of these is a restricted linear regression problem which can be solved explicitly, as discussed in Boswijk (1994). The scaled variant removes the normalization prior to estimation, and then reimposes it afterwards. During estimation, some scaling is applied at each step to prevent a situation such as α going to zero and β to infinity. This method requires linear and variation-free restrictions, where the α restrictions are simple and the β restrictions are homogenous (again, after the normalization has been removed).
- linear switching
  This method is similar to the previous one, but here the normalizations are not removed. It requires linear and variation-free restrictions.
- non-linear switching
  In PcFiml version 8, non-linear switching was the only available method. The principle is the same as in linear switching, but with each maximization step performed using non-linear optimization (BFGS, see Chapter 13). When the restrictions are linear, this is somewhat less efficient. With non-linear restrictions, the previous methods are not available.
- no switching
  No switching uses a hybrid Gauss–Newton/quasi-Newton method applied simultaneously to all the unknown parameters in both α and β. Initially, the generalized Gauss–Newton method is used with very weak convergence, after which the BFGS method takes over. When the restrictions are not identifying, the Hessian matrix in the Gauss–Newton is singular, and the generalized inverse is used. Similarly, the approximate Hessian in BFGS could become singular, leading to a Hessian reset.

All these methods may suffer from slow convergence, or even failure of convergence (when some parameters diverge to very large or to very small values, or both happen).

Convergence is decided as follows:

- beta switching
  Terminates when the change in the sum of the eigenvalues is less than $0.001\epsilon_1$. Whether or not the method has converged (strongly or weakly) is then based on the scores of the likelihood, as discussed in §13.3.5 and §13.3.6.
- other switching methods
  Convergence is verified whenever the relative increase in the likelihood is less than $0.001\epsilon_1$. Strong convergence (see §13.3.6) leads to termination, as does four successive occurrences of weak convergence.
- no switching
  Converges as with the standard BFGS method.

11.8 Identification

Deriving the degrees of freedom involved in these test is not straightforward, especially when α restrictions are involved. For example, version 8.0 of PcFiml would not always get it correct. When beta switching is allowed, the global method of Johansen (1995a) could be used. This will not work for more general restrictions, and the generic identification check of Doornik (1995b) is used instead.

It is important to bear in mind that the following situations may occur:

- some cointegrating vectors are identified, but others are not;
- although restrictions have been imposed, these are just rotations, not affecting the likelihood at all;
- restrictions have been imposed, but no identification achieved.

It is easy to illustrate the inherent complexity of counting restrictions. For simplicity, we assume that the identifying restrictions are imposed on $\boldsymbol{\beta}$. In the unrestricted case of rank p, there are np parameters in $\boldsymbol{\alpha}$ and $np-p^2$ in $\boldsymbol{\beta}$. Restrictions on $\boldsymbol{\beta}$ are only binding if they cannot be 'absorbed' by the $\boldsymbol{\alpha}$s, and vice versa. This is most easily seen for rank n: restricting $\boldsymbol{\beta}' = \mathbf{I}_n$ results in $\widehat{\boldsymbol{\alpha}} = \widehat{\mathbf{P}}_0$, whereas imposing $\boldsymbol{\alpha} = \mathbf{I}_n$ gives $\widehat{\boldsymbol{\beta}}' = \widehat{\mathbf{P}}_0$. But setting $\boldsymbol{\alpha} = \mathbf{0}$ imposes n^2 restrictions (which, of course, violate cointegration). Restrictions of the form $\theta_8 = 0$, or $\theta_8 = 0$ and $\theta_9 = 1$ in example (11.30) are not binding, because we may choose $\mathbf{L}$ such that $\theta_8 = \theta_{13} = 0$, $\theta_9 = \theta_{12} = 1$. However, imposing $\theta_8 = \theta_9 = 0$ would be binding, as it would require a singular $\mathbf{L}$; instead it involves one restriction, because only one of the zeros can be absorbed by a non-singular $\mathbf{L}$. The hypothesis $\theta_{10} = \theta_{11}, \theta_{14} = \theta_{15}$ equates two columns of $\boldsymbol{\beta}'$, one of which can be absorbed, resulting in two restrictions. This explains the number of restrictions involved in H_b, which amounts to fixing $(n-s)$ columns of p elements each. Fixing a row of $\boldsymbol{\beta}'$, as does H_c, constrains only $n-p$ parameters, as the first p may be absorbed by $\mathbf{L}$ (provided it can be done with a non-singular $\mathbf{L}$). Finally, some forms of constraint on $\boldsymbol{\alpha}$ and $\boldsymbol{\beta}$ can induce a failure of identification of the other under the null, in which case the tests need not have χ^2-distributions (see, for example, Toda and Phillips, 1993).

Chapter 12

Econometric Analysis of the Simultaneous Equations Model

12.1 The econometric model

The main criterion for the validity of the system:

$$\mathbf{y}_t = \boldsymbol{\Pi}\mathbf{w}_t + \mathbf{v}_t, \quad \mathbf{v}_t \sim \mathsf{IN}_n\left[\mathbf{0}, \boldsymbol{\Omega}\right], \quad t = 1, \ldots, T, \tag{12.1}$$

is its congruence, since that is a necessary condition for efficient statistical estimation and inference. Chapter 10 established notation and discussed the econometric techniques for estimation and evaluation of (12.1). An econometric model is a restricted version of a congruent system which sustains an economic interpretation, consistent with the associated theory. All linear structural models of (12.1) can be obtained by premultiplying (12.1) by a non-singular $(n \times n)$ matrix $\mathbf{B}$ which generates:

$$\mathbf{B}\mathbf{y}_t + \mathbf{C}\mathbf{w}_t = \mathbf{u}_t, \quad \mathbf{u}_t \sim \mathsf{IN}_n\left[\mathbf{0}, \boldsymbol{\Sigma}\right], \quad t = 1, \ldots, T, \tag{12.2}$$

with $\mathbf{u}_t = \mathbf{B}\mathbf{v}_t$, $\boldsymbol{\Sigma} = \mathbf{B}\boldsymbol{\Omega}\mathbf{B}'$ and $\mathbf{C} = -\mathbf{B}\boldsymbol{\Pi}$. We implicitly assume that the diagonal of $\mathbf{B}$ is normalized at unity to ensure a unique scaling in every equation: other normalizations are feasible. Further, the reformulation in I(0) space would have the same form. Then (12.2) can be written in compact notation as:

$$\mathbf{B}\mathbf{Y}' + \mathbf{C}\mathbf{W}' = \mathbf{A}\mathbf{X}' = \mathbf{U}'. \tag{12.3}$$

So $\mathbf{A} = (\mathbf{B} : \mathbf{C})$ and $\mathbf{X} = (\mathbf{Y} : \mathbf{W})$: these are $(n \times (n+k))$ and $(T \times (n+k))$ matrices respectively.

We shall require the matrices $\mathbf{R}$ and $\mathbf{Q}$:

$$\mathbf{R} = (\mathbf{I}_n : -\boldsymbol{\Pi}), \quad \mathbf{Q}' = (\boldsymbol{\Pi}' : \mathbf{I}_k).$$

This allows us to express the system (12.1) in matrix form as $\mathbf{R}\mathbf{X}' = \mathbf{V}'$. Comparing with $\mathbf{A}\mathbf{X}' = \mathbf{U}'$, we have $\mathbf{B}\mathbf{R} = \mathbf{A}$. This is usually expressed as $\mathbf{B}\boldsymbol{\Pi} + \mathbf{C} = \mathbf{0}$, but a more convenient form is obtained by $\mathbf{A}\mathbf{Q} = \mathbf{0}$.

When identities are present, the corresponding elements of $\{\mathbf{u}_t\}$ are precisely zero, so the model can be written as:

$$\mathbf{AX}' = \begin{pmatrix} \mathbf{A}_1 \\ \mathbf{A}_2 \end{pmatrix} \mathbf{X}' = \begin{pmatrix} \mathbf{U}_1' \\ \mathbf{0} \end{pmatrix}, \tag{12.4}$$

where $n = n_1 + n_2$, for n_1 stochastic equations and n_2 identities. The elements of $\mathbf{A}_2$ must be known, so do not need estimation. In much of what follows, we set $n_2 = 0$ for simplicity: however, the program handles identities by finding the value of $\mathbf{A}_2$ once the 'menu' of variables in each identity is known.

Given the system formulation, the model depends on the mapping between the unknown coefficients in the matrix $\mathbf{A}$ and the parameters of interest ϕ. This mapping can be written in many different notations: the one that follows is natural in a computer programming context, and is that used in PcFiml, namely $\phi = \mathbf{A}^{v_u}$. First we stack the rows of $\mathbf{A}$ as a vector (each row of $\mathbf{A}$ corresponds to an equation). From this vector, we select only unrestricted elements. Other than the elements of ϕ and the normalization that the diagonals of $\mathbf{B}$ are unity, the remaining elements of $\mathbf{A}$ are zero. Thus, $(\cdot)^{v_u}$ codes where in $\mathbf{A}$ the unrestricted elements occur and selects them in the right order. An example is given in Chapter 9.

12.2 Identification

Without some restrictions, the coefficients in $\mathbf{A}$ in (12.4) will not be identified. The matrix $\mathbf{B}$ used to multiply the system to obtain the model could in turn be multiplied by an arbitrary non-singular matrix, $\mathbf{D}$ say, and still produce a linear model, but with different coefficients. To resolve such arbitrariness, we need to know the form of $\mathbf{A}$ in advance, and it must be sufficiently restricted that the only admissible $\mathbf{D}$ matrix is $\mathbf{I}_n$. The *order condition* for identification concerns the number of unrestricted coefficients in $\mathbf{A}$. Since $\mathbf{\Pi}$ is $n \times k$, no more than k regressors can enter any equation, and no more than $n \times k$ unknowns in total can enter $\mathbf{A}$, where $k = n \times m + q \times (r+1)$ (m is the number of lags on $\mathbf{y}_t$, q is the number of variables in $\mathbf{z}_t$ and the model includes $\mathbf{z}_t, \ldots, \mathbf{z}_{t-r}$). This condition is easily checked by just counting the number of unrestricted elements of $\mathbf{A}$. However, to ensure that no equation can be obtained as a linear combination of other equations, these elements need to be located in the appropriate positions. This requires the exclusion of some variables and the inclusion of others in every equation. Since $\mathbf{Q}$ is the conditional expectation matrix of $\mathbf{x}_t$ given $\mathbf{w}_t$:

$$\mathsf{E}\left[\mathbf{x}_t \mid \mathbf{w}_t\right] = \mathsf{E}\left[\begin{pmatrix} \mathbf{y}_t \\ \mathbf{w}_t \end{pmatrix} \mid \mathbf{w}_t\right] = \begin{pmatrix} \mathbf{\Pi} \\ \mathbf{I}_k \end{pmatrix} \mathbf{w}_t = \mathbf{Q}\mathbf{w}_t, \tag{12.5}$$

it is unique, so that the identification of $\mathbf{A}$ rests on being able to uniquely solve for $\mathbf{A}$ from $\mathbf{AQ} = \mathbf{0}$. The order condition ensures a sufficient number of equations, and the *rank condition* that these equations are linearly independent. A rank condition can only be determined on a probability-one basis: if a variable is included in an equation, then its associated coefficient a_{ij} in the matrix $\mathbf{A}$ is assumed to be non-zero ($1+\delta$, where δ is a uniform random number), although in practice an estimate may be zero or there may exist linear combinations of coefficients that are collinear and hence lower the rank. An implication of this analysis is that any linear system like (12.1) can be interpreted as the unrestricted solved, or reduced, form of a just-identified structural econometric model (see Hendry and Mizon, 1993).

12.3 The estimator generating equation

Estimation methods in PcFiml are summarized by the estimator generating equation (EGE) based on Hendry (1976); for general discussions of simultaneous equations estimation, see, for example, Judge, Griffiths, Hill, Lütkepohl and Lee (1985, Chapter 15), Spanos (1986, Chapter 25), or Hendry (1995, Chapter 11). Consider the system of n structural simultaneous equations in (12.2), written as:

$$\mathbf{B}\mathbf{y}_t + \mathbf{C}\mathbf{w}_t = \mathbf{A}\mathbf{x}_t = \mathbf{u}_t \text{ with } \mathbf{u}_t \sim \mathsf{IN}_n\left[\mathbf{0}, \boldsymbol{\Sigma}\right]. \tag{12.6}$$

There are n endogenous variables $\mathbf{y}_t$ and k weakly exogenous or lagged variables $\mathbf{w}_t$ where the parameters of interest ϕ in (12.6) are assumed to be identified and $|\mathbf{B}| \neq 0$. In this section, we will only consider models in which $\mathbf{A}$ is a linear function of ϕ.

In fact, (12.6) is a useful way to view the claims of econometrics: a stochastic vector $\mathbf{x}_t$, multiplied by the correct constant matrix $\mathbf{A}$, is asserted to be a homoscedastic, normally distributed white-noise process $\mathbf{u}_t$. Expressed in that form, the claim is ambitious, and although $\mathbf{x}_t$ is a carefully selected vector, the claim does yield insight into econometrics as filtering data through a matrix $\mathbf{A}$ to produce an unpredictable component $\mathbf{u}_t \sim \mathsf{IN}_n[\mathbf{0}, \boldsymbol{\Sigma}]$. Large macro-econometric models are generally non-linear in both variables and parameters, so are only approximated by (12.6), but in practice linearity seems a reasonable first approximation.

The statistical structure of (12.6) is expressed in (12.5) through the conditional expectation:

$$\mathsf{E}\left[\mathbf{x}_t \mid \mathbf{w}_t\right] = \mathbf{Q}\mathbf{w}_t \tag{12.7}$$

and we now interpret $\boldsymbol{\Pi}$ as $-\mathbf{B}^{-1}\mathbf{C}$, so that:

$$\mathbf{y}_t \mid \mathbf{w}_t \sim \mathsf{N}_n\left[\boldsymbol{\Pi}\mathbf{w}_t, \boldsymbol{\Omega}\right] \text{ with } \boldsymbol{\Omega} = \mathbf{B}^{-1}\boldsymbol{\Sigma}\mathbf{B}'^{-1}. \tag{12.8}$$

These relationships are the inverse of those associated with (12.2). Whenever confusion is likely, we shall write $\boldsymbol{\Pi}_u$, $\boldsymbol{\Omega}_u$ for the unrestricted reduced form coefficients (obtained by multivariate least squares), and $\boldsymbol{\Pi}_r$, $\boldsymbol{\Omega}_r$ for the restricted reduced-form coefficients, obtained out of $\mathbf{B}$, $\mathbf{C}$, $\boldsymbol{\Sigma}$ from the simultaneous equations model (which itself is derived from the URF by imposing (over-)identifying restrictions).

The likelihood function is that of the multivariate normal distribution dependent on $(\mathbf{\Pi}, \mathbf{\Omega}) = f(\boldsymbol{\phi}, \mathbf{\Sigma})$, namely $\ell(\mathbf{\Pi}, \mathbf{\Omega})$. We wish to maximize $\ell(\cdot)$ with respect to $\boldsymbol{\phi}$, so first map to $\ell(\boldsymbol{\phi}, \mathbf{\Sigma})$. Then $\boldsymbol{\phi}$ corresponds to $\boldsymbol{\theta}_1$ and $\mathbf{\Sigma}$ corresponds to $\boldsymbol{\theta}_2$ in $\ell(\boldsymbol{\theta}_1, \boldsymbol{\theta}_2)$. However, $\mathbf{Q}$ will also be part of $\boldsymbol{\theta}_2$ (see Hendry, 1976). Consider the condition:

$$\mathsf{E}[\mathbf{w}_t \mathbf{u}_t'] = \mathbf{0} \tag{12.9}$$

entailed by the fact that the $\mathbf{w}_t$ are the conditioning variables, and so are uncorrelated with the $\mathbf{u}_t$. Since (12.7) implies that $\mathbf{Q}\mathbf{w}_t$ (the best predictor of $\mathbf{x}_t$ given $\mathbf{w}_t$) is also uncorrelated with $\mathbf{u}_t$:

$$\mathsf{E}[\mathbf{Q}\mathbf{w}_t \mathbf{u}_t'] = \mathbf{0}. \tag{12.10}$$

But $\mathbf{u}_t' = \mathbf{x}_t'\mathbf{A}_t'$, so (12.10) becomes:

$$\mathsf{E}[\mathbf{Q}\mathbf{w}_t \mathbf{x}_t'\mathbf{A}'] = \mathbf{0}. \tag{12.11}$$

However, $\mathbf{u}_t$ is generally heteroscedastic across equations (it is assumed homoscedastic over time), and its variance-covariance matrix is $\mathbf{\Sigma}$, so to obtain a suitably-weighted function of $\mathbf{u}_t$, postmultiply $\mathbf{u}_t$ by $\mathbf{\Sigma}^{-1}$:

$$\mathsf{E}\left[\mathbf{Q}\mathbf{w}_t \mathbf{x}_t'\mathbf{A}'\mathbf{\Sigma}^{-1}\right] = \mathbf{0}. \tag{12.12}$$

Finally (12.12) has to hold for all t. Thus, sum over the sample, and transpose the result for convenience, to obtain the EGE:

$$\mathsf{E}\left[\mathbf{\Sigma}^{-1}\mathbf{A}\mathbf{X}'\mathbf{W}\mathbf{Q}'\right] = \mathbf{0}. \tag{12.13}$$

Dropping the expectations operator, (12.13) is in fact the conditional score equation $\mathbf{q}_1(\boldsymbol{\theta}_1|\boldsymbol{\theta}_2)$, where $\boldsymbol{\theta}_1$ corresponds to $\mathbf{A}(\boldsymbol{\phi})$ and $\boldsymbol{\theta}_2$ to $(\mathbf{\Sigma}, \mathbf{Q})$. All known linear simultaneous equations estimation methods are generated by special cases of (12.13).

The next section gives a formal derivation.

12.4 Maximum likelihood estimation

12.4.1 Linear parameters

Starting from the log-likelihood (10.17) and substituting $\mathbf{\Omega}^{-1} = \mathbf{B}'\mathbf{\Sigma}^{-1}\mathbf{B}$ and $\mathbf{\Pi} = -\mathbf{B}^{-1}\mathbf{C}$:

$$\begin{aligned} \ell(\mathbf{\Pi}, \mathbf{\Omega} \mid \mathbf{X}) &= K + \tfrac{T}{2}\log\left|\mathbf{\Omega}^{-1}\right| - \tfrac{1}{2}\operatorname{tr}\left(\mathbf{\Omega}^{-1}\mathbf{V}'\mathbf{V}\right) \\ &= K + \tfrac{T}{2}\log\left|\mathbf{\Sigma}^{-1}\right| + T\log\|\mathbf{B}\| - \tfrac{1}{2}\operatorname{tr}\left(\mathbf{\Sigma}^{-1}\mathbf{U}'\mathbf{U}\right) \end{aligned} \tag{12.14}$$

where $\|\mathbf{B}\|$ is the modulus of $|\mathbf{B}|$ and the last right-hand term can also be written as:

$$-\ \tfrac{1}{2}\operatorname{tr}\left(\mathbf{\Sigma}^{-1}(\mathbf{B}\mathbf{Y}' + \mathbf{C}\mathbf{W}')(\mathbf{Y}\mathbf{B} + \mathbf{W}\mathbf{C})\right) = -\ \tfrac{1}{2}\operatorname{tr}\left(\mathbf{\Sigma}^{-1}\mathbf{A}\mathbf{X}'\mathbf{X}\mathbf{A}'\right),$$

If $\mathbf{B}$ is not square, as in an incompletely-specified system with fewer than n equations, the term $\frac{T}{2}\log|\mathbf{B}'\mathbf{\Sigma}^{-1}\mathbf{B}|$ is retained in place of the two middle right-hand terms in (12.14).

Concentrating with respect to $\mathbf{\Sigma}$ requires differentiating (12.14) with respect to $\mathbf{\Sigma}^{-1}$, which yields $\mathbf{\Sigma}_c = T^{-1}\mathbf{U}'\mathbf{U} = T^{-1}\mathbf{AX}'\mathbf{XA}'$ (see the derivation of (10.18) above), and the resulting concentrated likelihood function (CLF):

$$\ell_c\left(\mathbf{A}\left(\phi\right) \mid \mathbf{X};\mathbf{\Sigma}\right) = K_c - \frac{T}{2}\log\left|T^{-1}\mathbf{AX}'\mathbf{XA}'\right| + T\log||\mathbf{B}||. \tag{12.15}$$

The constant K_c is given in (10.23).

We first proceed as if we are interested in $\mathbf{A}$ rather than ϕ, and differentiate the log-likelihood $\ell_c\left(\mathbf{B},\mathbf{C}|\mathbf{X};\mathbf{\Sigma}\right)$ with respect to $\mathbf{B}$ and $\mathbf{C}$, evaluating the outcome at $\mathbf{\Sigma}_c = T^{-1}\mathbf{AX}'\mathbf{XA}'$:

$$\frac{\partial \ell_c}{\partial \mathbf{B}} = T\mathbf{B}'^{-1} - \mathbf{\Sigma}_c^{-1}\mathbf{U}'\mathbf{Y} \tag{12.16}$$

and:

$$\frac{\partial \ell_c}{\partial \mathbf{C}} = -\mathbf{\Sigma}_c^{-1}\mathbf{U}'\mathbf{W}. \tag{12.17}$$

The trick to solving these two equations together was discovered by Durbin (presented in 1963, published as Durbin, 1988). From the function for $\mathbf{\Sigma}_c$ at the first step, we have:

$$\mathbf{\Sigma}_c = T^{-1}\mathbf{AX}'\mathbf{XA}', \tag{12.18}$$

which on premultiplication of both sides by $\mathbf{\Sigma}_c^{-1}$ and postmultiplication of both sides by $T\mathbf{B}'^{-1}$ implies that:

$$T\mathbf{B}'^{-1} = \mathbf{\Sigma}_c^{-1}\mathbf{AX}'\mathbf{XR}' \tag{12.19}$$

since $\mathbf{R} = \mathbf{B}^{-1}\mathbf{A} = (\mathbf{I}_n : -\mathbf{\Pi})$ and hence $\mathbf{XR}' = \left(\mathbf{Y} - \mathbf{W\Pi}'\right) = \mathbf{V}$ is the matrix of reduced-form errors. Thus, in (12.19), since $\mathbf{AX}' = \mathbf{U}'$:

$$T\mathbf{B}'^{-1} - \mathbf{\Sigma}_c^{-1}\mathbf{U}'\mathbf{Y} = \mathbf{\Sigma}_c^{-1}\mathbf{U}'\mathbf{XR}' - \mathbf{\Sigma}_c^{-1}\mathbf{U}'\mathbf{Y} = -\mathbf{\Sigma}_c^{-1}\mathbf{U}'\mathbf{W\Pi}'. \tag{12.20}$$

Combining the two derivatives in (12.16) and (12.17) using (12.20):

$$\frac{\partial \ell_c}{\partial \mathbf{A}}_{\rfloor \mathbf{\Sigma}_c,\mathbf{Q}_c} = -\left(\mathbf{\Sigma}_c^{-1}\mathbf{U}'\mathbf{W\Pi}_c' : \mathbf{\Sigma}_c^{-1}\mathbf{U}'\mathbf{W}\right) = -\mathbf{\Sigma}_c^{-1}\mathbf{AX}'\mathbf{WQ}_c' \tag{12.21}$$

which is the EGE discussed in (12.13) above. With the selection operator explicitly present:

$$\left(\frac{\partial \ell_c}{\partial \mathbf{A}}\right)^{v_u} = \frac{\partial \ell_c}{\partial\left(\mathbf{A}^{v_u}\right)} = \frac{\partial \ell_c}{\partial \phi} = \mathbf{q}_1^c\left(\phi\right) \tag{12.22}$$

we find $\widehat{\phi}$ as the solution to:

$$\mathbf{q}_1^c\left(\phi\right)_{\rfloor \mathbf{\Sigma}_c,\mathbf{Q}_c} = -\left(\mathbf{\Sigma}^{-1}\mathbf{AX}'\mathbf{WQ}'\right)^{v_u}_{\rfloor \mathbf{\Sigma}_c,\mathbf{Q}_c} = \mathbf{0}. \tag{12.23}$$

The variance of $\widehat{\phi}$ depends on $-T^{-1}$ times the inverse Hessian:

$$-T^{-1}\frac{\partial^2 \ell_c}{\partial\phi\partial\phi'}\bigg\rfloor_{\Sigma_c,\mathbf{Q}_c} = \frac{\partial}{\partial\phi'}\left(\Sigma^{-1}\left[T^{-1}\mathbf{U}'\mathbf{W}\right]\mathbf{Q}'\right)^{v_u}_{\rfloor_{\Sigma_c,\mathbf{Q}_c}} \tag{12.24}$$

which must take account of the dependence of $\mathbf{Q}_c$ and Σ_c on ϕ. However, the central term in $\mathrm{q}_1^c(\phi)$ is $\left[T^{-1}\mathbf{U}'\mathbf{W}\right]$ which has an expectation, and a probability limit, of zero, so the effects of changing ϕ on Σ_c and $\mathbf{Q}_c$ are negligible asymptotically, since the resulting terms are multiplied by a term that vanishes. The only non-negligible derivative asymptotically is that owing to $\mathbf{A}^{v_u}$, which is an identity matrix. Further, $\operatorname{plim} T^{-1}\mathbf{X}'\mathbf{W} = \operatorname{plim}\, T^{-1}\mathbf{Q}\mathbf{W}'\mathbf{W}$, since $\operatorname{plim} T^{-1}\mathbf{U}'\mathbf{W} = \mathbf{0}$. Thus, the asymptotic variance $\mathsf{AV}[\cdot]$ of $\sqrt{T}(\widehat{\phi}-\phi)$ is (here $(\cdot)^u$ simply crosses out unwanted rows and columns):

$$\mathsf{AV}\left[\sqrt{T}\left(\widehat{\phi}-\phi\right)\right] = \left(\left(\Sigma^{-1}\otimes\mathbf{Q}\mathbf{S}_W\mathbf{Q}'\right)^u\right)^{-1} \quad \text{where } \mathbf{S}_W = \operatorname*{plim}_{T\to\infty} T^{-1}\mathbf{W}'\mathbf{W}. \tag{12.25}$$

Consequently, it does not matter for asymptotic efficiency what estimates of Σ_c^{-1} or $\mathbf{Q}_c$ are used in evaluating the EGE, providing they converge to their population values. In fact, even inappropriate $\widehat{\mathbf{Q}}$ or $\widehat{\Sigma}^{-1}$ will suffice for consistent estimates of $\mathbf{A}$ in (12.21) if they converge to non-zero, finite values $\mathbf{Q}^*$ and Σ^{*-1} since such choices cannot affect the fact that $\mathbf{w}_t$ is uncorrelated with $\mathbf{u}_t$. There is an infinite number of estimators that we can get by choosing different $\widehat{\mathbf{Q}}$ and $\widehat{\Sigma}$.

12.4.2 Non-linear parameters

Reconsider the model in (12.6):

$$\mathbf{A}(\phi)\,\mathbf{x}_t = \mathbf{u}_t \sim \mathsf{IN}_n\left[\mathbf{0},\Sigma\right]. \tag{12.26}$$

The log-likelihood is given by (12.21), namely:

$$\ell(\phi,\Sigma) = K + \frac{T}{2}\log\left|\Sigma^{-1}\right| + T\log\|\mathbf{B}(\phi)\| - \tfrac{1}{2}\operatorname{tr}\left(\Sigma^{-1}\mathbf{A}(\phi)\mathbf{X}'\mathbf{X}\mathbf{A}(\phi)'\right). \tag{12.27}$$

The score equation cannot now be written generally, since the mapping from $\mathbf{A}$ to ϕ could cross-relate many elements, but it remains similar to that obtained above. Differentiate $\ell(\cdot)$ with respect to ϕ_i and equate to zero for a maximum:

$$\frac{\partial\ell}{\partial\phi_i} = \operatorname{tr}\left(T\mathbf{B}(\phi)'^{-1}\frac{\partial\mathbf{B}(\phi)}{\partial\phi_i} - \Sigma^{-1}\mathbf{A}(\phi)\mathbf{X}'\mathbf{X}\frac{\partial\mathbf{A}(\phi)'}{\partial\phi_i}\right). \tag{12.28}$$

Further, as in (12.19) (omitting the conditioning on the maximizing functions for Σ etc.):

$$T\mathbf{B}(\phi)'^{-1} = \Sigma^{-1}\mathbf{A}(\phi)\mathbf{X}'\left(\mathbf{Y}-\mathbf{W}\Pi'\right). \tag{12.29}$$

Thus, we obtain an expression similar to that of the previous EGE:

$$\mathrm{tr}\left(\boldsymbol{\Sigma}^{-1}\mathbf{A}\left(\phi\right)\mathbf{X}'\mathbf{W}\mathbf{Q}'\mathbf{J}_i\right) = \mathbf{0} \quad \text{where } \mathbf{J}_i = \frac{\partial \mathbf{A}\left(\phi\right)'}{\partial \phi_i} \quad \text{for } i = 1, \ldots, p. \tag{12.30}$$

The earlier analysis of linear parameters set $\mathbf{J}_i$ equal to a matrix that was zero except for unity in the position associated with the relevant parameter. Thus, the same analysis goes through, but both the symbols and the solution are somewhat more awkward.

12.5 Estimators in PcFiml

As an example of the EGE, consider two-stage least squares (2SLS), which is just a special case of instrumental variables (IV). In 2SLS, the variance-covariance matrix is ignored by setting $\widehat{\boldsymbol{\Sigma}}^{-1} = \mathbf{I}_n$, which is certainly inconsistent and potentially could be very different from $\boldsymbol{\Sigma}$ in general. But because $\boldsymbol{\Sigma}$ is part of $\boldsymbol{\theta}_2$, that inconsistency does not affect the consistency of $\boldsymbol{\theta}_1$ as long as $\widehat{\boldsymbol{\Sigma}}$ converges (as it does here). Next, 2SLS estimates $\mathbf{Q}$ by regression:

$$\widehat{\mathbf{Q}}' = \left(\mathbf{W}'\mathbf{W}\right)^{-1}\mathbf{W}'\mathbf{X}, \tag{12.31}$$

which is often called the first stage of 2SLS. The predicted $\mathbf{X}$ is given by:

$$\widehat{\mathbf{X}} = \widehat{\mathbf{Q}}\mathbf{W}. \tag{12.32}$$

Solve the EGE expression (12.21) for $\mathbf{A}$ using (12.31) and $\boldsymbol{\Sigma} = \mathbf{I}_n$ to obtain:

$$\left(\mathbf{A}\mathbf{X}'\mathbf{W}\left(\mathbf{W}'\mathbf{W}\right)^{-1}\mathbf{W}'\mathbf{X}\right)^{v_u} = \mathbf{0}, \tag{12.33}$$

which is 2SLS applied simultaneously to every equation. The asymptotic distribution of 2SLS can be established directly, but is easily obtained from EGE theory. Writing (12.33) as $(\mathbf{A}\mathbf{X}'\mathbf{W}\widehat{\mathbf{Q}}') = (\mathbf{U}'\mathbf{W}\widehat{\mathbf{Q}}') = \mathbf{0}$, 2SLS is consistent and has an asymptotic variance matrix given by $\sigma_{ii}(\mathbf{Q}\mathbf{S}_W\mathbf{Q}')^{-1}$ for the ith equation.

Next, we examine the full-information maximum likelihood (FIML) estimator, which requires $\widehat{\boldsymbol{\theta}}_2$ and bases $\widehat{\boldsymbol{\theta}}_1$ explicitly on $\mathbf{h}(\widehat{\boldsymbol{\theta}}_2)$, the entailed function from the CLF. However, $\widehat{\boldsymbol{\theta}}_2$ requires $\widehat{\mathbf{Q}}$ which requires $\widehat{\boldsymbol{\Pi}}$, which requires $\widehat{\mathbf{B}}$ and $\widehat{\mathbf{C}}$, which obviously require $\widehat{\mathbf{A}}$. Likewise, $\widehat{\boldsymbol{\Sigma}}$ is quadratic in $\mathbf{A}$, because:

$$\widehat{\boldsymbol{\Sigma}} = T^{-1}\widehat{\mathbf{A}}\mathbf{X}'\mathbf{X}\widehat{\mathbf{A}}'. \tag{12.34}$$

Therefore, both $\mathbf{Q}$ and $\boldsymbol{\Sigma}$ are complicated non-linear functions of $\mathbf{A}$, and we have to solve the whole EGE expression (12.21) for $\widehat{\mathbf{A}} = (\widehat{\mathbf{B}} : \widehat{\mathbf{C}})$ simultaneously:

$$\left(\left(T^{-1}\mathbf{A}\mathbf{X}'\mathbf{X}\mathbf{A}'\right)^{-1}\mathbf{A}\mathbf{X}'\mathbf{W}\left(-\mathbf{C}'\mathbf{B}'^{-1} : \mathbf{I}_k\right)\right)^{v_u} = \mathbf{0}. \tag{12.35}$$

Trying to solve that highly non-linear problem slowed the progress of econometrics in the 1940s, because FIML seemed too complicated to apply with existing computers. As a result, econometrics somewhat digressed to inventing methods that were easier to compute, and have since transpired to be other EGE solutions. The revolution in computer power has rendered most of these short-cut solutions otiose.

We now summarize all the estimators available in PcFiml, beginning with an overview of all their acronyms:

- Single-equation OLS (1SLS);
- Two-stage least squares (2SLS);
- Three-stage least squares (3SLS);
- Limited-information instrumental variables (LIVE);
- Full-information instrumental variables (FIVE);
- Full-information maximum likelihood (FIML);
- Constrained FIML (CFIML);
- Limited-information maximum likelihood (LIML);
- Seemingly unrelated regression equations (SURE).

The maximum likelihood methods (FIML and CFIML) are available recursively. OLS is, of course, inconsistent in a simultaneous system, both in the statistical sense of converging to an inappropriate parameter, and logically in that endogenous variables in one equation are treated conditionally in another. However, for large systems with little interdependence or small samples, it is often used. The general estimation formulation is based on the EGE, from which all estimators are derived. For 2SLS, 3SLS, LIVE and FIVE, the EGE can be solved analytically, taking $\mathbf{\Sigma}_{in}$ and $\mathbf{\Pi}_{in}$ as input and yielding $\mathbf{\Sigma}_{out}$, $\mathbf{A}_{out}$ (and hence $\mathbf{\Omega}_{out}$, $\mathbf{\Pi}_{out}$) as output. A more formal statement of the estimation methods supported by PcFiml (other than 1SLS) is given in Table 12.1.

Table 12.1 Model estimation methods.

		Input $\widetilde{\mathbf{\Sigma}}$	Input $\widehat{\mathbf{\Pi}}$	Output $\widetilde{\mathbf{\Sigma}}$	Output $\widehat{\mathbf{\Pi}}$
0	system (URF)	n/a	n/a	$\mathbf{\Sigma}_{URF}$	$\mathbf{\Pi}_{URF}$
1	2SLS	$\mathbf{I}_n$	$\mathbf{\Pi}_{URF}$	$\mathbf{\Sigma}_{2SLS}$	$\mathbf{\Pi}_{2SLS}$
2	3SLS	$\mathbf{\Sigma}_{2SLS}$	$\mathbf{\Pi}_{URF}$	$\mathbf{\Sigma}_{3SLS}$	$\mathbf{\Pi}_{3SLS}$
3	LIVE	$\mathbf{I}_n$	$\mathbf{\Pi}_{2SLS}$	$\mathbf{\Sigma}_{LIVE}$	$\mathbf{\Pi}_{LIVE}$
4a	FIVE after 2SLS	$\mathbf{\Sigma}_{2SLS}$	$\mathbf{\Pi}_{2SLS}$	$\mathbf{\Sigma}_{FIVE1}$	$\mathbf{\Pi}_{FIVE1}$
4b	FIVE after 3SLS	$\mathbf{\Sigma}_{3SLS}$	$\mathbf{\Pi}_{3SLS}$	$\mathbf{\Sigma}_{FIVE2}$	$\mathbf{\Pi}_{FIVE2}$
4c	FIVE after LIVE	$\mathbf{\Sigma}_{LIVE}$	$\mathbf{\Pi}_{LIVE}$	$\mathbf{\Sigma}_{FIVE3}$	$\mathbf{\Pi}_{FIVE3}$
5	FIML solves $\mathbf{\Sigma}$ and $\mathbf{A}$ as mutually consistent functions of ϕ.				
6	CFIML is FIML with constraints on the parameters.				
o	LIML: as FIML with other equations in reduced form.				
o	SURE: formulate the equations and apply 3SLS.				

Table 12.2 Model coefficient variances.

		$\widetilde{\mathsf{V}[\widehat{\phi}]}$	$\widehat{\mathbf{\Pi}}$ used in $\mathbf{Q}$
0.	system (URF)	$\mathbf{\Omega}_{URF} \otimes (\mathbf{W}'\mathbf{W})^{-1}$	n/a
1.	2SLS	$\left(\left([\mathrm{dg}\mathbf{\Sigma}_{2SLS}]^{-1} \otimes \mathbf{QW}'\mathbf{WQ}'\right)^{u}\right)^{-1}$	$\mathbf{\Pi}_{URF}$
2.	3SLS	$\left((\mathbf{\Sigma}_{2SLS}^{-1} \otimes \mathbf{QW}'\mathbf{WQ}')^{u}\right)^{-1}$	$\mathbf{\Pi}_{URF}$
3.	LIVE	$\left((\mathbf{\Sigma}_{LIVE}^{-1} \otimes \mathbf{QW}'\mathbf{WQ}')^{u}\right)^{-1}$	$\mathbf{\Pi}_{LIVE}$
4a.	FIVE after 2SLS	$\left((\mathbf{\Sigma}_{FIVE1}^{-1} \otimes \mathbf{QW}'\mathbf{WQ}')^{u}\right)^{-1}$	$\mathbf{\Pi}_{FIVE1}$
4b.	FIVE after 3SLS	$\left((\mathbf{\Sigma}_{FIVE2}^{-1} \otimes \mathbf{QW}'\mathbf{WQ}')^{u}\right)^{-1}$	$\mathbf{\Pi}_{FIVE2}$
4c.	FIVE after LIVE	$\left((\mathbf{\Sigma}_{FIVE3}^{-1} \otimes \mathbf{QW}'\mathbf{WQ}')^{u}\right)^{-1}$	$\mathbf{\Pi}_{FIVE3}$
5.	FIML	$\left((\mathbf{\Sigma}_{FIML}^{-1} \otimes \mathbf{QW}'\mathbf{WQ}')^{u}\right)^{-1}$	$\mathbf{\Pi}_{FIML}$
6.	CFIML uses $\mathbf{J}\widetilde{\mathsf{V}[\widehat{\phi}]}\mathbf{J}'$ with $\mathbf{J}$ computed analytically.		

It is not sensible to compute a lower after a higher method (for example 2 after 5) although this option is allowed. FIML and CFIML are non-linear estimation methods and require numerical optimization. CFIML requires prior estimation of FIML, together with a specification of the constraints. Recursive implementation of FIML and CFIML require iterative optimization at every sample point, so can take a long time to calculate.

The estimated variance of $\mathbf{u}_t$ is:

$$\widetilde{\mathbf{\Sigma}} = \frac{\widehat{\mathbf{A}}_1\mathbf{X}'\mathbf{X}\widehat{\mathbf{A}}_1'}{T-c} = \frac{\widehat{\mathbf{U}}_1'\widehat{\mathbf{U}}_1}{T-c}. \tag{12.36}$$

A degrees of freedom correction, c, is used which equals the average number of parameters per equation (rounded towards 0); this would be k for the system. The estimated parameter variances as computed by PcFiml are given in Table 12.2.

12.6 Recursive estimation

A brute force method of recursive estimation is simply repeating the estimation procedure for each sample size. Computationally, this is not as efficient as the method employed for the system (see §10.3), but numerically, it is more stable than the rank-one updating technique for the inverse employed for RLS. The naive brute force method is used by PcFiml for recursive estimation of FIML, albeit with some time-saving devices (the coefficients and Hessian approximation of the previous step are reused in the next). Often this method is surprisingly fast.

System parameter constancy tests are readily computed from the recursive likelihood, as described in §10.8.1. As discussed there, this amounts to removing observations using dummy variables. Single-equation constancy tests are not a direct product of the recursive estimation: successive innovations are not independent. Even though they can be reconstructed as $\mathbf{V}'_{t+1}\mathbf{V}_{t+1} - \mathbf{V}'_t\mathbf{V}_t$, we do not end up with independent Wishart distributed variates from which to construct the single equation tests in the same way as for the system. In the model it is possible that $RSS_T - RSS_{T_1}$ is negative (cf. equation (10.118)). A dummy variable method is still possible: omit the dummy variable from equation i for the period of interest.

12.7 Computing FIML

FIML and CFIML estimation all require *numerical optimization* to maximize the likelihood $\log \mathsf{L}(\boldsymbol{\theta}) = \ell(\boldsymbol{\theta})$ as a non-linear function of $\boldsymbol{\theta}$. PcFiml maximization algorithms are based on the Newton scheme. These are discussed in detail in Chapter 13, but we now note their form:

$$\boldsymbol{\theta}_{i+1} = \boldsymbol{\theta}_i + s_i\mathbf{Q}_i^{-1}\mathbf{q}_i \qquad (12.37)$$

with

- $\boldsymbol{\theta}_i$ parameter value at iteration i;
- s_i step length, normally unity;
- $\mathbf{Q}_i$ symmetric positive-definite matrix (at iteration i);
- $\mathbf{q}_i$ first derivative of the log-likelihood (at iteration i) (the score vector);
- $\boldsymbol{\delta}_i = \boldsymbol{\theta}_i - \boldsymbol{\theta}_{i-1}$ is the change in the parameters;

PcFiml uses the quasi-Newton method developed by Broyden, Fletcher, Goldfarb, Shanno (BFGS) to update $\mathbf{K} = \mathbf{Q}^{-1}$ directly:

(1) BFGS with analytical first derivatives;
The derivatives are calculated analytically (FIML and CFIML). For CFIML, this method computes $(\partial\ell(\boldsymbol{\phi})/\partial\phi_i)$ together with analytical derivatives of the parameter constraints $(\partial\boldsymbol{\phi}/\partial\theta_i)$. This is the preferred method and the only one allowed for recursive FIML and CFIML.

(2) BFGS with numerical first derivatives.
Uses numerical derivatives to compute $\partial\ell\left(\boldsymbol{\phi}\left(\boldsymbol{\theta}\right)\right)/\partial\theta_i$. The numerical scores are less accurate than analytical scores, and usually more costly to obtain.

Starting values are determined as follows. Immediately after a system estimation, the starting values are $\boldsymbol{\theta}_0 = \boldsymbol{\theta}_{2SLS}$. If the model has been estimated before, the most recent parameters are used (2SLS or 3SLS provide excellent starting values). $\mathbf{K}$ is initialized to $\mathbf{I}_n$ every time the optimization process starts. So if the proces is aborted (for example, by pressing `Esc`) and then restarted, the approximate Hessian is reset to $\mathbf{I}_n$.

Recursive FIML and CFIML is computed backwards: starting from the full sample values for $\boldsymbol{\theta}$ and $\mathbf{K}$, one observation at a time is dropped. At each sample size, the previous values at convergence are used to start with.

Owing to numerical problems, it is possible (especially close to the maximum) that the calculated $\boldsymbol{\delta}_i$ does not yield a higher likelihood. Then an $s_i \in [0,1]$ yielding a higher function value is determined by a line search. Theoretically, since the direction is upward, such an s_i should exist; however numerically it might be impossible to find one. When using BFGS with numerical derivatives, it often pays to scale the data so that the initial gradients are of the same order of magnitude.

The *convergence* decision is based on two tests. The first uses likelihood elasticities $(\partial\ell/\partial\log\boldsymbol{\theta})$:

$$\begin{aligned} |q_{i,j}\theta_{i,j}| &\leq \epsilon \quad \text{for all } j \text{ when } \theta_{i,j} \neq 0, \\ |q_{i,j}| &\leq \epsilon \quad \text{for all } j \text{ with } \theta_{i,j} = 0. \end{aligned} \tag{12.38}$$

The second is based on the one-step-ahead relative change in the parameter values:

$$\begin{aligned} |\delta_{i+1,j}| &\leq 10\epsilon\, |\theta_{i,j}| \quad \text{for all } j \text{ with } \theta_{i,j} \neq 0, \\ |\delta_{i+1,j}| &\leq 10\epsilon \quad \text{for all } j \text{ when } \theta_{i,j} = 0. \end{aligned} \tag{12.39}$$

12.8 Restricted reduced form

From any selected estimator, the MLE of the restricted reduced form is:

$$\widehat{\mathbf{\Pi}} = -\widehat{\mathbf{B}}^{-1}\widehat{\mathbf{C}}. \tag{12.40}$$

The covariance matrix of the restricted reduced-form residuals for the subset of stochastic equations is obtained by letting:

$$\mathbf{B}^{-1} = \begin{pmatrix} \mathbf{B}^{11} & \mathbf{B}^{12} \\ \mathbf{B}^{21} & \mathbf{B}^{22} \end{pmatrix}, \tag{12.41}$$

where $\mathbf{B}^{11}$ is $n_1 \times n_1$ and so on. Then:

$$\widetilde{\mathbf{\Omega}} = \begin{pmatrix} \mathbf{B}^{11} \\ \mathbf{B}^{21} \end{pmatrix} \widetilde{\mathbf{\Sigma}} \left(\mathbf{B}^{11\prime} : \mathbf{B}^{21\prime}\right), \tag{12.42}$$

and $\mathbf{\Omega}_{11} = \mathbf{B}^{11}\mathbf{\Sigma}\mathbf{B}^{11\prime}$ is the part corresponding to the stochastic equations.

The variance-covariance matrix of the restricted reduced-form coefficients is:

$$\mathsf{V}\left[\widetilde{\text{vec}\widehat{\mathbf{\Pi}}'}\right] = \widehat{\mathbf{J}}\mathsf{V}\left[\widetilde{\widehat{\phi}}\right]\widehat{\mathbf{J}}' \quad \text{where } \mathbf{J} = \frac{\partial \text{vec}\mathbf{\Pi}'}{\left(\partial\widehat{\phi}\right)'} = \left(-\mathbf{B}^{-1} \otimes (\mathbf{\Pi}' : \mathbf{I}_k)\right)^u. \tag{12.43}$$

In $\mathbf{J}$, we choose only those columns corresponding to unrestricted elements in $\mathbf{A}$. The derivation of $\mathbf{J}$ is the same as in (10.90). The estimated variances of the elements of $\widehat{\phi}$ are given in Table 12.2.

12.9 Unrestricted variables

Variables that are included unrestrictedly in all equations of the model, such as dummy variables for the constant term, seasonal shift factors, or trend, can be concentrated out of the likelihood function. This reduces the dimensionality of the parameter vector, and enhances numerical optimization. The stochastic part of the model is written as:

$$\mathbf{A}_1\mathbf{X}' + \mathbf{D}\mathbf{S}' = \mathbf{U}', \tag{12.44}$$

where $\mathbf{D}$ is the $n_1 \times s$ unrestricted matrix of coefficients of the unrestricted variables and $\mathbf{S}$ is the $T \times s$ matrix of observations on these seasonal dummies. Then (see Hendry, 1971):

$$\begin{aligned} \ell\left(\mathbf{A}_1, \mathbf{\Sigma} \mid \mathbf{X}, \mathbf{S}\right) = \; & K + T \log ||\mathbf{B}|| - \tfrac{T}{2} \log |\mathbf{\Sigma}| \\ & - \tfrac{1}{2} \mathrm{tr}\left(\mathbf{\Sigma}^{-1}\left(\mathbf{A}_1\mathbf{X}'\mathbf{X}\mathbf{A}_1' + 2\mathbf{A}_1\mathbf{X}'\mathbf{S}\mathbf{D}' + \mathbf{D}\mathbf{S}'\mathbf{S}\mathbf{D}'\right)\right). \end{aligned} \tag{12.45}$$

Since $\mathbf{D}$ is unrestricted, maximizing $\ell(\cdot)$ with respect to $\mathbf{D}$ yields:

$$\widehat{\mathbf{D}}' = \left(\mathbf{S}'\mathbf{S}\right)^{-1} \mathbf{S}'\mathbf{X}\widehat{\mathbf{A}}_1'. \tag{12.46}$$

Let $\check{\mathbf{X}} = \left(\mathbf{I}_T - \mathbf{S}\left(\mathbf{S}'\mathbf{S}\right)^{-1}\mathbf{S}'\right)\mathbf{X} = \mathbf{M}_S\mathbf{X}$, namely the residuals from the least-squares regression of $\mathbf{X}$ on $\mathbf{S}$, denote the 'deseasonalized' data, then the concentrated likelihood function is:

$$\ell_c\left(\mathbf{A}_1, \mathbf{\Sigma} \mid \mathbf{X}, \mathbf{S}; \mathbf{D}\right) = K_c + T \log ||\mathbf{B}|| - \frac{T}{2} \log |\mathbf{\Sigma}| - \tfrac{1}{2} \mathrm{tr}\left(\mathbf{\Sigma}^{-1}\mathbf{A}_1\check{\mathbf{X}}'\check{\mathbf{X}}\mathbf{A}_1'\right). \tag{12.47}$$

From (12.46), the variance-covariance matrix of the $\widehat{\mathbf{D}}$ coefficients is:

$$\widetilde{\mathsf{V}\left[\mathrm{vec}\widehat{\mathbf{D}}'\right]} = \widetilde{\mathbf{\Sigma}} \otimes \left(\mathbf{S}'\mathbf{S}\right)^{-1} + \widehat{\mathbf{J}}_S \widetilde{\mathsf{V}\left[\widehat{\boldsymbol{\phi}}\right]} \widehat{\mathbf{J}}_S' \text{ where } \mathbf{J}_S = \left(\mathbf{I}_{n_1} \otimes \left(\mathbf{S}'\mathbf{S}\right)^{-1}\mathbf{S}'\mathbf{X}\right)^u \tag{12.48}$$

which is similar to (10.36) for the system.

12.10 Derived statistics

When the model encompasses the system, other derived statistics can usefully highlight the properties of the estimated model. Such statistics include forecast tests, static long run, etc. The results for forecasting and dynamic analysis derived for the system (sections §10.5 and §10.6) carry over after replacing $\mathbf{\Pi}_u$, $\mathbf{\Omega}_u$ by $\mathbf{\Pi}_r$, $\mathbf{\Omega}_r$. The forecast error variance for a single step ahead is:

$$\widetilde{\mathsf{V}[\mathbf{e}_{T+i,1}]} = \widetilde{\mathbf{\Omega}}_r + \left(\mathbf{I}_n \otimes \mathbf{w}_{T+i}'\right)\widehat{\mathbf{J}}\widetilde{\mathsf{V}\left[\widehat{\boldsymbol{\phi}}\right]}\widehat{\mathbf{J}}'\left(\mathbf{I}_n \otimes \mathbf{w}_{T+i}\right), \tag{12.49}$$

where $\mathbf{J}$ is given in (12.43).

The same holds to a large extent for mis-specification tests: the residuals involved in the tests are the RRF residuals. This is straightforward for the portmanteau statistic and the normality test. For both heteroscedasticitytests, the model is treated as if it were a system, albeit with coefficients $\boldsymbol{\Pi}_r$, $\boldsymbol{\Omega}_r$. This implies that these tests are likely to reject if the test for over-identifying restrictions fails. The vector error autocorrelation test re-estimates the model after the lagged structural residuals are partialled out from the original regressors, using the auxiliary system:

$$\mathbf{BY}' + \mathbf{CW}' - \mathbf{R}_r\widehat{\mathbf{U}}_r' - \cdots - \mathbf{R}_s\widehat{\mathbf{U}}_s' = \mathbf{E}'. \tag{12.50}$$

This involves recourse to numerical optimization for tests in models estimated by FIML or CFIML.

Tests at the level of the model may have more power to reject owing to the (often much) smaller number of free parameters estimated.

12.10.1 General restrictions

PcFiml allows you to test general restrictions on parameters. Restrictions are entered in the constraints editor.

Given the estimated coefficients $\hat{\boldsymbol{\theta}}$, and their covariance matrix $\widetilde{\mathsf{V}[\hat{\boldsymbol{\theta}}]}$, we can test for (non-) linear restrictions of the form:

$$\mathbf{f}(\boldsymbol{\theta}) = \mathbf{0}; \tag{12.51}$$

A Wald test is reported, which has a $\chi^2(r)$ distribution, where r is the number of restrictions (that is, equations entered in the restrictions editor). The null hypothesis is rejected if we observe a significant test statistic.

For example, the two restrictions implied by the long-run solution of:

$$Ya = \beta_0 Ya_1 + \beta_1 Yb + \beta_2 Yb_1 + \beta_3 Yc + \mu \tag{12.52}$$

are expressed as:

$$\begin{aligned} (\beta_1 + \beta_2)/(1 - \beta_0) &= 0; \\ \beta_3/(1 - \beta_0) &= 0; \end{aligned} \tag{12.53}$$

which has to be fed into PcFiml as (since coefficient numbering starts at 0):

```
(&1 + &2) / (1 - &0) = 0;
      &3  / (1 - &0) = 0;
```

12.11 Progress

The Progress command reports on the progress made during a general-to-simple modelling strategy (the Progress dialog can be used to exclude systems/models from the default model nesting sequence).

PcFiml keeps a record of the sequence of systems, and for the most recent system the sequence of models (which could be empty). It will report the likelihood-ratio tests indicating the progress in system modelling, the progress in model modelling, and the tests of over-identifying restrictions of all models in the system.

In the following discussion, *model* refers to both model and system. A more recent model (Model 2) is nested in an older (Model 1) if:

(1) Model 2 is derived from a parameter restriction on Model 1.

This entails:

(2) Model 2 is estimated over the same period.
(3) Model 2 has fewer coefficients than Model 1.
(4) Model 2 has a lower likelihood than Model 1.

But not necessarily:

(5) Both models have the same dependent variable, and the set of explanatory variables of Model 2 is a subset of that of Model 1.

PcFiml will offer you a default nesting sequence based on (2), (3), (4) and (5), but since it cannot decide on (1) itself, you will have the opportunity to change this nesting sequence. However, model sequences that do not satisfy (2), (3) or (4) will always be deleted.

Consider, for example, Model 2:

$$\Delta Ya_t = \mu + \gamma \Delta Yb_t \tag{12.54}$$

which is nested in Model 1:

$$Ya_t = \beta_0 + \beta_1 Ya_{t-1} + \beta_2 Yb_t + \beta_3 Yb_{t_1} \tag{12.55}$$

through two restrictions: $\beta_1 = 1$ and $\beta_3 = -\beta_2$. This nesting doesn't satisfy point (5), and hence is not recognized by PcFiml. You can mark Model 2 for inclusion in the progress report.

Chapter 13

Numerical Optimization and Numerical Accuracy

13.1 Introduction to numerical optimization

Any approach to estimation and inference implicitly assumes that it is feasible to obtain a maximum likelihood estimator (MLE) in situations of interest. For any fixed set of data and a given model specification, the log-likelihood function $\ell(\cdot)$ depends only on the parameters $\boldsymbol{\theta}$ of the model. Consequently, obtaining the MLE entails locating the value $\widehat{\boldsymbol{\theta}}$ of $\boldsymbol{\theta}$ which maximizes $\ell(\boldsymbol{\theta})$, and this is a numerical, not a statistical, problem – a matter of computational technique – which could be considered peripheral to econometrics.

However, optimization algorithms differ dramatically in their speeds of locating $\widehat{\boldsymbol{\theta}}$, and hence their computational costs. A statistical technique that needed (say) ten hours of computer time could not expect routine application if a closely similar statistical method required only one second on the same computer. Moreover, algorithms have different computer memory requirements, and certain methods may be too inefficient in their memory requirements for the available computers. Next, some algorithms are far more robust than others, that is, are much more likely to obtain $\widehat{\boldsymbol{\theta}}$ and not fail for mysterious reasons in the calculation process. While all of these points are in the province of numerical analysis and computing, in order to implement new methods, econometricians need to be aware of the problems involved in optimization.

There is also an intimate connection between the statistical and the numerical aspects of estimation. Methods of maximizing $\ell(\boldsymbol{\theta})$ yield insight into the statistical properties of $\widehat{\boldsymbol{\theta}}$. Some algorithms only calculate an approximation to $\widehat{\boldsymbol{\theta}}$, say $\widetilde{\boldsymbol{\theta}}$, but if they consist of well-defined rules that always yield unique values of $\widetilde{\boldsymbol{\theta}}$ from given data, then $\widetilde{\boldsymbol{\theta}}$ is an estimator of $\boldsymbol{\theta}$ with statistical properties that may be similar to those of $\widehat{\boldsymbol{\theta}}$ – but also may be very different. Thus, computing the maximum of $\ell(\boldsymbol{\theta})$ only approximately can have statistical implications: the discussion of the estimator-generating equation in Chapter 12 showed that different estimators can be reinterpreted as alternative numerical methods for approximating the maximum of $\ell(\boldsymbol{\theta})$.

There is a vast literature on non-linear optimization techniques (see, among many others, Fletcher, 1987, Gill, Murray and Wright, 1981, Cramer, 1986, Quandt, 1983 and Thisted, 1988). Note that many texts on optimization focus on minimization, rather than maximization, but of course $\max \ell(\boldsymbol{\theta}) = -\min\{-\ell(\boldsymbol{\theta})\}$.

13.2 Maximizing likelihood functions

A first approach to obtaining the MLE $\widehat{\boldsymbol{\theta}}$ from $\ell(\boldsymbol{\theta})$ is to consider solving the score equations, assuming the relevant partial derivatives exist:

$$\nabla\ell(\boldsymbol{\theta}) = \frac{\partial\ell(\boldsymbol{\theta})}{\partial\boldsymbol{\theta}} = \mathbf{q}(\boldsymbol{\theta}). \tag{13.1}$$

Then $\mathbf{q}(\widehat{\boldsymbol{\theta}}) = \mathbf{0}$ defines the necessary conditions for a local maximum of $\ell(\boldsymbol{\theta})$ at $\widehat{\boldsymbol{\theta}}$. A sufficient condition is that:

$$\nabla^2\ell(\boldsymbol{\theta}) = \frac{\partial^2\ell(\boldsymbol{\theta})}{\partial\boldsymbol{\theta}\partial\boldsymbol{\theta}'} = \frac{\partial\mathbf{q}(\boldsymbol{\theta})'}{\partial\boldsymbol{\theta}} = \mathbf{H}(\boldsymbol{\theta}) = -\mathbf{Q}(\boldsymbol{\theta}) \tag{13.2}$$

also exists, and is negative definite at $\widehat{\boldsymbol{\theta}}$ (minimization would require positive definiteness). If $\mathbf{H}(\cdot)$ is negative definite for all parameter values, the likelihood is concave, and hence has a unique maximum; if not, there could be local optima or singularities. When $\mathbf{q}(\boldsymbol{\theta})$ is a set of equations that can be transformed to be linear in $\boldsymbol{\theta}$, (13.1) can be solved explicitly for $\widehat{\boldsymbol{\theta}}$. In such a situation, it is easy to implement the estimator without recourse to numerical optimization. To maximize $\ell(\cdot)$ as a non-linear function of its parameters requires numerical optimization techniques.

13.2.1 Direct search methods

A more prosaic approach views the matter as one of hill climbing. A useful analogy is to consider the likelihood function $\ell(\boldsymbol{\theta})$ as a two-dimensional hill as in Figure 13.1. This is a well-behaved function: it is continuous, differentiable and has a unique maximum. To maximize $\ell(\cdot)$, we need to climb to the top of the hill. Start somewhere on the hill, say at θ_1, and take a step of length δ. The step will go either down the hill or up the hill: in computing terms, move some distance δ each way and compute the functions $\ell_1 = \ell(\theta_1)$ and $\ell_2 = \ell(\theta_1 + \delta)$. Depending on $\ell_1 \geq \ell_2$ or $\ell_2 \geq \ell_1$, we discover in which direction to continue: here $+\delta$ as $\ell_2 \geq \ell_1$ ($-\delta$ otherwise). Take a second step of δ in the appropriate direction, compute $\ell(\theta_1 + 2\delta)$ and repeat until we go downhill again, and have overshot the maximum, at $\theta_1 + k\delta$, say. The maximum will be inside the bracket $[\theta_1 + (k-1)\delta, \theta_1 + k\delta]$. Take a step of $\delta/2$ back, compute the function, and fit a quadratic through the three points. Select θ_2 which maximizes the quadratic as the approximation to the value maximizing the function, reduce the step-length δ, and recommence from θ_2. This is a simple method for finding maxima without derivatives.

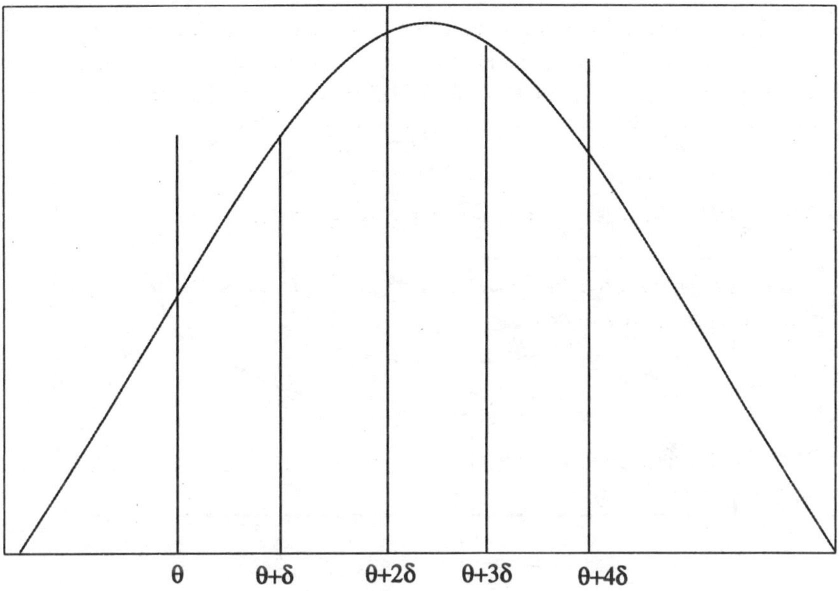

Figure 13.1 Two-dimensional hill.

We can extend this approach to the case of climbing a three-dimensional hill, applying exactly the same principles as above, but using two-dimensional iso-likelihood contours to represent a three-dimensional hill as in Figure 13.2.

Start from the origin, and apply the above method to find the maximum point along one line, say along the θ_a axis as in Figure 13.2 (the graph is equivalent to an indifference curve map, where the tangent to the highest indifference curve locates the maximum). Next, turn 90° to the previous path at the point θ_a^1 and search again until the highest point in the θ_b direction is reached. Turn 90° again, check for the uphill direction and climb, and keep iterating the procedure. In this way, we will finally get to the top of the hill.

We can of course extend this approach to situations with more than three dimensions, but expensively, since it is not a very intelligent method. A better method would be to utilize the information that accrues as we climb the hill. After changing direction once and finding the highest point for the second time, we find that we could have done much better by taking the direction corresponding to the hypotenuse instead of walking along the two sides of the hill. The average progress along the first two directions corresponds to a better path than either alone, and is known as the direction of total progress (see Figure 13.3). We could get from the second path on to the direction of total progress and climb either vertically or horizontally until the highest position. Then we can find the second direction of total progress and use that, providing a better method of climbing to the top of the hill.

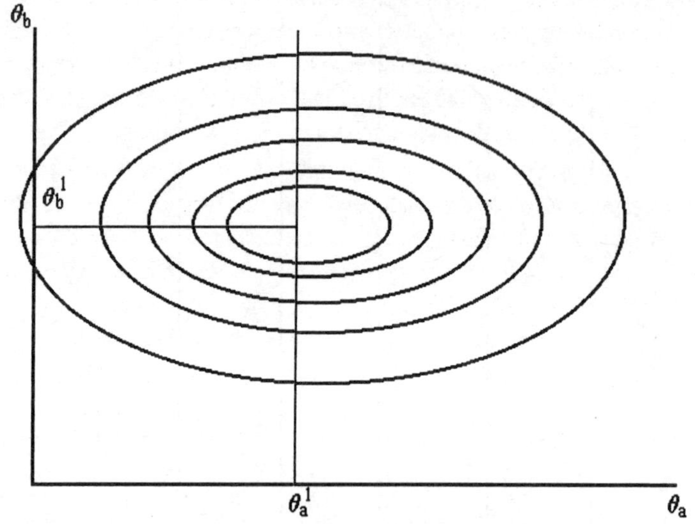

Figure 13.2 Projection of three-dimensional hill.

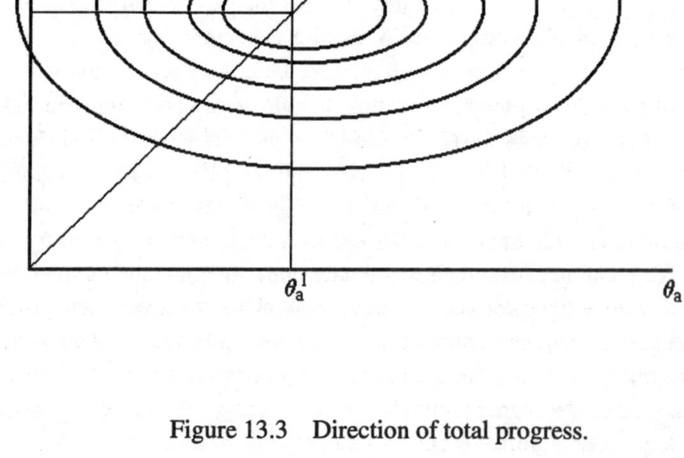

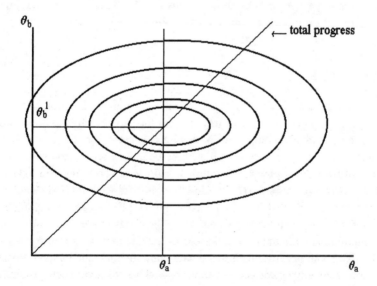

Figure 13.3 Direction of total progress.

This method (called conjugate directions) makes use of a Euclidean theorem: the line joining any two parallel tangent points of two concentric ellipses goes through their centre. So if a bivariate likelihood surface is elliptical, and we find one tangent of an iso-likelihood ellipse, then another tangent to a higher contour and follow the direction of total progress, we will get straight to the maximum of the likelihood.

A second way of climbing a hill is to exploit information at the starting point about the steepness of the slope: if the gradient is known, it seems worth trying to climb along the direction of steepest ascent. In many cases, the method progresses rapidly and beats the previous methods. However, there are a couple of *caveats*. First, the slope of a hill is not necessarily uniform, and a gradient method might be poor if the slope changes too much. Secondly, in the starting neighbourhood, the slope might be too flat or even point in the wrong direction. However, the obvious solution to that problem is to provide decent initial values. An EGE will often do so for FIML. For example, 2SLS initial values are an excellent set from which to commence FIML, and 3SLS are even better yet do not require iterative solution.

13.2.2 Newton type methods

We saw above that $\mathbf{q}(\widehat{\boldsymbol{\theta}}) = \mathbf{0}$ defines the necessary condition for a local maximum of $\ell(\boldsymbol{\theta})$ at $\widehat{\boldsymbol{\theta}}$, whereas a sufficient condition is that the negated Hessian matrix, $\mathbf{Q}(\boldsymbol{\theta}) = -\mathbf{H}(\boldsymbol{\theta})$, is positive definite at $\widehat{\boldsymbol{\theta}}$. When $\mathbf{q}(\boldsymbol{\theta})$ is a set of equations that are linear in $\boldsymbol{\theta}$, then $\mathbf{q}(\widehat{\boldsymbol{\theta}}) = \mathbf{0}$ can be solved explicitly for $\widehat{\boldsymbol{\theta}}$, as in the multiple regression model. More generally, $\mathbf{q}(\boldsymbol{\theta})$ is non-linear, yielding a problem of locating $\widehat{\boldsymbol{\theta}}$ which is no more tractable than maximizing $\ell(\boldsymbol{\theta})$. Thus, we consider iterative approaches in which a sequence of values of $\boldsymbol{\theta}$ (denoted $\boldsymbol{\theta}_i$ at the ith iteration) is obtained approximating $\mathbf{q}(\boldsymbol{\theta}_i) = \mathbf{0}$, and corresponding to non-decreasing values of the criterion function $\ell(\cdot)$, so $\ell(\boldsymbol{\theta}_{i+1}) \geq \ell(\boldsymbol{\theta}_i)$:

$$\boldsymbol{\theta}_{i+1} = \mathbf{h}\left(\boldsymbol{\theta}_i\right) \text{ for } i = 1, 2, \ldots, I \leq N \tag{13.3}$$

where N is a terminal maximum number of steps, from an initial value $\boldsymbol{\theta}_0$ (such as 2SLS). A convergence criterion is used to terminate the iteration, such as $\mathbf{q}(\boldsymbol{\theta}_{i+1}) \simeq \mathbf{0}$ or $|\ell(\boldsymbol{\theta}_{i+1}) - \ell(\boldsymbol{\theta}_i)| \leq \epsilon$. If convergence does not occur, try using a looser convergence criterion. These implementation-specific aspects are discussed below.

There is no optimal choice for $\mathbf{h}\left(\cdot\right)$, since optimization methods differ in their robustness, in the time taken to calculate successive values of $\boldsymbol{\theta}_i$, in the number of iterations required to achieve any given accuracy level (which may differ between problems), and in the effort needed to write a computer program to calculate $\mathbf{h}\left(\cdot\right)$. Moreover, an algorithm that performs excellently for a small number of parameters may be hopeless for a large number. The direct search methods just discussed only require $\ell\left(\cdot\right)$ to be programmed, and are robust but often require a large number of iterations.

Expand $\mathbf{q}(\widehat{\boldsymbol{\theta}}) = \mathbf{0}$ in a first-order Taylor's series:

$$\mathbf{q}\left(\widehat{\boldsymbol{\theta}}\right) \simeq \mathbf{q}(\boldsymbol{\theta}_1) + \mathbf{H}(\boldsymbol{\theta}_1)(\boldsymbol{\theta} - \boldsymbol{\theta}_1) = \mathbf{0}, \tag{13.4}$$

written as the iterative rule:

$$\boldsymbol{\theta}_{i+1} = \boldsymbol{\theta}_i - \mathbf{H}(\boldsymbol{\theta}_i)^{-1}\mathbf{q}(\boldsymbol{\theta}_i), \tag{13.5}$$

or alternatively:

$$\begin{aligned} &\text{solve} \quad \mathbf{Q}(\boldsymbol{\theta}_i)\boldsymbol{\delta}_i = \mathbf{q}(\boldsymbol{\theta}_i) \quad \text{for } \boldsymbol{\delta}_i, \\ &\text{set} \quad \boldsymbol{\theta}_{i+1} = \boldsymbol{\theta}_i + \boldsymbol{\delta}_i. \end{aligned} \tag{13.6}$$

The gradient, $\mathbf{q}(\boldsymbol{\theta}_i)$, determines the direction of the step to be taken, and $\mathbf{Q}(\boldsymbol{\theta}_i)^{-1}$ modifies the size of the step which determines the metric: this algorithm is the Newton–Raphson technique, or *Newton's method.* Even when the direction is uphill, it is possible to overstep the maximum in that direction. In that case, it is essential to add a line search to determine a step length $s_i \in [0, 1]$:

$$\boldsymbol{\theta}_{i+1} = \boldsymbol{\theta}_i + s_i\boldsymbol{\delta}_i, \tag{13.7}$$

where s_i is chosen to ensure that $\ell(\boldsymbol{\theta}_{i+1}) \geq \ell(\boldsymbol{\theta}_i)$.

Replacing the matrix $\mathbf{Q}(\cdot)$ by the unit matrix $\mathbf{I}_r$ is known as the method of *steepest ascent* (steepest descent when minimizing) since the step is in the direction of the gradient vector $\mathbf{q}(\cdot)$ – and so is useful only if $\boldsymbol{\theta}$ is sensibly scaled. Using $\mathbf{Q}_\mu(\cdot) = \mathbf{Q}(\cdot) + \mu\mathbf{I}_r$ (where $\mu > 0$ is chosen to ensure that $\mathbf{Q}_\mu(\cdot)$ is positive definite) is known as *quadratic hill climbing* (see Goldfeld and Quandt, 1972) or as the Levenberg–Marquardt method: note that $\mathbf{Q}_\mu(\cdot)$ varies between $\mathbf{Q}(\cdot)$ (Newton–Raphson) and $\mathbf{I}_r$ (steepest ascent) as μ increases from zero.

When we maximize a log-likelihood function and look back to the variance estimates given in (10.101), two additional methods suggest themselves. Of these, $\mathbf{Q} = -\mathbf{H}(\boldsymbol{\theta})$ is Newton's method discussed above. The method of scoring replaces $\mathbf{Q}(\cdot)$ by the information matrix $\mathcal{I} = \mathsf{E}[\mathbf{Q}(\cdot)]$; and the method which uses the outer product of the gradients is sometimes called the method of Berndt, Hall, Hall and Hausman (see e.g., Berndt, Hall, Hall and Hausman, 1974).

An important class of methods are the so-called variable metric or *quasi-Newton* methods. These approximate the matrix $\mathbf{Q}(\boldsymbol{\theta}_i)^{-1}$ by a symmetric positive definite matrix $\mathbf{K}_i$ which is updated at every iteration but converges on $\mathbf{Q}(\cdot)^{-1}$. The two most commonly used are the Davidon–Fletcher–Powell approach (DFP), and the Broyden–Fletcher–Goldfarb–Shanno (BFGS) update, where the latter is generally the preferred quasi-Newton method. Advantages of quasi-Newton methods over Newton–Raphson are that $\mathbf{K}_i$ is guaranteed to be positive definite, and only first derivatives are required. In the Newton–Raphson case, there could be parameter values for which the Hessian matrix is not negative definite. However, if the Hessian is negative definite for all parameter values, and not too costly to derive (in terms of derivation, programming time, and computational time), it tends to outperform the quasi-Newton methods.

Let $\mathbf{d} = s_i\delta_i = \boldsymbol{\theta}_i - \boldsymbol{\theta}_{i-1}$ and $\mathbf{g} = \mathbf{q}(\boldsymbol{\theta}_i) - \mathbf{q}(\boldsymbol{\theta}_{i-1})$, then the BFGS update is:

$$\mathbf{K}_{i+1} = \mathbf{K}_i + \left(1 + \frac{\mathbf{g}'\mathbf{K}_i\mathbf{g}}{\mathbf{d}'\mathbf{g}}\right)\frac{\mathbf{d}\mathbf{d}'}{\mathbf{d}'\mathbf{g}} - \frac{\mathbf{d}\mathbf{g}'\mathbf{K}_i + \mathbf{K}_i\mathbf{g}\mathbf{d}'}{\mathbf{d}'\mathbf{g}}. \tag{13.8}$$

This satisfies the quasi-Newton condition $\mathbf{K}_{i+1}\mathbf{g} = \mathbf{d}$, and possesses the properties of hereditary symmetry ($\mathbf{K}_{i+1}$ is symmetric if $\mathbf{K}_i$ is), hereditary positive definiteness, and super-linear convergence. There is a close correspondence between the logic underlying the earlier RLS procedure for recursive (rank-one) updating of the inverse second-moment matrix as the sample size increases, and the BFGS method for sequential updating of the inverse Hessian approximation by rank-two updates as the number of iterations increases.

13.2.3 Derivative-free methods

When the analytic formula for $\mathbf{q}(\boldsymbol{\theta})$ cannot be obtained, so that only function values are available, the choice is between a conjugate-directions method and a quasi-Newton method using finite differences. BFGS using a numerical approximation to $\mathbf{q}(\cdot)$ based on finite difference approximations seems to outperform derivative-free algorithms in many situations while providing an equal degree of flexibility in the choice of parameters in $\ell(\cdot)$. The numerical derivatives are calculated using:

$$\frac{\ell(\boldsymbol{\theta} + \epsilon\boldsymbol{\iota}) - \ell(\boldsymbol{\theta} - \delta\epsilon\boldsymbol{\iota})}{\mu} \simeq \frac{\partial\ell(\boldsymbol{\theta})}{\partial(\boldsymbol{\iota}'\boldsymbol{\theta})} \tag{13.9}$$

where $\boldsymbol{\iota}$ is a unit vector (for example, $(1\ 0\ldots0)'$ for the first element of $\boldsymbol{\theta}$), ϵ is a suitably chosen step length, and δ is either zero (forward difference) or unity (central difference) depending on the accuracy required at the given stage of the iteration. Thus, ϵ represents a compromise between round-off error (cancellation of leading digits when subtracting nearly equal numbers), and truncation error (ignoring terms of higher order than ϵ in the approximation). Although PcFiml chooses ϵ carefully, there may be situations where the numerical derivative performs poorly.

It is worth noting that numerical values of second derivatives can be computed in a corresponding way using:

$$\frac{\ell(\boldsymbol{\theta} + \epsilon_1\boldsymbol{\iota}_1 + \epsilon_2\boldsymbol{\iota}_2) + \ell(\boldsymbol{\theta} - \epsilon_1\boldsymbol{\iota}_1 - \epsilon_2\boldsymbol{\iota}_2) - \ell(\boldsymbol{\theta} - \epsilon_1\boldsymbol{\iota}_1 + \epsilon_2\boldsymbol{\iota}_2) - \ell(\boldsymbol{\theta} + \epsilon_1\boldsymbol{\iota}_1 - \epsilon_2\boldsymbol{\iota}_2)}{4\epsilon_1\epsilon_2} \tag{13.10}$$

where $\boldsymbol{\iota}_1$ or $\boldsymbol{\iota}_2$ is zero except for unity in the ith or j^{th} position. When computed from the MLE $\widehat{\boldsymbol{\theta}}$, (13.10) yields a reasonably good approximation to $\mathbf{Q}(\widehat{\boldsymbol{\theta}})$ for use in calculating the covariance matrix of $\widehat{\boldsymbol{\theta}}$.

13.2.4 Conclusion

The present state of the art in numerical optimization, and the computational speeds of modern computers are such that large estimation problems can be solved quickly and cheaply. Many estimators which were once described as 'computationally burdensome' or complex are now as easy to use as OLS but are considerably more informative. Thus, the complexity of the appropriate estimator is no longer a serious constraint, although it is simple to invent large, highly non-linear problems which would be prohibitively expensive to solve.

13.3 Practical optimization

The discussion of numerical optimization above is rather abstract. Practical aspects such as choice of convergence criteria, line search algorithm, and potential problems are discussed in this section, with reference to the actual implementation in PcFiml.

13.3.1 Maximization methods

PcFiml maximizes the likelihood $\ell(\boldsymbol{\phi}(\boldsymbol{\theta}))$ as an unconstrained non-linear function of $\boldsymbol{\theta}$ using a Newton scheme:

$$\boldsymbol{\theta}_{i+1} = \boldsymbol{\theta}_i + s_i \mathbf{Q}(\boldsymbol{\theta}_i)^{-1} \mathbf{q}(\boldsymbol{\theta}_i) \qquad (13.11)$$

where BFGS is used to update $\mathbf{Q}^{-1}$ directly. Two methods are available:

(1) *BFGS with analytical first derivatives*
The derivatives $\partial\ell/\partial\theta_i$ are calculated analytically. If the form of these derivatives is not known, this method employs a mixture of analytical $(\partial\ell(\boldsymbol{\phi})/\partial\phi_i)$ and numerical $(\partial\boldsymbol{\phi}/\partial\theta_i)$ derivatives. The numerical part, which corresponds to the Jacobian of the transformation, is computed by a central finite difference approximation. Where possible (as in CFIML and restricted cointegration analysis), the Jacobian matrix is computed analytically.

(2) *BFGS with numerical first derivatives*
This method uses central finite difference approximations to the derivatives $\partial\ell/\partial\theta_i$. It is slower than using analytical first derivatives, but the only method available if the analytical scores are unknown.

13.3.2 Line search

It is possible (especially close to the maximum) that the calculated parameter update $\boldsymbol{\delta}_i = \mathbf{Q}(\boldsymbol{\theta}_i)^{-1}\mathbf{q}(\boldsymbol{\theta}_i)$ does not yield a higher likelihood. Then an $s_i \in [0,1]$ yielding a higher function value is determined by a line search. Theoretically, since the direction is upward, such an s_i should exist; however, numerically it might be impossible to find one.

The line search implemented in PcFiml is quadratic, and employs derivative information: see Fletcher (1987, Section 2.6). Initially, we have the bracket $[a_0 = 0, b_0 = 1]$ which contains the maximum, $f(s_i^m) = \ell(\boldsymbol{\theta}_i + s_i^m \boldsymbol{\delta}_i)$. Using the function values at the end points, $f(0) = \ell(\boldsymbol{\theta}_i)$ and $f(1) = \ell(\boldsymbol{\theta}_i + \boldsymbol{\delta}_i)$, together with the derivative $f'(0)$:

$$f'(s_i) = \boldsymbol{\delta}_i' \mathbf{q}(\boldsymbol{\theta}_i + s_i \boldsymbol{\delta}_i),$$

we can tie down the polynomial and find its maximum, p_m say. If $p_m \in [a_0, b_0]$, we take $s_i^1 = p_m$, otherwise we take the maximum of two points on the polynomial, one a bit to the right of a_0, the other to the left of b_0. Depending on the function values and derivatives at a_0 and s_i^1, the new bracket $[a_1, b_1]$ will be $[a_0, s_i^1]$ or $[s_i^1, b_0]$. This is repeated until convergence, which occurs at iteration j if $f(s_i^j) > f(0) + 0.01 s_i^j f'(0)$ and $f(s_i^j) > f(a_{j-1})$ and $f'(s_i^j) \leq 0.2 f'(0)$. If the quadratic line search fails to improve, which occurs if $f'(a_{j-1})(s_i^j - a_{j-1}) < 10^{-6}$, the search is continued linearly ($s_i^{j+1} = s_i^j/2$) until convergence ($f(s_i^j) > f(0)$) or $s_i^j < 10^{-12}$.

13.3.3 Starting values

Immediately after a system estimation, the starting values are $\boldsymbol{\theta}_0 = \boldsymbol{\theta}_{2SLS}$. If the model has been estimated before, the most recent parameters are used (2SLS and especially 3SLS provide excellent starting values). $\mathbf{H}$ is initialized to $\mathbf{I}_r$.

13.3.4 Recursive estimation

Recursive estimation works as follows: starting values for $\boldsymbol{\theta}$ and $\mathbf{H}$ for the first estimation (M observations) are the full sample values (T observations); then at each sample size, the previous values for $\boldsymbol{\theta}$ and $\mathbf{H}$ at convergence are used to start with. Often only four steps are required, making recursive application of the optimization process very efficient relative to the size of the problem.

13.3.5 Convergence

The convergence decision is based on two tests. The first is based on likelihood elasticities ($\partial\ell/\partial\log|\theta_j|$), writing $\boldsymbol{\theta}_i = (\theta_{i,,j})$, $\mathbf{q}(\boldsymbol{\theta}_i) = (q_{i,,j})$, $\boldsymbol{\delta}_i = (\delta_{i,,j})$:

$$\begin{aligned} |q_{i,,j}\theta_{i,,j}| &\leq \epsilon \quad \text{for all } j \text{ with } \theta_{i,,j} \neq 0, \\ |q_{i,,j}| &\leq \epsilon \quad \text{for all } j \text{ with } \theta_{i,,j} = 0. \end{aligned} \tag{13.12}$$

The second is based on the one-step ahead relative change in the parameter values:

$$\begin{aligned} |\delta_{i+1,,j}| &\leq 10\epsilon\ |\theta_{i,,j}| \quad \text{for all } j \text{ with } \theta_{i,,j} \neq 0, \\ |\delta_{i+1,,j}| &\leq 10\epsilon \quad \text{for all } j \text{ with } \theta_{i,,j} = 0. \end{aligned} \tag{13.13}$$

If convergence fails, it is possible to retry using a larger convergence criterion if you still want output. However, this could also be a result of model mis-specification or under-identification.

13.3.6 End of iteration process

The status of the iterative process is contained in the following messages:

(1) *Press Estimate to start iterating!*
No attempt to maximize has been taken yet.

(2) *Aborted: no convergence!*
The process was halted by the user.

(3) *Function evaluation failed: no convergence!*
This is rare in FIML, but could occur in other estimation problems. It indicates that the program failed to compute the function value at the current parameter values. The cause could be a singular matrix, or illegal argument to a function such as $\log(\cdot)$.

(4) *Maximum number of iterations reached: no convergence!*
The maximum number can be increased and the search resumed from the previous best values; the Hessian is reset to the identity matrix when restarting.

(5) *Failed to improve in line search: no convergence!*
The step length s_i has become too small. The convergence test (13.12) was not passed, using tolerance ϵ_2.

(6) *Failed to improve in line search: weak convergence*
The step length s_i has become too small. The convergence test (13.12) was passed, using tolerance ϵ_2.

(7) *Strong convergence*
Both convergence tests (13.12) and (13.13) were passed, using tolerance ϵ_1.

The chosen default values for the tolerances are:

$$\epsilon_1 = 10^{-4}, \ \epsilon_2 = 5 \times 10^{-3}. \tag{13.14}$$

13.3.7 Process control

When the maximization fails, or for teaching purposes, you wish to experiment with the maximization procedure, you can:

(1) set the initial values of the parameters;
(2) set the maximum number of iterations;
(3) write iteration output;
(4) change the convergence tolerance;
(5) choose the maximization algorithm;
(6) plot a grid of the log-likelihood for each parameter, holding the remaining parameters constant at their present value (these are one-dimensional projections of the likelihood surface). A grid may reveal potential multiple optima. See the next section for an example.

Options (1), (5) and (6) are mainly for teaching optimization. The multiple grid facility is especially useful for this purpose.

13.4 Numerical accuracy

Any computer program that performs numerical calculations is faced with the problem of (loss of) numerical accuracy. It seems a slightly neglected area in econometric computations, which to some extent could be owing to a perception that the gradual and steady increase in computational power went hand in hand with improvements in accuracy. This, however, is not true. At the level of software interaction with hardware, the major (and virtually the only) change has been the shift from single precision (4-byte) floating point computation to double precision (8-byte). Not many modern computer programs have problems with the Longley (1967) data set, which severely tests single precision implementations. Of course, there has been a gradual improvement in the understanding of numerical stability of various methods, but this must be offset against the increasing complexity of the calculations involved.

Loss of numerical accuracy is not a problem, provided we know when it occurs and to what extent. Computations are done with finite precision, so it is always possible to design a problem with analytical solution which fails numerically. Unfortunately, most calculations are too complex to precisely understand to what extent accuracy is lost. So it is important to implement the most accurate methods, and increase understanding of the methods used. The nature of economic data will force us to throw away many correct digits, but only at the end of the computations.

Real numbers are represented as *floating point* numbers, consisting of a sign, a mantissa, and an exponent. A finite number of bytes is used to store a floating point number, so only a finite set can be represented on the computer. The main storage size in PcFiml is 8 bytes, which gives about 15 significant digits. Two sources of error result. The first is the *representation error*: most numbers can only be approximated on a computer. The second is *rounding error*. Consider the *machine precision* ϵ_m: this is the smallest number that can be added to one such that the result is different from one:

$$\epsilon_m = \underset{\epsilon}{\operatorname{argmin}} \left(1 + \epsilon \neq 1\right).$$

So an extreme example of rounding error would be $(1 + \epsilon_m/10) - 1$, where the answer would be 0, rather than $\epsilon_m/10$. In PcFiml: $\epsilon_m \approx 2.2 \times 10^{-16}$.

Due to the accumulation of rounding errors, it is possible that mathematically-equivalent formulae can have very different numerical behaviour. For example, computing $\mathsf{V}[x]$ as $\frac{1}{T}\sum x_i^2 - \bar{x}^2$ is much less stable than $\frac{1}{T}\sum (x_i - \bar{x})^2$. In the first case, we potentially subtract two quite similar numbers, resulting in cancellation of significant digits. A similar cancellation could occur in the computation of inner products (a very common operation, as it is part of matrix multiplication). To keep the danger of cancellation to a minimum, PcFiml accumulates these in 10-byte reals. PcFiml allows the constant term to be entered unrestricted in the system. This corresponds to taking deviations from the mean, and hence to the second variance formula.

An interesting example of harmless numerical inaccuracies is in the case of a grid plot of an autoregressive parameter based on the concentrated likelihood function of an AR(k) model. Rounding errors make the likelihood function appear non-smooth (not differentiable). This tends to occur in models with many lags of the dependent variable and a high autoregressive order. It also occurs in an AR(1) model of the Longley data set, see Figure 13.4, which is a grid of 2000 steps between -1 and 0, done in PcGive (ignoring the warning that numerical accuracy is endangered).

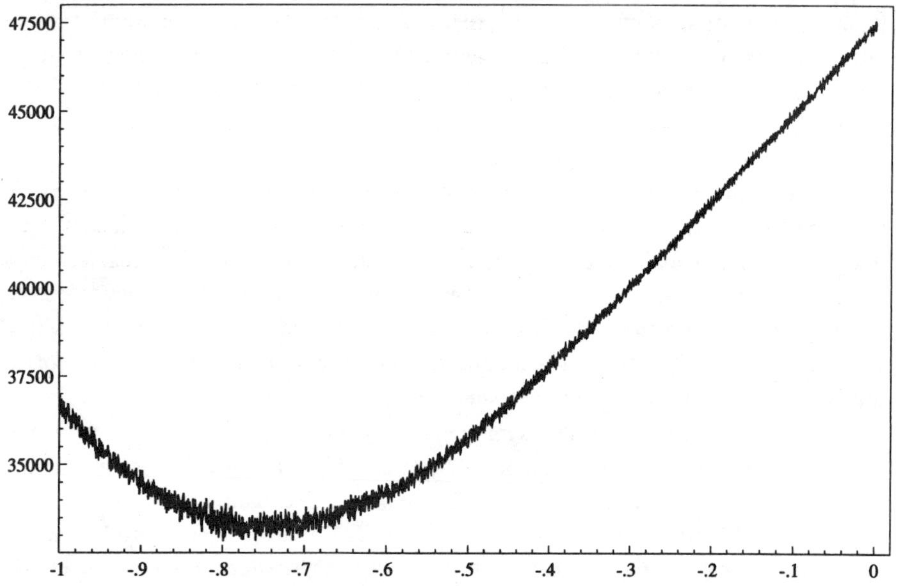

Figure 13.4 AR(1) grid of Longley data.

It is important to distinguish numerical accuracy from other problems that may occur. Multicollinearity, for example, is first and foremost a statistical problem. A certain parameterization of a model might make the estimates of one or more parameters statistically imprecise (see the concept of 'micronumerosity' playfully introduced by Goldberger in Kiefer, 1989). This imprecision could be changed (or moved) by altering the specification of the model, for example by linear or orthogonal transforms of the variables. Multicollinearity could induce numerical instability, leading to loss of significant digits in some or all results.

Another example is the determination of the optimum of a non-linear function that is not concave. Here it is possible to end up in a local optimum. This is clearly not a problem of numerical stability, but inherent in non-linear optimization techniques. A good example is provided by Klein model I. Figure 13.5 provides a grid plot of the FIML likelihood function for each parameter, centred around the maximum found with the 2SLS estimates as a starting point.

These grids are of a different type from the AR grid. In the former all parameters but one are kept fixed, whereas the AR grid actually graphs the concentrated likelihood. In the case of one autoregressive parameter, the correct optimum may be read off the graph, as is the case in the AR grid plot above.

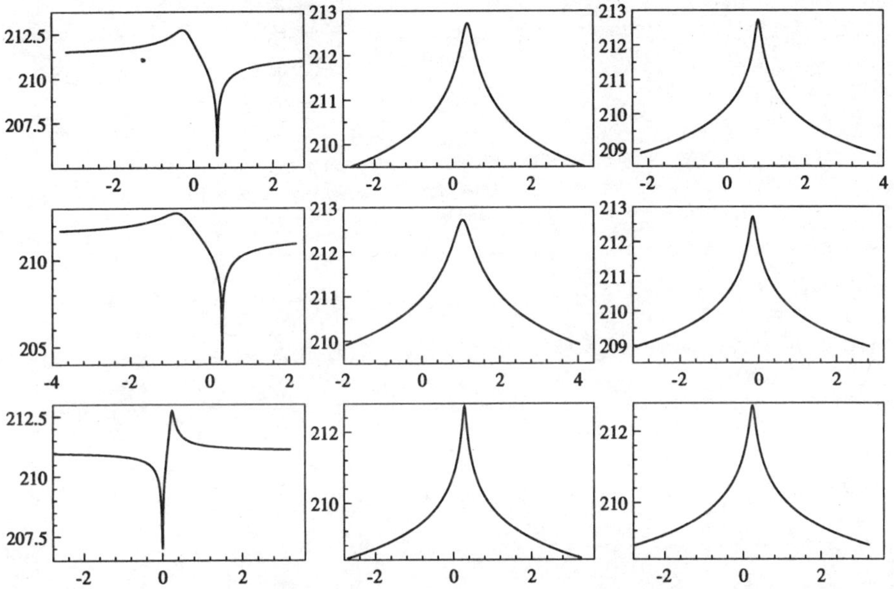

Figure 13.5 Likelihood grid of Klein model I.

Part IV

The Statistical Output of PcFiml

Chapter 14

PcFiml Statistical Output

14.1 Introduction

This chapter explains the statistics computed and reported by PcFiml for dynamic systems, cointegration analysis and model analysis. A brief summary of the underlying mathematics is given in this chapter, but for a comprehensive overview the reader is referred to Chapters 10, 11 and 12. The order is similar to that in the computer program. We first briefly describe system formulation in §14.2 to establish notation, then system estimation in §14.3, followed by graphic evaluation in §14.4, and dynamic analysis and long-run multipliers in §14.5. Section 14.6 considers testing, both at the single equation level as well as at the system level. Sections 14.7–14.9 discuss estimating the cointegrating space, related graphs and tests of restrictions on the space. Model formulation, estimation and related issues such as the restricted reduced form are discussed in §14.10 and §14.11. Model evaluation follows a similar order of presentation to that of the system, §14.12–§14.14. Finally §14.15 considers the progress made during system and model development.

14.2 System formulation

In PcFiml, a linear system, often called the *unrestricted reduced form* (URF), takes the form:

$$\mathbf{y}_t = \sum_{i=1}^{m} \boldsymbol{\pi}_i \mathbf{y}_{t-i} + \sum_{j=0}^{r} \boldsymbol{\pi}_{m+j+1} \mathbf{z}_{t-j} + \mathbf{v}_t \text{ for } t = 1, \ldots, T, \tag{14.1}$$

where $\mathbf{y}_t$, $\mathbf{z}_t$ are respectively $n \times 1$ and $q \times 1$ vectors of observations at time t on the endogenous and non-modelled variables. The $\{\boldsymbol{\pi}_i\}$ are unrestricted, except perhaps for columns of zeros, which would exclude certain $\mathbf{y}_{t-i}$ or $\mathbf{z}_{t-j}$ from the system. Hence each equation in the system has the same variables on the right-hand side. The orders m and r of the lag polynomial matrices for $\mathbf{y}$ and $\mathbf{z}$ should be specified so as to ensure that $\{\mathbf{v}_t\}$ is an innovation process against the available information when the $\{\boldsymbol{\pi}_i\}$ matrices are constant over t. Given a data set $\mathbf{x}_t$, then $\mathbf{y}_t$ is defined as the vector of endogenous variables and $(\mathbf{z}_t \ldots \mathbf{z}_{t-r})$ must be set as non-modelled (so they need to be at least weakly exogenous for the $\{\boldsymbol{\pi}_i\}$). A system in PcFiml is formulated by:

(1) which variables $\mathbf{y}_t, \mathbf{z}_t$ are involved;
(2) the orders m, r of the *lag polynomials*;
(3) classification of the ys into *endogenous* variables and *identity (endogenous)* variables;
(4) any *non-modelled* variable may be classified as *restricted* or as *unrestricted* (Constant, Seasonals and Trend are labelled as such by default). The latter variables are separately estimated (partialled out) to reduce the dimensionality of the parameter space. Their coefficients will be reconstructed afterwards, as described in §10.4.

A *vector autoregression* (VAR) arises when there are no z variables in the statistical system (14.1) ($q = 0$, but there could be a constant, seasonals or trend) and all y have the same lag length (no columns of $\boldsymbol{\pi}$ are zero).

PcFiml encourages you to transform the system to *equilibrium correction form*, where all endogenous variables and their lags are transformed to differences, apart from the first lag:

$$\Delta \mathbf{y}_t = \sum_{i=1}^{m-1} \delta_i \Delta \mathbf{y}_{t-i} + \mathbf{P}_0 \mathbf{y}_{t-1} + \sum_{j=0}^{r} \boldsymbol{\pi}_{m+j+1} \mathbf{z}_{t-j} + \mathbf{v}_t \text{ for } t = 1, \ldots, T. \quad (14.2)$$

Returning to the notation of (14.1), a more compact way of writing the system is:

$$\mathbf{y}_t = \boldsymbol{\Pi} \mathbf{w}_t + \mathbf{v}_t, \quad (14.3)$$

where $\mathbf{w}$ contains $\mathbf{z}$, lags of $\mathbf{z}$, and lags of $\mathbf{y}$: $\mathbf{w}_t' = \left(\mathbf{y}_{t-1}', \ldots, \mathbf{y}_{t-m}', \mathbf{z}_t', \ldots, \mathbf{z}_{t-r}'\right)$. This can be further condensed by writing $\mathbf{Y}' = (\mathbf{y}_1\, \mathbf{y}_2 \ldots \mathbf{y}_T)$, and $\mathbf{W}'$, $\mathbf{V}'$ correspondingly:

$$\mathbf{Y}' = \boldsymbol{\Pi} \mathbf{W}' + \mathbf{V}', \quad (14.4)$$

in which $\mathbf{Y}'$ is $(n \times T)$, $\mathbf{W}'$ is $(k \times T)$ and $\boldsymbol{\Pi}$ is $(n \times k)$.

14.3 System estimation

Since the $\{\boldsymbol{\pi}_i\}$ are unrestricted (except perhaps for excluding elements from $\mathbf{w}_t$) the system (14.1) can be estimated by multivariate least squares, either directly (OLS) or recursively (often denoted RLS). These estimators are the multivariate analogues of OLS and RLS in PcGive. Analogously, estimation of (14.1) requires $\mathbf{v}_t \sim \mathsf{ID}_n(\mathbf{0}, \boldsymbol{\Omega})$, where $\boldsymbol{\Omega}$ is constant over time. However, $\boldsymbol{\Omega}$ may be singular owing to identities linking elements of $\mathbf{x}_t$, and these are handled by estimating only the subset of equations corresponding to stochastic endogenous variables. If $\mathbf{v}_t \sim \mathsf{IN}_n[\mathbf{0}, \boldsymbol{\Omega}]$, OLS coincides with MLE, and estimation of (14.1) is discussed in Chapter 10; for notation, we note that the estimated coefficients are:

$$\widehat{\mathbf{\Pi}}' = (\mathbf{W}'\mathbf{W})^{-1}\mathbf{W}'\mathbf{Y}, \tag{14.5}$$

with residuals:

$$\widehat{\mathbf{V}}' = \mathbf{Y}' - \widehat{\mathbf{\Pi}}\mathbf{W}' \tag{14.6}$$

and estimated covariance matrix:

$$\mathsf{V}\left[\widehat{\mathrm{vec}\widehat{\mathbf{\Pi}}'}\right] = \widetilde{\mathbf{\Omega}} \otimes (\mathbf{W}'\mathbf{W})^{-1}, \tag{14.7}$$

where:

$$\widetilde{\mathbf{\Omega}} = \widehat{\mathbf{V}}'\widehat{\mathbf{V}}/(T-k). \tag{14.8}$$

In the likelihood-based statistics, we shall scale by T:

$$\widehat{\mathbf{\Omega}} = \widehat{\mathbf{V}}'\widehat{\mathbf{V}}/T. \tag{14.9}$$

A listing of the system output now follows. Items marked with a * are only printed on request, as set in the Options dialog. When choosing the columnar representation, PcFiml reports items (2) and (3) equation by equation, otherwise it prints (2) in matrix form.

(1) **Prior coefficients of unrestricted variables*
The coefficients of the regressions of all variables on all unrestricted variables.

(2) *URF coefficients and standard errors*
The coefficients $\widehat{\mathbf{\Pi}}$, and their standard errors $\sqrt{(\mathsf{V}[\widehat{\mathrm{vec}\widehat{\mathbf{\Pi}}'}])_{ii}}$. Any variables marked as unrestricted appear here too.

(3) t-*value and* t-*probability*
These statistics are conventionally calculated to determine whether individual coefficients are significantly different from zero:

$$\text{t-value} = \frac{\widehat{\pi}_{ij}}{\mathsf{SE}\left[\widehat{\pi}_{ij}\right]} \tag{14.10}$$

where the null hypothesis H_0 is $\pi_{ij} = 0$. The null hypothesis is rejected if the probability of getting a value at least as large is less than 5% (or any other chosen significance level). This probability is given as:

$$\text{t-prob} = 1 - \text{Prob}\left(|\tau| \leq |\text{t-value}|\right), \tag{14.11}$$

in which τ has a Student t-distribution with $T-k$ degrees of freedom.
When H_0 is true (and the model is otherwise correctly specified), a Student t-distribution is used since the sample size is often small, and we only have an estimate of the parameter's standard error: however, as the sample size increases, τ

tends to a standard normal distribution under H_0. Large values of t reject H_0; but, in many situations, H_0 may be of little interest to test. Also, selecting variables in a model according to their t-values implies that the usual (Neyman-Pearson) justification for testing is not valid (see Judge, Griffiths, Hill, Lütkepohl and Lee, 1985, for example).

(4) *Equation standard error ($\widetilde{\sigma}$) and residual sum of squares (RSS)*
The square root of the residual variance for each equation:

$$\sqrt{\widetilde{\mathbf{\Omega}}_{ii}} \text{ for } i = 1, \ldots n. \tag{14.12}$$

The RSS is $(T - k)\,\widetilde{\mathbf{\Omega}}_{ii}$, that is, the diagonal elements of $\widehat{\mathbf{V}}'\widehat{\mathbf{V}}$.

(5) *Correlation of URF Residuals*
A typical element of this matrix is:

$$\mathsf{c}_{ij} = \frac{\widetilde{\mathbf{\Omega}}_{ij}}{\sqrt{\widetilde{\mathbf{\Omega}}_{ii}}\sqrt{\widetilde{\mathbf{\Omega}}_{jj}}}. \tag{14.13}$$

So the diagonal consists of ones.

(6) *Standard deviations of URF residuals*
The square root of the residual variance for each equation collected together:

$$\sqrt{\widetilde{\mathbf{\Omega}}_{ii}} \text{ for } i = 1, \ldots n. \tag{14.14}$$

(7) *Likelihood and measures of goodness of fit*
The log-likelihood value is (up to a constant):

$$\widehat{\ell} = -\frac{T}{2} \log \left|\widehat{\mathbf{\Omega}}\right|. \tag{14.15}$$

Then ℓ constitutes the highest attainable likelihood value in the class (14.4) (unless either the set of variables or the lag structure is altered), and hence is the statistical baseline against which simplifications can be tested. In textbook econometrics, (14.4) is called the unrestricted reduced form (URF) and is usually derived from a structural representation. Here, the process is reversed: the statistical system (14.4) is first specified and tested for being a congruent representation; only then is a structural (parsimonious) interpretation sought. If, for example, (14.4) is not congruent, then (14.15) is not a valid baseline, and subsequent tests will not have appropriate distributions. In particular, any just-identified structural representation has the same likelihood value as (14.4), and hence will be invalid if (14.4) is invalid: the 'validity' of imposing further restrictions via a model is hardly of interest.

Define $\check{\mathbf{Y}}$ as $\mathbf{Y}$ after removing the effects of the unrestricted variables, and let:

$$\widehat{\mathbf{\Omega}}_0 = \left(\check{\mathbf{Y}}'\check{\mathbf{Y}}/T\right)^{-1}. \tag{14.16}$$

PcFiml reports:

(a) loglik, this is the log-likelihood (14.15);
(b) $\log|\widehat{\Omega}|$;
(c) $|\widehat{\Omega}|$;
(d) T, the number of observations used in the estimation;
(e) $\log|\check{\mathbf{Y}}'\check{\mathbf{Y}}/T| = \log|\widehat{\Omega}_0|$.

Various measures of the *goodness of fit* of a system can be calculated. The two reported by PcFiml are:

(a) R^2(LR)
Reports $\mathsf{R}^2_r = 1 - |\widehat{\Omega}||\widehat{\Omega}_0|$, which is an R^2 based on the likelihood-ratio principle. For a single equation system this statistic is identical to:
(b) R^2(LM)
Reports $\mathsf{R}^2_m = 1 - \frac{1}{n}\mathrm{tr}(\widehat{\Omega}\widehat{\Omega}_0)$, which derives from the Lagrange Multiplier principle.

Note that these are relative to the unrestricted variables. Both measures coincide with the traditional R^2 in a single equation, provided that the constant is the only unrestricted variable.

(8) F-*tests*
Significance at 5% is marked with a *, at 1% with **. Reported are:

(a) F-*tests against unrestricted regressors*
This uses Rao's F-approximation (see §10.8) to test the significance of R^2_r, which amounts to testing the null hypothesis that all coefficients are zero, except those on the unrestricted variables. In a single-equation system, with only the constant unrestricted, this is identical to the F-statistic reported by PcGive.
(b) F-*tests on retained regressors*
F-tests are shown for the significance of each column of $\widehat{\mathbf{\Pi}}$ together with their probability values (inside square brackets) under the null hypothesis that the corresponding column of coefficients is zero. So these test whether the variable at hand is significant in the system. The statistics are $\mathsf{F}(n, T-k+1-n)$.

Further F-tests of general to specific system modelling are available through the progress report: see §14.15.

(9) *Correlation of actual and fitted*
Prints the correlation between y_{it} and $\widehat{y}_{it}$ for each equation $i = 1, \ldots, n$.

(10) *1-step (ex post) forecast analysis*
The 1-step forecast errors (from $T+1$ to $T+H$) are defined as:

$$\mathbf{e}_{T+i} = \mathbf{y}_{T+i} - \widehat{\mathbf{\Pi}}\mathbf{w}_{T+i} = \left(\mathbf{\Pi} - \widehat{\mathbf{\Pi}}\right)\mathbf{w}_{T+i} + \mathbf{v}_{T+i} \qquad (14.17)$$

with estimated variance

$$\widetilde{\mathsf{V}[\mathbf{e}_{T+i}]} = \widetilde{\boldsymbol{\Omega}} \left(1 + \mathbf{w}'_{T+i} \left(\mathbf{W}'\mathbf{W}\right)^{-1} \mathbf{w}_{T+i}\right) = \widetilde{\boldsymbol{\Psi}}_{T+i}. \tag{14.18}$$

The forecast error variance matrix for a single step-ahead forecast is made up of a term for coefficient uncertainty and a term for innovation errors, as discussed in §10.5. Three types of parameter constancy tests are reported, in each case as a $\chi^2(nH)$ for n equations and H forecasts and an $\mathsf{F}(nH, T-k)$ statistic:

(a) *using* $\boldsymbol{\Omega}$.
This is an index of numerical parameter constancy, ignoring both parameter uncertainty and intercorrelation between forecasts errors at different time periods. It corresponds to ξ_1 and η_1 of (10.46).

(b) *using* $\mathsf{V}[\mathbf{e}]$.
This test is similar to (a), but takes parameter uncertainty into account, corresponding to ξ_2 and η_2 of (10.46).

(c) *using* $\mathsf{V}[\mathbf{E}]$.
Here, $\mathsf{V}[\mathbf{E}]$ is the full variance matrix of all forecast errors $\mathbf{E}$, which takes both parameter uncertainty and inter-correlations between forecast errors into account. This test is ξ_3 and η_3 of (10.46).

(11) **Descriptive statistics of forecast errors*
Reports the means, standard deviations, and correlation matrix of the forecast errors.

(12) **Matrix of forecast standard errors*
Reports the forecast standard errors as given by (14.18).

(13) **Forecast tests, single chi*^{2} $(\cdot)$
These are the individual test statistics underlying (a) and (b) above, for $i = 1, \ldots, H$:

$$\begin{array}{ll} \text{using } \boldsymbol{\Omega} & \mathbf{e}'_{T+i}\widetilde{\boldsymbol{\Omega}}^{-1}\mathbf{e}_{T+i}, \\ \text{using } \mathsf{V}[\mathbf{e}] & \mathbf{e}'_{T+i}\widetilde{\boldsymbol{\Psi}}^{-1}_{T+i}\mathbf{e}_{T+i}, \end{array} \tag{14.19}$$

this time distributed as $\chi^2(n)$. They can also be viewed graphically.

14.4 Graphical evaluation of the system

14.4.1 Graphic analysis

Graphic analysis focuses on graphical inspection of individual equations. Let y_t, $\widehat{y}_t$ denote respectively the actual (that is, observed) values and the fitted values of the selected equation, with residuals $\widehat{v}_t = y_t - \widehat{y}_t$, $t = 1, \ldots, T$. If H observations are retained for forecasting, then $\widehat{y}_{T+1}, \ldots, \widehat{y}_{T+H}$ are the 1-step forecasts.

Nine different types of graph are available:

(1) *Actual and fitted values*
This is a graph showing the fitted ($\widehat{y}_t$) and actual values (y_t) of the dependent variable over time, including the forecast period.

(2) *Cross-plot of actual and fitted values*
$\widehat{y}_t$ against y_t, including the forecast period.

(3) *Scaled residuals*
$(\widehat{v}_t/\widetilde{\sigma})$, where $\widetilde{\sigma}^2$ is the estimated equation error variance, plotted over $t = 1, \ldots, T+H$.

(4) *Forecasts and outcomes*
The 1-step forecasts can be plotted in a graph over time: y_t and $\widehat{y}_t$, $t = T+1, \ldots, T+H$, are shown with error bars of $\pm 2\mathsf{SE}\,(e_t)$, and centred on $\widehat{y}_t$ (that is, an approximate 95% confidence interval for the 1-step forecast). Corresponding to (14.17) the forecast errors are $e_t = y_t - \widehat{y}_t$ and $\mathsf{SE}\,[e_t]$ is derived from (14.18). The error bars can be replaced by bands, set in Options, and the number of pre-forecast observations can be selected.

(5) *Residual correlogram*
This plots the series $\{\mathsf{r}_j\}$ where r_j is the correlation coefficient between $\widehat{v}_t$ and $\widehat{v}_{t-j}$. The length of the correlogram is specified by the user, leading to a Figure that shows $(\mathsf{r}_1, \mathsf{r}_2, \ldots, \mathsf{r}_s)$ plotted against $(1, 2, \ldots, s)$ where for any j:

$$\mathsf{r}_j = \frac{\sum_{t=j+1}^{T} (v_t - \bar{v}_0)(v_{t-j} - \bar{v}_j)}{\sqrt{\sum_{t=j+1}^{T} (v_t - \bar{v}_0)^2 \sum_{t=j+1}^{T} (v_{t-j} - \bar{v}_j)^2}}, \tag{14.20}$$

where $\bar{v}_0 = \frac{1}{T-j}\sum_{t=j+1}^{T} v_t$ is the sample mean of v_t, $t = j+1, \ldots, T$, and $\bar{v}_j = \frac{1}{T-j}\sum_{t=j+1}^{T} v_{t-j}$ is the sample mean of v_{t-j}.

(6) *Residual density optionally with histogram*
Given a data set $\{x_t\} = (x_1 \ldots x_T)$ which are observations on a random variable X, write z_t for the standardized xs:

$$z_t = \frac{x_t - \bar{x}}{\widehat{\sigma}_x}, \quad \text{where } \bar{x} = \frac{1}{T}\sum_{t=1}^{T} x_t \quad \text{and } \widehat{\sigma}_x = \frac{1}{T}\sum_{t=1}^{T} (x_t - \bar{x}).$$

The range of $\{z_t\}$ is divided into N intervals of length h, with h defined below. Then the proportion of z_t in each interval constitutes the histogram; the sum of the proportions is unity on the scaling in PcFiml. The density can be estimated as a smoothed function of the histogram using a normal, or Gaussian, kernel. This can then be summed ('integrated') to obtain the estimated cumulative distribution function (CDF).
Denote the actual density of Z at z by $\mathsf{f}_\mathsf{z}(z)$. This is estimated from the sample

by:

$$\widehat{\mathsf{f}_{\mathsf{z}}(z)} = \frac{1}{Th}\sum_{t=1}^{T} K\left(\frac{z - z_t}{h}\right), \tag{14.21}$$

where h is the *window width* or smoothing parameter, and $K(\cdot)$ is a *kernel* such that:

$$\int_{-\infty}^{\infty} K(x)\,\mathrm{d}x = 1.$$

PcFiml sets $h = 1.06\widehat{\sigma}_z/T^{0.2}$ $(= 1.06/T^{0.2}$ as $\widehat{\sigma}_z = 1)$ as a default, and uses the standard normal density for $K(\cdot)$:

$$K\left(\frac{z - z_t}{h}\right) = \frac{1}{\sqrt{2\pi}}\exp\left[-\tfrac{1}{2}\left(\frac{z - z_t}{h}\right)^2\right]. \tag{14.22}$$

$\widehat{\mathsf{f}_{\mathsf{z}}(z)}$ is usually calculated for 128 values of z, but since direct evaluation can be somewhat expensive in computer time, a fast Fourier transform is used (we are grateful to Dr Silverman for permission to use his algorithm). The estimated CDF of Z can be derived from $\widehat{\mathsf{f}_{\mathsf{z}}(z)}$; this is shown with a standard normal CDF for comparison. An excellent reference on density function estimation is Silverman (1986).

By default, the estimated density of the residuals $\widehat{v}_t$, $t = 1, \ldots, T$, namely $\widehat{f_{\mathsf{v}}(\cdot)}$ is graphed, using the settings described above. The histogram and a standard normal density can be added for comparison.

(7) *Residual distribution*

The estimated cumulative density function, $\widehat{F_{\mathsf{v}}(\cdot)}$, of the residuals is shown with a standard normal for comparison.

(8) *Forecast chow tests.*

These are the Chow tests using $\mathsf{V}[\mathsf{e}]$ of (14.19), available from $T+1$ to $T+H$, together with a fixed 5% critical value from $\chi^2(n)$. These are not scaled by their critical values, unlike the graphs in recursive graphics.

(9) *Residual cross-plots*

Let $\widehat{v}_{it}$, $\widehat{v}_{jt}$ denote the residuals of equation i and j. This graph shows the cross-plot of $\widehat{v}_{it}$ against $\widehat{v}_{jt}$ for all marked equations ($i \neq j$), over $t = 1, \ldots, T+H$.

14.4.2 Recursive graphics

When RLS is selected, the $\mathbf{\Pi}$ matrix is estimated at each t $(1 \le M \le t \le T)$ where M is user-selected. Unlike previous versions, there is no requirement that $k \le M$. So OLS is used for observations $1 \ldots M-1$, RLS for $M \ldots T$. The calculations proceed exactly as for the single equation case in PcGive since the formulae for updating are unaffected by $\mathbf{Y}$ being a matrix rather than a vector. Indeed, the relative cost over single equation

RLS falls; but the huge number of statistics ($nk(T-M+1)$ coefficients alone) cannot be stored in PcFiml. Consequently, the graphical output omits coefficients and their t-values. Otherwise the output is similar to that in PcGive, but now available for each equation in the system. In addition, system graphs are available, either of the log likelihood, or of the system Chow tests. At each t, system estimates are available, for example coefficients $\mathbf{\Pi}_t$ and residuals $\mathbf{v}_t = \mathbf{y}_t - \mathbf{\Pi}_t \mathbf{w}_t$. Unrestricted variables have their coefficients fixed at the full sample values. Define $\mathbf{V}_t'$ as $(\mathbf{v}_1 \mathbf{v}_2 \ldots \mathbf{v}_t)$ and let y_t, v_t and $\mathbf{w}_t$ denote the endogenous variable, residuals and regressors of equation i at time t.

The following graphs are available for the system (the information can be printed on request):

(1) *Residual sum of squares*
The residual sum of squares RSS_t for equation i is the ith diagonal element of $\widehat{\mathbf{V}}_t' \widehat{\mathbf{V}}_t$ for $t = M, \ldots, T$.

(2) *1-Step Residuals* $\pm 2\widetilde{\sigma}$ for equation i at each t:
The 1-step residuals $\widehat{v}_t$ are shown bordered by $0 \pm 2\widetilde{\sigma}_t$ over $M, \ldots, T$. Points outside the 2-standard-error region are either outliers or are associated with coefficient changes.

(3) *Log-likelihood/T*

$$\widehat{l}_t = -\ \tfrac{1}{2}\ \log\left|\frac{t}{T}\widehat{\mathbf{\Omega}}_t\right| = -\ \tfrac{1}{2}\ \log\left|T^{-1}\widehat{\mathbf{V}}_t'\widehat{\mathbf{V}}_t\right|,\ t = M, \ldots, T. \qquad (14.23)$$

Per definition: $\widehat{l}_t \geq \widehat{l}_{t+1}$. This follows from the fact that both can be derived from a system estimated up to $t+1$, where $\widehat{l}_t$ obtains from the system with a dummy for the last observation (see §10.8.1), so that $\widehat{l}_{t+1}$ is the restricted likelihood. On the other hand: $\widehat{\ell}_t \ngeq \widehat{\ell}_{t+1}$, as this would still require the sample size correction as employed in $\widehat{l}_t$.

(4) *Single equation chow Tests*

(a) *1-step* F*-tests* (1-step Chow-tests)
1-step forecast tests are $\mathsf{F}(1, t-k-1)$ under the null of constant parameters, for $t = M, \ldots, T$. A typical statistic is calculated as:

$$\frac{(RSS_t - RSS_{t-1})(t-k-1)}{RSS_{t-1}}. \qquad (14.24)$$

Normality of y_t is needed for this statistic to be distributed as an F.

(b) *Break-point* F*-tests* ($N\!\downarrow$-step Chow-tests)
Break-point F-tests are $\mathsf{F}(T-t+1, t-k-1)$ for $t = M, \ldots, T$. These are, therefore, sequences of Chow tests and are called $N\downarrow$ because the number of forecasts goes from $T-M+1$ to 1. When the forecast period exceeds the estimation period, this test is not necessarily optimal relative to

the covariance test based on fitting the model separately to the split samples. A typical statistic is calculated as:

$$\frac{(RSS_T - RSS_{t-1})\,(t-k-1)}{RSS_{t-1}\,(T-t+1)}. \tag{14.25}$$

This test is closely related to the CUSUMSQ statistic in Brown, Durbin and Evans (1975).

(c) *Forecast* F-*tests*. ($N\uparrow$-step Chow-tests)
Forecast F-tests are $\mathsf{F}\,(t-M+1, M-k-1)$ for $t = M, \ldots, T$, and are called $N\uparrow$ as the forecast horizon increases from M to t. This tests the model over 1 to $M-1$ against an alternative which allows any form of change over M to T. Thus, unless $M > k$, blank graphs will result. A typical statistic is calculated as:

$$\frac{(RSS_t - RSS_{M-1})\,(M-k-1)}{RSS_{M-1}\,(t-M+1)}. \tag{14.26}$$

(5) *System Chow tests*

(a) *1-step* F-*tests* (1-step Chow-tests)
This uses Rao's F-approximation (see §10.8), with the R^2 computed as:

$$1 - \exp\left(-2\widehat{l}_{t-1} + 2\widehat{l}_t\right), \quad t = M, \ldots, T. \tag{14.27}$$

(b) *Break-point* F-*tests* ($N\downarrow$-step Chow-tests)
This uses Rao's F-approximation, with the R^2 computed as:

$$1 - \exp\left(-2\widehat{l}_{t-1} + 2\widehat{l}_T\right), \quad t = M, \ldots, T. \tag{14.28}$$

(c) *Forecast* F-*tests* ($N\uparrow$-step Chow-tests)
This uses Rao's F-approximation, with the R^2 computed as:

$$1 - \exp\left(-2\widehat{l}_{M-1} + 2\widehat{l}_t\right), \quad t = M, \ldots, T. \tag{14.29}$$

The statistics in (4) and (5) are variants of Chow (1960) tests: they are scaled by one-off critical values from the F-distribution at any selected probability level as an adjustment for changing degrees of freedom, so that the significance values become a straight line at unity. Selecting a probability of 0 or 1 results in unscaled statistics. Note that the first and last values of (14.24) respectively equal the first value of (14.26) and the last value of (14.25); the same relation holds for the system tests. When the system tests of (5) are computed for a single equation system, they are identical to the tests computed under (4).

14.4.3 Dynamic forecasting

Dynamic (or multi-period or *ex ante*) system forecasts can be graphed. Commencing from period T as initial conditions:

$$\widehat{\mathbf{y}}_t = \sum_{i=1}^{m} \widehat{\boldsymbol{\pi}}_i \widehat{\mathbf{y}}_{t-i} + \sum_{j=0}^{r} \widehat{\boldsymbol{\pi}}_{j+m+1} \mathbf{z}_{t-j} \quad \text{for } t = T+1, \ldots, T+H, \tag{14.30}$$

where $\widehat{\mathbf{y}}_{t-i} = \mathbf{y}_{t-i}$ for $t - i \leq T$.

Such forecasts require data on $(\mathbf{z}_{T+1} \ldots \mathbf{z}_{T+H})$ for H-periods ahead (but the future values of ys are not needed), and to be meaningful also require that $\mathbf{z}_t$ is strongly exogenous and that $\boldsymbol{\Pi}$ remains constant. Dynamic forecasts can be viewed with or without 'error bars' (or bands) based on the equation error-variance matrix only, where the variance estimates are given by the $(n \times n)$ top left block of:

$$\begin{aligned} \widetilde{\mathsf{V}[\mathbf{e}^*_{T+1}]} &= \widetilde{\mho}, \\ \widetilde{\mathsf{V}[\mathbf{e}^*_{T+2}]} &= \widetilde{\mho} + \widehat{\mathbf{D}}\widetilde{\mho}\widehat{\mathbf{D}}', \\ &\cdots \\ \widetilde{\mathsf{V}[\mathbf{e}^*_{T+H}]} &= \sum_{i=0}^{H-1} \widehat{\mathbf{D}}^i \widetilde{\mho} \widehat{\mathbf{D}}^{i\prime}. \end{aligned} \tag{14.31}$$

Optionally, parameter uncertainty can be taken into account when computing the forecast error variances (but not for h-step forecasts): this is allowed only when there are no unrestricted variables. Using the companion matrix, which is $(nm \times nm)$:

$$\widehat{\mathbf{D}} = \begin{pmatrix} \widehat{\boldsymbol{\pi}}_1 & \widehat{\boldsymbol{\pi}}_2 & \cdots & \widehat{\boldsymbol{\pi}}_{m-1} & \widehat{\boldsymbol{\pi}}_m \\ \mathbf{I}_n & \mathbf{0} & \cdots & \mathbf{0} & \mathbf{0} \\ \mathbf{0} & \mathbf{I}_n & \cdots & \mathbf{0} & \mathbf{0} \\ \vdots & \vdots & \ddots & \vdots & \vdots \\ \mathbf{0} & \mathbf{0} & \cdots & \mathbf{I}_n & \mathbf{0} \end{pmatrix} \quad \text{and} \quad \widetilde{\mho} = \begin{pmatrix} \widetilde{\boldsymbol{\Omega}} & \mathbf{0} & \cdots \\ \mathbf{0} & \mathbf{0} & \cdots \\ \vdots & \vdots & \ddots \end{pmatrix}, \tag{14.32}$$

see §10.5.2.

Thus, uncertainty owing to the parameters being estimated is presently ignored (compare this to the parameter constancy tests based on the 1-step forecasts). If $q > 0$, the non-modelled variables could be perturbed as in 'scenario studies' on non-linear models, but here with a view to assessing the robustness or fragility of *ex ante* forecasts to possible changes in the conditioning variables. If such perturbations alter the characteristics of the $\{\mathbf{z}_t\}$ process, super exogeneity is required.

It is also possible to graph h-step forecasts, where $h \leq H$. This uses (14.30), but with:

$$\widehat{\mathbf{y}}_{t-i} = \mathbf{y}_{t-i} \quad \text{for} \quad t - i \leq \max(T, t-h). \tag{14.33}$$

To be consistent with the definition of h-step forecasts in §10.5, what is graphed is the sequence of $1, \ldots, h-1$ step forecasts for $T+1, \ldots T+h-1$, followed by h-step forecasts from $T+h, \ldots T+H$. In other words: up to $T+h$ are dynamic forecasts, from then on h-step forecasts up to $T+H$. Thus, unless there is available data not used in estimation, the h-step forecasts are just dynamic forecasts up to the value of h: this data can be reserved by using a shorter estimation sample, or setting a non-zero number of forecasts. After h forecasts, the forecast error variance remains constant at $\sum_{i=0}^{h-1} \widehat{\mathbf{D}}^i \widetilde{\mho} \widehat{\mathbf{D}}^{i\prime}$. For example, 1-step forecasts use $\widehat{\mathbf{y}}_{t-i} = \mathbf{y}_{t-i}$ for $t - i \leq \max(T, t-1)$, and hence never use forecasted values (in this case $\max(T, t-1) = t-1$, as $t \geq T+1$). The 1-step forecast error variance used here is $\widetilde{\Omega}$, which differs from (14.18) in that it ignores the parameter uncertainty. Selecting $h = H$ yields the dynamic forecasts.

To summarize, the following graphs are available:

(1) *Dynamic forecasts* over any selected horizon H for closed systems, and the available sample for open (with non-modelled variables, but no identities).
Graphs can be without standard errors; or standard errors can be plotted as the forecast ±2SE, either error-variance based or parameter-variance based (i.e., full estimation uncertainty, if no unrestricted variables).

(2) *h-step forecasts* up to the end of the available sample, which is dependent on the presence or absence of non-modelled variables. In the former case, data must exist on the non-modelled variables; in the latter, the horizon $H \geq h$ is at choice.
Graphs can be without standard errors; or error-variance based standard errors can be plotted as the forecast ±2SE.

The forecasts and standard errors can be printed. Although dynamic forecasting is not available for a system with identities, it can be obtained by mapping the system to a model of itself and specifying the identity equations.

14.4.4 Dynamic simulation

The system can be dynamically simulated from any starting point within sample, ending at the last observation used in the estimation. Computation is as in (14.30), with $T+1$ replaced by the chosen within-sample starting point. Given the critiques of dynamic simulation as a method of evaluating econometric systems in Hendry and Richard (1982) and Chong and Hendry (1986), this option is included to allow users to see how misleading simulation tracks can be as a guide to selecting systems. Also see Pagan (1989). Like dynamic forecasting, dynamic simulation is not available for a system with identities, but can be obtained by mapping the system to a model of itself and specifying the identity equations.

Let $y_t, \widehat{y}_t, \widehat{s}_t$ denote respectively the actual (that is, observed) values, the fitted values (from the estimation) and the simulated values of the selected equation, $t = M, \ldots, M+H$. H is the number of simulated values, starting from M, $1 \leq M < T$.

Four different types of graph are available:

(1) *Actual and simulated values*
This is a graph showing the simulated ($\widehat{s}_t$) and actual values (y_t) of the dependent variable over time.
(2) *Actual and simulated cross-plot*
Cross-plot of $\widehat{y}_t$ against $\widehat{s}_t$.
(3) *Fitted and simulated values*
$\widehat{y}_t$ and $\widehat{s}_t$ against time.
(4) *Simulation residuals*
Graphs $(y_t - \widehat{s}_t)$ over time.

Impulse response analysis disregards the non-modelled variables and sets the history to zero, apart from the initial values $\mathbf{i}_1$:

$$\widehat{\mathbf{i}}_t = \sum_{i=1}^{m} \widehat{\boldsymbol{\pi}}_i \widehat{\mathbf{i}}_{t-i} \quad \text{for } t = 2, \ldots, H, \tag{14.34}$$

where $\widehat{\mathbf{i}}_1$ are the initial values, and $\widehat{\mathbf{i}}_t = \mathbf{0}$ for $t \leq 0$. This generates n^2 graphs, where the jth set of n graphs gives the response of the n endogenous variables to the jth initial values. These initial values $\mathbf{i}_{1,j}$ for the jth set of graphs can be chosen as follows:

(1) unity
$\mathbf{i}_{1,j} = \mathbf{e}_j$: 1 for the jth variable, 0 otherwise.
(2) standard error
$\mathbf{i}_{1,j} = \widetilde{\sigma}_j$: the jth residual standard error for the jth variable, 0 otherwise.
(3) orthogonalized
Take the Choleski decomposition of $\widetilde{\boldsymbol{\Omega}}$, $\widetilde{\boldsymbol{\Omega}} = \mathbf{PP}'$, so that $\mathbf{P} = (\mathbf{p}_1 \ldots \mathbf{p}_n)$ has zeros above the diagonal. The orthogonalized initial values are $\mathbf{i}_{1,j} = \mathbf{p}_j$. Thus, the outcome depends on the ordering of the variables.

Graphing is optionally of the accumulated response: $\sum_{t=1}^{h} \widehat{\mathbf{i}}_t$, $h = 1, \ldots, H$.

14.5 Dynamic analysis

After estimation, a dynamic analysis of the unrestricted reduced form (system) can be performed. Consider the system (14.2), but replace the $\boldsymbol{\pi}_{m+j+1}$ by $\boldsymbol{\Gamma}_j$:

$$\mathbf{y}_t = \sum_{i=1}^{m} \boldsymbol{\pi}_i \mathbf{y}_{t-i} + \sum_{j=0}^{r} \boldsymbol{\Gamma}_j \mathbf{z}_{t-j} + \mathbf{v}_t, \quad \mathbf{v}_t \sim \mathsf{IN}_n\left[\mathbf{0}, \boldsymbol{\Omega}\right], \tag{14.35}$$

with $\mathbf{y}_t$ $(n \times 1)$ and $\mathbf{z}_t$ $(q \times 1)$. Use the lag operator L, defined as $L\mathbf{y}_t = \mathbf{y}_{t-1}$, to write this as:

$$\left(\mathbf{I} - \boldsymbol{\pi}\left(L\right)\right)\mathbf{y}_t = \boldsymbol{\Gamma}\left(L\right)\mathbf{z}_t + \mathbf{v}_t. \tag{14.36}$$

So $\pi(1) = \pi_1 + \cdots + \pi_m$, with m the longest lag on endogenous variable(s); and $\mathbf{\Gamma}(1) = \mathbf{\Gamma}_0 + \cdots + \mathbf{\Gamma}_r$, with r the longest lag on non-modelled variable(s). $\widehat{\mathbf{P}}_0 = \widehat{\pi}(1) - \mathbf{I}_n$ can be inverted only if it is of rank $p = n$, in which case for $q > 0$, $\mathbf{y}$ and $\mathbf{z}$ are fully cointegrated. If $p < n$, only a subset of the ys and zs are cointegrated, see Chapter 11. If $\widehat{\mathbf{P}}_0$ can be inverted, we can write the estimated static long-run solution as:

$$\widehat{\mathbf{y}} = -\widehat{\mathbf{P}}_0^{-1}\widehat{\mathbf{\Gamma}}(1)\,\mathbf{z}. \tag{14.37}$$

If $q = 0$, the system is closed (that is, a VAR), and (14.37) is not defined. However, $\mathbf{P}_0$ can still be calculated, and then p characterizes the number of cointegrating vectors linking the ys: again see Chapter 11. $^+$ denotes that the outcome is reported only if there are non-modelled variables.

If there are no identities PcFiml computes:

(1) *Lag-1 multipliers*: $\widehat{\pi}_1(\widehat{\mathbf{\Gamma}}_0 \ldots \widehat{\mathbf{\Gamma}}_r)$;$^+$
(2) *Mean-lag matrix*: $\widehat{\mathbf{\Psi}} = \sum_{i=1}^{m} i\widehat{\pi}_i$: only shown if there is more than one lag.
(3) *Long-run matrix*: $\widehat{\pi}(1) - \mathbf{I}_n = \widehat{\mathbf{P}}_0$;
(4) *Long-run covariance*: $\widehat{\mathbf{P}}_0^{-1}\widetilde{\mathbf{\Omega}}\widehat{\mathbf{P}}_0^{-1\prime}$;
(5) *Long-run multipliers*: $-\widehat{\mathbf{P}}_0^{-1}(\widehat{\mathbf{\Gamma}}_0 \ldots \widehat{\mathbf{\Gamma}}_r)$;$^+$
(6) *Static long run*: $-\widehat{\mathbf{P}}_0^{-1}\widehat{\mathbf{\Gamma}}(1)$;$^+$
(7) *Standard errors of static long run*;$^+$
(8) *Eigenvalues of* $\widehat{\pi}(1) - \mathbf{I}_n$;
(9) *Eigenvalues of companion matrix*, $\widehat{\mathbf{D}}$, given in (14.32).

Thus (1) and (5)–(7) are only available if $q > 0$. Dynamic analysis is not available for a system with identities, but again can be obtained by making the model identical to the system.

14.6 System testing

14.6.1 Introduction

Many test statistics in PcFiml have either a χ^2 distribution or an F distribution. F-tests are usually reported as:

```
F(num,denom)   =   Value   [Probability]   /*/**
```

for example:

```
F(1, 155)      =   5.0088 [0.0266] *
```

where the test statistic has an F-distribution with one degree of freedom in the numerator and 155 in the denominator. The observed value is 5.0088, and the probability of getting a value of 5.0088 or larger under this distribution is 0.0266. This is less than 5% but more than 1%, hence the star. Significant outcomes at a 1% level are shown by two stars.

χ^2 tests are also reported with probabilities, as for example:

```
Normality Chi²(2)= 2.1867 [0.3351]
```

The 5% χ^2 critical values with two degrees of freedom is 5.99, so here normality is not rejected (alternatively, Prob($\chi^2 \geq 2.1867$) = 0.3351, which is more than 5%).

The probability values for the F-test are calculated using an algorithm based on Majunder and Bhattacharjee (1973a) and Cran, Martin and Thomas (1977).[1] Those for the χ^2 are based on Shea (1988). The significance points of the F-distribution derive from Majunder and Bhattacharjee (1973b).

Some tests take the form of a likelihood ratio (LR) test. If ℓ is the unrestricted, and ℓ_0 the restricted, log-likelihood, then under the null hypothesis that the restrictions are valid, $-2(\ell_0 - \ell)$ has a $\chi^2(s)$ distribution, with s the number of restrictions imposed (so model ℓ_0 is nested in ℓ).

Many diagnostic tests are done through an auxiliary regression. In the case of single-equation tests, they take the form of $T\mathsf{R}^2$ for the auxiliary regression, so that they are asymptotically distributed as $\chi^2\,(s)$ under their nulls, and hence have the usual additive property for independent $\chi^2 s$. In addition, following Harvey (1990) and Kiviet (1986), F-approximations of the form:

$$\frac{\mathsf{R}^2}{1-\mathsf{R}^2}\cdot\frac{T-k-s}{s} \sim \mathsf{F}\,(s, T-k-s) \qquad (14.38)$$

are calculated because they may be better behaved in small samples.

Whenever the vector tests are implemented through an auxiliary multivariate regression, PcFiml uses vector analogues of the χ^2 and F statistics. The first is an LM test in the auxiliary system, defined as $Tn\mathsf{R}^2_m$, the second uses the F approximation based on R^2_r, see §10.9.2 and §10.8. The vector tests reduce to the single-equation tests in a one-equation system. All tests are fully described in Chapter 10; we give a summary below.

14.6.2 Single equation diagnostics

Diagnostic testing in PcFiml is performed at two levels: individual equations and the system as a whole. Individual equation diagnostics take the residuals from the system, and treat them as PcGive would, ignoring that they form part of a system. Usually this means that they are only valid if the remaining equations are problem-free.

(1) *Portmanteau statistic*

This is a degrees-of-freedom corrected version of the Box and Pierce (1970) statistic. It is only a valid test in a single equation with strongly exogenous variables. If s is the chosen lag length and m the lag length of the dependent variable, values $\geq 2(s-m)$ could indicate residual autocorrelation. Conversely, small values of this statistic should be treated with caution as residual autocorrelations are biased

[1] As recommended in Cran *et al.* (1977), the approach in Pike and Hill (1966) is used for the logarithm of the gamma function.

towards zero when lagged dependent variables are included in econometric equations. An appropriate test for residual autocorrelation is provided by the LM test for autocorrelated residuals. The autocorrelation coefficients r_j, see (14.20), are also reported.

(2) *LM test for autocorrelated residuals*
This test is performed through the auxiliary regression of the residuals on the original variables and lagged residuals (missing lagged residuals at the start of the sample are replaced by zero, so no observations are lost). Unrestricted variables are included in the auxiliary regression. The null hypothesis is no autocorrelation, which would be rejected if the test statistic is too high. This LM test is valid for systems with lagged dependent variables and diagonal residual autocorrelation, whereas neither the Durbin–Watson nor the residual correlogram provide a valid test in that case. The χ^2 and F-statistic are shown, as are the error autocorrelation coefficients, which are the coefficients of the lagged residuals in the auxiliary regression.

(3) *LM test for autocorrelated squared residuals*
This is the ARCH test (AutoRegressive Conditional Heteroscedasticity: see Engle, 1982) which in the present form tests the joint significance of lagged squared residuals in the regression of squared residuals on a constant and lagged squared residuals. The χ^2 and F-statistic are shown, in addition to the ARCH coefficients, which are the coefficients of the lagged squared residuals in the auxiliary regression.

(4) *Test for normality*
This is the test proposed by Doornik and Hansen (1994), and amounts to testing whether the skewness and kurtosis of the residuals correspond to those of a normal distribution. Before reporting the actual test, PcFiml reports the following statistics of the residuals: mean (0 for the residuals), standard deviation, skewness (0 in a normal distribution), excess kurtosis (0 in a normal distribution), minimum and maximum.

(5) *Test for heteroscedasticity*
This test is based on White (1980), and involves an auxiliary regression of the squared residuals on the original regressors and all their squares. The null is unconditional homoscedasticity, and the alternative is that the variance of the error process depends on the regressors and their squares. The output comprises TR^2, the F-test equivalent, and the coefficients of the auxiliary regression plus their individual t-statistics to help highlight problem variables. Unrestricted variables are excluded from the auxiliary regression, but a constant is always included. Variables that are redundant when squared or collinear are automatically removed.

14.6.3 Vector tests

The present incarnation of PcFiml has various formal system mis-specification tests for within-sample congruency.

(1) *Vector portmanteau statistic*
This is the multivariate equivalent of the single-equation portmanteau statistic (again using a small-sample correction), and only a valid asymptotic test in a VAR.

(2) *Vector error autocorrelation test*
Lagged residuals (with missing observations for lagged residuals set to zero) are partialled out from the original regressors, and the whole system is re-estimated, providing a Lagrange-multiplier test based on comparing the likelihoods for both systems.

(3) *Vector normality test*
This is the multivariate equivalent of the aforementioned single equation normality test, see §10.9.2. It checks whether the residuals at hand are normally distributed as:

$$\mathbf{v}_t \sim \mathsf{IN}_n\left[\mathbf{0}, \boldsymbol{\Omega}\right] \tag{14.39}$$

by checking their skewness and kurtosis. A $\chi^2(2n)$ test for the null hypothesis of normality is reported, in addition to the transformed skewness and kurtosis of the rotated components.

(4) *Vector heteroscedasticity test (using squares)*
This test amounts to a multivariate regression of all error variances and covariances on the original regressors and their squares. The test is $\chi^2(sn(n+1)/2)$, where s is the number of non-redundant added regressors (collinear regressors are automatically removed). The null hypothesis is no heteroscedasticity, which would be rejected if the test statistic is too high. Note that regressors that were classified as unrestricted are excluded.

(5) *Vector heteroscedasticity test (using squares and cross-products)*
This test is similar to the heteroscedasticity test, but now cross-products of regressors are added as well. Again, the null hypothesis is no heteroscedasticity (the name functional form was used in version 8 of PcGive and PcFiml).

14.6.4 Testing for general restrictions

Writing $\widehat{\boldsymbol{\theta}} = \mathrm{vec}\widehat{\boldsymbol{\Pi}}'$, with corresponding variance-covariance matrix $\mathsf{V}[\widehat{\boldsymbol{\theta}}]$, we can test for (non-) linear restrictions of the form:

$$\mathbf{f}\left(\boldsymbol{\theta}\right) = \mathbf{0}. \tag{14.40}$$

The null hypothesis H_0: $\mathbf{f}(\boldsymbol{\theta}) = \mathbf{0}$ will be tested against H_1: $\mathbf{f}(\boldsymbol{\theta}) \neq \mathbf{0}$ through a Wald test:

$$\mathsf{w} = \mathbf{f}\left(\widehat{\boldsymbol{\theta}}\right)' \left(\widehat{\mathbf{J}}\widetilde{\mathsf{V}\left[\widehat{\boldsymbol{\theta}}\right]}\widehat{\mathbf{J}}'\right)^{-1} \mathbf{f}\left(\widehat{\boldsymbol{\theta}}\right) \tag{14.41}$$

where $\mathbf{J}$ is the Jacobian matrix of the transformation: $\mathbf{J} = \partial \mathbf{f}(\boldsymbol{\theta})/\partial \boldsymbol{\theta}'$. PcFiml computes $\widehat{\mathbf{J}}$ by numerical differentiation. The statistic w has a $\chi^2(s)$ distribution, where s is the number of restrictions (that is, equations in $\mathbf{f}(\cdot)$). The null hypothesis is rejected if we observe a significant test statistic.

Output consists of:

(1) *Wald test for general restrictions*, this is the statistic w with its p-value;

(2) **Restricted variance*, the matrix $\widehat{\mathbf{J}}\widetilde{\mathsf{V}[\widehat{\boldsymbol{\theta}}]}\widehat{\mathbf{J}}'$.

14.7 Cointegration analysis

When the system is closed in the endogenous variables, express $\mathbf{P}_0$ in (14.2) as $\boldsymbol{\alpha}\boldsymbol{\beta}'$, where $\boldsymbol{\alpha}$ and $\boldsymbol{\beta}$ are $(n \times p)$ matrices of rank p. Although $\mathbf{v}_t \sim \mathsf{IN}_n[\mathbf{0}, \boldsymbol{\Omega}]$, and so is stationary, the n variables in $\mathbf{y}_t$ need not all be stationary. The rank p of $\mathbf{P}_0$ determines how many linear combinations of $\mathbf{y}_t$ are stationary. If $p = n$, all variables in $\mathbf{y}_t$ are stationary, whereas $p = 0$ implies that $\Delta\mathbf{y}_t$ is stationary. For $0 < p < n$, there are p cointegrated (stationary) linear combinations of $\mathbf{y}_t$. The rank of $\mathbf{P}_0$ is estimated using the maximum likelihood method proposed by Johansen (1988), fully described in Chapter 11 and summarized here.

First, partial out from $\Delta\mathbf{y}_t$ and $\mathbf{y}_{t-1}$ in (14.2) the effects of the lagged differences $(\Delta\mathbf{y}_{t-1} \dots \Delta\mathbf{y}_{t-m+1})$ and any variables classified as unrestricted (usually the Constant or Trend, but any other variable is allowed as discussed below). This yields the residuals $\mathbf{R}_{0t}$ and $\mathbf{R}_{1t}$ respectively. Next compute the second moments of all these residuals, denoted $\mathbf{S}_{00}$, $\mathbf{S}_{01}$ and $\mathbf{S}_{11}$ where:

$$\mathbf{S}_{ij} = \frac{1}{T}\sum_{t=1}^{T} \mathbf{R}_{it}\mathbf{R}_{jt}' \text{ for } i, j = 0, 1. \tag{14.42}$$

Now solve $|\lambda\mathbf{S}_{11} - \mathbf{S}_{10}\mathbf{S}_{00}^{-1}\mathbf{S}_{01}| = 0$ for the p largest eigenvalues $1 > \widehat{\lambda}_1 > \dots > \widehat{\lambda}_p \dots > \widehat{\lambda}_n > 0$ and the corresponding eigenvectors:

$$\widehat{\boldsymbol{\beta}} = \left(\widehat{\boldsymbol{\beta}}_1, \dots, \widehat{\boldsymbol{\beta}}_p\right) \text{ normalized by } \widehat{\boldsymbol{\beta}}'\mathbf{S}_{11}\widehat{\boldsymbol{\beta}} = \mathbf{I}_p. \tag{14.43}$$

Then, tests of the hypothesis of p cointegrating vectors can be based on the *trace statistic*:

$$\eta_p = -T \sum_{i=p+1}^{n} \log\left(1 - \widehat{\lambda}_i\right) \tag{14.44}$$

or on the *maximum eigenvalue statistic*:

$$\xi_p = -T \log\left(1 - \widehat{\lambda}_{p+1}\right). \tag{14.45}$$

The cointegrating combinations $\beta' \mathbf{y}_{t-1}$ are the $\mathsf{I}(0)$ linear combinations of the $\mathsf{I}(1)$ variables which can be used as equilibrium correction mechanisms (ECMs).

Any non-endogenous variables $\mathbf{z}$ can enter in two ways:

(1) *Unrestricted*: they are partialled out prior to the ML procedure: denote these q_u variables by $\mathbf{z}^u$.
(2) *Restricted*: the q_r variables $\mathbf{z}^r$ are forced to enter the cointegrating space, which can then be written as $\beta'(\mathbf{y}_{t-1} : \mathbf{z}^r_{t-1})$, with β' now a $(p \times (n+q_r))$ matrix.

If lagged values $\mathbf{z}_t, \ldots, \mathbf{z}_{t-m}$ enter, reparameterize as $\Delta\mathbf{z}^u_t, \ldots, \Delta\mathbf{z}^u_{t-m+1}, \mathbf{z}^r_{t-1}$.

Output of the cointegration estimation is:

(1) *Eigenvalues* $\widehat{\lambda}_i$ and the log-likelihood for each rank:

$$\ell^*_c = -\frac{T}{2}\log|\mathbf{S}_{00}| - \frac{T}{2}\sum_{i=1}^{p}\log\left(1-\widehat{\lambda}_i\right), \quad p=0,\ldots,n. \tag{14.46}$$

(2) **Recursive eigenvalues* $\widehat{\lambda}_{it}$. These are automatically computed when the system is estimated recursively, and can be inspected graphically. Unrestricted variables and short-run dynamics can be fixed at their full-sample coefficients, or partialled out at each sample size.
(3) *Test statistics* The test statistics are given with 95% critical values (* and ** mark significance at 95%, 99%), based on a response surface fitted to the results of Osterwald-Lenum (1992). Critical values are available for the following cases:

Constant	Trend
none	none
restricted	none
unrestricted	none
unrestricted	restricted
unrestricted	unrestricted

Strictly speaking, separate critical values should be computed for all other cases. Reported are the maximum eigenvalue statistics:

$$-T\log(1-\widehat{\lambda}_p) \text{ and } -(T-nm)\log(1-\widehat{\lambda}_p),\ p=1,\ldots n. \tag{14.47}$$

This tests H_0: p cointegrating vectors (cvs) against H_1: $p+1$ cvs. So the first row tests H_0: $p=0$ against H_1: $p=1$. If this is significant H_0 is rejected.
Also reported are the trace statistics:

$$-T\sum_{i=p+1}^{n}\log(1-\widehat{\lambda}_i) \text{ and } -(T-nm)\sum_{i=p+1}^{n}\log(1-\widehat{\lambda}_i). \tag{14.48}$$

This tests H_0: p cointegrating vectors against H_1: $> p$ cvs. So the first row tests H_0: $p = 0$ against H_1: $p > 0$. If this is significant H_0 is rejected, and the next row tests H_0: $p = 1$ against H_1: $p > 1$.
The second form of both tests uses a small-sample correction, obtained by replacing T in η_p and ξ_p by $T - nm$.

(4) *Standardized $\widehat{\beta}'$ eigenvectors*, standardized on the diagonal.
(5) *Standardized $\widehat{\alpha}$ coefficients*, corresponding to the standardized $\widehat{\beta}'$.
(6) *Long-run matrix* $\widehat{\mathbf{P}}_0 = \widehat{\alpha}\widehat{\beta}'$, rank n.

14.8 Cointegration graphics

For generality, assume that the variables $\mathbf{z}_r$ were restricted to lie in the cointegrating space. Let α_0, β_0' denote the original *standardized* loadings and eigenvectors; α_r, β_r' are obtained after imposing further restrictions on the cointegrating space. In the unrestricted graphs, the analysis proceeds as if no rank has been chosen yet, corresponding to n eigenvectors. The restricted analysis requires selection of p, the rank of the cointegrating space, thus resulting in fewer graphs.

Let $(\mathbf{y}_t : \mathbf{z}_r)$ denote the original levels of the endogenous variables and the variables restricted to lie in the cointegrating space; $\mathbf{r}_{1t} = (\breve{\mathbf{y}}_{t-1} : \breve{\mathbf{z}}_r)$ are the residuals from regressing $(\mathbf{y}_{t-1} : \mathbf{z}_r)$ on the short-run dynamics $(\{\Delta\mathbf{y}_{t-i}\})$ and unrestricted variables $(\mathbf{z}_u)$. The following graphical output can be obtained after the cointegration analysis (for all graphs except recursive eigenvalues there are two variants, depending on whether or not 'restricted components' have been selected):

(1) *Cointegration relations*
$\widehat{\beta}_0'(\mathbf{y}_t : \mathbf{z}_r)$, or $\widehat{\beta}_0'\mathbf{r}_{1t}$. Write the standardized i^{th} eigenvector as $(\beta_1 \cdots \beta_n\ \beta_{n+1} \cdots \beta_{n+q_r})'$, standardized so that $\beta_i = 1$. The ith cointegration relation graph is: $\sum_j \beta_j y_{jt} + \sum_k \beta_k z_{kt}$ and using concentrated components: $\sum_j \beta_j \breve{y}_{jt-1} + \sum_k \beta_k \breve{z}_{kt}$.
(2) *Actual and fitted*
The graphs of the cointegrating relations are split into two components: the actuals $\mathbf{y}_t$ and the fitted values $\mathbf{y}_t - \widehat{\beta}_0'(\mathbf{y}_t : \mathbf{z}_r)$. All lines are graphed in deviation from mean. Alternatively: the $\breve{\mathbf{y}}_{t-1}$ and the fitted values $\breve{\mathbf{y}}_{t-1} - \widehat{\beta}_0'\mathbf{r}_{1t}$, in deviation from mean. Considering the ith graph of actual and fitted, using the above notation for the standardized i^{th} eigenvector: y_{it} and $y_{it} - \sum_j \beta_j y_{jt} - \sum_k \beta_k z_{kt} = -\sum_{j\neq i} \beta_j y_{jt} - \sum_k \beta_k z_{kt}$ whereas using concentrated components: y_{it} and $-\sum_{j\neq i} \beta_j \breve{y}_{jt-1} - \sum_k \beta_k \breve{z}_{kt}$.
(3) *Components of relation*
Graphs all the components of $\widehat{\beta}_0'(\mathbf{y}_t : \mathbf{z}_r)$ or $\widehat{\beta}_0'\mathbf{r}_{1t}$, matched by means. For the ith graph: $y_{it}, \beta_j y_{jt}\ (j \neq i), \beta_k z_{kt}$ all in deviation from their means. Using concentrated components: $\breve{y}_{it}, \beta_j \breve{y}_{jt-1}\ (j \neq i), \beta_k \breve{z}_{kt}$ also in deviation from means.

(4) *Recursive eigenvalues*
Only available if the system was estimated recursively.
(5) $-\log|\mathbf{\Omega}|$ for the maximum rank.
Only available if the system was estimated recursively.

The following are available after restrictions have been imposed:

(1) *Restricted relations*
$\widehat{\boldsymbol{\beta}}_r'(\mathbf{y}_t : \mathbf{z}_r)$ or $\widehat{\boldsymbol{\beta}}_r'\mathbf{r}_{1t}$.
(2) *Restricted actual and fitted*
The graphs of the restricted cointegrating relations are split into two components: the actuals $\mathbf{y}_t$ and the fitted values $\mathbf{y}_t - \widehat{\boldsymbol{\beta}}_r'(\mathbf{y}_t : \mathbf{z}_r)$. Or $\check{\mathbf{y}}_{t-1}$ and $\check{\mathbf{y}}_{t-1} - \widehat{\boldsymbol{\beta}}_r'\mathbf{r}_{1t}$. All lines are graphed in deviation from mean.
(3) *Restricted components*
Graphs all the components of $\widehat{\boldsymbol{\beta}}_r'(\mathbf{y}_t : \mathbf{z}_r)$ or $\widehat{\boldsymbol{\beta}}_r'\mathbf{r}_{1t}$, matched by means.
(4) *Recursive* $\boldsymbol{\beta}$*s* with ±2SE.
Only available if the system was estimated recursively.
(5) $-\log|\mathbf{\Omega}|$ for the restricted rank.
Only available if the system was estimated recursively.
(6) χ^2 test for the restrictions; its critical value is also shown.
Only available if the system was estimated recursively: the p-value can be set.

14.9 Cointegration restrictions

Following the cointegration analysis, tests for restrictions on $\boldsymbol{\alpha}$ and $\boldsymbol{\beta}$ can be performed in PcFiml:

(1) restricted $\boldsymbol{\alpha}: \ \boldsymbol{\alpha}_r = \mathbf{A}\boldsymbol{\theta}$;
(2) restricted $\boldsymbol{\beta}: \ \boldsymbol{\beta}_r = \mathbf{H}\boldsymbol{\phi}$;
(3) known $\boldsymbol{\beta}: \ \boldsymbol{\beta}_r = [\mathbf{H} : \boldsymbol{\phi}]$;
(4) (1) and (2) jointly;
(5) (1) and (3) jointly;
(6) any (non-linear) restrictions on $\boldsymbol{\alpha}$ and $\boldsymbol{\beta}'$.

PcFiml requires you to choose the rank p. For (1)–(5), the restrictions are expressed through the **A** and/or **H** matrix. The general restrictions of (6) are expressed directly in terms of the elements of $\boldsymbol{\alpha}$ and $\boldsymbol{\beta}'$. Examples of these tests are given in §11.6.

Output of the restricted cointegration estimation depends on the particular type of restrictions being imposed, but in general comprises:

(1) *Eigenvalues* $\widehat{\lambda}_i$ and the log-likelihood for each rank.
(2) $\widehat{\boldsymbol{\beta}}_r'$ *eigenvectors*, standardized as set by the user.
(3) *Standard errors* of the unrestricted elements of $\widehat{\boldsymbol{\beta}}_r'$.

(4) $\widehat{\alpha}_r$ *coefficients*, corresponding to the standardizations imposed on $\widehat{\beta}_r'$.
(5) *Standard errors* of the unrestricted elements of $\widehat{\alpha}_r$.
(6) *Restricted long-run matrix* $\widehat{\mathbf{P}}_0 = \widehat{\alpha}_r\widehat{\beta}_r'$, rank p.
(7) *Standard errors of the restricted long-run matrix* (only if no restrictions on α).
(8) *Reduced form* $\widehat{\beta}_r'$. This is (14.50) below, based on $\widehat{\beta}_r'$.
(9) *Moving-average impact matrix* $\mathbf{C}(1)$ based on Ψ in §14.5, the mean-lag , where

$$\mathbf{C}(1) = \beta_{\perp}\left(\alpha_{\perp}'\Psi\,\beta_{\perp}\right)^{-1}\alpha_{\perp}'$$

where $\alpha_{\perp}$ and $\beta_{\perp}$ are the orthogonal complements of α and β respectively (see Chapters 9 and 12).
(10) *LR-test* χ^2 test for the imposed restriction; the general restrictions test also reports the log-likelihoods on which the test is based. Note that the degrees of freedom as reported for the general restrictions test are approximate and cannot be guaranteed to be correct for all possible restrictions.

Also available is the reduced rank $\widehat{\mathbf{P}}_0$, which prints out the long-run matrix $\widehat{\mathbf{P}}_0\,(p) = \widehat{\alpha}\widehat{\beta}'$, based on a user-selected rank p (obtained by only using the first p columns of $\widehat{\alpha}$ and $\widehat{\beta}$). Note that this uses the original $\widehat{\alpha}$ and $\widehat{\beta}'$, unlike the restricted reduced rank $\widehat{\mathbf{P}}_0$ of 4 above. Also printed is the reduced form $\widehat{\beta}'$. Partition $\widehat{\beta}'$ as:

$$\begin{pmatrix} \widehat{\beta}_{11}' & \widehat{\beta}_{12}' \\ \widehat{\beta}_{21}' & \widehat{\beta}_{22}' \end{pmatrix} \tag{14.49}$$

where $\widehat{\beta}_{11}'$ is the top left $(p \times p)$ block of $\widehat{\beta}'$, then when $\widehat{\beta}_{11}'$ is non-singular, the reduced form matrix is:

$$-\left(\widehat{\beta}_{11}'\right)^{-1}\widehat{\beta}_{12}'. \tag{14.50}$$

14.10 Model formulation

Once a statistical system has been adequately modelled and its congruency satisfactorily evaluated, an economically meaningful structural interpretation can be sought. The relevant class of model has the form:

$$\mathbf{B}\mathbf{y}_t + \mathbf{C}\mathbf{w}_t = \mathbf{u}_t,\ \ \mathbf{u}_t \sim \mathsf{IN}_n\left[\mathbf{0}, \boldsymbol{\Sigma}\right],\ t = 1, \ldots, T. \tag{14.51}$$

The diagonal of $\mathbf{B}$ is normalized at unity. More concisely:

$$\mathbf{B}\mathbf{Y}' + \mathbf{C}\mathbf{W}' = \mathbf{A}\mathbf{X}' = \mathbf{U}', \tag{14.52}$$

with $\mathbf{A} = (\mathbf{B} : \mathbf{C})$ and $\mathbf{X} = (\mathbf{Y} : \mathbf{W})$. PcFiml accepts only linear, within-equation restrictions on the elements of $\mathbf{A}$ for the initial specification of the identified model, but allows for further non-linear restrictions on the parameters (possibly across equations).

The order condition for identification is enforced, and as discussed in §12.2, the rank condition is required to be satisfied for arbitrary (random) non-zero values of the parameters.

A subset of the equations can be identities, but otherwise $\boldsymbol{\Sigma}$ is assumed to be positive definite and unrestricted. When identities are present, the model to be estimated is written as:

$$\mathbf{AX}' = \begin{pmatrix} \mathbf{A}_1 \\ \mathbf{A}_2 \end{pmatrix} \mathbf{X}' = \begin{pmatrix} \mathbf{U}' \\ \mathbf{0} \end{pmatrix} \tag{14.53}$$

where $\mathbf{A}_1\mathbf{X}' = \mathbf{U}'$ is the subset of n_1 stochastic equations and $\mathbf{A}_2\mathbf{X}' = \mathbf{0}$ is the subset of n_2 identities with $n_1+n_2 = n$. PcFiml requires specification of the variables involved in the identities, but will derive the coefficients $\mathbf{A}_2$.

14.11 Model estimation

Let ϕ denote the vector of unrestricted elements of vec($\mathbf{A}_1'$): $\phi = \mathbf{A}_1^{v_u}$. Then $\ell(\phi)$ is to be minimized as an unrestricted function of the elements of ϕ. On convergence, we have the maximum likelihood estimator (MLE) of ϕ:

$$\widehat{\phi} = \underset{\phi \in \Phi}{\operatorname{argmax}}\, \ell(\phi) \tag{14.54}$$

and so have the MLE of $\mathbf{A}_1$; as all other elements of $\mathbf{A}_2$ are known, we have the MLE of $\mathbf{A}$. If convergence does not occur, reset the parameter values, and use a looser (larger) convergence criterion to obtain output.

The estimated variance of $\mathbf{u}_t$ is:

$$\widetilde{\boldsymbol{\Sigma}} = \frac{\widehat{\mathbf{A}}_1\mathbf{X}'\mathbf{X}\widehat{\mathbf{A}}_1'}{T - c}, \tag{14.55}$$

which is $(n_1 \times n_1)$. There is a degrees-of-freedom correction c, which equals the average number of parameters per equation (rounded towards 0); this would be k for the system.

From $\mathbf{A}$, we can derive the MLE of the restricted reduced form:

$$\widehat{\boldsymbol{\Pi}} = -\widehat{\mathbf{B}}^{-1}\widehat{\mathbf{C}} \tag{14.56}$$

and hence the estimated variances of the elements of $\widehat{\phi}$:

$$\widetilde{\mathsf{V}[\widehat{\phi}]} = \left\{ \left(\widetilde{\boldsymbol{\Sigma}}^{-1} \otimes \widehat{\mathbf{Q}}\mathbf{W}'\mathbf{W}\widehat{\mathbf{Q}}' \right)^{u} \right\}^{-1} \tag{14.57}$$

where, before inversion, we choose the rows and columns of the right-hand side corresponding to unrestricted elements of $\mathbf{A}_1$ only, and $\mathbf{Q}' = (\boldsymbol{\Pi}' : \mathbf{I})$.

The covariance matrix of the restricted reduced form residuals is obtained by writing:

$$\mathbf{B}^{-1} = \begin{pmatrix} \mathbf{B}^{11} & \mathbf{B}^{12} \\ \mathbf{B}^{21} & \mathbf{B}^{22} \end{pmatrix}, \tag{14.58}$$

where $\mathbf{B}^{11}$ is $(n_1 \times n_1)$. Then:

$$\boldsymbol{\Omega} = \begin{pmatrix} \mathbf{B}^{11} \\ \mathbf{B}^{21} \end{pmatrix} \boldsymbol{\Sigma} \left(\mathbf{B}^{11\prime} : \mathbf{B}^{21\prime}\right), \tag{14.59}$$

with:

$$\widetilde{\boldsymbol{\Omega}}_{11} = \widehat{\mathbf{B}}^{11} \widetilde{\boldsymbol{\Sigma}} \widehat{\mathbf{B}}^{11\prime} \tag{14.60}$$

corresponding to the stochastic equations. The estimated variance matrix of the restricted reduced form coefficients is:

$$\mathsf{V}\left[\widetilde{\mathrm{vec}\widehat{\boldsymbol{\Pi}}'}\right] = \widehat{\mathbf{J}}\mathsf{V}\left[\widetilde{\boldsymbol{\phi}}\right]\widehat{\mathbf{J}}' \text{ where } \mathbf{J} = -\left(\mathbf{B}^{-1} \otimes (\boldsymbol{\Pi}' : \mathbf{I})\right)^{u}. \tag{14.61}$$

Model estimation follows the successful estimation of the unrestricted reduced form. The sample period and number of forecasts carry over from the system.

The following information is needed to estimate a model:

(1) The *model* formulation.
(2) The *method* of estimation:

 Single equation OLS (1SLS);
 Two stage least squares (2SLS);
 Three stage least squares (3SLS);
 Limited information instrumental variables (LIVE);
 Full information instrumental variables (FIVE);
 Full information maximum likelihood (FIML);
 Constrained FIML (CFIML).

(3) The number of observations to be used to *initialize* the recursive estimation (FIML and CFIML).
(4) For CFIML: prior estimation by FIML.

All model estimation methods in PcFiml are derived from the *estimator-generating equation* (EGE), see Chapter 12. We require the reduced form to be a congruent data model, for which the structural specification is a more parsimonious representation.

The model output coincides to a large extent with the system output:

(1) *Identities*
 Gives the coefficients of the n_2 identity equations, together with the R^2 of each equation, which should be 1 (values $\geq .99$ are accepted).

(2) *Structural coefficients and standard errors,* $\widehat{\phi}$ and $\sqrt{(\widetilde{\mathsf{V}[\widehat{\phi}]})_{ii}}$, given for all n_1 equations.

(3) t-*value and* t-*probability*
The t-probabilities are based on a Student t-distribution with $T - c$ degrees of freedom. The correction c is defined below equation (14.55).

(4) *Heteroscedastic-consistent standard errors*
HCSE for short; computed for FIML only, but not for unrestricted variables. These provide consistent estimates of the regression coefficients' standard errors even if the residuals are heteroscedastic in an unknown way. Large differences between the HCSE and SE are indicative of the presence of heteroscedasticity, in which case the HCSE provides the more useful measure of the standard errors (see White, 1980). They are computed as: $\mathbf{Q}^{-1}\mathcal{I}\mathbf{Q}^{-1}$, $\mathbf{Q} = \mathsf{V}[\widehat{\phi}]$, $\mathcal{I} = \sum_{t=1}^{T} \mathbf{q}_t\mathbf{q}_t'$, the outer product of the gradients.

(5) *Equation standard error* (σ)
The square root of the structural residual variance for each equation:

$$\sqrt{\widetilde{\Sigma}_{ii}} \text{ for } i = 1, \ldots, n_1. \tag{14.62}$$

(6) *Likelihood*
The log-likelihood value is (up to a constant):

$$\widehat{\ell} = -\frac{T}{2}\log\left|\widetilde{\boldsymbol{\Sigma}}\right| + T\log\left||\widehat{\mathbf{B}}|\right| = -\frac{T}{2}\log\left|\widehat{\boldsymbol{\Omega}}_{11}\right|. \tag{14.63}$$

Reported are $\widehat{\ell}$, $\log|\widehat{\boldsymbol{\Omega}}_{11}|$, $|\widehat{\boldsymbol{\Omega}}_{11}|$ and the sample size T.

(7) *LR test of over-identifying restrictions*
This tests whether the model is a valid reduction of the system.

(8) *Correlation of residuals*
A typical element of this matrix is:

$$\mathsf{c}_{ij} = \frac{\widetilde{\boldsymbol{\Sigma}}_{ij}}{\sqrt{\widetilde{\boldsymbol{\Sigma}}_{ii}}\sqrt{\widetilde{\boldsymbol{\Sigma}}_{jj}}}. \tag{14.64}$$

(9) **Restricted reduced form*, consisting of:

(a) RRF coefficients;
(b) standard errors of RRF coefficients;
(c) correlation of RRF residuals;
(d) standard deviations of RRF residuals.

(10) *1-step (ex post) forecast analysis*
Static forecasting proceeds as for the system, but based on the restricted reduced form. Two types of parameter constancy tests are reported, in each case as a $\chi^2(nH)$ for n equations and H forecasts and an $\mathsf{F}(nH, T-k)$ statistic:

(a) *using* $\mathbf{\Omega}$.
This an index of numerical parameter constancy, ignoring both parameter uncertainty and intercorrelation between forecasts errors at different time periods. It corresponds to ξ_1 and η_1 of (10.46).

(b) *using* $\mathsf{V}[\mathsf{e}]$.
This test is similar to (a), but takes parameter uncertainty into account, corresponding to ξ_2 and η_2 of (10.46).

(11) **Descriptive statistics of forecast errors*
Reports the means, standard deviations, and correlation matrix of the forecast errors.

(12) **Matrix of forecast standard errors*
Reports the forecast standard errors.

(13) **Forecast tests, single chi*^{2} $(\cdot)$
These are the individual test statistics underlying (a) and (b) of (11) above. They can also be viewed graphically.

(14) **Variance of coefficients,* $\mathsf{V}[\widetilde{\widehat{\phi}}]$

14.12 Graphic evaluation of the model

14.12.1 Graphic analysis

Graphic analysis focuses on graphical inspection of individual restricted reduced form equations. Let y_t, $\widehat{y}_t$ denote respectively the actual (that is, observed) values and the fitted values of the selected equation, with RRF residuals $\widehat{v}_t = y_t - \widehat{y}_t$, $t = 1, \ldots, T$. If H observations are used for forecasting, then $\widehat{y}_{T+1}, \ldots, \widehat{y}_{T+H}$ are the 1-step forecasts.

The following graph are available:

(1) *Actual and fitted values*
This is a graph showing the fitted $(\widehat{y}_t)$ and actual values (y_t) of the dependent variable over time, including the forecast period.

(2) *Cross-plot of actual and fitted values*
$\widehat{y}_t$ against y_t, including the forecast period.

(3) *Scaled residuals*
$(\widehat{v}_t/\widetilde{\sigma})$, where $\widetilde{\sigma}^2$ is the estimated equation error variance, plotted over $t = 1, \ldots, T + H$.

(4) *Forecasts and outcomes*
The 1-step forecasts can be plotted in a graph over time: y_t and $\widehat{y}_t$ for $t = T + 1, \ldots, T + H$, are shown with error bars (or bands) of $\pm 2\mathsf{SE}[e_t]$ centred on $\widehat{y}_t$.

(5) *Residual correlogram* as for system graphics, but using RRF residuals $\widehat{v}_t$.

(6) *Residual density optionally with histogram* as for system graphics, but using RRF residuals $\widehat{v}_t$. By default, the estimated density of the residuals $\widehat{v}_t$, $t = 1, \ldots, T$,

namely $\widehat{f_v(\cdot)}$ is graphed. The histogram and a standard normal density can be added for comparison.

(7) *Residual distribution*
The estimated cumulative density function, $\widehat{F_v(\cdot)}$, of the residuals is shown, with a standard normal for comparison.

(8) *Forecast chow tests.*
These are the Chow tests using V [e] of (14.19), available from $T+1$ to $T+H$, together with a fixed 5% critical value from $\chi^2(n)$. These are not scaled by their critical values, unlike the graphs in recursive graphics.

(9) *Residual cross-plots*
Let $\widehat{v}_{it}$, $\widehat{v}_{jt}$ denote the residuals of equation i and j. This graph shows the cross-plot of $\widehat{v}_{it}$ against $\widehat{v}_{jt}$ for all marked equations ($i \neq j$), over $t = 1, \ldots, T+H$.

14.12.2 Recursive graphics

When recursive FIML or CFIML is selected, the ϕ and Σ matrices are estimated at each t $(k \leq M \leq t \leq T)$ where M is user selected. For each t, the RRF can be derived from this.

The following graphs are available for the model (the information can be printed on request):

(1) *Residual sum of squares*
The residual sum of squares RSS_t for equation i $(i = 1, \ldots, n_1)$ is the ith diagonal element of $\widehat{\mathbf{V}}_t'\widehat{\mathbf{V}}_t$ for $t = M, \ldots, T$.

(2) *1-Step residuals* $\pm 2\widetilde{\sigma}$ for equation i $(i = 1, \ldots, n_1)$ at each t
The 1-step RRF residuals $\widehat{v}_t$ are shown bordered by $0 \pm 2\widetilde{\sigma}_t$ over $M, \ldots, T$. Points outside the 2 standard-error region are either outliers or are associated with coefficient changes. Now $\widetilde{\sigma}_t$ is the ith diagonal element of the RRF $\widetilde{\mathbf{\Omega}}_{11,t}$.

(3) *Log-likelihood/T*

$$\widehat{l}_t = -\ \tfrac{1}{2}\log\left|\frac{t}{T}\widehat{\mathbf{\Omega}}_{11,t}\right| = -\ \tfrac{1}{2}\log\left|T^{-1}\widehat{\mathbf{V}}_t'\widehat{\mathbf{V}}_t\right|,\ t = M, \ldots, T. \quad (14.65)$$

As for the system, we have $\widehat{l}_t \geq \widehat{l}_{t+1}$.

(4) *Encompassing tests*
Let $\widehat{\ell}_t$ be the log-likelihood of the URF, and $\widehat{\ell}_{0,t}$ the log-likelihood of the RRF. This option graphs the tests for over-identifying restrictions, $2(\widehat{\ell}_t - \widehat{\ell}_{0,t})$, with a line graphing the critical value from the $\chi^2(s)$ distribution (s is the number of restrictions) at a chosen significance level. So these are not scaled by their critical values. These can be graphed even if the system was not estimated recursively, but the model was, since the latter now re-computes the former as it proceeds.

(5) *System Chow tests*

These are described in §14.4.2. They are scaled by one-off critical values from the F-distribution at any selected probability level as an adjustment for changing degrees of freedom, so that the significance values become a straight line at unity. Selecting a probability of 0 or 1 results in unscaled statistics.

14.12.3 Dynamic forecasting and dynamic simulation

These proceed as for the system, but based on the restricted reduced form. Graphs are available for identity equations.

14.13 Dynamic analysis

This is as for the system, but taking identities into account. In the case of a 'redundant' specification (such as a cointegrated system in I(0) space with both the first differences and the cointegration vectors then defined by identities), a singular long-run matrix results, so a message will be presented and only the subset of the calculations not involving $\mathbf{P}_0$ will be written.

14.14 Model testing

The vector error autocorrelation test partials lagged structural residuals out from the original regressors, and re-estimates the model. All other tests take the residuals from the RRF, and operate as for the system.

Note, however, that application of single-equation autocorrelation and heteroscedasticity tests in a model will lead to all reduced-form variables being used in the auxiliary regression. If the model is an invalid reduction of the system, this may cause the tests to be significant. Equally, valid reduction combined with small amounts of system residual autocorrelation could induce significant single-equation model autocorrelation. The usual difficulty of interpreting significant test outcomes is prominent here.

A similar feature operates for the vector heteroscedasticity tests, where all reduced-form variables (but not those classified as unrestricted) are used in the auxiliary regression.

14.15 Progress

PcFiml can be used in two ways: for general-to-specific modelling, and for unordered searches.

In the general-to-specific approach:

(1) Begin with the dynamic system formulation.

(2) Check its data coherence and cointegration.
(3) Map the system to I(0) after cointegration analysis.
(4) Transform to a set of variables with low intercorrelations, but interpretable parameters.
(5) Check the validity of the system by thorough testing.
(6) Move to the dynamic model formulation.
(7) Delete unwanted regressors to obtain a parsimonious model.
(8) Check the validity of the model by thorough testing, particularly parsimonious encompassing.

Nothing commends unordered searches:

(1) No control is offered over the significance level of testing.
(2) A 'later' reject outcome invalidates all earlier ones.
(3) Until a model adequately characterizes the data, standard tests are invalid.
(4) If the system displays symptoms of mis-specification, there is little point in imposing further restrictions on it.

PcFiml does not enforce a general-to-simple modelling strategy, but it will automatically monitor the progress of the sequential reduction from the general to the specific, and will provide the associated likelihood-ratio tests.

More precisely, the program will record a sequence of systems, and for the most recent system the sequence of models (which could be empty). The program gives a list of the selected systems and models, reporting the estimation method, sample size (T), number of coefficients (k), the log-likelihood ($-\frac{2}{T}\log|\widehat{\Omega}|$). Three *information criteria* are also reported: the Schwarz criterion, the Hannan–Quinn criterion and the Akaike criterion. These are defined as:

$$\begin{aligned}\mathsf{SC} &= \log\left|\widehat{\Omega}\right| + k\log(T)T^{-1},\\ \mathsf{HQ} &= \log\left|\widehat{\Omega}\right| + 2k\log(\log(T))T^{-1},\\ \mathsf{AIC} &= \log\left|\widehat{\Omega}\right| + 2kT^{-1}.\end{aligned} \tag{14.66}$$

For a discussion of the use of these and related scalar measures to choose between alternative models in a class, see Judge *et al.* (1985) or Lütkepohl (1991).

Following this, PcFiml will report the F-tests (based on Rao's F-approximation) indicating the progress in system modelling, as well as likelihood-ratio tests (χ^2) of the progress in modelling that system (tests of over-identifying restrictions).

Part V

Appendices

Appendix A1

PcFiml Languages

PcFiml is mostly menu-driven for ease of use. To add flexibility, certain functions can be accessed through entering commands. The syntax of these commands, which can be seen as little languages, is described in this chapter.

Algebra is described in the GiveWin manuals. Algebra commands are executed in GiveWin, via the Calculator, the Algebra editor, or as part of a batch run.

A1.1 General restrictions

Restrictions have to be entered when testing for parameter restrictions and for imposing parameter constraints for estimation. The syntax is similar to that of algebra, albeit more simple.

Restrictions code may consist of the following components:

(1) *Comment*

(2) *Constants*

(3) *Arithmetic operators*

These are all identical to algebra. In addition there are:

(4) *Parameter references*

Parameters are referenced by an ampersand followed by the parameter number. Counting starts at 0, so, for example, `&2` is the third parameter of the model. What this parameter is depends on your model. Make sure that when you enter restrictions through the batch language, you use the right order for the coefficients. In case of system estimation, PcFiml will reorder your model so that the endogenous variables come first.

Consider, for example, the following unconstrained model:

$$\mathrm{CONS}_t = \beta_0\mathrm{CONS\_1}_t + \beta_1\mathrm{INC}_t + \beta_2\mathrm{INC\_1}_t + \beta_3\mathrm{INFLAT}_t + \beta_4 + u_t.$$

Then `&0` indicates the coefficient on CONS_1, etc.

Table A1.1 lists the precedence of the operators available in restrictions code, with the highest precedence at the top of the table.

Table A1.1 Restrictions operator precedence.

Symbol	Description	Associativity
&	Parameter reference	
-	Unary minus	Right to left
+	Unary plus	
^	Power	Left to right
*	Multiply	Left to right
/	Divide	
+	Add	Left to right
-	Subtract	

A1.1.1 Restrictions for testing

Restrictions for *testing* are entered in the format: $f(\theta) = 0$;. The following restrictions test the significance of the long-run parameters in the unconstrained model given above:

```
(&1 + &2) / (1 - &0) = 0;
&3 / (1 - &0) = 0;
```

A1.1.2 Restrictions for estimation

PcFiml allows estimation of two types of non-linear models: FIML with parameter constraints (CFIML), and restricted cointegration analysis (RCOINT). Examples were given in the tutorial chapters.

Parameter constraints for estimation are written in the format: $\theta^* = g(\theta)$;. First consider an example which restricts parameter 0 as a function of three other parameters, creating a model which is non-linear in the parameters:

```
&0 = -(&1 - &2) * &3;
&4 = 0;
```

Tests for general restrictions on the α and β matrices from the cointegration analysis can be expressed directly in the elements of α and β'. Consider a system with three variables and cointegrating rank of 2. Then the elements are labelled as follows:

$$\alpha = \begin{pmatrix} \&0 & \&1 \\ \&2 & \&3 \\ \&4 & \&5 \end{pmatrix}, \quad \beta = \begin{pmatrix} \&6 & \&7 & \&8 \\ \&9 & \&10 & \&11 \end{pmatrix}.$$

To test the necessary conditions for weak exogeneity, for example, set:

```
&1 = 0;  &2 = 0; &4 = 0;
```

Starting values may be supplied as follows:

```
&1 = 0;  &2 = 0; &4 = 0;
start = 1 -1 1 -1 2 4 3 5 6;
```

A value is listed for each unrestricted parameter, so &0 starts with the value 1, &3 with -1, etc. here the starting values were picked randomly. Of course, it is only useful to specify starting values if these are better than the default values.

A1.2 PcFiml batch language

PcFiml allows models to be formulated, estimated and evaluated through batch commands. Such commands are entered in GiveWin. Certain commands are intercepted by GiveWin, such as those for loading and saving data, as well as blocks of algebra code. The remaining commands are then passed on to the active module, which is PcFiml in this case.

This section gives an alphabetical list of the PcFiml batch language statements. There are two types of batch commands: function calls (with or without arguments) terminated by a semicolon, and commands, which are followed by statements between curly brackets.

Anything between `/*` and `*/` is considered comment. Note that this comment cannot be nested. Everything following `//` up to the end of the line is also comment.

GiveWin allows you to save the current model as a batch file, and to rerun saved batch files. If a model has been created interactively, it can be saved as a batch file for further editing or easy recall in a later session. This is also the most convenient way to create a batch file.

If an error occurs during processing, the batch run will be aborted and control returned to GiveWin. A warning or out of memory message will have to be accepted by the user (press `Enter`), upon which the batch run will resume.

In the following list, function arguments are indicated by *words*, whereas the areas where statement blocks are expected are indicated by .... Examples follow the list of descriptions. For terms in double quotes, the desired term must be substituted and provided together with the quotes. A command summary is given in Table A1.2. For completeness, the Table A1.2 also contains the commands which are handled by GiveWin. Consult the GiveWin book for more information on those commands.

`constraints {...}`

Impose constraints for constrained estimation (CFIML). This command must appear before `estmodel`.

`dynamics;`

Do the dynamic analysis.

`estmodel("`*method*`", `*init*`);`

Estimate a model.

The *method* argument is one of: 1SLS, 2SLS, 3SLS, LIVE, FIVE, FIML, CFIML. *init* is the number of observations to use for initialization of recursive estimation (so a nonzero here will do recursive FIML or CFIML).

Table A1.2 Batch language syntax summary.

```
algebra {...}
appenddata("filename", "group");
appresults("filename");
break;
constraints {...}
database(year1, period1, year2, period2, frequency);
derived {...}
dynamics;
estmodel("method", init);
estsystem("method", year1, period1, year2, period2, forc, init, 0);
exit;
loaddata("filename");
model {...}
module("name");
option("option", argument);
progress;
savedata("filename");
saveresults("filename");
store("name");
system { Y=...; I=...; Z=...; U=...;}
testcoint {rank...}
testcointknown {rank...}
testcointrestr {rank...}
testrestr {...}
testsummary;
usedata("databasename");
```

`estsystem("`*method*`", `*year1*`, `*period1*`, `*year2*`, `*period2*`, `*forc*`, `*init*`, 0);`

Estimate a system.

The *method* argument is one of: OLS, COINT, RCOINT.

year1(period1) – year2(period2) is the estimation sample. Setting year1 to zero will result in the earliest possible year1(period1), setting year2 to zero will result in the latest possible year2(period2).

forc is the number of observations to withhold from the estimation sample for forecasting.

init is the number of observations to use for initialization of recursive estimation. A positive number will switch recursive estimation on.

The final argument is 0 for compatibility with previous versions of PcFiml.

`model {...}`

Specify the model. There must be an equation for each endogenous and identity endogenous variable specified in the system statement. An example of an equation is: `CONS=CONS_1,INC;`. Note that PcFiml reorders the equations of the model into the order they had in the system specification. Right-hand-side variables are not reordered.

`option("`*option*`", `*argument*`);`

This sets the options which are available in the Options dialog:

option	*argument*	*value*
`Automax`	automatic maximization	0 to switch off, 1 on,
`ColModel`	columnar format for system	0 to switch off, 1 on,
`ColSystem`	columnar format for model	0 to switch off, 1 on,
`Covariance`	print covariance matrix	0 to switch off, 1 on,
`ForcStats`	individual forecast statistics	0 to switch off, 1 on,
`PriorCoeffs`	prior coefficients	0 to switch off, 1 on,
`RRF`	restricted reduced form	0 to switch off, 1 on,
`Summary`	summary statistics only	0 to switch off, 1 on,
`Weak`	set weak convergence tolerance	default: 0.0001,
`Strong`	strong convergence tolerance	default: 0.005,
`print`	print every # iteration	0: do not print,
`maxit`	maximum number of iterations	default: 1000,
`shortrun`	re-estimate shortrun	1: re-estimate, 0: fixed,
`cointmethod`	set default restrictions method	
		0: beta switching
		1: linear switching, scaled
		2: linear switching
		3: no switching

`progress;`

Reports the modelling progress.

`store("`*name*`");`

Use this command to store residuals, etc. into the database, the default name is used. The *name* must be one of:

`residuals`	residuals
`fitted`	fitted values
`structres`	structural residuals (model only)
`res1step`	1-step residual (after recursive estimation)
`rss`	RSS (after recursive estimation)
`loglik`	log-likelihood (after recursive estimation)
`coieval`	eigenvalues (after recursive cointegration analysis)
`coivec`	cointegration vectors (after recursive cointegration)
`coiresvec`	cointegration vectors (recursive restricted cointegration)

`system` { `Y=...; I=...; Z=...; U=...;`}

Specify the system, consisting of the following components:

`Y` endogenous variables;
`I` identity endogenous variables (optional);
`Z` non-modelled variables;
`U` unrestricted variables (optional).

The variables listed are separated by commas, their base names (that is, name excluding lag length) must be in the database. Only variable names that would be valid in an algebra expression can be used here (invalid names must be enclosed in double quotes, e.g. `"x*10"`). The following special variables are recognized: Constant, Trend, Seasonal and CSeason.

Note that PcFiml reorders the system as follows: first the endogenous variables and their lags: endogenous variables, identity endogenous variables, first lag of these (variables in the same order), second lag, etc. then each exogenous variable with its lags. For example, with y, c endogenous, i identity and w, z exogenous:

$y_t\ c_t\ i_t\ y_{t-1}\ c_{t-1}\ i_{t-1}\ y_{t-2}\ c_{t-2}\ w_t\ w_{t-1}\ z_t\ z_{t-1}$

This reordering is relevant when specifying restrictions.

`testcoint` { *rank* ...}

First the assumed cointegrating rank is specified. This is followed by the restrictions, which are directly expressed in terms of the elements of $\boldsymbol{\alpha}$ and $\boldsymbol{\beta}'$.

This command must appear before `estsystem`.

`testcointknown` { *rank* ...}

First the assumed cointegrating rank is specified. **A** is the matrix of restrictions on $\boldsymbol{\alpha}$, namely $\boldsymbol{\alpha} = \mathbf{A}\boldsymbol{\theta}$. **H** is the matrix of known $\boldsymbol{\beta}$, to test $\boldsymbol{\beta} = [\mathbf{H} : \boldsymbol{\phi}]$. The **A** and **H** are specified in the same way as a matrix in a matrix file: first the dimensions are given, then the contents of the matrix. Note that 0 0 indicates a matrix of dimension 0×0, that is, absence of the matrix. This can be used to have either $\boldsymbol{\alpha}$ or $\boldsymbol{\beta}$ unrestricted.

This command must appear before `estsystem`.

`testcointrestr` { *rank* ...}

First the assumed cointegrating rank is specified. **A** and **H** are matrices of restrictions on α and β for cointegration tests: $\alpha = \mathbf{A}\theta$ and/or $\beta = \mathbf{H}\phi$. The matrices are specified as in testcointknown.

This command must appear before `estsystem`.

`testrestr {...}`

Used to test for general restrictions: specify the restrictions between { }, conforming to §A1.1.

testsummary;

Do the test summary.

Two points are worth stressing. First, that an error will lead to abortion of the batch run. If we had written line 6 as:

```
A = OUTPU, OUTPUT_1;
```

this would result in the following three error messages:

OUTPU not found in database data.in7

PcFiml Batch error: system: failed to get data and sample

Batch error: error on line 1

Note that the line number reported in the error message is that of the start of the command.

We finish with an annotated example using most commands.

```
loaddata("..\data.in7");    // Load the tutorial data set.
                            // (Assumes that the files are
                            // one directory lower).
module("PcFiml");           // activate PcFiml
usedata("data.in7");        // use data.in7 for modelling
algebra
{                           // Create SAVINGSL in database.
    SAVINGSL = lag(INC,1) - lag(CONS, 1);
}
system
{
    Y = CONS, INC, INFLAT;  // Three endogenous variables;
    I = SAVINGSL;           // one identity endogenous variable;
    Z = CONS_1, CONS_2,     // the non-endogenous variables; the
        INC_1,INC_2,        // lagged variables need not (better:
        INFLAT_1, INFLAT_2; // should not) exist in the database.
    U = Constant;           // the constant enters unrestricted.
}
estsystem("OLS", 1953, 3, 1992, 3, 8, 0, 0);
                    // Estimate the system by OLS over 1953(2)-
                    // 1992(3), withhold 8 forecasts,
                    // no observations used for initialization.
testcointrestr
{
    2               // Rank of cointegrating space.

    0 0             // (0 x 0) matrix: no A matrix, that is,
                    // no restrictions on the loadings.
```

```
    3 2              // Dimensions of H matrix.
    1 0              // Contents of H matrix:
   -1 0              // first two variables enter the
    0 1              // cointegrating vector with opposite sign.
}
estsystem("RCOINT", 1953, 3, 1992, 3, 8, 0, 0);
testcoint            // The previous restrictions, expressed in
{                    // terms of loadings (a 3 x 2 matrix) and
                     // eigenvectors (in rows, a 2 x 3 matrix).

    2                // Rank of cointegrating space.
                     // Elements 0-5 are the loadings.
    &6 = -&7;
    &9 = -&10;
}
estsystem("RCOINT", 1953, 3, 1992, 3, 8, 0, 0);
testcointknown
{
    2                // Rank of cointegrating space.

    3 2              // Dimensions of A matrix.
    1 0              // Contents of A matrix:
    0 1              // none of the cointegrating vectors
    0 0              // enter the third equation.

    3 1              // Dimensions of H matrix
    1                // Contents of H matrix:
   -1                // pretend we know the first vector.
    6
}
estsystem("RCOINT", 1953, 3, 1992, 3, 8, 0, 0);
testcoint            // The previous restrictions.
{
    2                // Rank of cointegrating space.
                     // Elements 0-5 are the loadings.
    &0 = 0;
    &1 = 0;

    &6 = 1;          // Restrictions on ECMs;
    &7 = -1;         // elements 6-8 are coefficients of 1st ECM
    &8 = 6;          // elements 9-11 of second ECM.
}
estsystem("RCOINT", 1953, 3, 1992, 3, 8, 0, 0);

estsystem("OLS", 1953, 3, 1992, 3, 8, 0, 0);
testsummary;         // Do the test summary.
testrestr            // Test for parameter restrictions.
{                    // Restrictions are on the INFLAT equation:
    &12 = 0;         // coefficient of CONS_1
    &13 = 0;         // coefficient of CONS_2
    &14 - &15 = 0; // coefficient of INC_1 - coeff. of INC_2.
}
```

```
model                   // Specify the equations in the model,
{                       // including the identity.
    CONS = INC, SAVINGSL, INFLAT_1;
    INC = INC_1, INC_2, CONS;
    INFLAT = INFLAT_1, INFLAT_2;
    SAVINGSL = INC_1, CONS_1;
}
estmodel("FIML", 0); // Estimate the model by FIML; no observa-
                        // tions required for initialization.
dynamics;               // Do dynamic analysis.
constraints             // Impose constraints for constrained
{                       // estimation.
    &4 = 0;             // Delete INC_2 from INC equation.
}
estmodel("CFIML", 0);// Estimate the constrained model by CFIML;
                        // no observations required for
                        // initialization.
progress;               // Report the modelling progress.
```

Appendix A2

Numerical Changes From Previous Versions

Changes between version 8 and 9

The major change is the adoption of the QR decomposition with partial pivoting to compute OLS and IV estimates. There are also some minor improvements in accuracy, the following tests are the most sensitive to such changes: encompassing, heteroscedasticity and RESET. The heteroscedasticity tests could also differ in the number of variables removed owing to singularity. To summarize:

- QR decomposition in all regressions;
- analytical differentiation of restrictions;
- singular value based cointegration analysis;
- standard errors in (restricted) cointegration analysis take all parameters into account;
- new algorithms for restricted cointegration analysis;
- slightly improved error recovery in BFGS;
- reset every 50 observations in RLS and better handling of singular subsamples;
- recursive FIML now done backward.

Changes between version 6 and 8

The numerical results generated by PcFiml version 8 (version 7 was never officially released) will not always be identical to those of version 6. This is mainly caused by the increase in accuracy: all data are now stored in eight byte reals, while accumulation of certain temporary results is done in ten byte precision. The increased precision will be especially noticeable in the recursive estimation procedures. Also note that results from iterative optimization are sensitive to the convergence tolerance used.

Additional differences are:

- The system and model statistics are now corrected for degrees of freedom. So equation standard errors, coefficient standard errors, t-values, etc. are different from version 6. Likelihoods (and hence likelihood ratio tests) are not, unless explicitly stated.
- RLS ends with a full sample OLS, so that the end results are always identical to just OLS. Version 6 reported the RLS results.
- The second degrees of freedom argument in the F test on retained regressors is different, affecting the test statistics.
- Version 7 uses a new normality test.
- PCFIML 6 computed FIVE using different inputs for $\mathbf{\Pi}$ (compare this with Table 12.1):

		Input $\widehat{\mathbf{\Sigma}}$	Input $\widehat{\mathbf{\Pi}}$	Output $\widehat{\mathbf{\Sigma}}$	Output $\widehat{\mathbf{\Pi}}$
4a.	FIVE after 2SLS	$\mathbf{\Sigma}_{2SLS}$	$\mathbf{\Pi}_{URF}$	$\mathbf{\Sigma}_{FIVE1}$	$\mathbf{\Pi}_{FIVE1}$
4b.	FIVE after 3SLS	$\mathbf{\Sigma}_{3SLS}$	$\mathbf{\Pi}_{URF}$	$\mathbf{\Sigma}_{FIVE2}$	$\mathbf{\Pi}_{FIVE2}$
4c.	FIVE after LIVE	$\mathbf{\Sigma}_{LIVE}$	$\mathbf{\Pi}_{2SLS}$	$\mathbf{\Sigma}_{FIVE3}$	$\mathbf{\Pi}_{FIVE3}$

- PCFIML 6 computed and used some coefficient variances different from PcFiml 7. Compare this with Table 12.2. The last column indicates which coefficient variance is used for reconstructing the variance of unrestricted variables and of 1-step forecast errors. Writing $\mathbf{D}$ for $\mathbf{QMQ}'$, and $\odot$ for the Hadamard product:

	$\widetilde{\mathsf{V}[\widehat{\theta}]}$	$\widehat{\mathbf{\Pi}}$ used in $\mathbf{Q}$
1. 2SLS	same as version 7	
2. 3SLS	same as version 7	
3. LIVE	$\left(\left(\left(\mathbf{\Sigma}_{LIVE}^{-1} \odot \mathbf{I}\right) \otimes \mathbf{D}\right)^{u}\right)^{-1}$	$\mathbf{\Pi}_{2SLS}$

	$\widetilde{\mathsf{V}[\widehat{\theta}]}$ used in $\widetilde{\mathsf{V}[\widehat{\mathsf{e}}]}$	$\widehat{\mathbf{\Pi}}$ used in $\mathbf{Q}$
1. 2SLS	$\left(\left(\mathbf{\Sigma}_{2SLS}^{-1} \otimes \mathbf{D}\right)^{u}\right)^{-1}$	$\mathbf{\Pi}_{2SLS}$
2. 3SLS	$\left(\left(\mathbf{\Sigma}_{3SLS}^{-1} \otimes \mathbf{D}\right)^{u}\right)^{-1}$	$\mathbf{\Pi}_{3SLS}$
3. LIVE	same as version 7	

References

Anderson, T. W. (1984). *An Introduction to Multivariate Statistical Analysis* 2nd edition. New York: John Wiley & Sons.

Banerjee, A., Dolado, J. J., Galbraith, J. W. and Hendry, D. F. (1993). *Co-integration, Error Correction and the Econometric Analysis of Non-Stationary Data.* Oxford University Press.

Banerjee, A. and Hendry, D. F. (1992). Testing integration and cointegration, *Oxford Bulletin of Economics and Statistics*, **54**. Special issue.

Bårdsen, G. (1989). The estimation of long run coefficients from error correction models, *Oxford Bulletin of Economics and Statistics*, **50**.

Berndt, E. K., Hall, B. H., Hall, R. E. and Hausman, J. A. (1974). Estimation and inference in nonlinear structural models, *Annals of Economic and Social Measurement*, **3**, 653–665.

Boswijk, H. P. (1992). *Cointegration, Identification and Exogeneity*, Vol. 37 of *Tinbergen Institute Research Series*. Amsterdam: Thesis Publishers.

Boswijk, H. P. (1994). Identifiability of cointegrated systems, Mimeo, Department of Actuarial Sciences and Econometrics, University of Amsterdam.

Bowman, K. O. and Shenton, L. R. (1975). Omnibus test contours for departures from normality based on $\sqrt{b_1}$ and b_2, *Biometrika*, **62**, 243–250.

Box, G. E. P. and Pierce, D. A. (1970). Distribution of residual autocorrelations in autoregressive-integrated moving average time series models, *Journal of the American Statistical Association*, **65**, 1509–1526.

Brown, R. L., Durbin, J. and Evans, J. M. (1975). Techniques for testing the constancy of regression relationships over time (with discussion), *Journal of the Royal Statistical Society B*, **37**, 149–192.

Calzolari, G. (1987). Forecast variance in dynamic simulation of simultaneous equations models, *Econometrica*, **55**, 1473–1476.

Campbell, J. Y. and Perron, P. (1991). Pitfalls and opportunities: What macroeconomists should know about unit roots, In Blanchard, O. J. and Fischer, S. (eds.), *NBER Macroeconomics annual 1991*. Cambridge, MA: MIT press.

Chong, Y. Y. and Hendry, D. F. (1986). Econometric evaluation of linear macro-economic models, *Review of Economic Studies*, **53**, 671–690. Reprinted in Granger, C. W. J. (ed.) (1990), *Modelling Economic Series*. Oxford: Clarendon Press.

Chow, G. C. (1960). Tests of equality between sets of coefficients in two linear regressions, *Econometrica*, **28**, 591–605.

Clements, M. P. and Hendry, D. F. (1994). Towards a theory of economic forecasting, in Hargreaves (1994), pp. 9–52.

Clements, M. P. and Hendry, D. F. (1997). *The Marshall Lectures on Economic Forecasting*. Cambridge: Cambridge University Press. Forthcoming.

Cramer, J. S. (1986). *Econometric Applications of Maximum Likelihood Methods*. Cambridge: Cambridge University Press.

Cran, G. W., Martin, K. J. and Thomas, G. E. (1977). A remark on algorithms. AS 63: The incomplete beta integral. AS 64: Inverse of the incomplete beta function ratio, *Applied Statistics*, **26**, 111–112.

D'Agostino, R. B. (1970). Transformation to normality of the null distribution of g_1, *Biometrika*, **57**, 679–681.

Davidson, J. E. H., Hendry, D. F., Srba, F. and Yeo, J. S. (1978). Econometric modelling of the aggregate time-series relationship between consumers' expenditure and income in the United Kingdom, *Economic Journal*, **88**, 661–692. Reprinted in Hendry, D. F. (1993).

Dhrymes, P. J. (1984). *Mathematics for Econometrics* 2nd edition. New York: Springer-Verlag.

Doornik, J. A. (1995a). *Econometric Computing*. Oxford: University of Oxford. Ph.D Thesis.

Doornik, J. A. (1995b). Testing general restrictions on the cointegrating space, Nuffield College.

Doornik, J. A. (1995c). Testing vector autocorrelation and heteroscedasticity in dynamic models, Mimeo, Nuffield College.

Doornik, J. A. (1996). *Object-Oriented Matrix Programming using Ox*. London: International Thomson Business Press and Oxford: http://www.nuff.ox.ac.uk/Users/Doornik/.

Doornik, J. A. and Hansen, H. (1994). A practical test for univariate and multivariate normality, Discussion paper, Nuffield College.

Doornik, J. A. and Hendry, D. F. (1992). *PcGive 7: An Interactive Econometric Modelling System*. Oxford: Institute of Economics and Statistics, University of Oxford.

Doornik, J. A. and Hendry, D. F. (1994a). *PcFiml 8: An Interactive Program for Modelling Econometric Systems*. London: International Thomson Publishing.

Doornik, J. A. and Hendry, D. F. (1994b). *PcGive 8: An Interactive Econometric Modelling System*. London: International Thomson Publishing, and Belmont, CA: Duxbury Press.

Durbin, J. (1988). Maximum likelihood estimation of the parameters of a system of simultaneous regression equations, *Econometric Theory*, **4**, 159–170. Paper presented to the Copenhagen Meeting of the Econometric Society, 1963.

Engle, R. F. (1982). Autoregressive conditional heteroscedasticity, with estimates of the variance of United Kingdom inflations, *Econometrica*, **50**, 987–1007.

Engle, R. F. and Granger, C. W. J. (1987). Cointegration and error correction: Representation, estimation and testing, *Econometrica*, **55**, 251–276.

Engle, R. F. and Hendry, D. F. (1993). Testing super exogeneity and invariance in regression models, *Journal of Econometrics*, **56**, 119–139.

Engle, R. F., Hendry, D. F. and Richard, J.-F. (1983). Exogeneity, *Econometrica*, **51**, 277–304. Reprinted in Hendry, D. F. (1993).

Engle, R. F., Hendry, D. F. and Trumbull, D. (1985). Small sample properties of ARCH estimators and tests, *Canadian Journal of Economics*, **43**, 66–93.

Ericsson, N. R., Hendry, D. F. and Mizon, G. E. (1997). Econometric issues in economic policy analysis, *Journal of Business and Economic Statistics*. Forthcoming.

Ericsson, N. R., Hendry, D. F. and Tran, H.-A. (1994). Cointegration, seasonality, encompassing and the demand for money in the United Kingdom, in Hargreaves (1994), pp. 179–224.

Ericsson, N. R. (1992). Cointegration, exogeneity and policy analysis, *Journal of Policy Modeling*, **14**. Special Issue.

Favero, C. and Hendry, D. F. (1992). Testing the Lucas critique: A review, *Econometric Reviews*, **11**, 265–306.

Fletcher, R. (1987). *Practical Methods of Optimization* 2nd edition. New York: John Wiley & Sons.

Gill, P. E., Murray, W. and Wright, M. H. (1981). *Practical Optimization*. New York: Academic Press.

Godfrey, L. G. (1988). *Misspecification Tests in Econometrics*. Cambridge: Cambridge University Press.

Goldfeld, S. M. and Quandt, R. E. (1972). *Non-linear Methods in Econometrics*. Amsterdam: North-Holland.

Granger, C. W. J. (1969). Investigating causal relations by econometric models and cross-spectral methods, *Econometrica*, **37**, 424–438.

Haavelmo, T. (1943). The statistical implications of a system of simultaneous equations, *Econometrica*, **11**, 1–12.

Haavelmo, T. (1944). The probability approach in econometrics, *Econometrica*, **12**, 1–118. Supplement.

Hansen, H. and Johansen, S. (1992). Recursive estimation in cointegrated VAR-models, Discussion paper, Institute of Mathematical Statistics, University of Copenhagen.

Hargreaves, C. (ed.)(1994). *Non-stationary Time-series Analyses and Cointegration*. Oxford: Oxford University Press.

Harvey, A. C. (1990). *The Econometric Analysis of Time Series* 2nd edition. Hemel Hempstead: Philip Allan.

Hendry, D. F. (1971). Maximum likelihood estimation of systems of simultaneous regression equations with errors generated by a vector autoregressive process, *International Economic Review*, **12**, 257–272. Correction in **15**, p.260.

Hendry, D. F. (1976). The structure of simultaneous equations estimators, *Journal of Econometrics*, **4**, 51–88. Reprinted in Hendry, D. F. (1993).

Hendry, D. F. (1979). Predictive failure and econometric modelling in macro-economics: The transactions demand for money, In Ormerod, P. (ed.), *Economic Modelling*, pp. 217–242. London: Heinemann. Reprinted in Hendry, D. F. (1993).

Hendry, D. F. (1986). Using PC-GIVE in econometrics teaching, *Oxford Bulletin of Economics and Statistics*, **48**, 87–98.

Hendry, D. F. (1987). Econometric methodology: A personal perspective, In Bewley, T. F. (ed.), *Advances in Econometrics*, Ch. 10. Cambridge: Cambridge University Press.

Hendry, D. F. (1988). The encompassing implications of feedback versus feedforward mechanisms in econometrics, *Oxford Economic Papers*, **40**, 132–149.

Hendry, D. F. (1993). *Econometrics: Alchemy or Science?* Oxford: Blackwell Publishers.

Hendry, D. F. (1995). *Dynamic Econometrics*. Oxford: Oxford University Press.

Hendry, D. F. and Doornik, J. A. (1994). Modelling linear dynamic econometric systems, *Scottish Journal of Political Economy*, **41**, 1–33.

Hendry, D. F. and Doornik, J. A. (1996a). *Empirical Econometric Modelling using PcGive 9 for Windows*. London: International Thomson Business Press.

Hendry, D. F. and Doornik, J. A. (1996b). *Empirical Econometric Modelling using PcGive for Windows*. London: Chapman and Hall.

Hendry, D. F. and Mizon, G. E. (1993). Evaluating dynamic econometric models by encompassing the VAR, In Phillips, P. C. B. (ed.), *Models, Methods and Applications of Econometrics*, pp. 272–300. Oxford: Basil Blackwell.

Hendry, D. F. and Morgan, M. S. (1995). *The Foundations of Econometric Analysis*. Cambridge: Cambridge University Press.

Hendry, D. F. and Neale, A. J. (1991). A Monte Carlo study of the effects of structural breaks on tests for unit roots, In Hackl, P. and Westlund, A. H. (eds.), *Economic Structural Change, Analysis and Forecasting*, pp. 95–119. Berlin: Springer-Verlag.

Hendry, D. F., Neale, A. J. and Srba, F. (1988). Econometric analysis of small linear systems using PC-FIML, *Journal of Econometrics*, **38**, 203–226.

Hendry, D. F., Pagan, A. R. and Sargan, J. D. (1984). Dynamic specification, In Griliches, Z. and Intriligator, M. D. (eds.), *Handbook of Econometrics*, Vol. 2–3, Ch. 18. Amsterdam: North-Holland. Reprinted in Hendry, D. F. (1993).

Hendry, D. F. and Richard, J.-F. (1982). On the formulation of empirical models in dynamic econometrics, *Journal of Econometrics*, **20**, 3–33. Reprinted in Granger, C. W. J. (ed.) (1990), *Modelling Economic Series*. Oxford: Clarendon Press and in Hendry D. F. (1993).

Hendry, D. F. and Richard, J.-F. (1983). The econometric analysis of economic time series (with discussion), *International Statistical Review*, **51**, 111–163. Reprinted in Hendry, D. F. (1993).

Hendry, D. F. and Richard, J.-F. (1989). Recent developments in the theory of encompassing, In Cornet, B. and Tulkens, H. (eds.), *Contributions to Operations Research and Economics. The XXth Anniversary of CORE*, pp. 393–440. Cambridge, MA: MIT Press.

Hendry, D. F. and Srba, F. (1980). AUTOREG: A computer program library for dynamic econometric models with autoregressive errors, *Journal of Econometrics*, **12**, 85–102. Reprinted in Hendry, D. F. (1993).

Hosking, J. R. M. (1980). The multivariate portmanteau statistic, *Journal of the American Statistical Association*, **75**, 602–608.

Hunter, J. (1992). Cointegrating exogeneity, *Economics Letters*, **34**, 33–35.

Johansen, S. (1988). Statistical analysis of cointegration vectors, *Journal of Economic Dynamics and Control*, **12**, 231–254.

Johansen, S. (1991). Estimation and hypothesis testing of cointegration vectors in Gaussian vector autoregressive models, *Econometrica*, **59**, 1551–1580.

Johansen, S. (1992a). Cointegration in partial systems and the efficiency of single-equation analysis, *Journal of Econometrics*, **52**, 389–402.

Johansen, S. (1992b). Testing weak exogeneity and the order of cointegration in UK money demand, *Journal of Policy Modeling*, **14**, 313–334.

Johansen, S. (1995a). Identifying restrictions of linear equations with applications to simultaneous equations and cointegration, *Journal of Econometrics*, **69**, 111–132.

Johansen, S. (1995b). *Likelihood-based inference in cointegrated vector autoregressive models*. Oxford: Oxford University Press.

Johansen, S. and Juselius, K. (1990). Maximum likelihood estimation and inference on cointegration – With application to the demand for money, *Oxford Bulletin of Economics and Statistics*, **52**, 169–210.

Johansen, S. and Juselius, K. (1992). Testing structural hypotheses in a multivariate cointegration analysis of the PPP and the UIP for UK, *Journal of Econometrics*, **53**, 211–244.

Johansen, S. and Juselius, K. (1994). Identification of the long-run and the short-run structure. An application to the ISLM model, *Journal of Econometrics*, **63**, 7–36.

Judge, G. G., Griffiths, W. E., Hill, R. C., Lütkepohl, H. and Lee, T.-C. (1985). *The Theory and Practice of Econometrics* 2nd edition. New York: John Wiley.

Kelejian, H. H. (1982). An extension of a standard test for heteroskedasticity to a systems framework, *Journal of Econometrics*, **20**, 325–333.

Kiefer, N. M. (1989). The ET interview: Arthur S. Goldberger, *Econometric Theory*, **5**, 133–160.

Kiviet, J. F. (1986). On the rigor of some mis-specification tests for modelling dynamic relationships, *Review of Economic Studies*, **53**, 241–261.

Kiviet, J. F. and Phillips, G. D. A. (1992). Exact similar tests for unit roots and cointegration, *Oxford Bulletin of Economics and Statistics*, **54**, 349–367.

Koopmans, T. C. (ed.)(1950). *Statistical Inference in Dynamic Economic Models*. No. 10 in Cowles Commission Monograph. New York: John Wiley & Sons.

Ljung, G. M. and Box, G. E. P. (1978). On a measure of lack of fit in time series models, *Biometrika*, **65**, 297–303.

Longley, G. M. (1967). An appraisal of least-squares for the electronic computer from the point of view of the user, *Journal of the American Statistical Association*, **62**, 819–841.

Lütkepohl, H. (1991). *Introduction to Multiple Time Series Analysis*. New York: Springer-Verlag.

Magnus, J. R. and Neudecker, H. (1988). *Matrix Differential Calculus with Applications in Statistics and Econometrics*. New York: John Wiley & Sons.

Majunder, K. L. and Bhattacharjee, G. P. (1973a). Algorithm AS 63. The incomplete beta integral, *Applied Statistics*, **22**, 409–411.

Majunder, K. L. and Bhattacharjee, G. P. (1973b). Algorithm AS 64. Inverse of the incomplete beta function ratio, *Applied Statistics*, **22**, 411–414.

Mizon, G. E. (1977). Model selection procedures, In Artis, M. J. and Nobay, A. R. (eds.), *Studies in Modern Economic Analysis*, Ch. 4. Oxford: Basil Blackwell.

Mizon, G. E. and Richard, J.-F. (1986). The encompassing principle and its application to non-nested hypothesis tests, *Econometrica*, **54**, 657–678.

Molinas, C. (1986). A note on spurious regressions with integrated moving average errors, *Oxford Bulletin of Economics and Statistics*, **48**, 279–282.

Mosconi, R. and Giannini, C. (1992). Non-causality in cointegrated systems: Representation, estimation and testing, *Oxford Bulletin of Economics and Statistics*, **54**, 399–417.

Ooms, M. (1994). *Empirical Vector Autoregressive Modeling*. Berlin: Springer-Verlag.

Osterwald-Lenum, M. (1992). A note with quantiles of the asymptotic distribution of the ML cointegration rank test statistics, *Oxford Bulletin of Economics and Statistics*, **54**, 461–472.

Pagan, A. R. (1987). Three econometric methodologies: A critical appraisal, *Journal of Economic Surveys*, **1**, 3–24. Reprinted in Granger, C. W. J. (ed.) (1990), *Modelling Economic Series*. Oxford: Clarendon Press.

Pagan, A. R. (1989). On the role of simulation in the statistical evaluation of econometric models, *Journal of Econometrics*, **40**, 125–139.

Pesaran, M. H., Smith, R. P. and Yeo, J. S. (1985). Testing for structural stability and predictive failure: A review, *Manchester School*, **3**, 280–295.

Phillips, P. C. B. (1986). Understanding spurious regressions in econometrics, *Journal of Econometrics*, **33**, 311–340.

Phillips, P. C. B. (1991). Optimal inference in cointegrated systems, *Econometrica*, **59**, 283–306.

Pike, M. C. and Hill, I. D. (1966). Logarithm of the gamma function, *Communications of the ACM*, **9**, 684.

Quandt, R. E. (1983). Computational methods and problems, In Griliches, Z. and Intriligator, M. D. (eds.), *Handbook of Econometrics*, Vol. 1, Ch. 12. Amsterdam: North-Holland.

Rao, C. R. (1952). *Advanced Statistical Methods in Biometric Research.* New York: John Wiley.

Rao, C. R. (1973). *Linear Statistical Inference and its Applications* 2nd edition. New York: John Wiley & Sons.

Reimers, H.-E. (1992). Comparisons of tests for multivariate cointegration, *Statistical Papers*, **33**, 335–359.

Richard, J.-F. (1984). Classical and Bayesian inference in incomplete simultaneous equation models, In Hendry, D. F. and Wallis, K. F. (eds.), *Econometrics and Quantitative Economics.* Oxford: Basil Blackwell.

Salkever, D. S. (1976). The use of dummy variables to compute predictions, prediction errrors and confidence intervals, *Journal of Econometrics*, **4**, 393–397.

Schmidt, P. (1974). The asymptotic distribution of forecasts in the dynamic simulation of an econometric model, *Econometrica*, **42**, 303–309.

Shea, B. L. (1988). Algorithm AS 239: Chi-squared and incomplete gamma integral, *Applied Statistics*, **37**, 466–473.

Shenton, L. R. and Bowman, K. O. (1977). A bivariate model for the distribution of $\sqrt{b_1}$ and b_2, *Journal of the American Statistical Association*, **72**, 206–211.

Silverman, B. W. (1986). *Density Estimation for Statistics and Data Analysis.* London: Chapman and Hall.

Sims, C. A. (1980). Macroeconomics and reality, *Econometrica*, **48**, 1–48. Reprinted in Granger, C. W. J. (ed.) (1990), *Modelling Economic Series.* Oxford: Clarendon Press.

Spanos, A. (1986). *Statistical Foundations of Econometric Modelling.* Cambridge: Cambridge University Press.

Spanos, A. (1989). On re-reading Haavelmo: A retrospective view of econometric modeling, *Econometric Theory*, **5**, 405–429.

Thisted, R. A. (1988). *Elements of Statistical Computing. Numerical Computation.* New York: Chapman and Hall.

Toda, H. Y. and Phillips, P. C. B. (1993). Vector autoregressions and causality, *Econometrica*, **61**, 1367–1393.

White, H. (1980). A heteroskedastic-consistent covariance matrix estimator and a direct test for heteroskedasticity, *Econometrica*, **48**, 817–838.

Winder, C. C. A. and Palm, F. I. (1989). Intertemporal consumer behaviour under structural changes in income, *Econometric Reviews*, **8**, 1–87.

Author Index

Subject Index